COLIN BAXTER ISLAND GUIDES

Shetland

Acknowledgements

I am grateful to so many people - Shetlanders, specialists, family and friends - without whose advice, information, patience, help and support this book could never have been written. The following names are not exclusive and I apologise for any which do not appear on the list, which could have filled a small book of their own: Neil Anderson, Julian Arculus, Ina Bairnson, Andrew Blackadder, Rhoda Bulter, John and Cissie Copland, Ronnie Eunson, Allen Fraser, Lollie Graham, Edith Grey, Jimmy Grey, Alistair Hamilton, Andrew Harmsworth, Paul Harvey, Janet Henderson, Derek Herning, Rhoda Hughson, Mary Isbister, Maggie Laurenson, Kevin Learmonth, Agnes Leask, Jane Mack, Vina Malcolmson, Jim Nicolson, Mary Ellen Odie, Dave Okill, Mike Pennington, George P.S. Peterson, Mary Peterson, Derek Rushton, Jean Sandison, June Sandison, John and Eileen Scott, Walter Scott, Margaret Slee, Brian Smith, Janis and Edward Smith, Mary Smith, Stella Sutherland, Jonathan Swale, Christian Tait, Ian Tait, Bobby Tulloch, Val Turner and Tammy Watt.

Archive photographs on pages 84 and 85 reproduced courtesy of The Shetland Museum, Lerwick.

Poem extracts, reproduced with permission:

Page 9: From 'Bide A Start Wi Me' by Rhoda Bulter. In *A Nev Foo A Coarn*, Thuleprint Ltd, 1977. © Rhoda Bulter 1977.

Page 15: From 'On a Raised Beach (to James H Whyte)' by Hugh MacDiarmid. In *Hugh MacDiarmid Selected Poetry*, edited by Alan Riach and Michael Grieve, Carcanet Press Ltd, 1992. © Hugh MacDiarmid 1992.

Page 58: From 'Löd A Langer' by Rhoda Bulter. In *Snyivveries. Shetland Poems*, The Shetland Times Ltd, 1986. © Rhoda Bulter 1986.

Page 61: From 'Burgawater' by Vagaland (TA Robertson). In *The Collected Poems of Vagaland*, The Shetland Times Ltd, 1975. © Vagaland 1975.

Page 96: From 'Shetlandic' by Rhoda Bulter. In *Link Stanes*, The Shetland Times Ltd, 1980. © Rhoda Bulter 1980.

Page 165: From 'Sunset Trowe Da Gaada Stack: A Response to a Photographic Image by Colin Baxter', by Christine De Luca. In *Plain Song*, The Shetland Library, 2002. © Christine De Luca 2002.

Page 169: From 'Macarism' by Rhoda Bulter. In *Snyivveries. Shetland Poems*, The Shetland Times Ltd, 1986. © Rhoda Bulter 1986.

Page 207: From 'The Clift Hills' by Christian Tait. In *Spindrift*, C.S. Tait, 1989. © Christian Tait, 1989.

First published in Great Britain in 2003 by
Colin Baxter Photography Ltd
Grantown-on-Spey, PH26 3NA Scotland

Reprinted 2007

www.colinbaxter.co.uk

Information used in the creation of the maps on pages 8, 12, 13, 98, 114, 124, 130, 146, 161, 164, 168, 200, 206 and 228 came from the Royal Commission on the Ancient and Historic Monuments of Scotland, The Macaulay Institute, Shetland Islands Council and Shetland Islands Tourism.

ISBN 978-1-84107-358-3

Front Cover Photograph: Sunset behind Muckle Roe and across Olna Firth to the north of Mainland Shetland. Back Cover Photograph: Atlantic Puffin ('Tammie Norie').
Page 1: Dragon head on the prow of replica Viking Longship or Galley, Up Helly Aa festival.
Page 3: Fair Isle North Lighthouse.

Printed in China

COLIN BAXTER ISLAND GUIDES

Shetland

Jill Slee Blackadder

Colin Baxter Photography, Grantown-on-Spey, Scotland

Wall of croft building, Papa Stour.

Contents

KEY FOR MAPS

- Nature reserve
- Museum/visitor centre
- Other ancient monument
- Castle
- Broch
- Lighthouse
- Cliffs
- Sandy beach
- Viewpoint
- Golf course
- Religious building
- Other place of interest
- Swimming pool/leisure centre

Preface

Islands are worlds in miniature. They have a wholeness, a completeness that wraps their inhabitants about with a deep sense of belonging. Shetland's islands are a cluster of over a hundred of these small worlds, each unique, each filled with a rich heritage of nature and history which is linked to its neighbours, yet entirely different from them. The shoreline defines the boundaries and marks the limit of land, tracing the profiles and character of each isle. The sea is an ever-changing presence, bringing, in quick succession, scenes of breathtaking wildness and calm, spellbinding beauty which have inspired poets, lured adventurers and provided a living for those who stayed.

Birds may have drawn people to Shetland first. No rock above sea level escapes the eye of a bird and Shetland has been home to hundreds of thousands of them for countless centuries. Whether to native seabirds, passing migrants or summer or winter visitors, Shetland affords shelter from the storm. The first human settlers, in all probability, were well aware of the birds' movements and also of the reasons for their journeys. After all, man was once – and in many lands still is – a migrating species. Birds were a source of food in themselves and their eggs were collected in large numbers until relatively recent times. But like Noah's dove, they were also reliable indicators of land, where restless tribes might settle. Seabirds might lead to food sources such as fish. It would have made great sense for early mariners to follow the feathered pilots as they headed north, or west, to see what rich pickings might be had over the horizon's mysterious curve.

No two people see Shetland in exactly the same way and my own experiences and perspective inevitably colour my reflection of the islands in the text. During the writing of this book I have been conscious of the debt that I owe all those to whom I have turned for information or advice, including the wealth of authors and experts whose knowledge and skill has furnished the islands with a rich store of literature of all kinds. Shetland is far bigger than many people at first realise and is crammed with history and an endless diversity of wildlife. It has proved impossible to do much more than touch briefly on the many facets of the islands. I apologise for any omissions, inaccuracies or faults, which are all my own.

Ketligill Head, Lang Ayre & Turls Head, North Mainland, Shetland.

Shetland

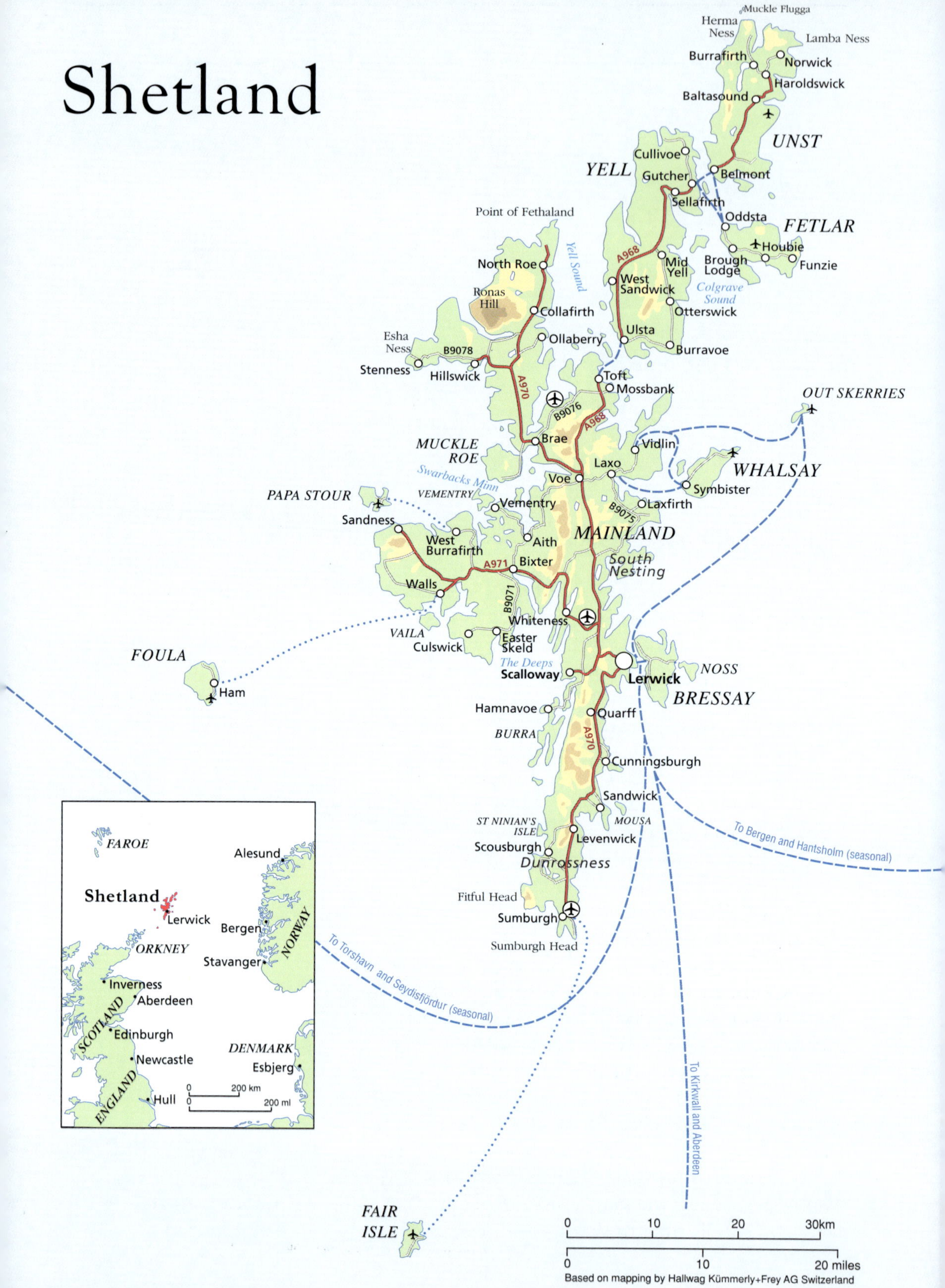

Muckle Flugga
Herma Ness
Lamba Ness
Burrafirth
Norwick
Haroldswick
Baltasound
UNST
Cullivoe
YELL
Gutcher
Belmont
Sellafirth
Oddsta
FETLAR
Houbie
Funzie
Brough Lodge
Point of Fethaland
Yell Sound
North Roe
A968
Mid Yell
West Sandwick
Colgrave Sound
Otterswick
Ronas Hill
Collafirth
Ulsta
Burravoe
Esha Ness
Ollaberry
B9078
Stenness
Hillswick
Toft
Mossbank
A970
B9076
OUT SKERRIES
MUCKLE ROE
Brae
Vidlin
Laxo
Voe
WHALSAY
Swarbacks Minn
Symbister
PAPA STOUR
VEMENTRY
Vementry
B9075
Laxfirth
Sandness
MAINLAND
West Burrafirth
Aith
A971
Bixter
South Nesting
Walls
B9071
Whiteness
VAILA
Easter Skeld
Culswick
FOULA
The Deeps
Scalloway
Lerwick
NOSS
Ham
BRESSAY
Hamnavoe
Quarff
BURRA
Cunningsburgh
Sandwick
ST NINIAN'S ISLE
MOUSA
Levenwick
Scousburgh
Dunrossness
To Bergen and Hantsholm (seasonal)
Fitful Head
Sumburgh
Sumburgh Head
To Torshavn and Seydisfjördur (seasonal)
To Kirkwall and Aberdeen
FAIR ISLE
0 10 20 30km
0 10 20 miles
Based on mapping by Hallwag Kümmerly+Frey AG Switzerland
FAROE
Alesund
Shetland
Lerwick
Bergen
ORKNEY
NORWAY
Stavanger
Inverness
Aberdeen
SCOTLAND
Edinburgh
DENMARK
Newcastle
Esbjerg
ENGLAND
Hull
0 200 km
0 200 ml

Introduction

Come, draa dee shair up ta da fire an bide a start wi me,
While I tell dee o da Hameland – da isles across da sea;
Whaar dir birds ta watch an fysh ta catch an heddir hills ta clim,
An times whin darkness niver faas idda laand o da Simmer Dim.

From *Bide A Start Wi Me* by Rhoda Bulter.

Shetland is a cluster of windswept islands which lie at the most northerly point of the British Isles. But that is only the beginning of the story. Far from being remote or peripheral, Shetland is at the hub of a great north Atlantic seaway. The Shetland Islands lie almost exactly at the centre of a triangle, with Norway approximately 200 miles to the east, Scotland slightly closer to the south and Faroe a similar distance away to the north-west. Shetland extends from latitude 59° 51' north to 61° north and from longitude 0° 45' west to 1° 45' west. The north of Unst lies, along with Anchorage in Alaska, Bergen in Norway and Leningrad in Russia, at about 61° north, the same latitude as Helsinki in Finland, and the southern tip of Greenland. Lerwick is in fact closer to the Arctic Circle than to London!

There has been much debate over the precise meaning and origins of the name 'Shetland'. References to the islands have been written more than twenty different ways in documents and on maps through the centuries. Experts may never agree on a single explanation. A selection of the variations found on records include: Syettelandia, Thule, Zetland, Hjaltland, Yeitlande, Hildland, Hiadtlandh, Hetlandt, Schytland and Hiatland. One possible derivation, 'land of the Cat tribe' has been suggested, relations perhaps of the tribe which may have given Caithness its name. Others include 'land of the story tellers', 'land of the sheltering or halting place', 'island of the sword hilt'. You can muse on all these and more; no one will ever know for certain.

Shetland is over 100 miles long from the Out Stack in the north to Fair Isle in the south. Yet despite its key location, its size and the number of islands, national maps and atlases often relegate Shetland to a corner of sea on a page showing Scotland several hundred miles further to the south. Shetlanders complain about these map-designers' distortions, yet often when making their own maps, commit the same crime by leaving Foula and Fair Isle inset into boxes many miles away from their true positions!

The distinctive silhouette of Foula seen from the north-east.

The Shetland archipelago consists of over 100 islands, seventeen of them inhabited at the turn of the new millennium, though a century ago it would have been twice that number. Its complex of islands, heavily indented by the sea, makes it difficult for visitors to orientate themselves.

The islands have been a historic centre for seafarers for thousands of years, an invaluable stepping stone between far-flung destinations. Sailors of many nationalities came and went, exchanging goods for fresh food and water. Here through the centuries, generations of islanders lived, fished and worked the land. Through the influences of new settlers, wars and increasing trade, language, culture and traditions of both Norse and Scots peoples have blended. Enriched through time with Dutch and German, Russian and Spanish, Shetland now has a community and culture of remarkable richness and diversity which is still evolving. Chinese, Thai, Indian, Filipino and Pakistani children mingle with Shetland Scots, English and other nationalities in island classrooms. With each fresh chapter in the histories of fishing, oil exploration and wildlife watching, new human migrants arrive and many stay and raise families. Some residents came first as visitors on holiday, so beware, you may fall under Shetland's spell yourself!

The first, distant glimpse of Shetland from the sea would have appeared little different all those years ago from that of sailors and passengers arriving here today. Fair Isle and the great bulk of Fitful Head stand proud of the sea for miles

Shapes from the land and sea of Northmavine.

if you reach Shetland from the south. Vikings from the east would have seen a different profile, with the impassive crest of Noss dominating the horizon long before the low-lying Out Skerries come into sight. Fishermen returning from the fishing grounds to the west would have seen Foula's great cliffs, second only in height to those of St Kilda. Early Arctic whaling ships on their way home would have seen the steep twin headlands of Hermaness and Saxavord in north Unst. But from whatever direction the first settlers came, the islands would have spelt rest, refreshment and shelter, for man and bird alike.

Despite, and maybe because of, its remoteness, the challenge of travelling to Shetland brings immense rewards. In today's modern and ever-changing world, Shetland can give a breathing space, a chance to connect with the past and reach out to the future with a refreshed spirit and renewed excitement.

This Guide falls into three main parts. It begins with a general account of the history of Shetland, starting with the rocks themselves and continuing with a simplified account of the evolving story of Shetland's wildlife and the human life which followed it, through to the present day. The second section covers the islands themselves, north to south, village by village. Lastly there are specific notes and checklists for visitors and those with special interests. Whether islander, incomer, visitor or browser, the book is intended to draw the reader to Shetland, its dramatic scenery, its fabulous wildlife, its spectacular archaeology, its history and people.

Shetland

0 5 10 km
0 5 10 miles
Muckle Flugga
Herma Ness
Lamba Ness
Norwick
Burrafirth
B9086
B9087
Haroldswick
The Nev
UNST
Baltasound
Balta
A968
Gloup Ness
Gloup
Cullivoe
B9082
YELL
Belmont
Gutcher
Uyea
Sellafirth
Ramna Stacks
Gruney
Nev of Stuis
Burra Ness
Oddsta
FETLAR
Point of Fethaland
Point of Bugarth
Hascosay
Camb
Brough Lodge
Uyea
Fugla Ness
Isbister
North Roe
Mid Yell
Houbie
B9088
Funzie
West Sandwick
B9081
Skelberry
A970
Muckle Ossa
The Faither
NORTH ROE
Otterswick
Ronas Hill
Collafirth
Ness of Gossabrough
Gossabrough
Lamba
Uynarey
Hamnavoe
Heylor
Ollaberry
Burravoe
Mio Ness
Esha Ness
B9078
Urafirth
Ulsta
Isle of Stenness
Tangwick
Stenness
Hillswick
Bardister
Bigga
Toft
Sullom Voe Oil Terminal
Samphrey
Mossbank
Sullom
Lunna Ness
Linga
Nibon
Scatsta
B9076
Bruray
Housay
Out Skerries
Egilsay
Lunna
Collafirth
Brae
Ve Skerries
Strom Ness
MUCKLE ROE
Busta
Vidlin
LUNNASTING
Skaw
Brough
Gillarona
Linga
Laxo
B9071
Tagon
WHALSAY
Grif Skerry
PAPA STOUR
Voe
East
Vementry
Symbister

Linga
Vementry
West Burrafirth
Sandness
Aith
Bixter
MAINLAND
AITHSTING
WEISDALE
NORTH NESTING
SOUTH NESTING
Hoo Kame
West
Mid
Bretabister
Gletness
Dale of Walls
Bridge of Walls
Walls
Gruting
Burrastow
VAILA
Kaliness
WHITENESS
Wormadale
Laxfirth
Kebister Ness
BRESSAY
Sand
Easter Skeld
Culswick
Silwick
Skelda Ness
Ustaness
Tingwall
LERWICK
Maryfield
Sound
NOSS
Kirkabister
Bard Head
Hildasay
Scalloway
Trondra
Oxna
Hamnavoe
WEST BURRA
Wester Quarff
Easter Quarff
EAST BURRA
Papil
Fladdabister
Cunningsburgh
Helli Ness
Kettla Ness
Houss Ness
South Havra
Leebotten
Mousa
Maywick
Sandwick
Bigton
St. Ninian's Isle
Levenwick
No Ness
Colsay
Dunrossness
Scousburgh
Boddam
Fitful Head
Quendale
Lady's Holm
Sumburgh
Horse Island
Sumburgh Head
Ham
FOULA
FAIR ISLE
Stonybreck
Fair Isle is 24 miles (39km) from Sumburgh head
To Torshavn and Seydisfjördur (seasonal)
To Bergen and Hantsholm (seasonal)
To Kirkwall and Aberdeen
To Fair Isle
A970
A971
B9071
B9075
B9073
B9074
B9122

The Landscape

These bare stones bring me straight back to reality.
I grasp one of them and I have in my grip
The beginning and the end of the world,

From *On A Raised Beach* by Hugh MacDiarmid.

Shetland owes its very existence to an extraordinarily rich underlying geology. Upon the ice and sea-worn, wind-battered rocks, soils of varying quality and chemistry have built up to support a unique community of plants and animals. This section of the Guide follows a sequence of topics through the evolving land- and seascapes of Shetland.

So how did Shetland come to be here at all? The islands have rocks of such remarkable variety, age and rarity, that a whole library could be filled with existing publications on the subject. But a simplified account is needed to set the stage for the subsequent human history of the islands. Without the 'auld rock', as Shetlanders affectionately call the islands, there would have been no story to tell. If the rocks could speak, what stories would they tell of the peoples who came first to the islands' shores and the fortunes of those who followed them?

GEOLOGY

For many people, it is enough simply to know where the most attractive beaches and the most spectacular cliffs can be found; Shetland's beaches alone are reason enough to make the journey here. There is a list of the best at the end of the book. As well as the miles of peaceful deserted sandy ones there are also endlessly engrossing pebble beaches where you can find sea-worn treasures for the pocket or the mantelpiece, not just indigenous pebbles either. Ballast in the form of stones from all over the world has been left on Shetland's beaches for centuries. But for those who would like to know more, a simplified account of Shetland's geology may help to explain how the islands came to be where and how they are today.

Rock is assumed to be solid, but to understand Shetland's geology, it must be thought of as a flexible, mobile material, constantly changing as a result of tension or stress of some kind, but mostly on a vast and slow timescale. You only have to glance at a geological map to see the enormous variety of rock types in Shetland and how far, through faulting, they have moved. So colourful and

Eshaness, Northmavine.

The north-east cliffs and stacks of Foula from Soberlie Hill.

decorative are the contrasting coloured bands and patterns of the rock alignments that some people buy one of these maps just to frame and hang on their walls. It is also useful to remember the three key words used by geologists: igneous (molten in origin), sedimentary (eroded and laid down in layers on sea beds by water action) and metamorphic (disturbed, altered by heat and pressure into rock of a very different appearance).

The rocks of which these islands are constructed are the surviving stumps of mountains formed about 420 million years ago during what is called the Caledonian Mountain building period. They were thrust up at the point where two great continental plates on the Earth's surface were gradually colliding. The new mountain ranges were built up over far older rocks, of which traces still remain. At Uyea in the north-west Mainland, and the Ve Skerries, north-west of Papa Stour, there are rocks from the Pre-Cambrian period. These are thought to be contemporary with the Lewisian gneisses, believed to have been formed at least 2000 million years ago.

The Caledonian Mountains would have been worn down, or eroded, by climatic conditions too violent and interminable to imagine. The land surface then was without life, so no roots held soil to protect the open land from the relentless assaults of water, wind and frost. Thunderstorms, thought to have lasted for countless years, rainstorms and ferocious winds eroded the lifeless landscape and washed the resulting vast quantities of rocks, pebbles, gravel, sand and mud down ancient river beds into ancient seas. Sea cliff erosion has exposed sections of river beds and alluvial fans to the north of Lerwick. So much rock was worn away that, through time, it buried all but the remaining higher hilltops. Erosion products from the mountains built up deep layers, forming what are now called the Old Red Sandstone, examples of which are found in the South Mainland and on Bressay and Noss.The sandstones can be found along much of Shetland's southern and eastern shores, where the strata are seen in the cliff faces. Here, in ledges carved by today's weather out of the varying bands of fine and coarse rock, Shetland's famous seabird colonies nest in spring. In Noss, Bressay and Sumburgh kittiwakes and guillemots, razorbills and fulmars jostle in the tiny pockets for shelter from the rain, wind and sea spray.

Although there is little geological evidence for life on the land surfaces of the earth, species of simple plants, invertebrates and primitive fish did live in the inland seas. Fossil traces can be found in rocks in Foula, Bressay and Sumburgh. Noss sandstones have signs of minute animal tracks, made perhaps by primitive worms or crustaceans. At Exnaboe, Walls and Sandness traces of Devonian fossil fish lie among finely banded shales. Seas supported life for millions of years, successive generations of creatures dying, their bones and shells building up to great depths.The calcium-rich sediments on these ancient seabeds, buried and altered in later times, may have formed the crystalline limestones which played such a key role in Shetland's human landscape and settlement patterns by giving rise to bands of fertile soils such as those of Whiteness and Tingwall.

Older sediments, under intense pressure beneath the roots of the Caledonian Mountains, had been so altered by heat that their quartz and felspar had partly dissolved and recrystallised, giving the ancient layers their fretworks of brightly coloured veins. What was once a sandstone can be 'cooked' into a coarse gneiss, with just the faint traces of banding left as witness to former sedimentary layers. Finer schists may have originated as silts, the finest of all becoming silvery phyllites, like the pebbles at St Ninian's Isle. Shetland is composed of vast masses of these metamorphic schists and the shining pebbles and glittering rock faces are very much a part of the landscape throughout Shetland, especially in Yell.

During periods of volcanic activity, the sediments would have collected particles of ash and eroded lavas then in the atmosphere, altering the chemistry of the sand and mudstones and producing, after millions of years of alteration, schists with quite different composition. Screes can be fused into breccias, pebble beds into conglomerates like those near Lerwick at Rova Head. In Fetlar, ancient pebble deposits have in turn been buried and reheated, altered, squashed out of shape and now form parts of new cliffs and shorelines. Eshaness in Northmavine and Papa Stour have cliffs cut through sections of volcanic rocks. Red granites of Muckle Roe and Ronas Hill are all fine examples of Shetland's igneous rocks.

Geological Sketch Map of Shetland

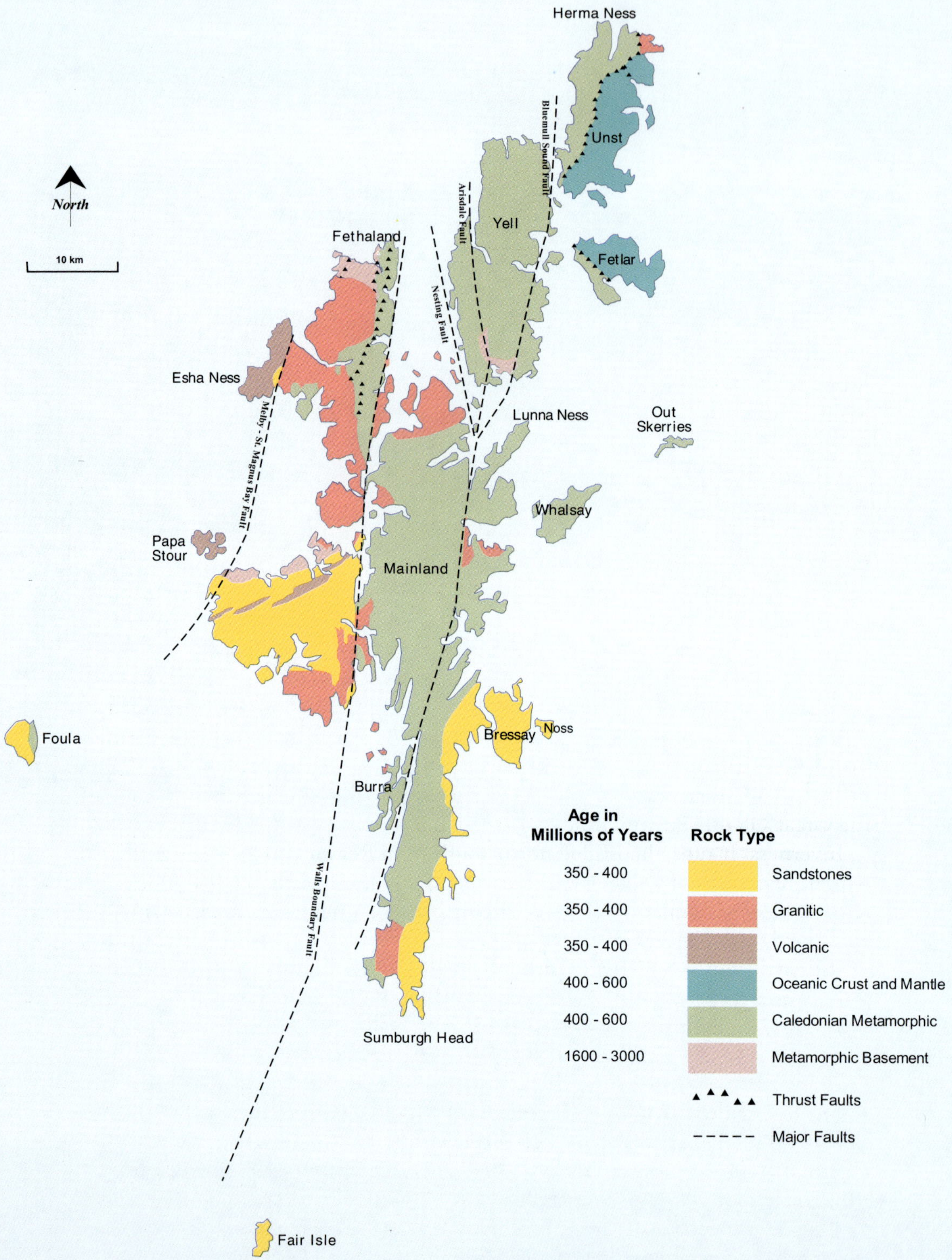

Red granite cliffs on the west of Muckle Roe, seen beyond Vementry.

Tensions in the Earth's crust which from time to time released themselves in massive splits and faults, created in Shetland some of the finest fault features found anywhere in Britain. One of the most important fault lines in Shetland, called the Walls Boundary Fault, is almost certainly the northernmost section of the Great Glen Fault which lies across northern Scotland from the Firth of Lorn to Inverness. It runs almost due north-south from Reawick to Brae and into Yell Sound. Just north of Ollaberry, a short section of tear fault is exposed in a remarkable and dramatic sheer face slicing out in an impressive wedge across a quiet sandy bay. Another long fault line, the Nesting Fault, runs parallel with it, to the east up Clift Sound and through north Central Mainland, along Yell's south-western shoreline. There are many other smaller fault lines.

Unst, too, displays some major faults and is famous for its serpentines and gabbros, giving rise to wonderful pebble beaches. Serpentines, rare exposures of ocean crust formed when the Iapetus Ocean closed, have moved from the deep seabed to Unst where they now form hills, exposed to the elements. This faulting has caused many very different rock types, formed far apart, to be brought close together, giving the islands' rocks a strongly defined north-south trend, with remarkably narrow bands of a whole variety of rocks lying alongside each other. The island is a geologist's dream. Talc, steatite and chromite have been quarried in the past and minute traces of gold and platinum have been detected.

'The Drongs', sea stacks near Hillswick, Eshaness.

During periods of climatic deterioration, ice caps and glaciers formed over the land surface of this part of Europe, ice advancing and retreating many times over thousands of years, each advance wiping out traces of earlier movements. Glaciers tore rocks from their beds and carried them great distances before they were dropped. Sometimes geologists can trace such 'erratic' boulders back to the rock they once came from. Most glacial erratics in Shetland are rocks of local origin. A single exception is the Dalsetter erratic, built into a South Mainland wall, which has been traced to Tonsberg in Norway. There is thought to have been a small, local ice cap near Voe which may have formed part of the last and most recent chapter of the Ice Age. Masses of large boulders can still be seen around the Loch of Voe, lying where they were dropped. The ice retreated from Shetland, leaving in its wake bare, scraped hills and valleys with, here and there, pockets of debris; clay, glacial till, boulder clay and erratic blocks. The Stanes of Stofast on Lunna Ness form one of the most spectacular clusters of erratics but there are thousands of smaller ones, often with their own local names and even legends attached.

Ice Ages came in waves and it is difficult to determine how each one affected Shetland. Sometimes clues can be found, however. At Fugla Ness in north-west Shetland, ancient peat layers have been exposed, buried beneath boulder clay from later ice movements. Traces of plants were preserved such as oak, Scots pine and Mediterranean heathers, indicating a much warmer climate at the time when they were growing, roughly 100,000 years ago. The last ice cover is believed to have retreated from Shetland about 10,000 years ago.

More recent peat deposits have formed since Shetland was first settled. Its acid depths, preserved remains of small trees, bark, hazel nuts, roots and branches have been and are often found when 'casting', or digging for peats. Peat levels can also preserve archaeological remains and even traces of volcanic ash and dust, datable evidence of eruptions in Iceland. Peat is still freely available but the number of households still casting and using peat for home use is steadily falling. This was the energy which was said traditionally to warm you three times; once when you cast (cut it from the peat banks and stacked it to dry), once when you raised it (lifted it and built it into stacks for drying) and once when you burned it.

Rivers can run under glaciers, sometimes forced through very restricted channels, wearing away the solid rocks of their beds. In Shetland short stretches of steep-sided ravines and gorges are thought to have been formed by these meltwater channels, notably the Daal of Lumbister in Yell, Valayre north of Brae, Fladdabister, Sundibanks and Tactigill on the Mainland. These gorges have been crucial in the preservation of Shetland's native wild trees, providing precious havens of protection from sheep. Only the hardest rock types, the strongest formations, resisted the ravages of ice and sea and these form the higher features of the present-day landscape. The 'Quarff Gap', visible as a deep notch in the hills from far out to sea from both east and west, prompts some geologists to argue that a massive river system once flowed east through the Gap, subsequent earth crust faulting leaving just this short section visible today.

Such depths of ice built up over Europe that the weight depressed much of the centre of the continent, allowing the fringes to rise up where ice and sea met. Now, the great ice masses which once weighed down the continent are melting and the landmass is rising. The edges, formerly forced up by downward pressure at the centre, are settling gently back down again. The rate of sinking is fairly slow, but in terms of the appearance of the islands today, it is significant. In a number of places, peat deposits, complete with fragments of ancient tree stumps, can be seen below low-tide mark; former moorland and scrub woodland has sunk and become shallow seabed habitat instead.

Shetland's geology is still evolving. Erosion wears away the higher outcrops and sea cliffs, and the sea washes the fragments along the coast and slowly down into deeper water. Because of the gradual sinking of the islands, a number of special features are found around Shetland. Bay head bars, ayres or shingle bars often form across the heads of the voes. Some become sealed off from the sea, allowing small salty or brackish lochs to fill up behind them. Saltmarshes can be found in a few shallow voe heads. Offshore islands are sometimes connected to the land by sand or shingle causeways or tombolos, such as the marvellous one at St Ninian's Isle near Bigton.

Sediments continue to settle ever deeper, like their ancient counterparts in the Old Red Sandstones. Minor earth tremors still occur, and are a serious factor taken into account by those responsible for designing safe tunnels, oil extraction and pipe-laying along the seabed. Modern development erodes inland sites even more quickly than natural weathering and, as tourism increases, public awareness and concern are growing factors where plans for new housing, industry and other

Flett, near Voe, Central Mainland.

developments are discussed. This will be an interesting area to watch in the coming years as employment patterns change and entrepreneurs cast greedy eyes at Shetland's wild spaces and seemingly limitless resources of aggregate-rich hills and cliffs.

A variety of different climatic elements controls the weathering of the Shetland island mass and a brief look at Shetland's weather may help set the scene for life on the land.

WEATHER AND CLIMATE

Throughout Shetland's history, climate change has directly affected human settlement, with swings from warmer to colder periods and back again.

As long as you are out of doors among the superb scenery, Shetland can be beautiful whatever the weather, but on a still, midsummer day it is exquisite. Winter days are short and dark, but in a roaring gale, with the sea crashing in towering clouds of spray against the streaming cliffs, it is magnificent. The sea to a large degree controls Shetland's weather. Warm it up in July and after a day or two of almost Mediterranean scenery and heat, fog descends. Cooled down, spring seas glitter under steady blue skies and you can see for 50 miles. The sun is above the horizon for almost 19 hours in midsummer and at night its light never leaves the sky. Lochs form their own mist patches and there is no stranger and

Gruney and Ramna Stacks from near West Sandwick, Yell.

more haunting sight than that of a deserted valley, filled with small lochs, from whose mirror surfaces, in the half light, mist rises in swirls into a deep blue-green sky. The 'Simmer Dim', as this time is called, is a natural spectacle not to be missed. Reflections in still voes at night are so perfect that a photograph could be inverted without detection.

A poor start is often followed by a rapid improvement and vice versa. Shetlanders adapt constantly to the changing weather conditions. A head teacher might allow a slightly longer playtime than usual on a hot sunny day and, contrastingly, wedding plans have bad weather fall-backs for photograph venues (though modern studios now have special effects technology which enables a couple to appear to be on a tropical beach, even if it is blowing a gale outside!). It is always advisable to go well prepared, however auspiciously a day may start. But should you be unlucky with a day of really bad weather, Shetland is small and diverse enough for there always to be places which will be calm and sheltered. If the wind is from the west, try to locate an east-facing bay and vice versa. The Best Beach Guide at the end of the book lists wind directions from which the beach may be best sheltered. Weather statistics can give an idea of typical conditions, but they can only give a general indication of what you might actually experience.

The Lerwick Observatory, which is perched on the top of a hill overlooking the town, experiences colder, windier, mistier conditions than those felt in the town, just a mile away. Wind speeds, chill factors and temperatures vary dramatically between sea level and hill tops. The changeability sometimes means that national radio weather forecasts, dependent on local reports, can be wrong, sometimes describing heavy rain or strong winds in Shetland, when it is actually dry and warm! Complaints are sometimes made about this, as these forecasts can obviously have an effect on prospective visitors. Radio Shetland broadcasts the best forecast from Monday to Friday at 5.30 pm. *Shetland in Statistics*, first published in March 1972 and each year since, gives detailed records of the weather as well as island distances, economic data and a wealth of other useful facts and figures.

One delightful advantage of the changeability of Shetland's weather is the rainbows. When it does rain, there is usually some sun about too, so frequent, vivid rainbows are something of a speciality. Hazy summer skies towards evening sometimes produce special effects such as 'gaas' – sun dogs, or false suns. Haloes, or 'brochs', around the moon as well as the sun are seen often enough to have their own dialect names. But the most magical of all the sky effects have to be the Mirrie Dancers, or the northern lights (aurora borealis), seen in northern skies in autumn and winter. When Shetland's weather is hot and sunny, landscapes rival the Greek islands for sheer loveliness, and are greener by far. People come out and make the best of every glorious day, never taking the next day's sunshine for granted.

But on the few occasions in the year when a real blaster of a tempest erupts over the islands, it is a very different matter. Ferocious gusts of wind can knock a grown man off his feet and houses creak and groan, the glass in their windows bowing and bending under the pressure. Thunderstorms are relatively rare, as are true heatwaves. Snow falls, but seldom for long enough to lie long and a good, snowy, sledging winter is every bairn's dream.

Some Shetland dialect words express the weather far better than their English equivalents. A 'day atween wadders' is a glorious day sandwiched between stormy periods. A 'blind moorie' is the name for blinding, gale-driven snow, a particularly dangerous winter feature. 'Flans' are vicious gusts of the kind that could easily overwhelm a small boat out at sea. People find the weather an endless source of interest and conversation and over the years, certain phrases and comments have become classics. Here are a few just for fun: 'If you don't like Shetland's weather, hang around for a few minutes!' 'In Shetland it rains between showers!' 'Shetland has four seasons in one day.' After a particularly fine day, you may be asked, tongue in cheek, 'did you enjoy the summer?' But for all the humour and cynicism, there is a pride in the hardiness and toughness of the island people who stay and make the best of every fine period, never wasting a moment's sun and calm. I will never forget the day I walked, head bent against a stiff, rain-filled breeze, and saw an old man striding towards me. 'Fine day!' he said and walked cheerfully by.

INLAND LANDSCAPE

The inland landscape may at first sight appear bare and treeless. Exposure to glaciation and the ravages of some of the worst seas around the British coastline have certainly taken their toll. But the ice also helped to shape superb valleys, freshwater lochs and magnificent gorges where foaming waterfalls cascade into pool after pool before reaching the sea. Miles of burns flow through the hills, trickling peacefully in summer, but foaming yellow and brown in winter spate.

Crofting still dominates the landscape, with sheep grazing most of the hills, moors and pastures of the islands, even the uninhabited ones. You can see herds of cattle in the richer pastures and wide fields of 'tatties' (potatoes) and 'neeps' (turnips) in the South Mainland. Here and there the odd pocket-handkerchief-size patch of silver-green Shetland oats, or dark green 'kale', or Shetland cabbage, is still grown for fodder. Many crofters augment their incomes, if they can, with part- and even full-time work in a different area of employment. Hill dykes can still be seen as great sweeping curves above the townships, but modern fencing methods have put an end to the well-maintained stone and turf barricades of their heyday. Much hill land has been taken out of the common grazing and straight lines cut starkly through the shifting shades of brown, leaving improved grazing, glaring green, in their wake, where as long as the application of the lime and seed mixtures continues, the heather is killed off.

A few corners of the islands remain much as they would have been 50 years ago, but most are increasingly overlain by the tracery of modern, technological life; fast roads, power lines, new housing estates, factories and business units. The old strip fields or 'rigs' of arable land once framed every township in Shetland, but sadly almost all small-scale cultivation has ceased. The area of land suitable for cultivation is roughly 871,000 acres (352,000 hectares), but much of this has returned to grass; the faint parallel lines of old shared cultivation strips showing clearly through the green. It has been estimated that 90 per cent of cultivated ground has been lost to the Shetland landscape in the last 50 years.

Hills and moorland rise dark and brooding over vivid lower pasture and grassland, broken here and there by magnificent wild inland cliffs with their rare flora and ferns. Blanket bog, one of Britain's rarest habitats, has built up in many places. Everywhere there are lochs, their surfaces glass still, reflecting the hills and skies; dark, or rippled, or wild with trailing streamers of spray, depending on the state of the wind. High ground in Shetland is a relative term. The highest hill, Ronas Hill, is only 1486 feet (453m) high at the summit, but because of the Shetland climate, conditions there are known to be equivalent to those at 3000 ft (915m) over on the mainland. Other hills dominate the skyline in the west, north and south of the island mass. To the far west, the sea cliffs of Foula are the second highest in the whole of Britain, St Kilda's cliffs beating them by only a few feet.

SHORE- AND SEASCAPES

The sea, reaching up where glaciers once flowed down, cuts deep into the land, creating superb scenery everywhere you go. The long, narrow inlets, called voes, have afforded splendid shelter for boats through the centuries. Most are relatively shallow, but Ronas Voe is exceptionally deep and long, more like a Norwegian

North and South Benelip, and Filla from Out Skerries with Bressay and Noss in the distance.

fjord, allowing two whaling stations to be established there at one time. There are miles upon miles of low, rocky shore, of fine, deserted sandy beaches where seals, otters and shoals of tiny fish enjoy the relatively warm shallows.

Seventeen islands were still inhabited at the start of the twenty-first century, the majority of the population living on the largest island, Mainland, with sizeable numbers of people living in Unst and Yell, Whalsay, two islands in the Out Skerries group, Bressay, Muckle Roe, Trondra and East and West Burra, with smaller numbers in Fair Isle, Fetlar, Papa Stour, Foula, Vaila and (by bird wardens in summer only) Noss. Many of the other islands were inhabited within living memory. Houses and outbuildings in some of them are still kept up by the descendants of those who once lived there and are used for short periods for seasonal work with sheep, and occasionally for holidays.

Smaller islands often have ruins and other remains, traces of early settlement, going back several thousand years. Vementry, Papa Little, Hascosay, Uyea, Mousa, Hildasay, Oxna, Papa, South Havra and Linga are all deserted, but a few former inhabitants are still living and keep the memories and stories alive. Balta, Huney, Haaf Gruney, Urie Linga, Brother Isle, Samphrey, Cheynies, North Havra, Colsay, Little Roe, Lamba, Egilsay, Nibon, Uynarey plus another half dozen Lingas are still home, if not to folk, at least to the seabirds and otters. The names of these now uninhabited islands read like a

Moo Stack and the cliffs of Eshaness in a storm.

line of ancient poetry and a summer's day spent in any of them is one of the most wonderful experiences to be had in Shetland.

Where the sea batters against higher ground, dramatic cliffs result, producing spectacular scenery, often providing marvellous seabird breeding habitats. Wild seas have torn at the coast, creating magnificent sea stacks and caves, natural arches and sea-carved tunnels. These are featured in many geography text books as classic examples of their kind. Each headland, or ness, jutting out into deeper water and every innermost beach differs subtly from every other. A wealth of Norse place names describes these differences with fascinating words: *houb*, *ayre*, *wick* and *geo* occur time and time again as part of coastal place names. In places the coast looks as if it has been slashed by a giant axe. These deep cuts, typical Shetland features, are called *geos* ('geo' is pronounced like 'go', with a small 'i' in the middle). They are havens for wild cliff flora and nesting seabirds. Winter seas drive air and water into the geos, often creating sea caves and blow holes. Such is the sea's force that the rock above occasionally weakens and collapses, creating great holes in the ground. The Holes of Scraada at Eshaness, Kirsten's Hole in Papa Stour and the Kirn of Cumlewick are fine examples of collapsed sea caves.

The sea is an endless source of interest in Shetland. Today's seascapes are filled with activity of all kinds. Fishing boats, with their high-tech catching gear and safety features, convenient and comfortable crew facilities and bright colours are a far cry from their open, six-oared ancestors. A few older, smaller boats still work for shellfish, but the big fleets can venture hundreds of miles and spend weeks at sea. Lerwick Harbour is busy with ships of every kind from tiny rowing boats, or 'punts' as they are called, to monster cruise ships, oil service boats, geo-survey ships and fisheries protection vessels, and flotillas of visiting yachts contrast with the occasional appearances of old sailing ships. The *Dim Riv*, a replica of a Viking longship, makes short trips round the harbour in Lerwick, and a restored 'zulu' fishing boat, the *Swan*, takes people on trips round the islands, and to Norway or St Kilda. Island seascapes often feature mussel rafts with rows of floats like enormous necklaces; salmon cages like giant floating hoops, little wooden salmon feed huts on rafts and salmon boats ferrying feed between them. But apart from modern shipping, there are more traditional things to look for.

THE SEA

The sea is the place to watch for incoming weather. Distant squalls approach in a white blur over far-flung islands, allowing enough time to bring the washing in before they sweep in over the whole scene. Glance at the sea in the morning and the colour, patterns and movement of the waves will tell you how much wind there is and from which airt, or direction, it is blowing. When winter gales reach a critical strength, the wave crests tear, sending white water flying ahead of them in smoking trails of spindrift. But on a calm summer night, you can see not only the sky, but reflected stars as well in the still surface. Sunrise over the eastern sea is a breathtaking blaze and sunsets can often transform the end of an otherwise dark day when the sun appears briefly out of the heavy cloud layer over the horizon, emerging in a glory of reddening waves and blinding light before sinking into the sea.

If you could venture down below the waves and explore the hidden panorama deep beyond the shoreline, you would discover Shetland's true nature, that of a small fragment of eroded hill system stretching out towards the deep Atlantic and reaching back towards the rest of Europe. Shetland is situated at a key point in the fishing atlas, where the North Sea and Atlantic meet. The North Atlantic Drift swings away from the Gulf Stream and washes our shores all year round. Arriving from the south, the warm currents from the Gulf Stream sweep past Shetland, meeting the colder Arctic currents, and veer away to the west, along the shores of Iceland. Here, the Irminger Current, as it is now called, swings south again as it approaches Greenland and is deflected eastwards, where it rejoins the North Atlantic Drift and the circular flow begins again.

The seabed around the islands is as full of varied habitats as the land. All submarine habitats have their unique range of wildlife and just as land masses have prevailing winds, so seabed territory has prevailing currents, which shift, seasonally, in much the same way as air currents in the world above the waves.

The currents carry with them the constant stream of plankton on which all sea life depends. As well as moving with the current, great masses of plankton rise towards the surface at night and sink again as day breaks, a process known as vertical migration. Flat sandy and muddy areas support young fish and are the seed beds of the Shetland fishing industry. Large areas of rocky, uneven seabed lie between jagged tangles of outcrops and boulders which could tear fishing nets if they were set in the wrong place. Here and there submarine ridges run far out to sea from the shoreline, one reaching from Shetland all the way to Fair Isle and Orkney. There are steep-sided gullies, disconnected ridges and strings of small mountain peaks, the crests of which make up many uninhabited offshore islands, stacks and skerries. Some areas of the seabed are covered by 'stonefields', rough tracts of boulder-strewn sand and mud where huge sea spiders and various species of fish are found.

Currents affect surface water conditions too, but less strongly than the tides, whose influence can be altered greatly by the prevailing wind situation. Tides which run between islands create powerful and fast-changing tidal streams, which can present problems for boats unfamiliar with Shetland waters, especially when visibility is poor. For several thousand years mariners have negotiated Shetland's beautiful but dangerous coastline, each new generation learning from the previous one how to navigate safely around the islands. Thorough knowledge of local underwater rocks, tidal patterns and weather conditions saved many a life in days before radar and navigation charts. Today, newcomers must study for certificates before they can take charge of even a small fishing craft. A copy of the *North Coast of Scotland Pilot* will give the casual reader a completely different perspective of island life, with its current and weather charts, shelter havens, and descriptions of the islands seen from the open sea.

Standing stone at Skellister, South Nesting.

Natural History

Islanders and visitors find Shetland's wildlife rich and spectacular, despite the fact that scientists often describe it as 'impoverished'! As a general rule, the greater the land mass, the greater the number of wild species found, thus leaving small islands with a narrower range of species than comparable areas of land elsewhere. But the wildlife which inhabits islands has a tendency to evolve slightly different features from those found on the mainland. Shetland has its own range of unique species and subspecies of plants and animals which greatly add to the interest for specialist and casual visitors alike. This chapter looks first at the wildlife and then at the introduced domestic species.

Soils vary in quality and chemistry in Shetland. In general, sandstone and limestone areas produce the most fertile soils and the richest growth of wild plants and crops. Moorland with its peat, heather, mosses and coarse grasses is acid and less productive. Small areas of late glacial sediments exist where local clays and gravels are found. Wherever the few good rich brown soils are found, farms have been built and fields established. The levels of many rigs and small fields were raised over centuries of wearying effort, baskets, or 'kishies', full of earth from pockets found here and there, being carried and tipped out on the land. Manuring and the use of seaweed as fertilizer each year also built up soil fertility and the green places remain long after cultivation has ceased.

WILD FLORA

Traditional crofting systems encouraged the rich growth of wild flower species. Shetland is a wild flower haven for plant lovers despite many changes and degradations to its landscape in recent years, and there are delights for the amateur and professional botanist alike. The unique position in the north Atlantic, close both to Europe and the Arctic Circle, has enabled plants from very different regions to grow here. However, despite the enormous numbers of wild flowers in certain places in spring, under present legislation it is an offence to uproot any wild plant unless you have a licence. Certain rare species are listed and these may not be picked or destroyed at all. One of the best ways to remember the flowers is to take close-up photographs. A small folding screen can be used to deflect the wind which might shake them, causing blurring of pictures.

Despite its treeless reputation, Shetland has a considerable amount of native woodland, but it is only a few inches high! Dwarf species of native

Atlantic Puffin ('Tammie Norie').

willow are common across much of the islands' clifftop pasture and some areas of heath. Native species of rowan, aspen, hazel, birch and even crab apple all exist, though in desperately fragile, tiny sites where sheep have not gained access. These sites are being afforded more protection and efforts at propagating and restoring native tree populations are beginning to bear fruit.

Edmondston's Chickweed.

Springtime conjures up images of flower masses; golden valleys drenched with kingcups, primroses and celandines; sea pinks carpeting the short coastal turf in June; meadows brimming with orchids; higher hills transformed into seas of blue with squill flowers, and roadside verges in Dunrossness flooded with bird's-foot trefoil and regal purple swathes of tufted vetch. But to get the most out of Shetland's flora, you need to look more carefully at the different habitats and the different soils which nurture them to discover the rarities and specialities in the islands. The following account of Shetland habitats begins at the highest places in the islands and works its way down to sea level.

Shetland's highest hills do not reach a very great altitude, but they are exposed to such severe weather conditions that the plant communities resemble those growing at 3000 feet in mainland Scotland. Shetland's highest point is the top of Ronas Hill, where the uppermost Shetland habitat is, literally speaking, bare rock. On the surfaces of all exposed rocks in Shetland, lichens of many kinds have become established, as they would have done after the ice retreated for the last time, about 12,000 years ago. Lichens, a life form composed of a remarkable combination of alga and fungus, are among the oldest of all Shetland's plants, and are a well-known indicator of clean, unpolluted air, of which Shetland has vast quantities. Natural dyes were extracted from lichens long ago and there has been a revival of interest in this old craft. Algae, liverworts, and club mosses can all be found within the environs of Ronas Hill. Ferns grow in the deep cracks between rocks and in sheltered gullies.

Between the weathered rocks, fellfield habitat has formed on the granite dome of Ronas Hill. Fellfield is an area of high, exposed, rocky ground where ice action causes the stones to shift little by little every year. A range of low, tough mountain plants grows here among the widespread woolly hair moss, including trailing azalea, bearberry, alpine bearberry, alpine lady's mantle, alpine clubmoss and juniper. Interesting grasses and sedges can be found here too, but so small and reduced as to prove difficult to identify for those familiar with their appearance in less harsh conditions. Fellfield has also formed on the serpentine of the Keen of Hamar in Unst and here you can find arctic sandwort, northern rock cress, fragrant orchid and the unique Edmondston's Chickweed, or Shetland mouse-ear, which has beautiful white starry flowers on short, furry stems.

Further down the lower slopes there is heath, where water drains freely through thin soils. Heather, crowberry and a range of grasses cover the ground, with here and there, bell heather and cross-leaved heath. Several tiny flowers, including tormentil, heath milkwort, eyebright and heath spotted orchids, all add splashes of colour.

Moorland differs from heath as it is formed over deep peat layers. Heather grows here too, as well as deer grass and cotton grass or bog cotton, which in Shetland rejoices in the wonderful name of *Luckaminnie's oo* (wool), Luckaminnie, or Luckie, being an old name of a legendary witch. Moorland is rich in moss species, especially sphagnums, as well as many fascinating sedges and rushes. Drainage gullies in the moorlands support different flora and you can find round-leaved sundew, lousewort, hard fern, butterwort and bog asphodel.

The term 'relict vegetation' refers to plant species that were common in Shetland long before humans and their grazing animals. Today, a few sites survive in places which are inaccessible to sheep. Gorges with steep sides where streams race through, inland cliff faces, outcrops of rocks, deep cracks in rock formations and small islands or holms in lochs all provide a safe foothold for some of Shetland's loveliest plants. Wild rose, honeysuckle, great woodrush, roseroot, meadowsweet, and even some small native trees can be found here, among a glorious display of other flowers. Look for (dwarf) golden rod, ferns, hawkweeds, sheep's bit and lady's bedstraw. The underlying rocks, whether schist, limestone or granite, sandstone or serpentine, all tend to support slightly different plant communities. One great rarity, common on mainland Scotland, is the harebell, or Scottish bluebell, which only survives in a few tiny sites in Shetland.

Fungi deserve a mention in their own right and a surprising variety are found in Shetland, many of them edible. 'Piddock stools', as they used to be called in Shetlandic, grow mainly in the autumn, especially on well-grazed coastal pasture. Field and horse mushrooms are common and a range of the wax caps, which come in scatters of shiny scarlet, yellow and orange, arrive slightly later. Shaggy ink caps occur in large numbers in certain years and puff-balls of several species can be found, including occasionally giant puff-balls of enormous size.

A number of fungi common on willow trees can be found growing apparently in grass, but on closer inspection can be seen to be growing on some of the tiny dwarf willows which flourish in many coastal areas. There are also many dwarf, delicate fungi, frequently found on sheep dung. Shetland naturalist Bobby Tulloch, famous for his bird photography, was also a keen observer of fungi and added many hundreds to Shetland's fungus record list in the 1980s.

Sea cliffs can produce superb displays of sea campion in white cascades, warm drifts of sea pinks, or thrift, the miniature hyacinth-blues of spring squill,

Thrift (Sea Pink).

and, early in the season, low pink cushions of the heavily scented moss campion. Stacks and skerries offshore are rich in vegetation and the steep-sided geos spill over gold with bird's-foot trefoil, rich glossy green Scottish lovage, purple thyme, eyebright and a wonderfully deep carmine, furry stemmed form of red campion, known affectionately as Shetland red campion.

Freshwater lochs and pools afford yet another habitat for wild plants. But here, even more than on land, the underlying rock chemistry dictates the nutrient richness and variety of the flora. There are four splendidly tongue-twisting names for the main types, in ascending order from poor to rich: dystrophic, oligotrophic, mesotrophic and eutrophic! In the nutrient-poor, peaty lochs with their deep-brown water, mosses, especially sphagnums, provide almost the only colour with a remarkable range of greens, yellows and maroons. A few may have colonies of 'carnivorous' bladderworts (they catch tiny water creatures inside underwater bladders) and perhaps bog bean. The latter deserves a more attractive name and if you do find it in flower, have a really good close-up look at the beautiful flowers with their intricate fringed petals. A few peaty lochs in the far west of Shetland have small populations of water lilies, with white, waxy petals enclosing dense clusters of yellow stamens.

By contrast, lochs over granite have exceptionally clear water. Also poor in nutrients, they support rather more species, of which water lobelia is particularly attractive. A whole range of different pondweeds and rushes tend to do well in the third category of loch, such as Sand Water in the Lang Kames with its waving forest of bullrushes. But the most interesting are those in the last, and in Shetland the rarest, category, the eutrophic lochs. The rich plant life supports an abundance of minibeasts. Waterfowl visit regularly on migrations, to feed before resuming their flights. Some of the best birdwatching in Shetland can be enjoyed here. Loch of Hillwell and Loch of Spiggie in the South Mainland and Loch of Clickimin in Lerwick are good examples. Look for water crowfoot, water forget-me-not, water speedwell and several different pondweeds, among many other species.

Burns (streams) and roadside ditches are great places for wild flowers, with an abundance of marsh-marigolds in the lower reaches in spring. But the flowers in fact grow mostly along the edges, rather than actually in the water. Marsh cinquefoil, water forget-me-not and lesser spearwort bloom in abundance and monkey flower or mimulus transforms ditches into dazzling golden trails in summer; it is a relatively recent incomer to the islands, but is certainly very successful. You may see the rich orange double version in a few places. In some peaty burns, a dark, almost black-green moss is found in shaggy cascades along the water edges. This is *fontinalis antipyretica*, a moss well known for having fire-resistant qualities, which was said to be packed in-between stones when building lums, or chimneys. Springs up in the hills often seep out across stony ground and are frequently surrounded by lush vegetation. Some interesting species can be found among these 'flushes', especially in more fertile areas, of which grass-of-Parnassus must be the finest.

Wetlands occur where water cannot freely escape. Marsh and bog plants grow here and yet again, the richness of diversity reflects the chemistry below. A sequence of rushes, mosses and sedges grows through the marshes from dryer conditions to wetter and then dryer again on the far side. Mosses, in particular, grow well and there are records of sphagnum being harvested during the First World War and dried for use as a medical aid in the war effort for both their absorbent and anti-fungal properties as well as for padding and protection. Blanket bogs occur in some areas of Shetland and are gradually becoming valued and protected as rare and special habitats in their own right. White drifts of bog cotton stand out brightly against the darker peat moors. But the richer swampy ground is a place in which to spend hours just revelling in the mass of different species and the sheer quantity of plants and colours: lady's smock and marsh bedstraw, marsh-marigold and yellow flag iris, northern marsh orchid, marsh lousewort and sneezewort, marsh cinquefoil and creeping forget-me-not, and the frilly carmine drifts of ragged robin, take the breath away.

There are several kinds of grassland in Shetland, almost all heavily affected by years of grazing or cultivating. Pastureland near the sea, rich in red fescue, creeping bent and Yorkshire fog (grass) is grazed nearly down to the roots and wild flowers tend to grow almost unrecognisably short and small. Cliff edges are mostly well fenced off and the contrast in size between a spring squill or a devil's-bit scabious flower on the cropped turf and one growing behind the protective fence is startling. In really exposed places, grass gives way entirely to sea pinks, scurvy grass, sea and buck's-horn plantain. Sea plantain leaves can be as little as half an inch in length here, whereas on a sheltered cliff face, or a small offshore island, the leaves can reach eight or nine inches and are wide and succulent. Where the sward approaches the sea it changes into saltmarsh and a whole new range of plants takes over.

On some ungrazed headlands and holms grass can grow almost knee high, threaded through here and there with narrow otter trails. Limestone grassland has a different range of flowers from granite and sandstone areas, and hay meadows are different again; rich in different species, they are a gradually diminishing sight, silage having become the preferred method of saving fodder for the winter, and there has been a consequent decline in many of the bird species which nested among the hay, notably the corncrake. There are many different grasses in Shetland but identifying them can be difficult. It is worth mentioning a few of the more striking and obvious ones for those who are interested.

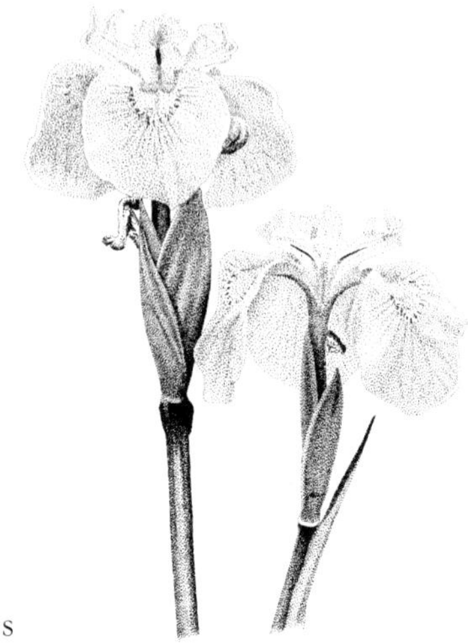
Yellow Iris.

Look out for viviparous fescue with its very heavy heads made up entirely of small grass seedlings. These tiny plantlets have minute tufts of leaves and little tangled roots, all ready to start growing the moment they fall from the parent plant. Wavy hair grass grows much taller and the delicate flowering heads glitter in low sunlight as each gleaming awn is illuminated on its tiny crimped stem. The short, bluish-purple moor grass can tint whole areas of hill when almost in flower. A grass to look out for in moorlands is mat grass, a short, tufty grass with flowering heads rather like narrow hair combs. Press a finger onto one and as it bends, the 'teeth' of the comb open and you can see them clearly. Cocksfoot grass grows very tall and lush, particularly along new roadside verges. Bents, with their minute awns, when growing in profusion, give a misty effect to the ground. Great tall stands of reed canary grass grow in some damper pastures, prized in days gone by for its qualities as a thatching grass. Meadow grass is often picked by Shetland children who hold up the flowering head and say, 'Look, a tree in spring', then strip the awns clear and hold up the skeletal stem, crying 'and now it's winter!'

Beaches are a Shetland speciality, but each supports very different vegetation, depending on its type. Sand dunes are good places to find marram grass and lyme grass, both excellent for stabilising the dunes against wind erosion, and they grow so tall that smaller plants can often be found in the sheltered spaces between them. Sea rocket makes a splash of colour on the seaward fringes of the dunes and the upper shore of sandy beaches, and there may be patches of sea sandwort and orache. Autumn gentian can sometimes be found in the grass above the beach.

Shingle beaches and bars often have an interesting population of small plants, as well as a good summer display of the yellow sow thistle, red campion and sea mayweed, often depicted in local artists' paintings of boats and sea-shore scenes. Nettles and goose grass, or cleavers, may grow onto the edges of the shingle, but, sadly, you are unlikely to find one of Shetland's loveliest but rarest plants, the oyster-plant, which has been declining in recent years. Saltmarshes occur at the head of some voes, but they tend to be fairly small. However, they support a range of curious and resilient plants which are well worth investigating. Pink flowering orache, glasswort, tasselweed, greater sea spurrey and sea arrow grass may be unfamiliar names, but they have a long Shetland pedigree. This habitat is an excellent place for indicating the degree of marine pollution in Shetland waters and certain sites have been regularly monitored ever since the oil terminal was constructed at Sullom Voe.

Eel grass is the only flowering plant actually to grow in the sea below low watermark. This is the territory of the seaweeds, marine algae, of which Shetland boasts well over 300 species. They fall loosely into three categories: the greens, the browns and the reds. Rock pools are often filled with yellow-green strands of gut weed, and bright green blades of sea lettuce are often cast up by the waves. Tangled masses of coarser seaweeds are thrown up onto shores after heavy seas and in former times would have been safely gathered in and spread on the land as fertilizer. From the 1720s until the late 1800s these were gathered, burnt and the resulting residue sold and transported south for industrial use to augment local incomes. But the most attractive stranded seaweeds are the red species. You can pick up a pink frond here and a small purple bunch there and examine the differences between their filmy fonds, fringed blades and fern-like trails. The changing sequences of marine habitats continue out of sight, deeper and deeper into increasingly unknown territory.

Another wild plant treasure found on Shetland's beaches is the sea bean. Rounded, flattened and chocolate brown, the seeds of the tropical vine *Entadas gigas*, known as Molucca beans, occasionally wash up on Shetland shores, having drifted all the way from the Caribbean via the Gulf Stream. Several other species have been found here; some have even sprouted when planted indoors and kept at high temperatures, but none has survived for long.

GARDENS

Gardens are increasing in popularity and size to such an extent that Shetland now has several full-time garden nurseries and landscaping businesses. Shelter has to be the watchword for gardening in the islands and there is an amazing range of tricks and strategies for keeping the wind off plants, from hedges to fish boxes, upside-down sweetie jars to expensive windbreak fencing. Until recent years the flower park in Lerwick was the only garden open to the public. But the late John Copland, a crofter from Islesburgh in Northmavine, opened a garden with a plant-sale section in the 1980s. His book *Hardy Plants of the North* sold out immediately and since then there has been a rising tide of interest. Many primary schools have been establishing gardens since the 1980s and in the late 1990s a community gardens initiative began to catch on; there is a splendid one at the Old Haa, Burravoe, in Yell.

Greenhouses have been constructed in increasing numbers in recent years and here and there you will see a geodesic dome. Pioneering initiatives came from some individual Shetlanders, such as the late John Williamson from Ollaberry, who grew much-admired peaches, plums, apples and cherries in tiny, interconnecting greenhouses. Several businesses, responding to the growing interest in gardening, have begun marketing new outdoor cultivation equipment and hardware. Tingwall has an annual garden fair which is well worth visiting if your stay happens to coincide. The Planticrub, a plant nursery and shop, was set up in the late 1980s and for many years supplied Shetland with much of its tomato and cucumber requirements. Strawberry cultivation was introduced commercially in Yell and for some years Tingwall Valley Herbs produced dried and fresh herbs, local pickles and chutneys.

Trees have been planted ever since the first of the 'big' houses began to establish their own gardens. Sycamores, first recorded in the early 1700s, grow very well, even managing to set seed. There are sizeable trees in walled gardens in Busta, Veensgarth, Tresta, Scalloway, Lerwick, Swinning, Voe, Kergord and in Baltasound at Halligarth, Britain's most northerly wood. As part of an agricultural experiment, substantial plantations were established in Shetland in 1913. In Weisdale, 'Kergord Forest' with its tall conifers, and the monkey puzzle pine in the garden of Kergord House, are on almost all tour-bus itineraries. There were several more shelter-belt plantation experiments in the 1920s, '50s and '60s.

The gardens of the big houses are an interesting facet of Shetland's garden history. Certain lairds clergy and lesser gentry vied with each other to lay out magnificent gardens in so far as it was possible. A number still retain many features from early design stages, but most have changed completely, deteriorated over the years or even vanished altogether. Gardie House in Bressay and Sandlodge in Sandwick open their gardens occasionally in the summer for charitable purposes. The once-famous garden in Vaila fell into decay and all but vanished, but is being gradually restored.

Look out for old varieties of daffodils and narcissi, which in much of mainland Britain have long since disappeared. Hedges of flowering currant, daisy bush, Japanese rose and fuchsia abound. Old favourites – bachelor's buttons, lupins, roses, primulas, mimulus and michaelmas daisies – thrive in older gardens. Magellan ragwort, or Australian daisy, is a curiosity from the South Atlantic, said to have been brought back by whalers. A species of grass from the Falklands, known as tushie girse, or tussock grass, also grows in a few places.

Exotic species and hardy hybrids appear as gardeners get more adventurous. Spring bulb flowers do especially well and the council has started planting daffodils along selected roadside embankments. Fruit bushes, especially blackcurrant, grow well in Shetland provided that they have reasonable shelter too, though raspberries are less successful. Strawberries can produce remarkably good harvests. Among the most successful is rhubarb, which grows so well that some plants are left uncut, their flowering stems reaching six feet high at times. The best place to appreciate the full range of Shetland garden produce is at a county agricultural show when the cherished produce of many a local gardener is arranged and displayed, potatoes neatly cut in halves and both fruit and vegetables glowing with mouthwatering freshness.

FAUNA

INSECTS

Minibeast- and insect-watchers are becoming almost as keen as birdwatchers in Shetland and the Shetland Entomological Group produces a regular report, listing migrant moths, butterflies and other insect groups, with contacts given for helping with identification of specific groups of insects. The lists of recorded species are growing, both for passing insects blown across to Shetland from the continent and for native breeding species. Occasionally insects make it into the news when, for instance, massive invasions hit the headlines, like the millions of Silver Y moths which, along with hordes of other insects, swept over the islands one summer. As with wild flowers and some subspecies of animals, there are a number of Shetland variations of insect too. A sizeable number of moth species have significantly darker markings than in those found in other places, and were much sought after during the great Victorian insect-collecting boom.

The geographical isolation of the island group means that there are bound to be fewer native species of insect than in an area of equivalent size on the mainland, but loss of certain habitats and their wild plants may increase and speed up these losses. Native small blue butterflies are recorded as having once inhabited the dune pasture behind Quendale beach but they seem to have died out. A number of butterflies lay eggs which hatch and pupate, but are unlikely to be able to overwinter here. South-easterly winds in summer often bring in 'falls' of peacock butterflies, painted ladies, red admirals, small tortoiseshells and an occasional Camberwell beauty.

Peacock Butterfly, migrant insect.

There are instances of strange imported insects arriving with timber, plants, vegetables or fruits, such as the banana stowaway moth. The only resident butterfly species now is the cabbage white, believed by many to have been introduced among cabbages imported during the Second World

War, though several reports of white butterflies are recorded by visiting scientists from earlier times. Vine weevils are a most unpopular recent accidental import, as is the dreaded New Zealand flatworm, which, though not an insect, prowls slowly through a small but increasing number of Shetland gardens seeking earthworms.

Earthworms are plentiful in the islands on cultivated land. Unfortunately for gardeners, so too are slugs, of which several species are found. Large black slugs, golden brown ones and an occasional stripy one can sometimes be found quite high up in the hills. But those creating most havoc in the gardens are tiny, grey-brown slugs with a passion for newly planted vegetable seedlings, primuli and daffodil petals! Snails are less widespread, but they are locally quite common. Sand dunes are good places to find the yellow and black stripy ones.

Hawk-moths migrate south through Europe and occasionally during south-easterly gales, a few are blown west and land on Shetland. Convolvulus hawk-moths are the most frequently recorded, but privet, humming bird and death's head hawk moths have also turned up. Large burying beetles are found every year, often clinging to salmon cages, having apparently been blown across the sea to Shetland. Ladybirds too can appear in some numbers, and shield bugs occasionally descend on certain areas apparently out of nowhere. Some dialect insect names are clearly Scottish in origin, others less so. 'Forky tail' is well known as a name for earwigs, shiny, large black beetles hurrying along are referred to as 'clocks' and many people call bluebottles and house flies 'bees' as opposed to 'buzzy bees' for bumble or honey bees. Shetland is not an easy place for bee-keepers to succeed, but there have been as many as eight registered bee-keepers in the past at one and the same time.

Wasps are a recent and unpopular coloniser of Lerwick but they have not yet reached large numbers. Midges do live in Shetland, but they tend to come out now and again for short periods and are not the constant blight of summer days that they can be in the Highlands. Mosquitoes, if they feature at all, are a rarity. I have never seen or heard one in twenty years of living in Shetland. The Shetland white-tailed bumble bee, on the other hand, is a familiar sight in the islands and long may it remain so. Bumble bees are declining in far too many areas in the south. A number of island-wide surveys of wildlife species began when the Shetland Biological Records Office was established in 1999, including one on bumble bees in May 2000. More surveys will follow as the whole of Shetland's range of wildlife comes under the spotlight.

BIRDS

Shetland is world famous for its seabird colonies, its rare and less rare native species and endlessly varied migrants. So it was strange once to hear a newcomer to the islands confessing to a surprised Shetlander, how much she missed the birds! Many of the commoner garden birds familiar to visitors from Scotland as well as England and Wales are missing altogether from the Shetland scene; no

Arctic Tern ('Tirrick').

use hanging up nut baskets for blue tits here. Members of the tit family, thrushes and chaffinches are seen only very fleetingly on their migrations to more gentle climes. Shetland has its own wren, a slightly larger fellow than its mainland British counterpart. There is no dawn chorus of the deafening kind enjoyed by those living in tree- and hedge-rich countryside further south in mainland Britain. Instead, you must seek the sea cliffs and be deafened by the hordes of noisy nesting seabirds, not to mention being overwhelmed by the smell!

Shetland's special bird life owes its existence to certain habitats and geological features in the islands. Sea cliffs have formed in ancient rocks, some of which, notably those at Sumburgh and Noss, have weathered into horizontal ledges, ideal for seabirds to nest on. Combinations of geology and climate have created moorlands which are home to important colonies of breeding waders, as well as merlin, pipits and wheatears. Nearly all Britain's whimbrel breed in Shetland and the exquisite red-necked phalarope breeds in Fetlar, home to the snowy owl not many years ago.

As autumn approaches, millions of wild birds begin to leave their breeding grounds in northern Europe (including Shetland) and the Arctic. There are parent birds, immatures and newly fledged young ones. They head steadily south for warmer wintering lands, where food will be plentiful until the following spring. They fly day and night to Britain, southern Europe, and some go as far as Africa. Arctic terns, Shetland's 'Tirricks', fly halfway round the world to the Antarctic. In spring the same thing happens in reverse. This time, flocks are heading north for the breeding season and are in peak condition for their journey after the long winter feed. They arrive as their breeding lands burst into flower and insects hatch out in large numbers.

Should bad weather arrive, with strong winds from the south-east, large numbers of birds will be driven off course, and after fighting the turbulence, lose height and, as they are driven out to sea, look desperately for somewhere to land. Ships at sea often find exhausted migrants perching on rails or in rigging; many almost certainly drown, but hundreds and thousands every year make a temporary, emergency landfall in Shetland, where the birdwatchers are ready for them.

Serious birdwatchers frequently travel up by plane when a rarity appears, sometimes even chartering a special flight just to be able to see it and tick it off their special list. These enthusiasts, or 'twitchers' as they are termed, can often

Black Guillemot ('Tystie').

be seen in clusters, green-clad, telescopes and 'bins', or binoculars, to their eyes, scanning the neighbourhood for a glimpse of an unusual migrant, or hiding behind walls making sibilant noises in an attempt to flush out a weary rarity.

Many birds are still referred to in Shetland by their local names. The red-throated diver is called the 'raingoose'; seagulls in particular are known as 'maas', with 'scories' as the term for immature gulls. 'Swaabies' are the great black-backed gulls. All the other gulls have local names too, but their use is declining. Great skuas are called 'bonxies' and this name has become the common name for them even among birding circles. Tirricks are the seabird equivalent of the swallow, Shetland's harbinger of summer. There is a checklist of birds with their Shetland names at the back of the book.

In spring and summer, the sight of a bonxie sweeping past overhead scarcely raises a second glance, as these birds, one of the rarest species in the rest of Britain, are common in Shetland, with their numbers rising steadily. In the evening, the peaceful summer light seems to go on for ever and the rapid, sharp, quack-like flight call of the red-throated diver is a familiar sound. This lovely bird is another national rarity, yet in Shetland a pair or even several pairs grace many a loch during the nesting season. It is one of the most protected of all Shetland's breeding birds, listed as a Schedule 1 species, and an official permit has to be obtained before you can photograph it. If you walk among the hills and remote lochs on misty days listen out for their haunting cries as they call across blank spaces, the plaintive sounds mingling with the drumming of snipe and the sad, falling notes of golden plover.

Puffins, or 'tammie nories', perhaps the most photographed of all Shetland's bird species, throng to Shetland each spring for their nesting season, before resuming their wandering seafarer lives in early August. Their small size often amazes people, many of whom expect them to be much larger. There are cliff tops in Foula, Unst, Fair Isle and Sumburgh where they can potter up to within a few feet of you if you keep still for long enough. They peer up at you, head tilted first one way, then another; even stopping for a quick preen. One once nibbled curiously round the toe of my wellington boot as I sat motionless on the thrift-carpeted cliff top overlooking a geo in Fair Isle. Listen patiently near their burrows and you might hear the curious growling, grumbling 'puffin speak' as they talk to their chick. Magical moments with wild birds are a Shetland speciality, free for those who are willing to watch and wait.

Fair Isle is the Mecca for birdwatchers. The newly designed Bird Observatory will continue to provide the same excellent study and accommodation features as its predecessor. You can use the library and also watch the bird warden and research staff catching and ringing, weighing and recording an amazing variety of birds. But there are superb bird cliffs everywhere in Shetland and for those coming between May and August, it would be a great mistake to miss seeing at least a few of them. Hermaness, Noss, Fetlar – these world-famous bird reserves act as magnets to the thousands of birdwatchers who visit Shetland each year. The Out Skerries are also excellent places to watch for newly arrived migrants. Individual sites are described later in more detail, in the regional and island descriptions.

A brief run through the Shetland bird year will help to set the birds in context.

January: the start of the year sees short, dark days and a wintry bird setting but plenty of colourful winter visitors. Great northern divers, whooper swans and sea ducks such as long-tailed ducks enliven the bird scene. Harbours attract seagulls and the observant watcher may spot glaucous or Iceland gulls foraging and wheeling among the more familiar herring and black-backed gulls.

February can see some of the leanest, meanest weather and the birds are hard-pressed. Herons stand knee-deep in the voes, motionless in icy shallows; curlews forage widely across grassland and open ground; ravens tumble and cavort in the skies, starlings battle for scraps with sparrows and blackbirds around the houses and crofts and the 'shalders', or oystercatchers, return.

Gradually, as March approaches, some birds will prepare themselves for the long haul to their summer breeding grounds. As they fly north, our winter visitors – long-tailed ducks, whooper swans and snow buntings – may well meet different species flying in the opposite direction. Among the migrants seen most frequently are waders, meadow pipits, skylarks, chaffinches, goldcrests, redwings, fieldfares and bramblings. There is always the possibility of seeing great rarities among these tiny birds, as now and again the odd individual arrives from America, or even the far east, having survived unbelievably long journeys. Ravens may still be displaying.

Skylark ('Laverock').

April brings to an end the winter residency of great northern divers and long-tailed ducks. Ravens begin to nest and so do lapwings and golden plover. The first skylark's song is a cause for celebration, signalling the ending of long, dark days. There is great competition in Shetland in late April and early May for the first recorded sighting of Arctic terns. Their sharp cries and dancing flight herald true spring at last. The local radio and newspaper announce their arrival as well as that of other species, bonxie, or great skua, Arctic skua and red-throated divers. The courtship, pairing and mating of birds gets underway in earnest and frantic nest-building begins in the islands.

May is the best month for watching spring migrants and the main nest-building effort goes into top gear. These days, Arctic terns in particular are carefully monitored as their breeding success has been subject to violent fluctuation over recent years. There has been a problem with sand eel populations (at one time heavily fished) which form the bulk of the tern chicks' diet and a debate as to which of many possible causes is responsible has been fierce at times. Other rarities include whimbrel, now protected by additional reserves, and red-necked phalarope, helped by the improvement of some of their breeding grounds in Fetlar. Migrants can still turn up, including an occasional waxwing, flycatchers and various warblers. The latter tend to be small and brownish, earning themselves the nickname of 'LBJs', ('Little Brown Jobs') among the birdwatching fraternity.

June is the most spectacular time to visit the seabird colony reserves, when there is a frantic, tireless traffic of parent birds flying to and from nest sites, threading their way through a moving maze of other parent birds, always with half an eye cocked for trouble. Danger is everywhere; jealous neighbours, unpredictable weather, wind turbulence around the cliffs, but most of all, the vicious and scheming attentions of the pirate skuas. These and several species of gull depend on scavenged free meals, whether of fish brought for chicks, or the chicks themselves. Even the adult birds aren't safe. Visitors to the seabird colonies face gruesome sights of nature at its reddest, in beak and claw. Fully grown puffins and kittiwakes are knocked into the sea and drowned, then eaten by their bigger, cannier predators.

July is the last month for reasonable seabird watching. Young guillemots and other seabird chicks are fledging and the parent birds are frantically trying to feed them and guard them at the same time. There is one small bird though which attracts visitors every year to witness a unique spectacle. Storm petrels are at sea all year round, either flying or swimming, except for a brief visit to land for breeding. They are shy, secretive birds and nest in a very few sites in Shetland, only appearing after dark. There are few experiences in Shetland more worthwhile than the storm petrel boat trips to Mousa at night. After dark, if the weather is favourable, the boat takes you across from Leebitton and you walk along the shore and sit inside the ancient broch out of the wind and wait. The first parent bird returning to feed her chick may pass unnoticed, but after long minutes of still, silent darkness, the stones begin to reverberate with a churring, creaking sound. From deep inside the old broch walls the fledglings are singing to their parents. Soon after midnight, as if at a secret signal, the sky is alive with them; tiny, silent, black and white birds, they streak out of nowhere. Each adult miraculously homes in on the precise crevice between two stones where its own young are waiting.

By August the activity has wound down to next to nothing and most of the parent birds and their young will be out at sea. Whimbrel and red-necked phalaropes are unlikely to be seen by the middle of the month and September will find most of the summer breeding visitors leaving. A few puffins may still be seen, to delight late summer tourists, but the main spectacular bird event of the year is all but over and the great cliffs of Noss and Hermaness are virtually silent.

September brings thrills of a different kind, with the start of the autumn migration. As one group leaves, another appears. Depending on weather and wind direction, Shetland can seem to fill up overnight with a vast mixed flock of newcomers, all taking a rest on their long journey to warmer climes. Rather than brace the south-easterly gales for several days, these autumn visitors will land, exhausted, and feed and forage desperately to rebuild their depleted energy stocks. Considerate birdwatchers will observe them carefully from a respectful distance, resisting the temptation to hound the weary strangers for a better view as they feed.

October too can still be a good month for the unexpected and the local newspaper keeps amateurs and fanatics alike abreast of each new arrival and departure. The *Braer* oil

Whimbrel ('Peerie whaap').

spill left at least one beneficial item behind in its wake, namely the Oiled Bird Unit in Tingwall. Here, under the watchful eye of the local SSPCA representative, weary or injured birds are often housed and tended while they recover. Their subsequent release is carefully planned and timetabled. Often a real rarity, such as an egret, osprey or hawk, is shipped or flown to a reserve further south.

November sees the return of the whooper swans and other wildfowl, geese and ducks migrating south from Iceland and further north. These winter visitors begin to coast in and seek out their favourite haunts. Fieldfares and redwings, snow buntings and twites are seen, often in large flocks. A flock of snow buntings can make a spectacular sight as they fly and then turn simultaneously, their wings all flashing silver at the same instant. Some roost for a night or two, then fly on. Others may stay a while longer, or even all winter. Gardens well endowed with trees and wet areas can attract water rails, moorhens, robins and some finches who may decide to stay right through until March or even early April.

December rolls down the daylight to a bare minimum, the sun barely skimming above the southern horizon as it glides through the short days. The bird year is complete.

Some wild breeding birds in Shetland, despite being locally quite common, are extremely rare on a worldwide scale. Their numbers are closely monitored, their breeding successes a matter of international importance; specific legislation has been introduced to help support their conservation. A number of laws exist specifically to ensure the upholding of international agreements designed to conserve and protect nature and wildlife. The following information is a summary of the main points.

The principal agreements are the 1979 Convention on the Conservation of European Wildlife and Natural Habitats (The Bern Convention); the 1979 European Community Directive on the Conservation of Wild Birds (The Birds Directive) and the 1992 European Community Directive on the Conservation of Natural Habitats and of Wild Fauna and Flora (The Habitats Directive). The 1981 Wildlife and Countryside Act offers various levels of protection to groups of listed species. In general, it is an offence to kill, injure, capture or keep *any* wild bird. It is also illegal to destroy or take birds' eggs, to sell or advertise for sale any wild bird or eggs. Destroying, taking away or damaging wild birds' nests while they are building or using them is also an offence.

In addition, a 'Schedule 1' list has been drawn up of rare species which it is an offence even to disturb while they are nest-building, sitting on eggs, or rearing young. The young birds are also protected until they are fully independent. Schedule 1 species in Shetland include red-throated diver, corncrake, long-tailed duck, peregrine falcon, scaup, merlin, whimbrel, whooper swan and red-necked phalarope. Scottish Natural Heritage in Lerwick (tel: 01595 693345) can provide advice on licences should you wish to photograph these birds.

Red-Throated Diver ('Raingoose').

WILD ANIMALS

Wild animals seen in Shetland today are thought to have been artificially introduced into the islands at one time or another during the past 6000 years. Even the otter, some people believe, is unlikely to have made the sea crossing unaided. Rabbits were introduced long ago and are plentiful, despite several serious attempts to reduce their numbers. What is certain is that there are now special Shetland subspecies of a number of wild, as well as domestic, animals which have evolved slight differences from others of the same species on the mainland. There are a number of distinct variations of Shetland mouse.

Field mice are widespread in Shetland. They have slightly redder fur than mainland mice and distinct island subspecies have been described from Yell, Foula and Fair Isle. Similarities with field mice in Norway suggest that Shetland field mice were inadvertently brought in by Viking settlers. Recent archaeological evidence, however, has shown that the house mouse was here far earlier, as remains have been found on an Iron Age site at Scatness. Both Shetland field mice and house mice have been found to be slightly larger than their equivalents in the rest of the UK and beyond. On a warm autumn evening mice are often seen in car headlights, racing across the road. They frequently nest in stone walls, as well as in byres and other buildings. In the days when hay and corn were grown, mice would gather in stacks and stooks, giving the sheepdogs cause for great excitement when the last of the store was removed.

Rats tend to live near the seashore, especially among the boulders arranged as sea defences, where they are sometimes seen, foraging and fighting. High tides and floods occasionally unseat these less well-loved animals and very rarely they may take up temporary residence in cellars, garages or outbuildings.

Shetland's wild otter population is said to be the highest of any county in the UK. The animals are often seen at close quarters and most easily at dawn and dusk. There are so many about that you might be lucky and catch a glimpse at almost any time of day. The most usual sight is that of a dark, streamlined shape in the sea, smaller than a seal and, unlike a seal, tending to disappear for a few minutes, reappearing a little further away. On still days a trail of bubbles in calm water immediately betrays the presence of an otter. If you sit still and wait you will almost certainly be rewarded with excellent views. The otter may surface unaware of your presence and, if not disturbed, may even come ashore and feed.

Shetland is rich in Otters.

It is not so many years since otters were far more timid, as they were regularly hunted for their skins, which fetched good prices; many a poor family benefited from the income brought by selling them. Traps were sometimes built on the routes which otters were known to take between loch and sea. You can still find otter traps in varying states of collapse in Shetland today. The well-known Shetland saying, 'Lat be for lat be', originated from the story of a man checking his otter trap one day and finding a live otter in it, clubbing it and carrying it home over his shoulder. Shortly afterwards, the otter, which had only been stunned, came round and sank its teeth into the man's backside. Crying 'Lat be for lat be!', the man let the otter go and, presumably, headed for home as fast as he was able.

For those really intent on watching wild otters, Lunna Ness, East Yell, Nesting and South Whiteness are the places I have most frequently had success. Find a suitable time – early evening, or very early morning – and a suitable place, such as a deserted stretch of low, rocky shore, with a reasonably sheltered, comfortable corner to sit in, and wait. Otters, surprisingly, have rather poor sight, but they can detect movement rapidly, so avoid being silhouetted against the horizon. Sadly, a growing number of otters are being killed on Shetland's roads. Every year, a number of these dead otters are sent south for tests; much valuable data about Shetland otters has been built up by researchers at the Banchory Institute of Terrestrial Ecology over the years.

Having originally escaped or been released, 'pole-ferrets' (a polecat-ferret cross) have multiplied and are a menace to poultry and ground-nesting wild birds. A trapping system has been introduced and the stock of traps is almost permanently in use by crofters. A number of these animals are knocked down by cars on the roads and you may see one lying on a verge. They are attractive creatures, with bodies varying from dark cream, through chestnut, almost to black, with little white faces and paws. But despite their appealing looks, they are bad news for wildlife and many people would like to see them eradicated.

Rabbits are present in large numbers in the islands. Don't be surprised if you should see black, piebald, albino or even bright apricot-coloured rabbits in the hills. Shetland's wild rabbits have only man as a major predator and their natural colour range has been able to flourish without selective reduction as tends to happen in mainland Britain. First recorded the early 1600s they have spread fast and periodically reach such numbers that attempts are made to reduce their numbers. Myxomatosis was introduced on more than one occasion and had an effect for a while. The recent rabbit viral disease seemed to have an effect only on pet rabbits as wild populations appeared to continue unaffected.

Hares are said to have been introduced for sport. Two species were found in the islands, both brown and mountain hare. The blue, or mountain, hare, famous for its white (or almost all white) winter coat thrived best. Shetland is seldom snow-covered and the poor animal is so noticeable, white against the dark moorland, that the camouflage could not be less appropriate. The brown hare eventually died out.

Hedgehogs are a relatively recently introduced species and have adapted well to the Shetland environment; their numbers have rocketed. Second broods are sometimes managed within a year, but the later offspring seldom manage to hibernate successfully as they are too small and light to withstand the long winter hibernation. They have acquired some popularity in recent years and their numbers have certainly risen dramatically, judging by the growing number of road casualties. Hedgehogs can be found on most of the inhabited islands and are greatly beloved of gardeners as they help reduce the vast slug population. Seagulls, curiously, have begun to evolve ways of keeping down the hedgehog population too. Several have been seen gripping small hedgehogs and flying up with them, then dropping them onto roads, and after several 'drops', eating the creatures.

By the time frogs were introduced to Shetland, local interest in wildlife and conscious attempts to experiment were increasing. There are a number of documented introductions and probably many more unreported ones. Several buckets of frogspawn were brought up from Aberdeen at the request of a couple of Shetlanders from Scalloway. They were released into a number of lochs, streams and ditches, and have spread widely. In late summer there is sometimes a reported mass movement of frogs, seen hopping across roads in their hundreds. The increasing popularity of gardening and pond making has allowed their numbers to grow still faster.

Clement Williamson from Scalloway told me the story of one of the first recorded local sightings of an adult frog. It was a few years after the frogspawn had been released and happened one late summer during the 1920s, when hay was being cut. One elderly lady from Blydoit near Scalloway must have disturbed a frog while scything her way through the hay. A frog jumped away from her and, being utterly unfamiliar and weird, it gave her the scare of her life. She apparently shrieked and ran to a neighbour who was cutting his own hay not far away, crying, 'Wullie, Wullie, der a baist in da mudoo!' (Willie, Willie, there's a beast in the meadow!)

Toads have been introduced experimentally from time to time, but appear not to have survived beyond a few months or a year or two. No evidence of toads came to light in surveys in the 1990s.

Stoats are widespread in much of Shetland. John Brand in part of his 1703 *A New Description of Orkney, Shetland*...etc, recounts a story he was told, about stoats being originally introduced to Shetland by 'the king's falconer' as revenge for the refusal of Shetlanders to continue the practice of providing hens for food for the royal hawks. Known as 'whitrits' (white rats) in Shetlandic, stoats are on record as having occasionally taken up residence in attics, where they have been very content, and it has taken a lot of determination to shift them.

A mink fur farm was established in Shetland at one time and a number of mink escaped. This could have presented Shetland with a major problem for its ground-nesting birds. Fortunately the animals were recaptured. There are no mink farms in Shetland now and it is highly unlikely that permission would ever be granted to set one up in the future.

Wild foxes are not found in Shetland, but a few introduced foxes have been seen on occasions over the years. They never seem to thrive and have never been known to breed, possibly as a result of hostile climate, or, perhaps more likely, have been eradicated by quiet but determined crofters. A dead red fox was found beside the main road in the late 1990s and a dead Arctic fox found in similar circumstances near Voe. Both were suspected of having been killed and dumped.

Feral cats have established tiny colonies here and there in a number of places in the islands in recent years and measures are taken to eradicate them. Particular efforts were made in Noss to remove a feral cat colony because of the damage to ground-nesting wild birds in the reserve and there is concern too for the Manx shearwater colony in Fetlar, similarly at risk.

Weasels are not found in Shetland, neither are deer, badgers, lizards, snakes, squirrels, voles, shrews or newts.

DOMESTIC ANIMALS

A working sheepdog stands among the special Shetland breeds, which is believed to have evolved in the islands in the same way as native cattle, sheep and ponies. Like them, it too is smaller than its southern collie counterparts and comes in a wide range of colour combinations. Tough, courageous, intelligent and hardy, the 'sheltie', as dog breeders call them, is ideally suited to working in Shetland. In 1909 the Shetland collie, or *Toonie Dog*, was officially recognised as a separate breed by the Scottish Shetland Sheepdog Club and by the

The unique Shetland Pony.

Kennel Club in 1914. When tourism increased in the early 1900s, many visitors bought a sheltie to take home with them. The breed eventually, like the Shetland pony, became more numerous on the mainland than in the islands.

Ponies have been in Shetland for over 4000 years. Horse teeth were found on the site of a Neolithic house at Ness of Gruting during an archaeological excavation in the 1950s and fragments of bone were found at Stanydale. Horse teeth have been found on other Neolithic sites, suggesting that they may well have been part of the early Shetland farming scene, along with oxen and sheep. Shetland ponies are well suited to the climate and they may have been here almost as long as human beings. They shouldered much of the hard labour of farming in the islands for the best part of 50 centuries, from pulling carts to ferrying peats back from the hills.

A whole range of harnesses and equipment was used, much of which can be seen in the Shetland Crofthouse Museum. There are places where horses are used occasionally for agricultural work and Shetland still has a blacksmith, but ploughing matches are no longer on the agricultural show programme. In 1842 the introduction of the Mines Act by the British government put an end to the use of women and children to drag coal wagons down the mines and Shetland ponies began to be bred for the purpose instead. There were several pony enclosures, or 'punds', large, square, stone enclosures with characteristically heightened corners and roofed stalls inside. Noss has a restored pony pund with an interpretive display featuring the pony-breeding history of the Marquis of Londonderry's stud, which was established in the 1870s.

Today, thankfully, the ponies no longer slave below ground and on land too Shetland ponies are less often worked, but are bred, shown, ridden and exported to breeders all round the world and have become a much-loved symbol of the islands. The pony sales in October are well worth seeing, but most visitors enjoy the herds of ponies in May when the tiny newborn foals are at their most irresistible. Horse riding has become popular and many breeds of riding horses are kept in the islands. Recent interest in Icelandic horses led to an indoor riding centre being established in Mid Walls.

Cattle have been part of the Shetland scene for as long as ponies, and oxen were used for centuries to pull carts and drag ploughs. Shetland cattle, or 'kye' as they are known, came originally, like Shetland sheep, ponies and poultry, in a variety of colours and patterns and were once universal in the islands. But they began to die out as larger, better milking breeds became available. Today a range of breeds of cattle are kept and Shetland is virtually self-sufficient in dairy produce. Recently, however, the Shetland kye began to make a comeback. It seems that overbreeding may have reduced the digestibility of beef flesh and fat, whereas Shetland cattle appear to have more digestible protein in their flesh and milk. As research continues into this subject, local herds are growing steadily in numbers. Today you are likely to see them only in black and white, as limited numbers of surviving Shetland bulls meant that the wide range of colours was no longer available for breeders.

Shetland sheep have their detractors but there are many who hold them in great regard. Their wool is exceptionally soft and the ewes are renowned for being wonderful mothers. Hardy and adaptable, able to steal a living from ill-fenced gardens as well as near-vertical cliff ledges, scavenging seaweed on beaches and ripping every blade of green from accessible acres and hills, they have largely created the treeless, barren slopes of the islands for thousands of years. Fencing and boundary walls have been essential through the centuries for anyone wishing to raise crops and the Shetland sheep has grown wily and inventive at finding ways through. They come in a bewildering variety and range of colours and patterns, most of which have ancient words to describe them: *moorit* for brown, *shaela* for grey are two well-known terms, but there are dozens more.

Shetland lamb meat, too, as with Shetland beef, has proved to have uniquely healthy qualities and may well soon be sold at a premium, unlike their fatter, whiter rivals, the Blackfaces, Suffolks and Cheviots which crowded into the islands after the Clearances. Famous long ago for their soft, fine wool, the fleeces are small and to increase the quantity, rams, or 'tups', of different, larger breeds were introduced. The *Shetland Flock Book* was established to try to preserve the pure breed. Shetland fleeces fetched poor prices for many years, but they deserve higher, rather than lower rates. New marketing initiatives began in the late 1990s with an international conference held in the islands. Perhaps this century will see greater rewards for Shetland sheep breeders.

'Shetland' pigs survived into the first decade of last century, but sadly, have become extinct. Thought to have derived from those brought in by the early Norse farmers, virtually every croft had its pig. During the summer the pigs ranged freely over the hills, feeding and sometimes breeding there. Later on they were brought in and kept in sties or even indoors during the winter. Sties had to be floored with stone or the pigs would tear their way out by tunnelling under the walls. Croft hill dykes had to be pig-proof too, as a pig could create havoc among crops.

Stories of these pigs still abound. They were said to be small, dark, hairy, full of character and voracious. There is one marvellous tale of two brothers visiting lady friends in a neighbouring district rather late at night. They waited until the old parents were seen to retire for the night before tapping on the window. The delighted lasses insisted that the men stayed the night, and woke them before daylight to allow them to return home before the old folk rose. To mingled horror and amusement, it was discovered that the house pig had shredded and eaten their clothing during the night.

A range of breeds of pig were kept in small numbers last century. Recent pig-rearing and butchering enterprises have been very popular and may prove successful.

A number of other animals have been introduced to Shetland over the years. Goats do well with care and extra shelter, as do angora rabbits and bees. Both earthworm- and snail-farming have been tried at various times. Resourceful Shetlanders and unwary newcomers are willing to try almost anything which seems to have a chance of success, so don't be surprised to find the unusual among the familiar wherever you go.

SEA LIFE AND FISH

Without fish, there would probably have been no permanent human settlement in Shetland. The earliest evidence of fishing – simple fish-catching tools, net sinkers and fish bones – comes from archaeological sites. In days gone by, a trained eye could detect a shoal of fish from the tell-tale patterning on the sea surface. A group of small feeding whales, their dorsal fins breaking the surface like small black sails, would make men head for their boats. You can watch for whales today too, or seals, otters and the ever-present seabirds. Initially, fish kept people alive, then as the centuries progressed, it became an increasingly vital element in the trade which fed the island economy. A particularly rich fishing area lay to the south-west, known as the Burra Haaf. Over 60 species have been recorded from recent landings in Shetland. The main commercial species are cod, haddock, mackerel and herring, ling, whiting, monkfish, halibut, plaice and sole.

Other fishing grounds include the Fetlar Firth, St Magnus Bay, and the Bressay and Bergen banks. It is believed that global warming may have increased the movement of some fish and other marine species from far to the south. Rarities occasionally end up in the nets of Shetland fishing boats, arousing much interest, whether unusual sharks, leatherback turtles, sunfish or even on one occasion a marbled electric ray. The protection of the spawning areas for cod, haddock and other species is of crucial importance. Each species of fish has its own specific life history of breeding areas, feeding and, in some cases, migrating patterns. More and more is being learned and discovered about the natural history of this hidden world and not before time, as fish stocks are desperately depleted.

Progress in fishing technology carries with it the seeds of its own destruction. Shellfish can be very sensitive to pollution and in places the techniques of one kind of fishery have created problems for another. As technology has advanced, the impact of increasingly efficient fish-location systems and catching-gear has resulted in fewer boats but greater numbers of fish caught by a single boat than ever before. This, and the growing number of foreign fleets fishing the same grounds, has had an increasing impact on fish stocks and one species after another has been fished to the brink. Efforts have been made to seek new species to catch, including deep-water fishing, which has brought new and strange fish to light. Boats these days are colossally expensive to equip and require massive investment. Once working, they and their crews cannot just be 'switched off' while stocks build up.

Conservation efforts are coming, but it is a controversial and complex business and far from resolved. Aquaculture is the main development area today. Salmon farming has brought in increasing income in recent years, but this industry too has its problems. Halibut and cod are now being commercially farmed. Shetland is at the forefront of research into the ecology of commercial fish and shellfish species and the next few years may well see major changes in the ways in which traditional fishing methods are used. Meanwhile, the future employment for children of traditional fishing families, following in their parents' footsteps, grows steadily less certain.

Traditionally, young Shetlanders were introduced to fishing from the shore from an early age. A jam jar for catching sticklebacks was discarded for a length of string with a bent pin on one end as a simple fishing line by young bairns, graduating to their own first 'waand' (rod) later. Favourite places for fishing along a rocky shore, known as 'craigs', still attract islanders in their spare time. This method of adding food items to the general pot must be one of the oldest skills in the islands. Limpets, traditionally ground up for bait, are abundant. Small bowl-shaped depressions, called so pots, can sometimes be found carved into solid rock at the sea's rim. Here, for centuries, limpets were pounded to pulp, the resulting mass was chewed and then 'frooshed', or spat out, over the sea to attract fish which could be caught by rod or net as they surged in to feed on the floating morsels.

In addition to fishing, shellfish gathering was important for the larder, especially during periods of low tides. Shetland's seashores are great places for finding seashells. Winkles, or 'whelks' as Shetlanders call them, are gathered in large quantities and sold at certain times of year, making a relatively lucrative pastime for youngsters as well as more serious adult gatherers. Some families actually earn their summer holiday money this way. Depending on the nature of the nearby seabed, a range of species of shellfish can be found. Small periwinkles, dog whelks, mussels and cockles, and grey-top shells and a range of small clams are frequently found. An oyster shell bed would be a rarity today, though oyster shell dumps found in the islands dating back long ago, prove that they were once common and have also been fished out.

Razor shells (known locally as 'spoots', owing to their tendency to squirt water rapidly upwards as they contract and dive under the sand where they live) are still an item on many a crofter's seasonal menu. A 'spootie ebb', an exceptionally low tide, is still used by many for gathering razor shells. You may see people on a calm evening at very low tide, walking slowly backwards over wet sand exposed by the low tide and watching closely for a spoot, or spurt of water, as the shellfish under the sand senses pressure above and starts to contract, drawing itself deeper away from danger. With a rapid downwards thrust of a finger, they can be pulled out; a simple-sounding process, but trickier than you might think.

Crabs, lobsters and scallops are fished inshore and sea urchins (known as 'Scaddiman's heads' in Shetland dialect) are plentiful in Shetland waters and may well become a commercial item in the future, as they are a delicacy in Europe. Mussel farming is common in Shetland and other species of shellfish are being trialled, with a view to farming them in the future. Fish factories process shellfish in the islands and the range of different methods of preservation, packaging and storage has increased dramatically in recent years. Seafood products are sent all over the world. One enterprising business was set up to use most of the waste scallop shells and some are used by the craft industry for ornaments and art work.

Traditionally, freshwater as well as saltwater fish have been caught in Shetland. The place where burns meet the sea can be good for catching 'flukes', or small flatfish and eels too which swim up the freshwater burns in season to spawn. There are literally hundreds of lochs in the islands; many are well stocked with fish and much frequented by Shetland's keen anglers. Many lochs are well stocked with brown trout, grilse too can be found and in the Loch of Girlsta there is a protected population of relict Artic char. Increasingly, escaped caged salmon as well as sea trout can be found in sea lochs.

Every loch in Shetland is different. Some are shallow and easily crossed in wading gear, others are boulder-strewn, or deep and treacherous. A new sport, 'loch-isleing', is gaining popularity, whereby anglers attempt to catch a trout in a loch on as many islands as they can. The Tourist Office in Lerwick has details of when and where to fish and how to obtain permits. They will have information on the best lochs, estuaries or shorelines and where to hire or buy fishing gear. There are also a number of sea-angling businesses. But there are mammals other than humans which depend on fish for their survival in Shetland.

SEA MAMMALS

Seals are possibly the only true native breeding mammals in Shetland. The ocean would have been no deterrent for this streamlined master of the seas. Common seals have rather dog-like, snub-nosed profiles, tend to be variable in colour, often blotched and spotted, and are slightly smaller than the grey seals, which have domed, Roman noses. Both species are

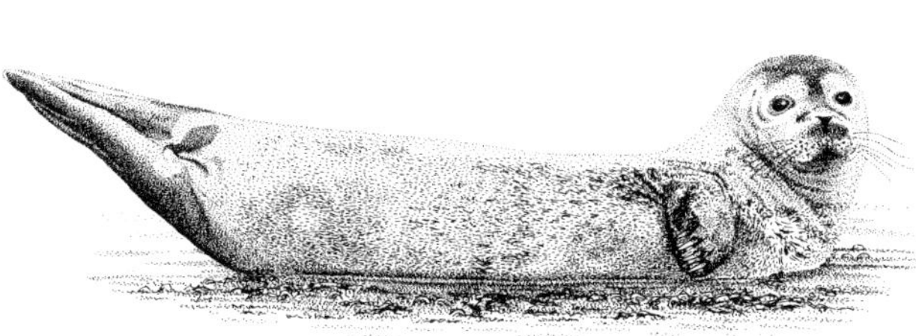

Common Seal.

numerous around the coastline, but other species do appear from time to time. Long-travelled strangers from far afield such as hooded seals, bearded seals, harp seals and even walruses have been found from time to time, hauled out on beaches or slipways and in some cases have been helped on their way back home.

Seals have become the subject of considerable controversy in Shetland in recent years. Traditionally, they were hunted for their fur and the sale of sealskins added to the family income for many folk. Following a serious decline in numbers, they became protected, since when their numbers have increased and their behaviour has become bolder and more confident. Where a seal might once have vanished at the sight of a human approaching the sea, they will now rise up and stare at you from amazingly close quarters. There are some who believe that seal numbers have grown so much out of balance that fish catches are affected. Seals seem to be fascinated by the sight of a party of humans and a walk along the banks can attract anything from one to several score seals at a time, all vying with each other to show off in front of their land-bound distant cousins.

Sometimes they swim remarkably close to the beach and just watch, 'bottling', or resting with their heads poking up out of the water, whiskers twitching, huge eyes goggling. They often make loud sneezing and snorting noises and, occasionally, moan like lost souls or wail like abandoned children. If you approach too close, they slap the water hard and dive, coming up again further out in deep water. But if you are good at sitting absolutely still for long periods, they will sometimes come right inshore to within a few yards of you. A party of children once settled themselves on some rocks right by the edge of the sea and waited, wrapped in black bin bags to keep out the spray and the cold. Several seals came so close that the group leader decided to call a retreat just in case. The nearest seal had been less than four feet from the group, so close that you could actually smell its fishy breath and almost count the eyelashes round each eye.

The common seal breeds in the summer but late autumn is the grey seals' breeding time. If you know your beaches, you can find the snow-white pups, waiting patiently, half-asleep, for their mothers' return with a new food supply. Young seal pups can be wonderful things to watch but only from a safe distance as bull seals will be patrolling the shore nearby. It is the young ones which catch at the heart; there is little more intensely appealing than these roly-poly waifs and it is easy to believe that they are marooned, abandoned, even injured, when all that has happened is that the approach of humans has frightened off their carers. Unguarded pups are greatly at risk. If approached, they turn wild with a vengeance; they will bite if touched, with fangs coated in germ-laden saliva, as seals carry nasty diseases. A frightened seal pup will often attempt to get down to the sea for safety, before it is old enough, only to die later. Mother seals can cover distance alarmingly fast, even on rough, bouldery beaches; they have immensely powerful jaws and no scruples. The father seal, the bull, is

Grey Seal pup.

never far away; angry and frightened seal pups make a terrific noise and seal hearing is sharp.

Whales are an increasing attraction in Shetland. Large numbers of cetaceans have been recorded in Shetland waters in recent years – a total of 23 different species, either alive, or dead and stranded. In times past, pilot whales, the commonest local species, were driven onto the shore and killed in large numbers for their meat, blubber and whalebone. Common porpoises, known as 'neesiks', are found in Shetland waters, though they are not as common as they once were. White-sided dolphins and Risso's dolphins turn up from time to time. But whales can be more difficult to plan for. Killer whales ('orcas') and minke whales (or 'herrin hogs') are the most likely species to be about, although sperm whales do make an occasional appearance and a white beluga whale was seen not many years ago. The Shetland Cetacean Group keeps detailed records of all sightings and there is now an annual whale-watching day in the summer which is well worth attending for the displays and videos, even if no whales actually turn up for the occasion! Humpback whales are sometimes seen surging out of the waves to turn, twist and crash back again, sending up fountains of spray. Equally dramatic, but less pleasant, are the sightings of killer whales attacking seals. Some bloodthirsty pictures have been taken by those who were in the right place at the right time.

Who are the Shetlanders?

O sing me a sang a da smack an da boom,
Gyaan aff ta da haaf idda simmer,
Whin da sails mirr an sing wi a fine room wind,
An da watter lachs back in a shimmer.

From *Löd a Langer* by Rhoda Bulter.

Shetland is home to a unique twenty-first century community, most of whom are still in close touch with their traditional crofting/fishing roots. The population stood at just over 23,000 as the twenty-first century began. Some Shetlanders consider themselves to be more Scandinavian than British, as these islands were home to Viking adventurers, farmers and raiders for some 800 years before the first formal Scottish rule was established. Shetland's native domestic animals – sheep, cattle, dogs, ponies and poultry – are special breeds, some closely related to those brought over by the Norsemen. Until Shetland became part of Scotland, 600 years ago, Norn, the Norse language spoken in the islands, was the only language. Norn songs, rhymes and sayings were still being used in some remote parts of Shetland as recently as a century ago.

The islands boast Europe's largest oil terminal on one hand, yet also one of Britain's densest networks of ancient archaeological sites on the other. Shetland is for ornithologists one of the world's most significant seabird breeding areas, the most important wild otter haven in the UK, a paradise for geologists, a key area for land and marine plant study, a magnet for traditional musicians from all over the world and a wonderful, safe and exciting place in which to live and bring up children.

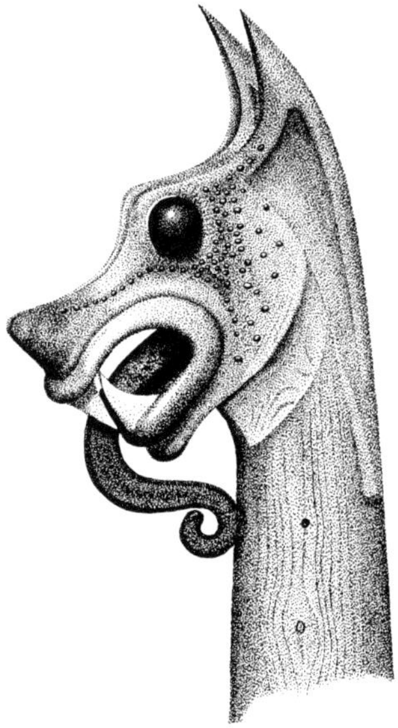

Detail from the replica Viking longship *Dim Riv*, Lerwick.

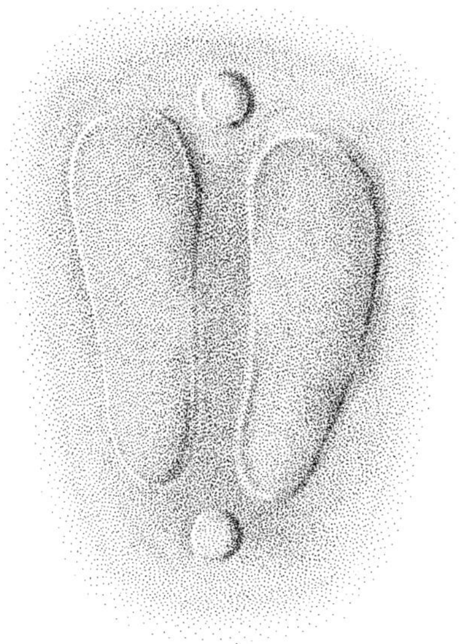

Carved footprints at Clickimin Broch.

But life in the islands has not always been so good. Many periods of poverty, famine and oppression of various kinds throughout history – invasions, disasters, emigrations – have tested islanders to their limits, but somehow they survived. Those who left, or their descendants, frequently find their way back again, especially for the Hamefarin celebrations, specially arranged for Shetlanders living abroad, held every 25 years.

Today's oil reserves have transformed many aspects of Shetland, its society and infrastructure. But the modern and the old, the high tech and the prehistoric here lie side by side. At every turn, Shetland's ancient past confronts you. Here a castle rubs shoulders with a fish and chip shop; there an Iron Age broch faces a garage. Tractors and lorries rumble past ancient standing stones and occasionally, new 'standing stones' have been erected to mark the completion of a major new stretch of road. In Shetland, where people have lived for possibly 6000 years in the same areas, building and rebuilding over the house sites of former generations happens all the time. Old buildings were rebuilt again and again on the same sites, but their foundations remain and countless ancient sites await discovery.

You can spend hours just watching the comings and goings of the fishing fleet, the oil service boats and fisheries patrol vessels. 'Klondykers', or factory ships from former 'Iron Curtain' countries, used to arrive in large numbers, especially during the mackerel season. Occasionally, special cable-laying, seismic survey or even Greenpeace ships may call in. At night, larger seashore communities look out, not over the pitch-black, moonlit or starlit sea, but over a dark expanse filled with shimmering reflections and a dazzling array of lights, warning buoys, and coloured navigation lights, some flashing at different speeds. You need to travel to remote corners and tiny coastal hamlets to find the former dark stillness and peace of a traditional Shetland sea at night.

Aeroplanes taxi into Sumburgh airport along the runway, which was built over the earliest burial site ever found in the islands; the Aberdeen ferry entering Lerwick harbour follows the same course as the Dutch ships whose crews, almost half a millennium ago, set fire to the Cromwellian fort overlooking the town; salmon cages sit moored where longships once lay at anchor and the changes which have shouldered out the old ways await their own eviction by fresh changes as yet undreamed of.

Human History

Above the ruins the gulls are crying
Where once the Pict-folk stayed.

From *Burgawater* by Vagaland (T. A. Robertson)

Despite its remoteness, climate and exposed terrain, Shetland has attracted people to its shores for thousands of years, not simply to visit, but to stay. The settlement patterns have changed gradually through time, but themes of cultivation, fishing, crafts and husbandry remain common to all of them. Each year that passes sees both new revelations about early life in the islands, and new ventures by present-day islanders, all as keen as their ancient forebears to make an improved living here for themselves, their families and communities.

An astonishing number of ancient sites are found in Shetland, preserved probably because of the nature of land use, which has left much of the land undisturbed. It is fascinating to walk through the islands searching for sudden changes in vegetation, rectangular or circular outlines in even plant cover, or the occasional half-buried mound of stone. Many Shetlanders, notably John Stewart from Whalsay, have become keen amateur archaeologists and walk systematically over their areas, noting and reporting on possible sites of interest. Since the mid 1980s Shetland has had its own professional archaeologist, Val Turner, and the sites and monuments list for Shetland has grown rapidly since field survey work has increased. Excavations take place whenever sites are threatened, and each one deepens our knowledge and understanding about the folk who lived here so long ago.

Research indicates that there have been critical times in the long distant past, when over-use has impoverished local soils, burning and grazing have drastically altered tree and other plant populations and, more recently, there has been a dramatic collapse of local fish stocks. Extremes of need, native ingenuity and rugged determination have ensured the islanders' survival before and it is hoped that, with new technology and information systems, disaster may be averted once again. The following section takes each period of ancient settlement in turn, in chronological order, and touches briefly on the buildings, agriculture, burial arrangements and trade, in so far as evidence has been found.

Clickimin Broch, Lerwick.

NEOLITHIC AND BRONZE-AGE SHETLAND

For me, there is nowhere better than Shetland in the whole of the British Isles for archaeology. The islands are believed to have several thousand prehistoric sites; more per square mile than anywhere else in the UK. Traditional crofting methods throughout many centuries have allowed vast areas of the islands to retain their ancient surface landscapes and skylines. Stripped long since of the tree and shrub cover which once grew here, the ground reveals traces of ancient habitation. Burial sites, cultivated areas and boundaries leave telltale patterns and undulations behind. Some areas have lost original soil and the ground with stones and rocks lies bare, with ancient foundations still visible. In other parts of Shetland peat has formed over old settled landscapes and buried the remains of buildings and field systems several feet below today's surface.

Following the ending of the last ice age about 10,000 years ago, the climate improved. Plants recolonised the denuded land and the presence of seabirds and fish, berries and scrub woodland may have made the islands attractive. Archaeological excavations in Europe have shown that travelling hunters and gatherers followed the migrating animals they depended on; making temporary camps, some of which have produced charcoal and evidence of tools and tool-working. Remains of dugout canoes found in Europe and ancient rock pictures of boats with skins stretched over wood from Sweden show that they were able to cross the sea. However, evidence of the Mesolithic, or Middle Stone Age, found in the Western Isles, and in Orkney too, has not yet come to light in Shetland. From the north of Orkney, people would just have been able to see Fair Isle, enticing them to travel further north. Any cave or seashore camp remains are almost certainly now lost to the rising sea levels, but evidence may yet come to light further inland, under the peat.

Carbon dating has so far placed the earliest Neolithic (New Stone Age) sites at roughly 3500 BC, or 5500 years ago. Archaeologists have discovered evidence of a remarkably mild climate during early settlement periods. A rise of even one or two degrees would make a big difference, with conditions at sea more conducive to crossings from mainland Scotland and the growing season extended, allowing more time for the ripening of cereal crops. Pollen analysis gives precise evidence of a large variety of plant species which grew at the time. Pollen grains can survive for thousands of years; some found deep in the present peat layers indicate that many plant, shrub and tree species once grew here where they can no longer exist under present-day Shetland conditions.

House sites of various sizes, mostly oval in outline, have been found throughout Shetland. Excavation of some sites has revealed a single room with recesses built into the thickness of the great walls. Traces of wood found beneath some Neolithic oval houses suggest that buildings of more perishable materials may well have predated the stone ones. Stone vessels have survived in large numbers. Charcoal and fragments of bone found during excavations indicate sites of fires and cooking. Pottery of various kinds has been preserved on some sites and recent research techniques enable far more information about Neolithic life to be gleaned from these fragments than was ever thought possible.

Where land is cultivated, stones are progressively cleared from fields and piled into heaps known as field clearance cairns, which occur widely throughout Shetland. Broken prehistoric tools have been found among stones at the base, while more recent items are sometimes found lying higher up. This suggests that some of these clearance cairns may have been used by Shetland farmers from prehistoric times right up to the present day. Ard points, or stone ploughshares, have been found and, on some sites, the deep scratches that they made in the subsoil, where ploughs have cut through the earth above, can sometimes be seen during excavations. On one site, a marvellously preserved hoard of charred barley was discovered in a midden where it had been buried. Some areas of Shetland which are currently covered in meagre, infertile soils, may in times long past have been intensively cultivated; the soils eventually becoming exhausted.

Evidence of land enclosure is widespread. Stone dykes or walls can be seen in many places, and some are thought to have been built to divide large tracts of land into smaller units, while others may have defined territorial boundaries. Shetland's native scrub woodland is thought to have been heavily used at this time.

Excavation at a Neolithic settlement at Scord of Brouster, near Walls, revealed several house sites spanning a period of 2000 years of habitation. Evidence of sheep and cattle was found and even a piece of red deer antler! The site of the biggest Neolithic building found so far, thought once to have been a temple or maybe a chief's house, is at Stanydale, close to a whole series of other smaller, contemporary house sites. These early Shetlanders were expert at working with stone. Some beautiful polished axes have been discovered. Look out for the remarkable 'Shetland knives', highly polished stone blades believed to have had great value, probably for symbolic or religious use rather than for practical purposes, in the Shetland Museum. Neolithic quarry sites have been identified in a few remote parts of the islands. Some stone tools found on the mainland have been traced back to Shetland quarries, demonstrating the extent of contact and trade during this period.

Some interesting burial sites from the Neolithic period are unique to these islands. Chambered cairns are found all over Scotland, but in Shetland they have a unique outline plan. They consist of a stone-built structure with an entrance-way leading to a small chamber with little recesses leading off it. The front is usually built into a flattened, slightly concave face of characteristic 'heel'-shaped appearance. The island of Vementry has a particularly fine one and there are many others, usually located on prominent hills. Heel-shaped cairns are thought to have contained the remains of a single individual. Burial cists or stone slab boxes appear to be a later method of disposing of the dead. Bones of several

Jarlshof, Sumburgh, South Mainland.

individuals have been found inside these cists, often accompanied by various items for their use in the afterworld. Shetland's earliest multiple burial site, dating from a little over 5000 years ago, was found at Sumburgh during the building of the airport and can be seen in the Shetland Museum.

About 4000 years ago a colder, wetter period began and farming seems to have become less dependable. Expanses of cultivated land became waterlogged and people abandoned them. Peat formed over much of the ancient landscape, obscuring many signs of habitation and cultivation. Evidence suggests that communities clustered into groups, often nearer to the sea. There are indications too that the population, which seemed to be high during the Neolithic period, began to decline. Round about 3800 years ago the first bronze appears on the scene and all sites and structures dated from this point on are termed Bronze Age.

Excavated in the 1950s, Clickimin Broch in Lerwick was found to have been built over a Bronze Age farmstead and Shetland Museum has extensive displays featuring the site excavation there. Jarlshof, Shetland's famous multi-period archaeological site, lies against the seashore at the southernmost tip of the mainland. Here, with almost the whole spread of Shetland's archaeological periods represented in one place, you can allow your imagination full rein as you follow the twists and turns of the paths. There are fine examples of Bronze Age houses and a smithy, where considerable evidence of bronze-working was found. You can borrow a torch from the interpretive centre and crawl into two souterrains, and be completely enclosed within the ancient stone-lined chamber. Wheelhouse and broch remains as well as Norse houses can be entered.

Scatness, a new multi-period site, is being excavated nearby and has even more metal-working remains including many moulds. Reconstructed prehistoric buildings and studies of Pictish and Viking remains from here are adding constantly to the understanding of this little-known period of Shetland's history. Over several summers, experts from The Living History TV programme experimented with local materials to produce tools, cloth and other items, demonstrating to visitors stone-working, weaving, iron- and copper-working and metal-working skills.

A remarkable feature associated with the Bronze Age is the 'burnt mound'. These intriguing, often crescent-shaped mounds of heat-shattered stones are found all over Shetland, always close to a fresh water source. Excavated examples have often revealed stone-and clay-lined trenches beneath them, as well as benches, conduits and other structures. Water may have been heated to boiling point by the throwing in of red-hot stones. Experiments have proved that it was possible, though extremely difficult, to cook whole animals in such trenches. Experts differ over the function of burnt mounds, believing they were group cooking places, or some form of sauna (common to many northern cultures) or perhaps locations for certain kinds of technology or treatment which required heat to process it. Perhaps they served a variety of purposes.

IRON-AGE AND PICTISH SHETLAND

The first evidence of iron working, bringing in the Iron Age in Shetland, dates from roughly 600 BC. Day-to-day agriculture and fishing may have continued much as it had before, but helped now by iron tools. A remarkable number of metal-working sites were revealed during excavations in the late 1990s. A variety of new features, including defensive sites, began to appear on the scene. This suggests that there may have been hostile groups against which communities needed protection, either from local, competitive groups in Shetland, or from raiding outsiders from across the sea. At this time, a number of seafaring raider groups were active. Although the Romans are known to have raided Scotland for slaves, there is as yet no evidence of their having reached Shetland.

The largest Iron Age buildings seem to have been brochs (double-walled stone towers or fortified houses), and blockhouse forts (defensive structures), the latter usually in very dramatic coastal sites. Some, like that on the Loch of Huxter in Whalsay, were built in lochs, connected to the shore by underwater causeways. The ones on Scatness and Burgi Geos in Yell, were constructed on high cliffs. Brochs were usually built within sight of others, which would have made it possible to light beacons and send signals rapidly from broch to broch across the isles, should a suspect ship be sighted. Smoke signals could have been sent by day. Few brochs have been excavated as yet, but those that have been reveal an increasingly complex society, accustomed to trading and contact with people far away from Shetland. Finds indicate a wider range of material goods than people possessed in earlier times.

Mousa Broch.

Mousa Broch, the largest and most complete broch in Britain, survives on the island of Mousa, just east of Sandwick in the South Mainland, and was probably saved from demolition by its remote island location. There is an account in the *Orkneyinga Saga* of Erlend the Young escaping from Orkney with Earl Harald's mother Margaret and staying in Mousa Broch under siege until Harald and Erlend were reconciled and departed for Orkney together. Most prehistoric buildings survive only as foundations or floor-level ruins, usually covered by the heap of collapsed stone walls above. But in Mousa you may stand where people stood thousands of years before, completely enclosed by the same drystone walls. You can climb the same narrow stairs as they did, inside the thickness of the walls, to the lookout at the top of the tower.

A new, rather roughly constructed style of dwelling called a wheelhouse began to be built at about the broch-building period. Their builders possibly used broch masonry and sometimes built within the enclosing walls of an earlier broch. Artefacts found on these sites suggest a relatively affluent society, and include jewellery, fine pottery and evidence of the use of both gold and silver. There are wheelhouses at Jarlshof and more at Scatness, where one has been reconstructed in an experiment to understand Iron Age drystone construction methods. Interestingly, wheelhouses have so far been found only in the South Mainland.

Shetland was an established part of the northern Pictish kingdom, which was centred around Inverness. Pictish Shetland, often known as Shetland's Dark Age, dates from the late Iron Age. Artefacts left behind by the Picts certainly reflect an artistic side to their life and work. Pictish carvings and jewellery inspire designers to this day. Theirs was a literate society with a script known as Ogam, a series of short lines in groups, set across a long central line, the meaning of which has remained a mystery. However, recently progress has been made in the translation of Pictish Ogam by Kathy Forsyth in Glasgow and this may shed some light on our understanding of the period.

Excavated finds reveal the existence of good links with mainland Scotland, Ireland and Scandinavia at this time. A remarkable number of carved stones have been found in Shetland, a few of which have Ogam inscriptions, the first actual written records in Shetland's history. Many have been found in the vicinity of Cunningsburgh, a name thought to mean 'king's fortified settlement'. The purpose of intriguing painted quartz pebbles from this period remains a mystery, as does the material from which the marks were made.

The symbols and designs on some stones resemble those found on Pictish sites on mainland Scotland. A very old carved symbol stone, known as the Brake Stone, was found in the South Mainland at Brake near Quendale. The Mail Stone, found in 1992 at Mail in Cunningsburgh, shows an animal-headed figure and is thought to date from 700. The curious logo used to represent Islesburgh Centre is taken from the Islesburgh Eagle Stone, found north of Brae by a farmer, John Copland, when he was burying a sheep. All three of these ancient stones can be seen in the Shetland Museum.

Some Pictish houses, unlike the larger wheelhouses built earlier, were smaller and were informally termed 'jelly baby houses', thought to be possible to build in a day. They were rounded and consisted of two parts. Very few of these houses have so far been found, suggesting that more buildings may have been built out of wood and other biodegradeable materials, long since rotted away. The Viking word for Pict was *Petta*, found in place names like Pettadale, Pettifirth, Pettister and Pettawater. Some islanders like to refer to the Picts as the forebears of the Shetlanders we know today; rich in art, music, skilled in crafts, metalwork, stonework, farming and seamanship. Children in Lerwick have for generations (incorrectly) called Clickimin Broch the 'Picts' Castle'.

Clickimin Broch, Lerwick.

CELTIC SHETLAND

Christianity was brought to Pictish Shetland well before the Vikings first arrived. The journeys of the seafaring, missionary monks from Celtic, Christian communities in Ireland, Iona and the West of Scotland are well documented. They are known to have reached as far north as Iceland, so it is not surprising to find evidence of their arrival in Shetland as well, dated roughly at about the year 500. Some place names record the presence of places of worship or residence of priests, or *papae* (Norse for priests). Papa Little (little priest's island) and Papa Stour (big priest's island) Papil and the island of Papa near Burra, Papil Bay, Papil Ness and Loch of Papil in Yell all suggest that Celtic Christian influence was widespread throughout Shetland.

Surviving Pictish carved stone slabs sometimes depict both Pictish and Christian symbols. There have been a remarkable number of significant finds of carved stones from both Christian and pre-Christian periods in the islands. Papil in Burra has produced some wonderful finds including both carved cross slabs and carved stone panels from the sides of corner post shrines. The Papil Stone depicts four monks, two carrying books, a lion figure and two extraordinary bird-headed men pecking at a human skull.The Monks' Stone, also from Papil, is a carved side panel from a corner post shrine. Five monks are carved, one on horseback, all apparently travelling towards a cross. Beneath their feet is a row of nine linked spirals, rather like waves, possibly symbolising a sea crossing.

The Bressay Stone, a replica of which now stands where it was found at the churchyard of St Mary's at Cullingsburgh in Bressay, resembles the Papil Stone, having figures of monks with books and also strange beasts. Both stones have elaborate cross designs at the top. A number of carved stones have on occasions in the past been lost or stolen. There is a story of an ancient carved stone being found in North Yell many years ago, but it is now assumed to be lost. Another fine carved stone is recorded from Sandness but that too was lost, possibly stolen. A copy of the design survives. Perhaps they may turn up at some time in the future. New carved stones may yet come to light on excavation sites.

The name 'St Ninian's Isle' may or may not indicate that the saint actually visited Shetland, but the presence of the name at all is significant. In many cases surviving place names indicate the existence of ancient church sites and remains of earlier Christian buildings are sometimes found. A new church would be built on the site of an older one, thus covering all evidence of the previous building, itself perhaps having been constructed over an even earlier one. During excavations in the

The Bressay Stone.

1950s the famous St Ninan's Isle Treasure was discovered along with evidence of an earlier church. Eleven-year-old Douglas Coutts was helping out on the dig. He lifted a large flat stone and a wooden box containing the exquisite silver hoard was revealed. Shetlanders hope one day to see the treasure returned to the islands from Edinburgh where it was taken for safe keeping. In 2000, more of the site was excavated.

Yet another kind of religious site exists in Shetland. On some stacks and remote headlands very small, rectangular outlines can be seen. These, sometimes single, and in other places built in groups, are believed to have been monastic sites. Exactly how and when these sites were used is unknown. Their perilous and precipitous situations make them very difficult to excavate, but a site on an offshore stack in Papa Stour was investigated in the summer of 2000 by a team of archaeologists from Glasgow University. Other sites can be found at the Kame of Isbister, the Birrier at West Sandwick in Yell, Burri Geo at Culswick, Brei Holm and Maiden Stack off Papa Stour and Strandibrough Ness in Fetlar. In the summer of 2000 a pilgrimage was made to three of these sites, to celebrate 2000 years of Christianity.

Boat design and building skills must have improved greatly by this time, judging by increasing evidence of communications between Shetland and mainland Britain. But the real mastery of the sea belongs in the Norse lands to the east, where metal tools and unlimited fine timber led to the birth of the Viking longship. These superb vessels must have created quite an impression when they first appeared on the eastern horizon. It is tantalising to know so little about how their arrival into the relatively peaceful Celtic, Christian Shetland was received. But whether it was gradual or sudden, peaceful or violent, it heralded the end of an era and Shetland was soon to become a very different place.

VIKING SHETLAND

Viking/Norse Shetland began just as a period of warmer climatic conditions arrived in the early ninth century. For some time there had been a general migration 'west over sea' out of Norway and Shetland became a staging post *en route* to Norse colonies in Faroe and Iceland. It is known that in Norway population expansion was creating increasing problems. Inherited land, shared between sons, resulted in ever smaller and less viable units.

Perhaps the last straw that led to mass emigration was King Harald Harfager's unification of Norway, when for the first time he required payment of *scat*, a tax for the upkeep of government, and the provision of service when required for the defence of the realm. Many objected so strongly that they left Norway and settled in many different parts of Europe, including Orkney and Shetland, some reaching Greenland and even America. According to legend, Shetland rebels plotted to overthrow the king, but were foiled when King Harald actually landed in Haroldswick and dealt with them, presumably very effectively.

Until the 1980s evidence of Viking life in Shetland came mainly from excavations at Jarlshof in the extreme south, Papa Stour in the far west and Underhoull in northernmost Unst. More recent Viking excavations at Soterberg and Belmont in Unst and a number of new sites are bringing in new information and already a fuller picture of the period is emerging. Traces of rectangular Viking longhouses contrast with the previous circular and rounded prehistoric building outlines. Evidence suggests that the Norse settlers very sensibly made use of existing houses as well as gradually adding buildings of their own. A new Viking Unst project will intensify research and interpretation with over 30 Norse sites now recorded in the island. Look out for displays and events.

Daily life in Norse times would have been similar to traditional Shetland crofting life in many ways. The tools and materials available were similar and the seasonal activities of fishing, cultivation, animal husbandry, harvests, pressures of weather, daylight and time are little different. Oats, bere (an old form of barley) and occasionally flax were grown. Sheep, cattle and pigs were kept and apart from metal, soapstone and jewellery, families would have been virtually self-sufficient. Blood feuds and raiding continued as recorded so vividly in the *Orkneyinga Saga*. Viking farmers sowed their cereal seed in the spring, and then set sail to spend their summers raiding coastal communities of northern Britain and its islands, returning in time to harvest the crops in the autumn. But despite the privations, life in general may well have been more comfortable and outward-looking than at any time in the preceding 3000 years.

Scattald, the Old Norse term for commonly held, open, unimproved land, is still used today and sheep can take shelter on whichever side of a hill is in the lee of the prevailing wind and rain. The different flocks mingle with each other as they feed and wander, making it difficult to sort them all out at shearing or lambing time. As with many aspects of traditional Shetland life, such as farming and fishing, a considerable amount of Old Norse vocabulary survives in the local Shetland dialects, and in terms for colours and patterns of colour in sheep fleeces: *moorit*, *shaela* or *sholmit*. A *crø* is an exclosure for sheep, *hentilaget* is a piece of shed wool.

A number of documents reveal tantalising glimpses of life in late Norse times. In *Shetland Documents 1195-1579* John Ballantyne and Brian Smith translate, among others, some wonderful property transfer documents dated from the very early 1400s. One list reads: '6 good beds with pillows of down which had good fringes...a rosary of pearls and silver...woven tapestries and glittering under-hangings and lace covers...jugs, dishes, pots...'. So there were spectacularly rich as well as poor even then. The Norsemen had access to iron, silver and gold, as well as the traditional materials, wood, stone, bone and leather. One kind of stone became very important in Shetland; steatite, or soapstone, had the advantage of being soft enough to carve, when quarried, and hardened later. It was worked in the quarry at Catpund near Cunningsburgh and exported all over Scotland.

A remarkable variety of burial methods have been discovered from the Norse period. The first Norsemen here, judging by their burials, were pagan, worshipping the Norse gods Odin, Thor and Freya and believing in the eternal life in Valhalla. Traditionally they buried their dead with grave goods, to equip them for the next world, a practice which was anathema to Christians. Several Viking graves were uncovered when Sumburgh airport was being constructed. The dialect names for bog cotton, *Luckie's oo*, and thongweed, *Loki's lines*, may have a connection with Loki the Norse god of mischief. Could it be that Viking children were warned off dangerous bogs, or swimming in places where thongweed could tangle round their feet and drown them, by associating them with a dangerous and powerful figure?

Norse incomers must have found Christianity already established in Shetland, and official conversion of the Earldom took place in 995. A bishopric of Orkney and Shetland was established in the eleventh century with a Shetland archdeacon who was based in Tingwall. Following this, churches were built all over the islands. Norse farms traditionally had their own small church. The church built at Tingwall in 1150 was magnificent for its time, larger than those at Papil in Burra and Ireland in Dunrossness, with a nave, chancel and a round tower of 60 or 70 feet high. The old chapel of St Olaf at Lund in Unst dates back to 1200.

Most of Shetland's place names are Norse in origin and are mainly descriptive. Wick, or *vik* in Norse, meaning bay, is found in scores of names like Lerwick, Haroldswick, Levenwick, Otterswick. Farm – *bolstadr* in Norse – gives the 'bister' suffix in Isbister, Fladdabister, and Outrabister. Pasture, or *saetr*, generates the many 'setter' names, such as Dalsetter, Aithsetter, and Culbinsetter. A Faroese philologist, Dr Jakob Jakobsen, carried out a detailed study of Shetland place names between 1893 and 1895, collecting over 50,000 words. His *Place Names of Shetland* was reprinted in 1993 and is still widely read. Ownership or function association generated other names, as did events or legends; they give the islands a very Scandinavian feel and are, in some cases, being translated on road signs, in an effort to assist interpretation and appreciation of the Norse heritage. A map of Viking place names was drawn up in the 1980s by Roy Grönneberg.

Many Shetland family names, too, derive from Norse names, notably those with a 'son' at the end such as Laurenson, Nicolson, Bairnson, Jacobsen, Anderson. The old system of patronymics required that each son took on his father's first name after his own. A girl took on her mother's surname. The language of Norn was Scandinavian and was spoken in Shetland long after the islands became Scottish. In 1774 Orkney minister George Low collected a few fragments of Norn in Foula. He wrote, 'nothing remains but a few names of things and two or three remnants of songs which one old man can repeat...'. Shetland, according to geologist Samuel Hibbert in 1822, was full of Norwegian ballads and had been 'from time immemorial, celebrated for its native poets'. Visitors often assume that Shetland shares with Scotland a Gaelic heritage, but this is far from the case. Some Pictish names have survived but Scottish Gaelic place names feature little, except occasionally as modern house names.

NORSE SHETLAND

Eventually Shetland and Orkney were given to Jarl Rognvald of More who became Earl Rognvald in the late 800s. He had several estates in Norway and so gave the islands to his brother Sigurd. The islands were used as a base from which Viking raids were made on territories further south. Shetland was only two days' sail from Norway, which was at that time evolving from free-booting Viking, to more organised and civilised Norse. The Norse estates were united and a separate 'earldom' of Orkney and Shetland was created. A tax, or skat, was paid to the Norwegian crown by all those who had land and all had to abide by laws which were drawn up. The system survived for several hundred years.

Norse rule was based on the *Book of Laws of St Olaf*. A 'Great Foude', or chief magistrate, appointed by the King of Norway, was assisted by a lawman to whom was entrusted the care of the *Book of Laws*. Shetland was divided into a dozen or so smaller units, each under the charge of an Under Foude who presided over local assemblies, and who was assisted by about ten local men of good reputation known as Ranselmen. The islands were visited in turn during each year and locally acceptable representatives called Lawrightmen in each district saw to the gathering of the land tax which was paid in material goods. Each year the Great Foude and his lawman went round every district, holding courts. Once a year the Lawting, main assembly of the parliment, was held at Tingwall; it continued to be held there until 1604: almost 800 years of Norse rule, several hundred years more than the Scots and English rule which has since followed. The ancient place name 'Ting' dates back to the Norse division of Shetland Mainland into manageable units, each with its own court, or 'Thing'. Six of the original names are still in use: Aithsting, Delting, Lunnasting, Nesting, Sandsting and Tingwall.

Udal law prevailed, wherein land was the property of the person who had first claimed and improved it, regardless of social status. If you come to Shetland in January to watch the Up Helly Aa fire festival, look at the very top of the mast of the galley before it is burned, for a severed hand motif. This is said to represent a Viking's hand, cut off and thrown onto the shore ahead of rivals when racing to beach their longships in a new country, the tradition being that the first to touch the land, laid claim to it from then on!

Land was valued in merks, a measurement based on productivity rather than physical size. This meant that however different in size two holdings might be, if they produced the same amount of crops, they had equal merks and equal land tax. Many people believe that this was a far fairer and more democratic system than any devised since.

Around 900 guizers with their burning torches surround the replica Viking longship (galley) prior to its burning at the Up Helly Aa Festival in Lerwick.

Between 900 and 1100, Viking adventurers sailed ever further. From their colony on Vinland in Newfoundland and Greenland in the north-west, to Russia and Byzantium in the east and as far south as Spain and Rhodes, Vikings now had access to goods from far and wide, whether traded or raided, and Shetland remained a key northern base for their journeyings. Shetland Museum has lamps and bowls, fishing weights, Norse bone combs and pins which have survived, along with tools and items of harness.

The Earldom of Orkney and Shetland created a political and legislative background to life in the islands and the two islands were closely connected for several hundred years. In 1194 this changed suddenly. Olaf, a kinsman of the then Earl, Harald Maddadarson, who had estates in Shetland, plotted with a band of Shetlanders and Orcadians to overthrow the Norse King Sverre Sigurdsson. The plot failed. Shetland was removed from the Earldom as a punishment and annexed to the Norwegian crown. For the next 300 years, the islands became a Scatland, or tributary province of Norway, overseen by a 'sysselman' or representative of the king.

While Shetland's ties with Norway strengthened, Norway's grip on former territories to the south was gradually weakening. In an attempt to regain control over former Viking territories, King Haakon fought King Alexander at the Battle of Largs in 1263, but neither side won and both remained in dispute. In a treaty drawn up in 1265, Norway ceded the Isle of Man and the Western Isles to Scotland in exchange for an annual rent of 400 merks. Orkney and Shetland were specifically exempted from this. Scotland failed to pay the yearly fee; had it done so, Shetland would still have belonged to Norway. But this was not to be.

Between 1200 and 1300 the climate deteriorated, greatly restricting the Vikings' northern sea routes to Iceland and Greenland. Ice floes would have blocked access to the north-west and increasingly bad weather would have restricted sailing ventures. The severe conditions must have had an impact on Shetland harvests and rural life and prayers may well have been said in the old churches in Shetland for a return to better weather and crops. Norse control over the seas was still strong, but other states and nations were edging into the trade and travel picture too. Fascinating and colourful stories from this period were told for generations and eventually written up in the fourteenth-century *Orkneyinga Saga*. Shetland's oldest surviving document is a letter written in 1299 by local lawmen, enquiring about allegations made by a woman from Papa Stour. The woman, Ragnhild Simunsdatter, had accused Thorvald Thoresson, then Sysselman in Shetland, of dirty dealing and claimed that he was a 'Judas'.

In 1319 Norway united with Sweden and in 1397 both united with Denmark. By the fifteenth century Shetland was divided up into five different land categories: Crown estates or Kingslands, Lordship lands of Shetland, udal lands, bishopric lands and kirklands, leading to complications and conflicts; one set of families rising to power, wheeling and dealing to maintain it and eventually being eclipsed by new ones. This period has been referred to as 'The Orkney and Shetland game of Monopoly'. Land ownership and sale can still be a contentious issue to this day.

A new method of preserving fish in barrels of salt was discovered which led to a big increase in fishing by the Germans who began to build up vast fortunes. Agents came to live in Shetland and built houses and trading booths, or 'böds', by the shore. Goods from far and wide were brought to Shetland and traded either for cash, or for butter, woollen garments, fish and livestock. Local people must have looked forward to the trading season and these booths, Shetland's earliest shops, were built by successions of traders over the next few centuries.

In the mid fifteenth century King Christian I of Denmark and Norway realised that there was little chance of retrieving the Scottish debts unless by force, which his own lack of funds prevented, and a strategic marriage was arranged as a substitute. In 1468 a marriage treaty was drawn up, setting at 60,000 florins the dowry required for Margaret his daughter to marry the young Prince James, shortly to become King James III of Scotland. This effectively cancelled the Scottish debt and placed Denmark 10,000 florins in debt instead. Two thousand florins were paid promptly, the remaining 8000 were to be paid in due course, and Shetland was pledged by way of a surety until the debt was settled. All subsequent efforts by Denmark to do this were deliberately ignored and sidestepped by Scottish officials, who thus skilfully enabled Scotland to retain the Shetland islands to the present day. There are still some in Shetland who feel strongly that the islands should be restored to Denmark.

Shetland was administered in much the same way as it had been under Norse control for almost another century, with Bergen as the most influential source of control. But eventually, things began to change. During this time, the traditional Shetland trading links with Bergen were shifting in favour of direct trading connections with Germany and later, Holland. The Hanseatic League dominated Shetland trade for many years. It had its own laws and conventions and on the whole was used and appreciated by the islanders. When changes in trading laws were introduced by the English king and parliament, the new requirements were largely ignored by Shetland and for many years things went on as they had done before. Norse influence is still much talked about in Shetland. Scottish influence spread only slowly, as the islands held on to their Norse laws and language for a long while. Norse manuscripts relating to Shetland were still being written several hundred years after the islands became effectively Scottish.

SHETLAND FROM 1500

An interesting insight into this time came when the foundations of a large stone building were revealed during an archeological excavation at Kebister, which proved to be a *teind*, or tithe barn, belonging to Henry Phankouth, Archdeacon of Shetland in 1500. The report which was published later is well worth reading by those who have an interest in this period.

The reformation of Shetland churches in 1560 was handled by Adam Bothwell, Bishop of Orkney, and Jerome Cheyne, the Archdeacon of Shetland. The Sinclair family too held powerful positions in the islands. James V's illegitimate son, Lord Robert Stewart, was granted the Earldom and Crown lands of Orkney and Zetland in 1564 by Mary, Queen of Scots, his half sister. Robert Stewart had a big house built at Sumburgh, the ruin of which was seen by Walter Scott on a visit to Shetland. He was inspired to write *The Pirate* and named the ruin 'Jarlshof', and the site has been known by that name ever since. In 1571 Robert Stewart delegated his position of Foud, or chief magistrate, to Laurence Bruce of Cultmalindie, a disaster for Shetland by all accounts. Complaints flooded in, resulting in the arrival of two royal commissioners who interviewed 760 people at Tingwall. But after a brief spell in prison, Bruce returned to Shetland, a far from reformed character. He built Muness Castle in Unst and many a tale of his ill-treatment of islanders can be read in the island's interpretive centre.

Shortly after Mary granted the earldom to Robert Stewart, she conferred on James Hepburn, Earl of Bothwell, her third husband, the title of Duke of Orkney. His enemies were numerous and when things began to get hot, he tried to take refuge in Orkney. This failed, so he sailed to Shetland, but, learning that he was being followed, he struck a deal with a Dutchman, Geert Hemelingk, who took him to Norway in his ship *The Pelican*. In a dramatic escape, the ship took a devious course out of the north mouth of Lerwick harbour, thus luring the

Muness Castle, Unst.

pursuing ship, *The Unicorn*, onto a dangerous rock, which has borne its name ever since. Bothwell finally arrived in Denmark, but past crimes caught up with him; his attempts to win favour failed and he was imprisoned. Bothwell died in prison and his corpse remained a gruesome visitor attraction until only a few decades ago, when his bones were finally buried.

The Spanish were at war with England in 1588, and after the Battle of the Armada a number of Spanish ships, attempting to return to Spain round Scotland, were wrecked on the Shetland coast. Stories of Spanish survivors still exist in various parts of Shetland. Some concern the building of chapels of thanksgiving. One records a Spanish ship dragging her anchor until her prow ground a huge, glass-smooth groove in the rough cliff face near Islesburgh which can still be seen. Another tale tells of a party of Spaniards landing, executing and burying a shipmate, then returning to sea. A Spanish supply ship from the Armada, the *El Gran Grifon*, was wrecked on Fair Isle and an account of the fate of the survivors was found among archives in Madrid. The short but fascinating piece graphically describes the physical appearance and meagre existence of the islanders of the time.

Robert Stewart handed the lordship over to his son Patrick and Earl Patrick Stewart took up his new position in 1593. He ordered the building of Scalloway Castle, reputedly using forced labour, where he lived in grand style by comparison with the Shetlanders. The court, held for so many years in Tingwall, was moved to Scalloway Castle. Experts differ over the degree to which Earl Patrick's reputation was manipulated by jealous contemporaries, but massive amounts of land and wealth were certainly accumulated. The *Court Book of Shetland 1602-4* records heavy fines imposed for minor offences and the confiscation of land and property. There was public anger at the increasing number of injustices and in 1609 Earl Patrick was arrested and his lands confiscated. In 1611 an Act of the Scottish privy council banned the use of Norse laws; only the newly revised Scottish laws were to be used. The old *Book of Laws* has been lost. After a failed attempt by influential landlords to regain their lands by force, both Patrick and his father were executed in Edinburgh in 1615. Sadly there were plenty of powerful clergy and landowners to continue and even increase exploitation and oppression of the islanders for generations to come.

Growing concern about the lawlessness of Scotland's poor led to resolutions to educate the people in the scriptures and to increase literacy throughout the population. A number of wealthy islanders appear to have had private tutors for their children, but an Act was passed in 1616, instructing the establishment of schools in all the parishes of Scotland. The Act had no powers of enforcement and little seems to have happened in Shetland as a result. Fragmentary references to schools appear in records, but nothing formal was organised for the best part of another century.

Gordon Donaldson's edited transcript of the *Court Book of Shetland 1615-29* makes enthralling reading. Cases of theft, gruesome accounts of assault and murder, the settling of disputes, unpaid debts, rent recovery, land ownership and details of inheritances, create vivid images of the life of the period. The best-known extracts concern cases of alleged witchcraft, leading to the gallows, and the famous order given on 7 November 1625 to demolish houses in Lerwick, in an attempt to end 'The great abominatioun and wickedness comittit yeirlie be the Hollendaris, and the cuntrie people, godles and profane persones'.

Dutch merchants had by this time established themselves in the islands, each with his own corner of suitable sheltered natural harbour and piece of land, for which they paid rent to the local landowner. In the stone trading booths which they built, various local goods such as knitted socks and caps, butter, fresh meat and eggs were traded for tobacco, spirits, cloth and meal. A number of their elaborate gravestones can still be seen in a few of the older graveyards. The riches reaped by the trade in salt herring helped to fund the Dutch East Indies ventures and Amsterdam was said to be 'built on herring

Window detail from Muness Castle, Unst.

bones'. Claes Jansen, a Dutch sea captain, was buried at St Mary's, at Cullingsburgh, Bressay, in 1636 and the tombstone can still be seen. His ship had struggled into Bressay Sound after a dreadful crossing from Mozambique, plagued by gales and disease. He died the following day.

These were times of great unrest in Europe and Shetland felt the ripples from battles and sea chases over many years as the focus of the fighting switched between the English, French, Dutch and Spanish. In 1640, four Spanish frigates surprised four Dutch men-of-war in Bressay Sound as they were waiting for a fleet to arrive from the Indies. A ferocious battle ensued and several ships were sunk. A cannon from one of them was dredged up in 1922 and now stands in Fort Charlotte in Lerwick.

In 1653 a Dutch East Indiaman, *Lastdrager*, was wrecked off Yell and in 1664 the *Kennermerland* was wrecked off the Out Skerries. Visit the Pier House exhibition in Whalsay to picture the busy scenes of the day. A fascinating glimpse into the lives of the poorer people at the time is provided by a young Dutchman, Jan Camphuijs, who survived the wreck of the *Lastdrager* and was washed up on the coast of Yell. He was given shelter by an old man and his son who shared what little they had without hesitation. He describes a large stone being rolled towards the fire as a stool and records how an oxhide bag carrying all the food they had was taken down and offered to him.

Shetlanders benefitted from their Dutch trading contacts and there must have been considerable resistance to the growing interference from the British government, for whom the Dutch were the enemy. National government concern about the Dutch led to the building of Fort Charlotte in Lerwick in 1665. The Dutch got their own back by burning the fort to the ground, along with part of the town, and hostilities continued for years. After 1667 Shetland's Scottish land tax was collected by the Commissioners of Supply, consisting of the landowning and power-wielding élite of the day, who also decided how it should be spent. It must have been agonising for local folk, accustomed to their seasonal friendly relations with the Dutch, to stand and watch while more of their ships were burned in 1677. Token storming of Scalloway Castle by Lerwick gentry is chronicled from the period. Troubles mounted up as the fisheries themselves began to decline and, as if this wasn't bad enough, French pirates began to

The south gate into Fort Charlotte, Lerwick.

make raids on Shetland, causing considerable disruption to trade. To add to the general misery, smallpox broke out, there were several bad harvests and serious famine hit the islands in the 1690s.

An Act for the Settling of Schools was passed in 1696, which enabled a fresh effort to be made towards the educating of the young people of the time. Some wonderful characters and individuals committed themselves to campaigning and working towards the setting up of schools in many parts of Shetland, sometimes helped and sometimes hindered by the Scottish Society for the Promotion of Christian Knowledge (SSPCK), the local presbytery and the Church authorities in Scotland. Shetlanders, despite (or maybe because of) their poverty and wretched circumstances, famine, disease and general suffering, proved to be very keen to see their children learn. Astonishing sums were sometimes raised in areas where money was desperately scarce. There is a vivid insight into this period in *A Vehement Thirst after Knowledge* by John Graham; particularly inspiring is the story of Happyhansel School in Walls.

In 1700 there were developments in the Christian arena between Presbyterian and Episcopalian factions within the church. A commission of ministers was sent to Shetland by the General Assembly of the Church of Scotland. Among these was the Revd John Brand, who wrote in an account of his visit (a wonderful, if not wholly accurate account of Shetland at the turn of the eighteenth century): 'The people are generally discreet and civil, not so rustic and clownish as would be expected in such a place of the world...'!

More wars in Europe affected Shetland and its trading patterns. During the War of the Spanish Succession, a fleet of French warships came on a large fleet of Dutch herring busses and cruisers in Lerwick harbour; 100 Dutch ships were burned.

In 1707 the Act of Union between Scotland and England sealed the fate of Shetland. Now, as an economic part of Great Britain, it would never return to Denmark. With the introduction of a stinging tax on imported salt, the keystone of the Hanseatic fish trade, money no longer flowed into the hands of Shetlanders and the era of Shetland-Holland alliance was over. As this resulted in removing the only source of income for the people to pay their rents, some lairds began to take over the role of merchant themselves. One of the most adventurous was Thomas Gifford of Busta, many of whose letters have survived and form a valuable insight into the problems and ideas of the time. Many of the gentry disapproved of the idea of actually handling money and dealing directly with the common populace!

Potatoes were introduced to Shetland in 1730 and other agricultural experiments and improvements were set up. The Greenland whaling began in the same year, attracting hundreds of men away from the islands for months at a time during the season, away from the drudgery and poverty, where even if you worked hard to improve your croft or your lot, the rent would simply be increased, as often as not, to reflect the added value. Lairds were much opposed to their tenants going to the whaling as each man who left was one less to join their fishing fleet.

Gifford built up markets in Spain for hard dried, lightly salted cod and ling, a trade which lasted into the next century. More Shetlanders turned to trading, some buying large ships and selling fish widely throughout Europe. The rise of the Shetland merchants had begun. Smuggling became widespread on these voyages. The Revd John Mill travelled to Shetland in 1754 and kept a detailed diary of his life as a minister in the islands. The diary makes very interesting reading and includes some vivid accounts of Mill's view of the depravity of the time.

The Greenland whaling was building up by 1750 and nearer to home, the Haaf fishery was beginning to gain momentum. Gradually, as well as owning the land and the crofts, lairds owned the boats, fishing gear and homes, and also the shops which provided every essential item for the survival of their tenants. Large families were encouraged, to breed more young fishermen, and extra land to feed the growing population was taken out of the hills. People worked all hours to catch fish, weave cloth and make butter simply to exchange it in the shop for the basic necessities of life. This was the infamous 'truck system'.

New smallpox epidemics killed large numbers of people, reducing the rise in population to 15,000 by 1755. It was still early days in preventive medicine. Links with the Scottish mainland were improving and after several years of a limited and irregular service, the first regular post began to travel between Lerwick and Leith, taken by the open packet ship *Isabel* on 6 May 1758, and the service continued for two years. Today E-mails fly between Shetland and the rest of the world every second of the day and night. In those days a journey to Aberdeen could take days or weeks, if the weather was bad.

By 1760 inoculation against smallpox had been developed, but a single dose cost more then than a whole year's wages for many. In 1761, 200 people died and severe frosts and loss of cattle added to the suffering. It was then that a remarkable Shetlander, John Williamson, developed a cure of his own for smallpox. He treated infected matter with peat smoke and buried it in camphor. A tiny amount was inserted under the skin and the cut wrapped in cabbage leaves. According to the medical practitioner in Lerwick at the time, 'Johnnie Notions', as he came to be called, never lost a patient.

While ever-larger boats were plying between Shetland and mainland Scotland, smaller sixereens, six-oared open boats, were working the Far Haaf (the open sea), rowing for 40 miles and more out to the west to catch ling. Boats from all over Shetland were working flat out between mid May and mid August. All round the coast, on gently shelving pebble beaches, especially in the north and west, fishing stations were set up where the split fish were dried and stacked. The men lived in small huts or lodges. Sometimes artificial beaches were built; stones were laid up on the grass until there was enough area of 'shingle' to lie the drying fish. Productivity rose dramatically and in 1763 a new method of curing fish was pioneered by Bruce of Symbister.

By 1770 Lerwick was growing fast, as was the population, which had begun to increase since the smallpox was brought under control. The industrial revolution began to get underway in Shetland in 1780 with a number of experimental ventures undertaken. Flax was grown for linen, copper was mined and kelp burning was tried along suitable stretches of coastline; the sale of the rich ash augmented many incomes. It was hard work for little reward and the labourers may well have stopped to rest their aching backs and gaze out to sea where the Haaf fishing was bringing in record catches. There are still remains of kelp-burning pits in places. Despite all the innovation and change, repeated bad harvests created high levels of poverty. George Lowe was commissioned to travel through and report on Shetland in 1774 for a writer called Pennant who had just completed an Orkney account. Lowe's Shetland writings were finally published in 1879, 85 years after his death.

By 1790 the Lodberries, small stone warehouses built out from the shore, were being constructed in Lerwick, trading and commerce having taken over a large proportion of the town's foreshore. For the first time, some Shetland merchants became richer than the landowners and tension between them began to mount. This dynamic time saw the production of one of Shetland's most important documents, *A Statistical Account of Shetland*, compiled from questionnaires sent to every parish minister in the islands. In 1809 Arthur Edmundston wrote his *Views of the Ancient and Present State of the Zetland Islands*.

The Napoleonic Wars saw an increased demand for seamen in the British navy. Captains knew that Shetlanders were superb sailors and despite the fact that the quota of 100 men (and more) was regularly met, sailed their men-of-war into every voe, lay in wait and resorted to the vilest of deceptions and brutalities in order to 'press' more and more men and even boys into service. Around the shores of the islands in 1810 the press gang were in action, sailing stealthily into bays and anchoring offshore, ready to launch small boats and capture as many

Old fishing station, Stenness, Eshaness.

Shetland Croft Museum, Boddam.

young skilled Shetland seamen as they could surprise. Men were taken from their own weddings, boys taken out of school. Stories abound of incidents with the press gang; escapes, hiding places, women carrying food and provisions across the hills and along dangerous cliff paths in the dark to their menfolk. Now and again successful tricks were played against the officers by local men, betrayed by unpopular landlords who knew which men were home from the fishing and which were not.

Samuel Hibbert, a geology student, arrived in Shetland in 1817 where he found chromite in commercial quantities. He explored Shetland thoroughly and in 1820 published a geological account of Shetland, complete with a colour map and then in 1822 published *A Description of the Shetland Islands*. A wonderful collection of extracts from his and other historical writings can be found in Derek Flinn's *Travellers in a Bygone Shetland*.

There were developments on Shetland's spiritual front at this time. The first Baptist Church was built in Dunrossness; Methodist preachers arrived a few years later and a number of other denominations added to the variety of Christian witness in the islands.

In the 1820s the first tenants were forcibly removed from their crofts to poorer land. *Rigga rendal*, or runrigs, which had fed families for a thousand years were ploughed up into large fields where fodder crops were grown. Cattle and vast numbers of sheep grazed over traditional croftlands. This was the start of the infamous Clearances. Sandlodge and Sumburgh farms were laid out. Landowners, no longer able to make their fortunes through the fishing, for which their tenants provided the labour, looked to sheep-raising as a more lucrative business. Over a quarter of the population of Shetland left the islands, most of them in the second half of the century, settling far away, often in New Zealand, America and Canada. Some merchants began to buy fish directly from local fishermen and lairds were said to keep watch on their small fleets, to prevent private sales of fish.

Shetland fishermen ventured as far as Greenland and Norway's North Cape looking for cod. Improved boats with decks enabled the men to split and salt the fish on board. Landlords no longer controlled the fishing scene and income increasingly went to the fishermen themselves. Chromite quarrying opened in Unst, and Hay and Ogilvy were established as shipbuilders, from which grew the twentieth-century Hay and Co. a business success story. The Shetland Bank was set up in 1821, producing its own notes, an indication of just how much money there was around by this time, at least in the coffers of a few. The Haaf fishing was still providing catches for processing at the fishing stations at Fethaland, Stenness, Gloup and Haaf Gruney. In 1832, disaster struck and 105 men were lost in one deadly gale, while out at sea. The boats afforded no shelter from the weather and there was nothing in the way of the safety equipment and rescue services we take for granted now.

In 1832 the Reform Bill was passed, giving some Shetlanders a right to vote; and in the same year communications to the mainland improved when the paddlesteamer *Sovereign*, the first steamer service to Shetland, began fortnightly summer calls into Lerwick. Shetland's first newspaper, *The Shetland Journal*, was launched. By the 1840s the Scottish landlords were beginning to derive more income from farms than from fishing and ceased trading in fish. Crofters could no longer sell fish to help pay the rent. Many moved to other districts or emigrated. Those first emigrants had no chance of returning. Now, many generations later, more and more of their descendants visit Shetland in search of their roots. Every 25 years a special 'Hamefarin' event is held to welcome them back. The Prime Minister of New Zealand in 2000 was Helen Clark, whose family originated from Cuckron in Stromfirth. She follows in the footsteps of emigrant and teacher Sir Robert Stout; born in Lerwick in 1844, he became Prime Minister of New Zealand in 1884.

The autumn of 1846 was the first of four years of failure of the potato crop, reducing the islanders to deeper levels of famine and poverty than ever before. Relief was sent up from Edinburgh in the form of supplies of meal in return for work building stone walls, or 'dykes', and also proper roads, for which there was a growing demand. The work was to be supervised by the army. All transport had previously been by sea around the coastal settlements. Overland journeys across the hills were made on foot or by pony. Over 100 miles of 'meal roads', as they came to be known, were built and in Papa Stour you can still see part of one. Many have disappeared under modern routes.

Gas lighting was introduced to Lerwick in 1856 and new technologies began to transform the traditional ways. A Lerwick man, Arthur Anderson, who started as a beach boy drying fish in Lerwick, proved a dynamic and creative businessman and philanthropist. He became the first Shetlander M.P. and made a great

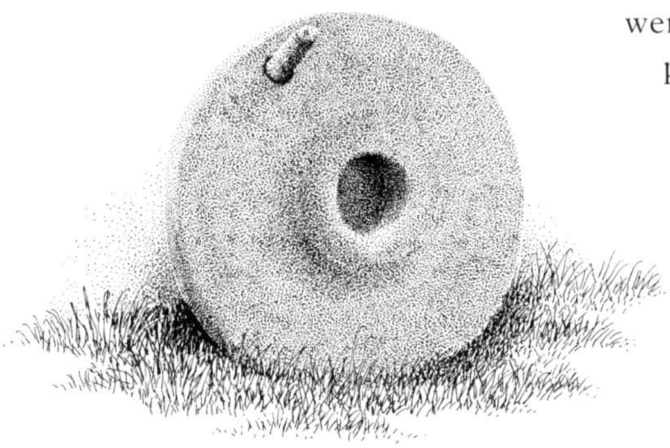

Mill stone.

Contemporary painting of Arthur Anderson's fishing station at Vaila in the 1840s.

impact on the lives and fortunes of Shetland people, the effects of which linger still. He devised an improved system for drying fish, jointly set up the P&O shipping company, started Shetland's first newspaper and in 1862, perhaps most importantly of all for Shetland, founded the Anderson Institute, a first-class school for Shetland's children.

In the same year, more Clearances took place, some families moving to Orkney but many opting to go further afield. In just ten years from 1871 close on 5000 people emigrated from Shetland. An attempt was made at last to bring relief to Shetland's poor and the unfair system of the lairds' shops was examined by the Truck Commission. The landmark Education Act was passed in 1872 requiring all children to attend school. Schools were built all through the islands, replacing the previous private and church schools.

In 1881 disaster struck the fishing communities again when another 58 fishermen were lost in a single night, this time off Yell. There were other smaller losses and gradually the Haaf fishery began to come to an end. The communities had been devastated by the deaths of so many young, active men, and some families had lost all their menfolk, leaving women and children destitute. In 1883 the Napier Commission visited Shetland to investigate the conditions of crofters. The reports made by Shetlanders were so grievous that they led to the setting up of the Crofters' Holdings Act of 1886. This gave crofters security of tenure, compensation for improvements, and a new, fair rent. In 1889 the Local Government (Scotland) Act established Zetland County Council as a representative body, to be elected by the Shetlanders themselves. This period marked a turning point in the security and welfare of the islanders.

A new insight into the times became possible as photography arrived in the islands. Prints reflect contemporary Shetland with views of people at work, crowds of steam drifters, rural scenes, villages with thatch-roofed houses and women with heavy 'kishies', or baskets, strapped to their backs, hands busy knitting while they walked. The new computer database in Shetland Museum enables you to select photographs from their enormous collection, glimpse life in hundreds of Shetland scenes and even buy a print to take home.

Woman knitting, with a kishie on her back.

The Shetland Pony Stud was established in 1890, reflecting the respect with which the breed was regarded.

For some time the herring fishery had been expanding with dramatic increases in catches of herring. Herring are a migrating species and in the summer months, move into Shetland waters. Alistair Goodlad's *Shetland Fishing Saga* covers this period very thoroughly. There were hundreds of herring boats and boat-building and repair businesses expanded rapidly. Herring stations multiplied along the Lerwick seafront during the great Shetland herring boom.

The Public Health Act of 1897 enabled a sanitary inspector in Lerwick to put assistants to work in every district to report on the conditions of houses and people's health. The Gilbert Bain Hospital was built in the same year.

THE LAST HUNDRED YEARS

By 1900 the herring fishery was prospering while the cod fishing was coming to an end. In 1905 the sail fleet is said to have peaked, with 1000 sail boats and nearly 300 steam drifters landing their catches at an incredible 170 fishing stations spread around the coast of Shetland from Boddam in the south to Baltasound in Unst in the north. A. Halcrow's *Sail Fishermen of Shetland*, reprinted in 1994, captures some of the atmosphere of this period.

The Smallowners (Scotland) Act passed in 1911 gave the Board of Agriculture power to establish smallholdings, with or without the landlord's consent. The current of reform and redistribution which had been in full flow was interrupted by the First World War. Shetland played a strategic role in the British defences. Great guns were built on Vementry and Bressay to guard the most important approaches to Shetland and large numbers of servicemen arrived to man the many military locations around the islands. Equally large numbers of islanders left for service abroad and many never returned. There were especially devastating losses on the Somme, with some families losing several members.

In 1919 the Land Settlement (Scotland) Act came in, giving the Board powers of compulsory purchase. In 1923 Veensgarth farm and a number of others in Shetland were broken up and the 19 new holdings and ten enlargements virtually restored the valley to the state it had been in 100 years before. This was revolutionary change for the better in the fortunes of the ordinary folk of the islands. It was hundreds of years since the last period of true independence had been enjoyed on the land.

There was an outbreak of scarlet fever in 1930. TB was still present in Shetland, but islanders' health and welfare generally were improving. Mains electricity, generated by a small diesel power station, was introduced in 1932, almost 80 years since the introduction of mains gas in Lerwick. Shetlanders saw their first aeroplane, which landed in 1933, followed in 1934 by the first commercial flight carrying passengers.

In 1939 the Second World War broke out and Shetland again assumed national importance. Once more servicemen flooded the islands and large numbers of Shetlanders left to serve in the forces. Casualties, despite being fewer in number than in the First World War, were, as before, higher in relation to the local population than anywhere else in the UK. Massive military construction work took place, building military air strips, barracks, various sea defences, air-raid shelters and gun emplacements. Public access to certain areas was restricted and the islands braced themselves for several years of wartime conditions. Echo sounders and Decca navigation systems were introduced at about this time, which were to have a major impact on the fishing.

A new chapter in relations with Norway opened with the 'Shetland Bus' resistance network, described later in the Scalloway section, page 189. Every Shetland family has a story to tell about the war and a full account of this period has still to be written. Shetland in many ways benefitted economically during the war and when the troops finally left, there was a period of real hardship.

By 1942, 63 miles of road had been constructed in Shetland, effectively bringing to an end the old pattern of communities linked only by sea. Some hamlets still without road access began to shrink, as first one, then another family left to live somewhere a little more accessible to the road network. The North of Scotland Hydro Electric Board was formed in 1946 for 'promoting social improvement and economic development...throughout the Highlands and Islands' by providing electrical power. The Board took over the old generating station, running it for nine years before building a new diesel power station out at Gremista. By 2000, there were over 1000 miles of supply lines in Shetland, compared to just ten in 1947!

Russian and Polish trawlers began to fish off Shetland. Lobster fishing increased significantly during the 1950s. In 1955 work began on a major redevelopment of Lerwick's waterfront and harbour facilities; a plan which had taken many years to draw up. Construction of a covered fish market was begun in 1959 and in 1960 the whole completed works were opened by Queen Elizabeth. Herring and mackerel processing, consisting of gutting and packing in salt, had been a familiar industry for decades but refrigeration in the 1960s created an expansion in fish processing. In 1965 the first Norwegian purse-seine netters arrived in Shetland. Almost every new development to the earlier ways of fishing met with resistance from the old guard; but the purse-seiners went further than usual, often catching 100 tons at a single cast in contrast to the five tons caught by a Shetland drifter in one night. Shetland's fishermen could not have survived against this degree of competition. By 1967 Shetland had its own purse-seiner and others followed.

There were some very different types of boats operating off Shetland during the late 1960s. They were oil survey vessels, testing the seabed and the geological formations below for the presence of oil. The increase in shipping around the islands began to present safety problems and in 1969 VHF radio sets were installed in the harbour office and the pilot boat in Lerwick. The pelagic (fish that swim in shoals of the same species, e.g. herring and mackerel) fishery took off, benefitting from continuing developments in catching technology, and other countries joined in the race. Fish-processing factories were doing well but by the early 1970s indications of over-fishing were becoming obvious. The herring stocks were so low that a total ban on catching them was imposed between 1977 and 1983.

New technology, as well as transforming fish catching, entered the world of accounting in the 1970s. The Computer Age arrived with the introduction to the Shetland Council's finance department of a Burroughs B 80 system which involved pre-programmed sheets with magnetic strips. MacDonald Douglas micro-computers were introduced in 1979 and they in turn were replaced. The current system consists of AS 400 PCs and covers all departments. Computers eventually entered the machine-knitting arena and designs can be typed onto a screen at one end of the process and emerge in a finished garment at the other.

Oil was eventually discovered to the east of Shetland and the oil boom which hit soon afterwards had a major impact on the course of development in the islands. Shetland had been experiencing a period of relative economic well-being just prior to the discovery of oil. Only a short time before this, things had looked pretty bleak, and an oil bonanza then would have been instantly welcomed. But coming when it did in 1971, there was considerable suspicion of its likely consequences. Traditional industries of knitwear and fishing had been helped to new levels of profitability with changes in economic support and marketing. A boom in the sale of knitwear to France made a real impact on the income in that sector; Shetland knitwear had become fashionable. The revival in the economy was parallelled by a growing confidence within the community.

Then local government reorganisation came in 1969. The first proposals for Shetland suggested that the islands be merged with a large part of mainland Scotland. This was vigorously and successfully opposed and Shetland along with Orkney and the Western Isles achieved all-purpose status in 1975. Thus they secured the powers of both tiers of local government, regional as well as district. The stakes rose, with opportunist incomers on the prowl for speculative land acquisition. These were exciting times and key local figures steered Shetland towards one of the best deals ever achieved with oil companies by a small community. The Zetland County Council Act was passed in 1974 and enabled the council to have greater control over new developments in the 'first phase of oil'. Shetland MP Jo Grimond was instrumental in driving the project through parliament. Land for an oil terminal was acquired and development plans drawn up. The Council drove a hard bargain with the oil companies, persuading them to contribute to the cost of port infrastructure and a disturbance fund, as well as fixing income per barrel from oil and agreeing on high standards of care of the environment through which the pipeline construction would pass.

SOTEAG (Shetland Oil Terminal Enviromental Advisory Group) was set up to monitor the impact of oil activities on the environment. Construction camps complete with self-contained catering and leisure facilities for up to 7000 workers were installed at Toft and Firth, with built-in safeguards for removing all buildings and restoring the land to agricultural condition after the phase was over. The oil terminal produces its own electricity from a power station built at Sullom Voe. It is the largest building in Shetland and has a capacity of 125 megawatts fuelled with waste gas from the oil fields, as well as diesel. The hordes of workers and incomers brought with them new foods and locals still chuckle about the courgettes and celery, green peppers and other 'unken' foods that 'cam in wi da oily men.'

By the end of the decade the 'oil invasion' was in full swing with the construction of the oil terminal, and new air and marine infrastructure. The oil companies courted popular approval and their funds supported many local projects. High wages paid for very basic work such as cleaning and bed making were tempting people out of their previous jobs and even luring older teenagers away from school. Skilled workers – electricians, bakers, plumbers and men and women from all walks of life – left their jobs in droves, heading for the terminal and the money! Shetland infrastructure rapidly began to feel the pinch and soon businesses were having to close. The island population swelled by 35 per cent with the families of oil workers from the south and the demand for new housing and schools, better roads and health facilities grew more urgent. Housing schemes for oil staff at Brae and Mossbank necessitated enlargement of local schools.

The advent of oil didn't end the use of other energy sources. Commercial extraction of peat, despite some misgivings, was introduced in the 1980s, and became widespread in Shetland. Between the wars 'windy lights', or small wind-driven generators, were installed privately across much of Shetland. Private diesel generators produced power for outlying islands and private homes until very recently and many people still hang onto their generators in case of winter power cuts on the mains. Only a few solar panels have so far been installed in new buildings despite the latitude with its long hours of summer daylight. The Council built a Waste to Energy plant during 1998 which supplies hot water to a district heating scheme. This sells and distributes piped hot water to a number of houses and other properties in Lerwick, including the hospital.

The first roll-on-roll-off ferry, *St Clair*, arrived at Holmsgarth terminal on Tuesday 5 April 1977. In the same year Radio Shetland went on air for the first time and has since become something of an institution. People see the radio as 'their' service, not the BBC's! There are regular news reports and special programmes on music, wildlife and archaeology. There are interviews and outside broadcast reports as well as opportunities for new poets and writers to have a wider audience. Shetland also has its own independent commercial radio station, SIBC 96.2 FM, locally owned by the Shetland Islands Broadcasting Company, which went on air in 1987 after a long campaign. Many local businesses use SIBC for advertising. SIBC broadcasts 24 hours a day, 7 days a week, with breaks for weather and for hourly local, national and Nordic news, doubling to half hourly at morning and afternoon drive times.

The 1980s were a time of peak activity. Computers were used in schools for the first time. Many social and economic changes in Shetland had been predicted. A total of 9000 oil-related jobs had been created. The oil terminal was officially opened by the Queen in 1982. New airport facilities were completed at Sumburgh, and at Sullom Voe the major construction activity of the 1970s came to an end, resulting in an increase in unemployment, and the population fell. However, the Council made use of its oil revenues to help develop the traditional sectors, as well as supporting new business ventures. Thus by the end of the 1980s the population had stabilised and many new jobs had been created. In particular, fish farming was proving very successful and grew from nothing in 1983, to a major source of income by the end of the decade. Agriculture and fisheries also benefitted from new investment. One unexpected bonus from the ending of the construction phase was the 'Grand Scran' or scavenge, when the workers' camps were dismantled and all the materials were gathered and carted off for use on crofts and around the homes and gardens of hundreds of local people. Vans, lorries, tractors and trailers made many a sortie, even across the sea to other islands before the available wood, metal, fittings and prefabricated sections had all gone.

Tourism was expanding and a wide range of new leisure facilities and interpretive attractions appeared. Individual craft businesses and small knitwear and jewellery firms were helped to promote their products and combine forces on Shetland stands at some of Europe's major trade fairs. Oil reached a turning point of activity in its 'fourth phase' and from this point on, a gradual decrease in jobs and services began. One benefit of incomers who stayed was their visitors, who seldom returned home without buying Shetland knitwear and other craft items. Shetland's unique wool and knitting designs received a boost with the registering of a trade mark and new designs were tried, as well as the traditional Fair Isle and Unst lace patterns. Young knitters excelled themselves in the college knitwear courses and showed their goods far and wide.

There was a significant oil spill in 1978 when within a month of the oil terminal opening to tankers, the *Esso Bernicia* lost 1174 tons of bunker oil into the sea. Some 4000 seabirds died and the seashore from North Brae to Fethaland was polluted. Ironically the most serious oil-spill disaster before 2000 was the wrecking of the *Braer* in 1993, a vessel which had nothing to do with Sullom Voe at all, but was simply passing by the islands. The ship broke her back on Garth's Ness near Sumburgh and sank, releasing 86,000 tons of oil. The emergency response arrangements were initially hampered by an almost total blocking of transport into the islands by media hacks, competing for disaster images and copy. Nineteen days of almost continuous gale-force winds followed the wrecking of the *Braer*, resulting in far less coastal damage than might otherwise have been the case.

Many questions remain unanswered about aspects of the accident; the condition of the ship, the suitability of the crew, the possible consequences and nature of the oil dispersants used. Many claims for compensation had still not been settled by 2001. It was seven years after the *Braer* that shellfish harvesting restrictions were lifted on the inshore areas where the spilled oil was believed to have collected and contaminated the seabed. There was a call for a special tug to be kept in Shetland in case of future tanker breakdowns at sea. It was several years before the government agreed to fund a suitable tug in the Northern Isles during the winter months. After the *Braer* oil spill, Shetland played a key role in European initiatives to tighten control over maritime safety.

Many of the gloomy predictions of the negative impact of oil on the Shetland way of life proved groundless. Many newcomers contributed to the revival of music and language. Improved roads and transport facilities increased mobility and people travelled about the islands for enjoyment as well as necessity.

Arts and leisure centres attracted growing numbers and sports activity increased. Teams attended the Inter Island Games. Community centres were built with the 'oil moneys' as well as extra support facilities for the elderly and disadvantaged. New groups and clubs sprang up and local community history projects gathered momentum. The Council's Leisure and Recreation department assisted the visits of many theatre groups, music groups and orchestras to the islands. Shetland Amenity Trust was founded to further interpretive, conservation and environmental work and the Shetland Arts Trust was established a few years later.

The 1990s saw yet another local government reorganisation. All the larger authorities were split into many smaller ones, but Shetland remained largely unchanged, retaining all-purpose status. Fire and police services continued as before but water and drainage services were hived off into separate quangos. In 1999 the first Scottish Parliament for 300 years was established and Shetland elected Tavish Scott as its first MSP. Jim Wallace, the former Westminster MP for the North Isles, became the MSP for Orkney and Deputy Leader of the Coalition. Alistair Carmichael became the Westminster MP for Orkney and Shetland. A number of government departments have offices in Shetland, such as Customs and Excise, Employment, Social Security and Agriculture and Fisheries.

Since the early 1980s, a steadily increasing impact of European Union assistance and support has been felt within the islands, despite the overwhelming rejection of entry into the EEC by Shetland in 1975. The EU now has a major effect on daily activities in Shetland through various policies on agriculture, fisheries and the environment. Perhaps the biggest impact has been through the access to funding for infrastructure and business developments. Now, EU grant aid acknowledgement signs can be found in many places; beside newly aligned, improved roads, outside factory premises and beside piers and interpretive facilities. Further education centres including the Shetland College and the North Atlantic Fisheries College have received considerable funds. Up until the end of 1999, it is estimated that well over £200m has come into the islands. There has also been EU funding for exchange projects involving island energy issues and school projects under the Comenius scheme which suports links and visits between UK and other European schools.

Shetland was in a strong position to dictate terms to the oil consortium in the 1970s. However, the tables were turned in the mid 1990s when the oil was said to be running out. One interesting item, apparently overlooked in the early and effective pre-oil negotiations, was the subject of rent of the terminal. At the negotiations which led to the Busta House Agreement in the late 1980s, the Council was in a much weaker position than it had been before the lease for the terminal was agreed and fared less well than many hoped. Similarly, in the mid 1990s, urgent negotiations to secure Sullom Voe in Shetland, rather than Orkney or other Scottish locations, as a base for the new oil extraction zone 'west of Shetland' met with far less success than the original deal in the 1970s.

Conservation (now a term included under the umbrella of 'environmental issues') became a major element in Shetland towards the end of the twentieth century. Initially introduced as a measure to prevent the extinction of rare birds (too late for the sea eagle, the peregrine falcon – and the Great Auk) it now has a part to play in almost every island equation. Government legislation and, more recently, European directives have placed statutory requirements upon all regions of the UK to set in place various protection, interpretation and monitoring systems. Scottish Natural Heritage has a base in the islands, which is jointly managed with Orkney. As time goes by, there is a growing appreciation of the complexity of conservation issues and of the rarity and value internationally of many of Shetland's habitats and wildlife species.The Council has its own Environmental Services department and other agencies and organisations play various parts in the growing debate including Shetland Crofting and Farming Wildlife Advisory Group, the Shetland Amenity Trust, The RSPB, Shetland Bird Club and an increasing range of special interest clubs, groups and trusts. A Biological Data Recording Unit was set up in 1998.

Growing concern over radioactive particles found near the nuclear reprocessing plant at Dounreay on the north coast of Caithness resulted in some very imaginative initiatives being taken in the islands. Shetland and other North Atlantic countries belong to KIMO (a Norwegian acronym), an organisation set up to discuss concerns about nuclear contamination and other factors governing the health and safety of northern seas.

Shetland Field Studies Group, set up in 1981, researches local areas in detail and provides interpreted guided walks which have been regularly written up in the magazine *Shetland Life*, and produce leaflets and maps for each walk undertaken. They welcome visitors on their programmed walks, which can be booked at the Tourist Office. They publish a small journal, *The Shetland Naturalist*, in which new research is presented to the general public, rather than remaining in academic obscurity. In 1983 the Shetland Field Studies Trust was established to promote and provide environmental and local studies in Shetland schools. Shetland Conservation Volunteers organise voluntary projects to enhance sites of special wildlife interest. The next decade may well see a growth of local interpretive initiatives based in local communities. Coastal paths and scenic way-marked routes are currently under consideration.

The annual Environmental Award scheme highlighted a wide range of environmentally friendly ventures and thus encourages people to attempt more still. You may see 'Dunna Chuck Bruck' signs, meaning 'don't throw litter', and stickers on sale in some places, designed to combat litter in the islands. Despite anti-dumping-at-sea legislation, tons of sea-borne litter washes up around the coasts every year. Inevitably, the wind picks it up and blows it all round the islands. Each spring since 1982 the Shetland Amenity Trust has organised a massive islands-wide litter collection day called 'Da Voar Redd Up' and an astonishing number of people join in. The Shetland Bird Club maintains detailed records of native and migrant birds in Shetland, publishing an annual *Shetland Bird Report*. The more recently set up Cetacean Group and Shetland Entomological Group follow a similar form, publishing reports of sightings and identifications in their newsletters. A growing number of businesses have been set up to help visitors enjoy the wild environment. Boat trips, tour companies and special holidays spring up every year as interest in wildlife tourism grows.

The last decade of the twentieth century saw a gradual consolidating of economic and interest groups through the islands. Oil money looked set to flow for a good few years yet, and a healthy debate was in full swing on the subject of fish stocks, quotas and protection measures. There was help for new businesses with assistance from Shetland Enterprise, the EU and local and national government. Welfare and health-care provision was at an all-time high and the older generation was cared for and valued. There were a number of social problems with drugs and alcohol, just as there were throughout the rest of the country, but youth workers and special projects were being well supported. There was a real celebration in 1999 when the Tall Ships Race visited Shetland, leaving behind unforgettable images of masts and sails and a general air of festivity.

SHETLAND TODAY

The new millennium found Shetland in good shape. The quality of life in the islands was arguably the best that it had ever been, for the population as a whole. The economy was healthy, unemployment low and the population stable. A network of wide, well-maintained roads, good air and sea links with the mainland and excellent services to the islands enabled people to travel more easily and quickly than ever before in the islands' history. Air and sea transport and freezers allow food of any kind to be ordered and delivered from Aberdeen often within hours. But island economies are very fragile and local people know well how quickly the picture could change.

Shetland Aerogenerators installed three 750-megawatt wind turbines in 2001, overlooking Dales Voe, and the beautifully tapered, curved blades began to turn, feeding clean power into the Shetland grid. They were a fitting symbol of confident 'green' progress for a new century, visible from far away in many directions.

The built landscape is vastly different from that of 50 years ago. New houses, built for views rather than shelter or good productive soils, lie scattered across increasing numbers of accessible, attractive seaward-facing hillsides. Efforts have been made to group dwellings and limit grossly out-of-character styles, with mixed success.

There is a strong tradition of right-to-build where and how people wish, born perhaps out of the surviving feelings of determination never again to be bullied by those in power which date back to Shetland's centuries of oppression. There are many fine new buildings, however, and some traditional crofthouses have been restored and gracefully extended. Norwegian 'kit' houses are common, and here and there curious little dwellings have been constructed as shells around an inner caravan. A number of imaginative, well-designed clusters of new dwellings have been built for low-income groups.

Support for Shetland dialect has grown and a steady increase in both poetry and prose writing has resulted in many tapes and books of Shetland poetry, children's stories and novels on sale. A Shetland Literary Award is presented each year to the author judged to have produced the finest new work. Local concert parties produce first-class local comedy and command large audiences. More serious work is reflected in the quarterly *New Shetlander*. A rich mixture of verse, stories and historical writing can be enjoyed every month in *Shetland Life* magazine. The end of the twentieth century saw a revival of live story-telling which is gaining momentum. Autumn 2001 saw Shetland's first Story-Telling Festival. A range of some of the best literature is well represented in the book *A Shetland Anthology*.

Each new generation is encouraged to keep cultural traditions alive, and the Council provides resources for traditional fiddle tuition, knitting and even Shetland dance in Shetland schools. Despite increasing numbers of closures during the last century, there are some 35 schools in Shetland. Of these, 29 are primary schools and eight are junior high schools, which have both primary and secondary departments. Nursery school provision is increasing and well-resourced and staffed playgroups still fulfil a major role in pre-school education. A number of small communities have single-teacher schools, but visiting specialist staff increase the staffing provision overall. The Further Education College in Lerwick provides a wide range of training services every year and the arts department has helped produce some of Shetland's best new knitwear designers. In Scalloway, the North Atlantic Fisheries College is at the forefront of developments in aquaculture, marine and fisheries research, attracting many students from all round the world.

There remains a tangible Shetland warmth, a generosity and openness which affect all who visit the islands. This hospitality and positive approach is reflected in particular in the involvement in third-world and other charities; with special commendation frequently given to local groups of national charities, for raising vastly over the national average in funds, for the size of area and population. Shetland supports many third world projects with trained volunteer work teams as well as funds and materials. Albania and Tamil Nadu have seen significant input in recent years.

The islands have an energetic, forward-looking society, which still retains strong links with its past. As a small community situated in a remote location and a hostile environment, it has triumphed over the many and rapid changes forced upon it in the past 30 years. The survival instinct is strong and the environment demands a toughness and vitality found not only in natives but in incomers who have stayed as well. These qualities will be tested to the full with each fresh challenge which the new millennium presents; conservation of fish stocks, future employment problems and the ever-present risk of marine accidents.

SHETLAND TOMORROW

A number of exciting and controversial changes in transport, energy and industry are appearing on the horizon as the twenty-first century begins. Inter-island ferries in some cases may be replaced by 'fixed links' (bridges or tunnels) and the long-campaigned-for new road out west has been built. The new Aberdeen ferry service started and prompted mixed feelings as P&O's long service to Shetland came to an end.

More renewable energy projects, both wind, wave and tidal, are being designed and trialled, but there is a growing realisation that 'green' energy developments will remain limited unless a mains cable link to mainland Scotland can be laid. New oil developments west of Shetland promise a reprieve for the island economy in the short term, provided that safety measures prevent more accidents from occurring. Sustainable industry is a goal to which many agencies are directing their support.

Fish farming is broadening out to include other species including cod, halibut, lobster and oyster farms and knowledge about how to control the sea lice without poisoning the seabed is increasing. Fears remain in some quarters that, in a search for employment, even bigger quarrying projects might lie ahead, as minute traces of both gold and platinum are found here, which would require vast amounts of rock extraction in order to recover economic quantities of these precious metals.

The market for cholesterol-reduced meat is growing, favouring traditional breeds such as Shetland sheep and cattle. The amount of organically grown and locally produced food is increasing and climate change may help or hinder this in times to come.

A brand new Anderson High School, designed and planned during the 1990s, will eventually be built. The newly built Shetland Museum will be opened and work completed on the new Archives controlled environment. New excavations will uncover yet more of Shetland's past, maybe even solving the riddle of the Bronze Age burnt mounds. Experts may discover just what was used to paint the Pictish pebbles and even decipher their mysterious Ogam inscriptions.

Shetland's internationally recognised outstanding geology may well be awarded Geo Park status soon. Less well supported locally, has been the Scottish executive's proposed Marine National Park idea, though Shetland's superb coastal wildlife more than meets the conditions and views may change through time. The island's bird life and flora will continue to be carefully monitored as climate changes begin to impact on the habitats throughout the islands.

Looking across Cribba Sound and the island of Vementry towards Neeans Neap, West Mainland, with Papa Stour in the distance.

The Islands

Sometimes I tink whin da Loard med da aert,
An He got it aa pitten tagidder,
Fan he still hed a nev-foo a clippens left ower,
Trimmed aff a dis place or da tidder,
An He hedna da hert ta baal dem awa,
For dey lookit dat boannie an rare,
Sae He fashioned da Isles fae da end o da aert,
An med aa-body fin at hame dere.

From *Shetlandic* by Rhoda Bulter.

There are many guides which begin their journey in Lerwick, but it is all too easy to drift into a view of Shetland as a big town with radiating minor routes, dotted with items of interest. The organisation of this Guide seeks to value each community and settlement in its own right and to visit Lerwick as a part of Shetland's whole in passing. Shetland, though small, is a lot bigger than many visitors realise. Finding your way around can be a challenge if you don't have good maps, and to avoid missing some of the less well-known highlights of the islands' treasure store of features, the following gazetteer is designed to help you explore with confidence. Shetland, being the furthest north of the British Isles, sees, in turn, Unst as its northernmost outpost. So this Guide begins with Unst and takes the reader gradually south through the outer isles, taking in village after village, feature after feature until we reach Fair Isle at the furthest southern limit.

In a book of this size, it is impossible to include every hamlet and settlement but most of Shetland is here. References to geology, botany and wildlife are made where particular locations merit a special mention, but not in any great detail, as these subjects have been covered in the introductory sections. Archaeological sites are mentioned in context, in order to make it easier to visit them when in the area. The routes from place to place are chosen to help those travelling by car, bike, or even on foot, to find their way, gain an understanding of and make the best use of their time in each area. Where appropriate, incidents from history are introduced roughly where they are believed to have happened, as a means of bringing the past to life.

From Unst, the Guide travels to Fetlar and then Yell. Whalsay and the Out Skerries follow, as these too count as northern isles. Northmavine comes next and introduces Mainland Shetland. The Guide breaks off at this point and focuses on the West Mainland, including the islands of Papa Stour and Foula. The text then returns to Brae and covers Mossbank and Voe, followed by the central and eastern landscape as far south as Tingwall. The Guide then leads the reader north-west to Weisdale and Kergord, to link up with the West side section covered earlier. Returning to Tingwall, we head south to Scalloway and the Scalloway islands, including Trondra and Burra, before covering Lerwick. Bressay and Noss then take centre stage, concluding this section of the Guide. The final part of the text is a broad scan southwards from Gulberwick to Scatness. Fair Isle forms the concluding elements of the islands-wide tour.

A short section on travel and holiday information follows, covering briefly a range of current topics, sports, music, exhibitions, eating out and other facilities with general advice for visitors. The final section consists of appendices, with lists for reference on Shetland's chronological history, plants and birds and other items of interest, including a best beach guide.

Out Stack
Muckle Flugga
Herma Ness
The Noup
200
Hermaness Hill
Hermaness National Nature Reserve
Burra Firth
Brei Wick
Saxa Vord
285
Skaw
Holm of Skaw
Wick of Skaw
Lamba Ness
Grunka Hellier
Tonga Stack
Tonga
Visitor Centre
Nor Wick
Norwick
170
Burrafirth
Unst Heritage Centre
B9087
Orknagable
Libbers Hill
Skeggie
Hill of Clibberswick
B9086
Boat Haven
Haroldswick
The Nev
North Holms
Wood Wick
Hevda Hill
116
Loch of Cliff
Harold's Wick
Nikka Vord
Hagdale Chromate Quarry
South Holms
Baliasta
Halligarth
The Rett
Keen of Hamar National Nature Reserve
Buness
Baltasound
Balta Sound
Balta
216
Valla Field
U N S T
Spoo Ness
Newgord
Hill of Colvadale
Huney
Gloup Holm
Gloup Ness
Wick of Breckon
Gloup Voe
Lunda Wick
Loch of Watlee
A968
Breckon
Westing
Brough Taing
Colvadale
North Neaps
Gloup
St. Olaf's Kirk
Underhoull
Sobul
West a Firth
Memorial
Mid Breck
Gunister
116
Blue Mull Sound
Vord Hill
112
Kussa Waters
Papil Bay
Lund
The Vere
Hill of Vigon
Cullivoe
Framgord
Loch of Snarravoe
Sand Wick
Stonganess
Mu Ness
B9084
Y E L L
B9082
Uyeasound
Clivocast
Muness Castle
97
Gossa Water
Wick of Belmont
Belmont
Uyea Sound
Skuda Sound
The Ward
Dalsetter
Linga
Gutcher
Uyea
Haaf Gruney
Hill of Dalsetter
95
A968
Wick of Belmont
Sellafirth
96
Wedder Holm
Colvister
Cunnister
Sound Gruney
Lochs of Lumbister
Urie Lingey
Burra Ness
Kirkabister
Tressa Ness
Basta Voe
Stack of Birrier
Loch of Vollister
Hamars Ness
Urie Ness
East Neap
Basta
Oddsta
Colgrave
Vord Hill
159
Strandburgh Ness
The Camb
Basta Ness
94
58
RSPB Reserve
North-A-Voe
Wick of Gruting
Brough Lodge
F E T L A R
Camb
Hascosay Sound
Sands of Sand
Skutes Water
Head of Hesta
Windhouse
Kaywick
B9088
A968
Mid Yell Voe
Hascosay
105
Houbie
Mid Yell
Hill of Lussetter
Interpretive Centre
The Tind
Loch of Vatsetter
Vatsetter
Papil Water
Tresta
Aith
Funzie
Sound
Loch of Funzie
Wick of Tresta
Laxa Burn
Birrier
Lamb Hoga
RSPB Reserve
B9081
North Aywick
Head of Lambhoga
The Snap
Aywick
Rams Ness
South Aywick
0
5 km
Hill of Arisdale
205
Queyon
Otterswick
White Wife
0
5 miles

Unst

You cannot get any further north in the British Isles than Unst. Only the stacks of Muckle Flugga with its famous lighthouse (built by Thomas Stevenson, father of Robert Louis Stevenson, and David Stevenson in 1858) and the battered rocks of the Out Stack lie a little further to the north – the only 'land' between here and the Arctic. The island, famous for its exquisite lace 'wedding ring' shawls, is just 12 miles long from north to south and five from east to west.

The ferry to Unst leaves from Gutcher in Yell and sails east across Blue Mull Sound to Belmont. This stretch of sea is thought to be the channel carved by a glacier towards the end of the last Ice Age. While you cross, keep an eye open for unusual birds swimming or fishing in the Sound, including white-throated divers which are sometimes seen here. The crew may know if there is anything interesting about. As the ferry approaches Belmont, it passes an ancient broch site on the left, high on the cliff-top. Iron Age Picts may have kept watch from here as the first Vikings arrived.

There is a substantial modern pier at Belmont, very much like one at Ulsta in Yell, but instead of having been excavated from schist, it is built out of the yellow/green and blue/green blocks of serpentine taken from the quarry behind the carpark. The recently renovated Belmont House, one of several old lairds' houses in Unst, stands four-square above the shore to the left as you approach the pier. Built in 1777 for one Thomas Mouat, the house has many architecturally interesting features and additional farm buildings behind it. Funds were raised for its renovation through the Belmont House Trust.

A short way north from the ferry, the Loch of Snarravoe comes into view to the west, with its ruined houses and outbuildings, last inhabited in the early 1950s. A windlass was used here to bring water up from the loch. This must have saved much back-breaking carrying of buckets. Old rig lines run down the green slopes to the shore of the loch, where anglers regularly catch trout. You can walk across the moors northwards to a second deserted homestead at Snabroch, with its ancient broch site and more scattered ruins, as far as Lunda Wick. A number of prehistoric sites have been found in this area and recent excavations have revealed much information about ancient settlement in Unst.

The road for Uyeasound turns right a mile or so north of the ferry, the isle of Uyea with its derelict house and chapel ruin visible across the sea to the south. A stranding of killer whales caused some excitement here in the early 1990s. There is a small hostel opposite the substantial pier, which is in constant use. The ruin of an old trading booth, Greenwell's Booth, still stands here and the houses facing the sea are thick-walled and sturdy. The Church of Scotland was built in 1843 originally as a United Free church, and has a belfry. Children at Uyeasound school were among the luckiest in the land when at one time they could watch a snowy owl from their classroom windows.

As you head east out of the village, look out for a tall prehistoric standing stone on the right. A few miles further along the southern coastline is Mu Ness, a headland full of interest for botanists, geologists and archaeologists. Explore Unst's most notable historic building, Muness Castle, which stood originally three storeys high. It was built in 1598 for Laurence Bruce, half-brother of Robert Stewart, the notorious illegitimate son of King James V, whose reputation for tyrannical rule he shared. Local fishermen say that some of the huge building stones fell into the sea while being unloaded and can still be found underwater. A key to the castle can be obtained from the nearby cottage.

If you have time and enjoy walking, there are fine views and much to discover on the coastal route north from Muness to Baltasound. Sandwick was the site of a large amount of Norse settlement, and artefacts are periodically washed up by the sea onto the wonderful sandy beach

Bordastubble Standing Stone, Unst.

here. Local fishermen claim that there are remains of walls under the waves, which snag their nets from time to time. Recent excavations on a Norse house site managed to establish a considerable amount of information before the last of the steadings was eaten away by the waves. The ruined church of St Mary's at Framgord dates back to Norse times. The graveyard, still in use today, has some very old 'keel stone' gravestones and the grave of Laurence Bruce from Muness. You can walk north along the coast from here to the deserted settlement of Colvadale, where the ground is still green and fertile, after centuries of human habitation and land improvement. Among the ruined crofthouses and stone walls can be found signs of prehistoric sites, earth banks, lines of once-cultivated ground and clearance cairns.

Head north from the Uyeasound junction, and turn left along a side road signed to Westing. About a mile along, turn left again, past the great standing stone of Bordastubble, said to be the largest in Shetland. The ruined house of Lund, built for John Ross in the eighteenth century, stands here. It was said to have been haunted and a number of wild tales exist about the place. The devil is said to have left an imprint of his hoof in the fireplace. The road continues to the ruined St Olaf's kirk, built around 1200, which was still in use in 1785. Notice the Pictish symbol stone carved into the lintel stone of one of its windows. The graveyard is still used and features two Hanseatic memorials, to merchants from Bremen; one Segebad Detkin and a Henrik Segeleken the Elder, dated 1585. The peaceful sandy beach here, always sheltered from south westerlies, is worth a visit in its own right. You can retrace your route and turn left past the Stone of Bordastubble.

Underhoull Broch earthworks lie to the left of the road just before it dips down into the Westing approach. Several ancient sites can be found locally, including a Norse farm and prehistoric house site as well as the broch. An excavation was undertaken here in the early 1960s which shed light on life and farming in Viking times in Shetland. The road carries on, ending at Westing itself. Here there is a fine shingle beach which forms the start of an interesting walk north along the coast past several abandoned townships. Not far offshore is a small island with yet another broch site on it. A burn runs down into the sea at Westing and a few hundred yards upstream, an old water mill can be seen. As you retrace your

Lunda Wick from Underhoull Broch.

route to the main road you appreciate how this whole area is sheltered from the east and south by the massive ridge of Vallafield.

A short way north of the Westing junction on the way to Baltasound, you can detour left to Gunnister where you can see another of Unst's remarkable prehistoric stones, but this one isn't standing. It lies rather like a massive cushion, well plumped-up in the middle, but with curious scalloped depressions like small bowls all round the outer edge. The purpose of this stone is unknown, but, however fanciful, ritual sacrifice springs to mind when you study those strange hollows and imagine them full of blood.

Baltasound is a large settlement clustered around the shore. The harbour is greatly protected against the worst of the heavy seas by the barricade of Balta Isle, which lies a few miles out to the east. At the beginning of the twentieth century Baltasound was a seething hive of commercial activity with all the herring traffic: boats, fishing stations, gutters and coopers and their accommodation sheds. Unst has never seen busier times. At that time, Balta itself had many fishing stations and working piers. Now only tattered fragments of concrete and iron remain to poke up from among the rocks and sand. Today, salmon farming is in full swing, a growing element of the local economy.

Baltasound is the main village in Unst, with a hotel, shop and garage in the centre of the village. High hills to the north shelter the community from the worst of the northerlies. On their south-facing slopes lies a circle of ancient stones. These were said to have been the place to which, long ago, people accused of certain crimes could run for sanctuary; that is if they managed to survive the gauntlet of violence meted out to them *en route* by a gathering of hostile individuals!

A fine leisure centre was built in Baltasound in 1988; an ideal solution to a day of bad weather. The junior high school has a wood and large pond, one of Shetland's first school wildlife areas. The primary school children from the recently closed Haroldswick school now attend here. An airport at Baltasound served both island and oil rigs until the end of the 1990s, when the oil companies which used it shifted their operations to Scatsta. Scheduled flights ceased in April 2001.

There are many pleasant walks around Baltasound and some interesting buildings to be seen. Buness dates back possibly to the seventeenth century and is an old haa (laird's or merchant's house) which has been considerably added to. It was here in 1817 that the Frenchman Jean Baptiste Biot carried out an experiment into gravitational acceleration at high latitude. The experiment was repeated in 1999 at a local festival. St John's Church is built on the site of an earlier church and several others have stood in the village in the past. Hillside Church at Balliasta, now a ruin, was identical to the Uyeasound church and the Old Kirk built in 1764 is also roofless, standing in its old graveyard. There is an ancient church site in Balta, too, but long since lost under the sand dunes and no one knows exactly where it stood.

Halligarth, in the north-east corner of Baltasound, once home to the Saxby and Edmondston families, is the site of Britain's most northerly woodland. In its heyday, the wood boasted many scores of different tree and shrub species, an avenue and gardens. In spring the ground beneath the trees is carpeted with bluebells. Migrant birds make straight for the sheltering branches when they struggle into Unst from the east after hours or days of battle with south-easterly winds. The shelter the trees provide is considerable and rare breeding birds have been recorded here on several occasions. Halligarth is part of a large estate which has been gifted to the National Trust for Scotland and includes many buildings, both historic and traditional, as well as croft land and peat moorland.

Woodwick, once the site of a fishing station, makes a lovely place for a walk west from Baltasound. As the name suggests, the sea here has washed in flotsam and jetsam, forcing it high up onto the beach. Immense quantities of timber can be found here, especially after westerly gales. The valley approaches are beautiful and in summer are full of birds and flowers.

Heading east and north from Baltasound, the land rises up to Hagdale, where chromate was once quarried. Signs lead you to the restored horse-mill which is well worth a visit. Just to the south is the Keen of Hamar, a National Nature Reserve, famous for the flora which grows on the Serpentine Fellfield here. Just as Shetland has greater geological variety than any other county in the UK, so Unst has the greatest variety in Shetland. These rocks break down to form interesting, mineral-rich soils which support some unusual plant species. At the Keen of Hamar these tend to grow smaller than usual, possibly because of the cocktail of minerals in the soil. Among the rarities found in early summer are Norwegian sandwort, northern rock cress, early purple orchid and a species of arctic chickweed, an exquisite flower unique to the island. The significance of the Shetland chickweed was first appreciated by the famous young Unst botanist Thomas Edmondston, who published a paper about it in 1843 at the age of 18, and the flower has been known as Edmondston's Chickweed ever since. Thomas was a remarkable young man who became a Professor of Botany at Glasgow University at the age of 20. Son of doctor and naturalist Laurence Edmonston, he died in a tragic accident barely a year later while on a scientific trip to Peru.

Norwegian Sandwort.

The road continues north,

descending past more quarries and Haroldswick comes in sight. This is said to be the site of a battle when King Harald Harfager landed here and slew the exile rebel Vikings who had taken to raiding the Norwegian coast. You can see the replica longship Skipblader, which a modern day Viking crew sailed to Shetland recently and abandoned it in Haraldswick. Here, opposite the community hall, was the most northerly school in Britain. This has been converted into the new Unst Heritage Centre and is a 'must' for every visitor to the island. There are several displays about life here in the past, including excellent displays of Unst's famous lace knitwear. An archive of local history, families and houses is also kept and worked on here.

You can walk for hours along the tiny roads which thread through the island here, and enjoy a snack in the do-it-yourself café in the shop. Behind the shop is the Unst Boat Haven, a splendidly designed and locally run maritime museum. For long a collector of old boats, Duncan Sandison dreamed of and worked towards the establishing of a museum to safeguard and interpret them for the future; this museum is now a reality. Look for the massive mural of an old fishing station painted by Liam O'Neil and wander among the boats, the exhibits of marine gear, shells, accounts of famous voyages and expeditions and model life-size fishermen. There are many fine walks north along the coastline, with superb views and more archaeological remains.

Early settlers quarried here, though only on a small scale, as was discovered when the talc quarry at Clibberswick was extended. Signs of ancient quarrying came to light, where the softer, freshly exposed rock had been chipped out into large bowls and troughs and hewn out intact for use in the ancient steadings in the isle. Other ancient steatite workings in Shetland are found at Catpund and Fethaland on the Mainland and in Fetlar.

Haroldswick had, until recently, Britain's most northerly post office, which sold postcards of itself and also franked letters with a special postmark. Now Baltasound has assumed the title and the service.

Norwick, to the north-west, has a beautiful beach, with interesting serpentine outcrops, giant boulders and expanses of sand. You can have a fine walk on a sunny day starting here and following the cliff-tops right round to the south, ending up back in Haroldswick. Remember to keep well back from the

Urda Stack and Flodda Stack, Hermaness, with Neap and Tonga in the distance.

cliff edges, use stiles whenever they are available and, if you have to use them, avoid damaging any gates or fences, taking great care to leave them exactly as you find them, whether open or closed. From Norwick the road leads up past Lamba Ness, a dramatic headland chosen for a radar station during the last war. Many of the structures still survive, but take care if you venture close, as floors are rotten.

At the end of the road from Norwick lies Skaw, literally the last and most northerly habitation in the UK. Minute shells strand along the beautiful beach where a stream runs out to sea. Prehistoric sites near cliff-tops in Shetland have sometimes been eroded by the sea and occasionally you may find items washed up on the beaches. A number of stone tools have been found here, so keep your eyes open.

Britain's northernmost house at Skaw, Unst.

Muckle Flugga and The Gord, Hermaness, from Saxavord.

Should you come across an ancient artefact or something which might be, remember to take it along to the Shetland Museum or the Archaeologist, as certain stones, if they prove to be prehistoric in origin, are classed as treasure trove and must be registered.

Saxavord is crowned by an RAF early warning station which had a massive white radar dome, which was blasted into the sea in 1991 by the 200 mph winds. The RAF base near Haroldswick contributed greatly to the population and employment in the island, even providing it with electricity, a dentist and a cinema, long before other Shetland communities caught up. Improvements to the buildings at the base include some houses with interesting architectural features and there is a beautiful new chapel built of wood. Recent cutbacks of staff have been a serious blow to the island. The future use of the base, once most of the personnel had left, is the subject of great concern and debate.

Burrafirth lies at the head of a long north-facing inlet sheltered from west and east by the high cliffs of Hermaness and Saxavord. The long sandy beach has to be accessed by track but is beautifully peaceful. Drift seeds – tropical plant seeds washed across the Atlantic by the currents – have sometimes been found here. The former lighthouse station now belongs to the RSPB and has a splendid interpretive centre for birdwatchers, complete with recorded bird calls of several different bird species. Shetland's largest loch, the Loch of Cliff, is surrounded by lush vegetation and rich flora in summer and is a favourite haunt of anglers.

Hermaness, a National Nature Reserve, is arguably Unst's most spectacular feature. According to one local legend, two giants, Herman and Saxa, fought, hurling huge rocks across Burra Firth at each other from their respective headlands. In the summer hundreds of thousands of seabirds congregate here to raise their young. Follow the well-marked route down the centre of the reserve, with footbridges and walkways built neatly over the boggiest parts, during the breeding season. Or you may choose to branch off to the cliffs and walk along the western or eastern margins of the Ness. A black-browed albatross from the southern hemisphere took up residence among one large colony of gannets here in the 1990s and stayed for some years. The relatively silent cliffs of winter become scenes of such thronging, screaming hordes in spring that they simply take the breath away. This is a time of great danger for the birds, with enemies at every turn and the endless battle for food and survival to be fought. There is murder in the air and in the water, with great skuas (bonxies) and great black-backed gulls (swaabies) attempting to steal food, chicks and even adults from among the ranks of puffin, guillemot and smaller gull colonies.

The cliff approaches require extreme care; remember in particular to stand or sit when using binoculars. It is all too easy to look through them as you walk, without realising how close you have come to the edge. Up on the high moorlands different species breed. Here you are constantly under surveillance, and often under attack, from the skuas and gulls. Bonxies tend to dive on you from a height, Arctic skuas tend to fly fast at ground level and head straight at you. But all of them, great black-backs too, can switch tactics occasionally. Keep a hat on, or hold up a stick or an arm and they are unlikely to cause a problem. However, they can sometimes strike you in passing, so avoid their nesting territories, or walk in a group where possible.

Fetlar

Fetlar takes a little planning to get to, but the rewards for making the effort to read the ferry timetable are endless. You need to get to Gutcher in north Yell, from where you will be taken to Oddsta in Fetlar, usually via Belmont pier in Unst! The island had a population of 900 during its heyday, but just under 100 live here today. Fetlar, which means 'fat land', is traditionally called the 'Garden of Shetland' and is roughly five miles by two and a half in size. There are public toilets at the ferry terminal; a camp site, a museum, a shop and a tiny primary school. The island rocked the bird establishment with the discovery by Bobby Tulloch in 1967, of a pair of breeding snowy owls. The RSPB have a bird reserve here with resident staff to protect the rarities and to help visitors watch and appreciate the bird life safely. A wonderful hide was built near Funzie, for watching the phalaropes feeding in the pools a few feet away. Apart from rare birds, Fetlar has spectacular geological features, wild flowers and a wealth of archaeological and historical remains.

The geology in Fetlar is very varied. A combination of metamorphic schists, serpentines and ancient conglomerates have left a rich legacy of fascinating and rare rock types. These have formed as great blocks and lie jammed together along fault lines. Where they are visible in cliff faces there are some stunning effects. The underlying drama of rock has created some very varied scenery and a wealth of different habitats. There are gentle rolling moors and high, bleak plateaux; wide sandy beaches and narrow shingle strands, low rocky shores and spectacular high cliffs and stacks. Beaches in Fetlar are full of interest and contrast.

Great Skua ('Bonxie').

Towards Papil Water, Lamb Hoga and Wick of Tresta, Fetlar.

Tresta, with its wide curve of sand, has striking pebbles banded with a kind of graphite with which you can actually draw on paper. A massive stone wall runs from Papil Water out along the edge of the ness, constructed under duress by semi-slave labour. Funzie (pronounced 'Finnie') has cliffs made from ancient pebble beds, greatly deformed by millions of years of heat and pressure.These pebble beds are thought to be almost 4000 ft (1200 m) thick. Aith, which was once the scene of a busy fish-curing station, has lovely green and yellow patterned serpentine pebbles. Talc and steatite or soapstone are also found in Fetlar and some of the outcrops show signs of having been worked in prehistoric times.

Soils vary over the different rock types, with acid peat moorland forming over the schists and marvellously green fertile areas over the conglomerate and lime-rich rocks. Wild flowers are at their best between late May and August, with especially fine displays along the roadside verges, sea cliffs and beside the burns. There are native willows and juniper, albeit very small and low-growing, and a host of mosses, sedges and rushes. Much of the pasture is surprisingly green. Apart from

The northern cliffs of Fetlar – Il Holm, East Neap and Busta Hill.

wild flowers in natural habitats, there is a history of famous gardens as well. Both Brough Lodge, now derelict, and Leagarth House were renowned for their extensive gardens in times past. Their cossetted plants flourished while many of the crofters' rigs, deprived by the Clearances of their seasonal tending, reverted to the wild. A few garden flowers have invaded wild places; look out in summer for the rich bronze double-flowered mimulus in some stream banks.

Fetlar's resident and summer-visiting birds attract large numbers of birdwatchers. Among the summer-visiting birds are rare red-necked phalaropes which nest among the freshwater loch margins in the Mires of Funzie, and new pools have been added to help boost their numbers. These birds are remarkably tame and you can watch them from quite close quarters as they swim and feed among the marsh plants. One of Britain's rarest waders, the whimbrel, breeds here too. Look out for golden plover, Arctic and great skuas, oystercatchers and curlews. Remote lochs are favoured breeding places for red-throated divers and ringed plover and dunlin will be seen along the shorelines. It should be possible to see fulmars, black

Ringed Plover ('Saandy Loo').

guillemots, kittiwakes, shags, several species of seagulls and puffins around the coasts on most days throughout late spring and summer. You might see otters playing around quiet piers and among seaweed-covered rocks at low tide.The less-frequented beaches around the north coast are havens for seals; some canoeists camping on a remote north-facing beach were woken by the screams of seals being attacked by killer whales.

There are many prehistoric house sites, standing-stone features and ancient stone walls. Perhaps the most impressive of these is the Finigert dyke which begins at the cliff-top above Muckle Funziegord Geo in the north and runs south between Vord Hill and Stackaberg. The intriguing Hjaltadans is a stone circle north of Skutes Water, which, according to legend, is made of stones which were once trows, who turned to stone when the sun rose and caught them all still dancing. Look out for a standing stone, known as the 'Ripple Stane', close to Leagarth House; further along the road to Funzie, an elongated mound known locally as the 'Giant's Grave' is thought possibly to conceal a Viking ship burial. Traces of a Neolithic chambered cairn remain on Vord Hill.

At Strandburgh Ness an offshore stack bears traces of buildings thought to have been an early Celtic Christian site. Monastic settlements were not uncommon in the Western and Northern Isles in the fifth and sixth centuries AD and this one has similarities with other sites in Shetland. The monks would have lived simply, by their faith, and would probably have grown their own food and had a small church and possibly a library in order to be self-supporting, not unlike the twentieth-century equivalent establishment founded in the early 1980s, now very much part of Fetlar. The Episcopalian religious community of SOLI (The Society of Our Lady of the Isles), stands at Aithness; the modern, almost boat-shaped chapel and house visible from miles around. People come and stay in the self-catering chalets here for the peace and quiet which is found in Fetlar, supported, if they wish, by the services of the religious community.

Today large areas of Fetlar still bear the scars of the Clearances. Many ruined buildings can still be found, along with the green vegetation over their once-cultivated land, clearance cairns, drains and walls. Countless stories survive in Fetlar of bitter quarrels, forced labour, particularly brutal evictions and revenge hauntings by resentful spirits. There are traces of early fishing industry ventures, old fish-drying beaches and fishing stations, as well as modern boat gear and facilities lying nearby. The 'big houses' still remain, as do those of some of their factors, agents and local merchants, and some extraordinary follies. Brough Lodge was built in 1820 for Arthur Nicolson. It was he who built the folly, resembling the castellated round tower of a small fort. He later built another oddity, a summer house with classical columns topped by a wooden structure, long since collapsed. The pillars survive, standing at rakish angles in a sea of nettles. Leagarth House, which had its own private electricity supply, was built in 1900 as the home of Sir William Watson Cheyne, assistant to Lord Lister.

The Fetlar kirk was built in 1790 and its graceful manse, with its beautiful landing window, stands nearby, surrounded by trees. The name of the nearby loch, Papil Water, or priest's water, suggests a place of early Christian influence. There are remains of 15 more old and ancient kirk sites in Fetlar, some visible, others remembered only by their place names. The span of Christian influence here goes back well over a thousand years.

Wildlife events are regularly held in the summer, with guided walks through the reserves and birdwatching hides available for use by the many visitors in the spring, summer and autumn. Do not miss the Fetlar Interpretive Centre which has developed into a marvellous exhibition, archive and information nerve-centre for visitors and islanders alike. Legends and traditional stories abound, as do a number of wonderful songs, fiddle tunes and poems. Here you can meet Fetlar residents and read about many of the island's more colourful and interesting characters and their lives.

Red-Necked Phalarope.

UNST
YELL
FETLAR
Gloup Holm
Gloup Ness
Gloup Voe
Wick of Breckon
Spoo Ness
Newgord
Valla Field
216
Loch of Watlee
Lunda Wick
Westing
A968
North Neaps
Breckon
Gloup
St. Olaf's Kirk
Underhoull
Gunister
Geo of Vigon
West a Firth
Memorial
Mid Breck
116
Papil Bay
Lund
Burgi Geo
Kussa Waters
Hill of Vigon
Cullivoe
Blue Mull Sound
Stonganess
Loch of Snarravoe
B9084
Geo of Markamouth
Uyeasound
Belmont
97
B9082
Wick of Belmont
Gossa Water
Uyea Sound
Skuda
The Ward
Dalsetter
Linga
Head of Bratta
Gutcher
Hill of Dalsetter
95
Sellafirth
96
Wick of Belmont
Uyea
Ramna Stacks
Nev of Stuis
Daal of Lumbister
Gruney
Colvister
Cunnister
Sound Gruney
Lochs of Lumbister
Whale Firth
Stuis of Graveland
Norther Geo
Burra Ness
Urie Lingey
Point of Fethaland
93
Kirkabister
Basta Voe
Loch of Vollister
Hamars Ness
Urie Ness
Oddsta
58
Whale Geo
The Herra
Basta
Colgrave Sound
Brough Lodge
Basta Ness
Point of Bugarth
114
Grimister
The Camb
North-A-Voe
94
Efstigarth
Camb
Kame of Isbister
Windhouse
Kaywick
Hascosay Sound
Sands of Sand
B9088
Birrier
Mid Yell Voe
Hascosay
105
Loch of Birriesgirt
A968
Mid Yell
Hill of Lussetter
Papil Water
Ness of Burravoe
Loch of Vatsetter
Vatsetter
Heracle
Holm of West Sandwick
Birrier
Muckle Holm
West Sandwick
Laxa Burn
Kame of Sandwick
162
Ness of Houlland
B9081
North Aywick
Aywick
Ness of West Sandwick
Little Holm
South Aywick
Queyon
Hill of Arisdale
205
Long Taing
Yell Sound
Head of Brough
Westbrough
Otterswick
White Wife
Otters Wick
Burn of Arisdale
East Yell
West Yell
Kirkhouse
Aris Dale
Ness of Gossabrough
A968
Gossabrough
New Town
Ness of Sound
Setter
Uynarey
Canis Dale
Loch of Kettlester
Lamba
Brother Isle
Clothan
Horse of Burravoe
Hamnavoe
Kettlester
Burravoe
Ulsta
Little Roe
Mio Ness
Brough
Old Haa of Burravoe
Hamna Voe
Heoga Ness
Copister
Gluss Isle
Skaw Taing
Orka Voe
Bigga
Orfasay
Brei Wick
Brough
Nature Reserve
Sullom Voe
Hill of Crooksetter
152
Toft
Tofts Voe
Samphrey
Sullom Voe Oil Terminal
0
5 km
5 miles
Mossbank
A968
Lunna Holm
Lunna Ness
Firths Voe
Fish Holm
Garths Voe
Voe of Scatsta
Scatsta Ness
B9076
Firth
Linga

Yell

The ferry for Yell leaves from the pier at Toft on Mainland Shetland and heads north across the notoriously moody stretch of sea known as Yell Sound. It takes a course halfway between Bigga to the west and Samphrey to the east, the two largest of the islands in the Sound. A number of other islands lie scattered between Yell and the Mainland and all are now uninhabited, save for sheep and seabirds. Each, though, has a unique history, with many stories of hardship and privation, as well as of adventure and heroism. Some have sites of prehistoric houses and ancient chapels.

The south coast of Yell stretches out ahead, with Copister, the southernmost settlement, in the foreground and the high hill of Arisdale beyond to the north. To the east and south as you cross, you can get fine views of Lunna Ness, Mossbank and other islands, while behind you, across Mioness, the flare stacks of the oil terminal at Sullom Voe glow fiercely as they burn off unused gases. Look out for seabirds as you cross Yell Sound. There are always a good selection busy fishing and if you are lucky, you may also glimpse dolphins, porpoises or even whales. The ferry lands you at Ulsta, where you can, if you need to, book a return ferry at the booking office. There are public toilets next door to the office. Make use of the splendid shop and filling station should you need fuel. The ferry assembly area is carved out of a hillside of iron-stained schist which gleams silver and red-gold when the sun shines onto its wet faces.

Yell is largely composed of schist and gneiss which lie now beneath peat – which is as much as 40 ft (12 m) deep in some places in the island. Blanket bog and heather moors cloak the hills from south to north, through which run channels of brown water between vivid banks of sphagnum moss. Here and there lochs and streams catch the light, lacing the landscape with silver trails. In places the streams turn suddenly into foaming torrents and rush through steep-sided gorges. Among these habitats you can find a wealth of wild flowers and birds can nest here in peace.

In spring, peat banks are flayed (stripped of turf) and cut, often by machine, but many still cast by traditional methods with the tushkar, a tool designed centuries ago for slicing regular blocks of wet peat and lifting them into courses to dry. Yell boasts some of the best peat-stacking skills in Shetland and if you are fortunate, you may still see expertly built, intricately patterned low walls of peats arranged to allow free passage of air between them. No two are quite alike, each reflecting the particular tradition or style of the caster.

From Ulsta you can choose whether to head north along the fast, improved A968 road to Mid Yell, with detours off to the west, or to take the smaller, quieter east route to Mid Yell via the B9081. The first is faster and wider, useful for drivers heading for the Unst ferry and it gives you easy access to several of the more interesting south-west corners of Yell. This Guide takes the east route first.

Copister, a settlement with a fine shingle beach that played an important part in the days of the Haaf fishing, is signed to the right just as you leave the ferry at Ulsta. There are remains of a broch just off the point of the Holm of Copister. Arisdale with its fine burn, almost a small river at its mouth, a favourite haunt of trout, lies a few miles further along the road towards Burravoe. Hamnavoe, a scattered hamlet, overlooks an exceptionally sheltered stretch of coastline, protected by the mass of Ness of Copister to the south and west. The small church of St Magnus stands here, built in 1838. The name 'Hamnavoe' occurs frequently in Shetland, and derives from the Old Norse for safe or sheltered harbour; a good description of the curving tongue of sea sheltered by the Ness of Galtagarth.

It is tempting to imagine the longships of early Viking settlers gliding in, sails being lowered and the scuff and drag of keel on shingle as they beached and settled against the land. Today a whole range of salmon farming buildings and gear dominates the scene. These shallow waters can often provide excellent birdwatching. Waders and many kinds of migrant duck feed here at different times of year. Beyond Hamnavoe and Houlland, the road curves round the Loch of Littlester on Burra Ness. The name 'Burra' frequently indicates the presence of a broch and there are several near here. One is sited very strikingly on a small island in the Loch of Kettlester about half a mile inland to the north.

Old Haa, Burravoe, Yell.

Burravoe appears next, facing south and well sheltered by the protective arm of Heoga Ness from the ravages of south-easterly seas. The village, with its great variety of buildings, was one of Yell's most important in the days of the Hanseatic trade. More recently it was a major link in the former Shetland-wide ferry service, and the next stop after Whalsay for passengers from Lerwick.

Especially interesting is the wonderful local museum, garden and interpretive centre in the Old Haa. This striking building has arched buttresses through which the road once passed. The buildings to which it was joined were demolished when the road was widened. The house dates back to 1672 when it was built by a Scottish merchant, Robert Tyrie. It was lovingly restored in the 1980s and a local group produce regular exhibitions of changing themes. As well as a café and craft shop there are thousands of carefully stored and catalogued items. Many local people work to save and study everything that can be found of Yell's past.

From Burravoe head north, deviating right into Gossabrough which has a fine, sandy beach. You can enjoy warm shelter should a fine day be plagued by westerly winds. A large mound marks the site of the broch and you can see the sadly neglected buildings of the two old haa houses, once grand and imposing.

The road towards Mid Yell splits north of Otterswick, and you can choose whether to take the high road, with its marvellous views down over the east Yell coast, or the low road through the settlements themselves. A quiet, peaceful place, Otterswick was the scene of a dramatic shipwreck in April 1924. The German ship the *Bohus* mistakenly entered the bay in poor visibility and was unable to turn round in time to avoid smashing into rocks on the north shore below Queyon. Brass portholes and items made of wood from the ship are among a

Horse of Burravoe on the east coast of Yell, with Fetlar beyond.

number of relics still treasured from the ship but the biggest relic of all, the figurehead, was erected just above the rocks as a memorial to those drowned. It is well worth visiting the recently restored figurehead, known as the *White Wife*, which was carved holding a Bible and gazing out to sea.

If you have time, explore Aywick, a community clustered in a half circle around the tiny bay, with all the rigs radiating out from the shore in a design as picturesque as it was practical. Another broch site remains here, on a magnificent setting above the cliffs a short way along the north coast. A mile or so north of the broch site is another important prehistoric site, that of an ancient fort at the Birrier, not far from Vatsetter with its excellent views of the islands of Hascosay and Fetlar beyond. This site, like that north of West Sandwick on the west coast of Yell, is inaccessible now, after centuries of erosion from the wild winter seas which rage here every year. Only a couple of miles north, the coastline turns sharply west, below Lussetter Hill towards Mid Yell.

Yell's largest village, Mid Yell has a secondary as well as a primary school, several factories, shops and many other

Loch of Scattlands and West Sandwick on the west coast of Yell.

facilities. A particularly beautifully designed care centre was built recently. St John's Kirk was built in 1832, but the old kirkyard down near the shore has the graveyard, where fragments of the earlier kirk can be seen, including part of a stone arch, and several interesting old memorial stones can be found.

Some old buildings still stand in Mid Yell, including Linkshouse, a merchant's house, near the pier, built in 1770; Lussetter House (former home of the late Bobby Tulloch, Shetland's famous naturalist) is an eighteenth-century manse with castellated outer walls. The Haa of Gardie at Gardiestaing dates back to the mid 1600s. Many events take place during the year in Mid Yell and it is always worth checking dates so as not to miss one. Whether fishing, sailing, lectures or sales, they are excellent opportunities to meet and talk with Yell folk. Make good use of the free information magazine when you come.

Yell is almost cut into two here, as Mid Yell Voe from the east and Whale Firth from the west almost meet below Windhouse, the dramatic ruin on the skyline, built in the early

Windhouse, Yell.

1700s and said to be haunted. At the foot of the track to Windhouse stands a camping böd converted from the old lodge. Mid Yell Voe is overlooked by Camb and North-a-Voe to the north, opposite and facing Mid Yell itself. You can walk north round the coast here, past the secluded bay of Kaywick and round Basta Ness to Basta, set above the massive arm of Basta Voe, and beyond to Dalsetter and Sellafirth. The sea can be very shallow here at times, and I learned from one Yell resident that as a child, he and his friends had sometimes waded across the sea to the old school at Colvister, often with younger brothers and sisters on their backs, to save over a mile of walking.

The steep-sided gorge of Lumbister and the old ruined settlement nearby make an interesting walk across the moors to the west past the Loch of Colvister. You will need waterproof footwear and a map, but will be well rewarded if you make the effort. There are some mysterious stone alignments here and local legends tell of strange events relating to drowned sailors buried nearby.

At the head of Basta Voe, there was once a choice of routes to the far north of Yell but the westernmost route, to Cullivoe, has been allowed to deteriorate, and is definitely a walking, not a driving option. Burra Ness, famous for otters, stretches out to the south-east and has a broch site. Substantial amounts of lichen-cloaked wall still stand, in which storm petrels nest in summer. The deserted settlement nearby tells another part of the sorry story of the Shetland Clearances. The road leads to Kirkabister where one of Shetland's pony studs once flourished. The curious stone pony enclosure with its four raised corners is one of several in Shetland. Whimbrel frequent this corner of Yell.

Gutcher is the ferry point for both Unst and Fetlar and there is a splendid café and shop, as well as a post office and public toilets. Cullivoe has a shop, too, and now boasts improved marina and harbour facilities. Further north, the road bends left heading for Gloup, but first there is Breckon.

Take a walk over the links to Breckon. The ancient kirk of St Olaf, dating back to pre-Reformation times, stands amid the gravestones at the recently refurbished cemetery here. But beyond these to the north lies a stretch of ground inhabited at various points throughout several thousand years of history. Archaeologists believe there to have been prehistoric as well as Norse dwellings. Many tantalising features still survive, poking through the dense dune grasses and the large, rocky beach stones to the east. The area is full of a sense of the past. Whole human skeletons were discovered during the excavation of an eroding grave site. One, it was claimed (by a local man of considerable standing, who was present at the excavation as a boy), was seven feet long and had two identical bony outgrowths, like short horns, on his skull, one above each temple.

Take the narrow road west, past the modern strawberry farm with its tough polythene tunnels, noticing the Haa of Houlland on the skyline to the left, built around 1735, as was the Haa of Midbrake to the right. The road ends at Gloup, a busy farm whose fields overlook a historic scene of tragedy. Here the Gloup memorial, the stone statue of a woman and child, stands gazing blankly out to sea where, on 20 July 1881, 58 men lost their lives in a horrific summer gale. It brings into sharp focus the harshness of Shetland life in former times. The event still shadows many families today, whose forebears were among those lost. Gloup Haa, built in the eighteenth century and much restored, stands on higher ground to the south.

Gloup Voe strikes south here, following a fault line, in a steep-sided fjord-like slash through the coast. There are beautiful gorges and stream gulleys at the head, with wild roses and honeysuckle growing in abundance, but the walking can be a strain; steep-angled ground surface and narrow path. There is wonderful moorland above and beyond with many lochs, some thought to have been dammed by ice during the retreating

Sands of Breckon, north Yell.

glaciers in the last ice age. Across the voe can be seen the deserted settlements of West-a-Firth and Graven. The more hardy walkers can take a long route west as far as Yell's west coast past the remote ruin of Vigon. There was a shop right out here, long ago. The precarious remnants of a prehistoric fort are found at Burgi Geos.

The Guide now returns to Ulsta, and describes the western route to Mid Yell. The road heads north from the ferry terminal with its pier, toilets, shop and garage and runs along between the cultivated land with the old settlements of Clothan, Freedom and Setter and the steeper hills to the east. You could walk down to the attractive Ness of Sound with its tombolo, the wide strips of shingle connecting it to the shore like a sheep on a tether. The uninhabited islands of Uynarey and Brother Isle just beyond lie a short distance away offshore and away across Yell Sound you can see Ronas Hill and take in the impressive seascapes towards the eastern cliff faces of Ollaberry, North Roe and Fethaland on Mainland. To their north lies the seldom accessible, wild cluster of the Ramna Stacks, an RSPB bird reserve. To the south is the distant expanse of Mioness and moorland stretching out of sight between Graven and Voe. A little to the west stand the massive, cylindrical tanks of stored oil on Calback Ness, and the flare stack from Sullom Voe oil terminal flickers and surges above the scene.

The road carries on north, overlooking West Yell, Newhouse, Foreland, Kirkhouse, Everhoull, Laggins and Westbrough with its ruined broch on a small, projecting headland. Stone-walled enclosures and scattered dwellings lie below the road, some with remarkable gardens and surprisingly mature trees. Here and there the lines of old cultivation rigs and fenced or stone-walled strip fields bear witness to the intense agricultural labour of former times. Now the road begins to descend as Southladie Voe and West Sandwick come into view.

Southladie Voe, protected by the Ness of West Sandwick, was a safe anchorage for ships in days gone by and the eighteenth-century North Haa still stands, surveying the sea approaches. West Sandwick is well worth a picnic stop, with its magnificent sand dunes, sandy beach and the burn where otters often play. There has been considerable sand extraction here in the past and the issue has been the subject of much debate in the islands. Sand dune and machair habitats are relatively rare in Shetland and they support several rare plants. A short way to the south there is an impressive broch site, accessible with extreme care. A mile or so to the north of West Sandwick beach you reach Heracle, or Harkland, and the Loch of Birriesgirt, where another broch site still stands. A mile or so north along the coast, connected to the cliffs by a tortuous tumble of rocks, are the remains of an ancient monastic settlement at Birrier, from which the loch gets its name. Hardy walkers might like to continue north to the Stuie of Graveland, the headland which narrows to a point opposite Gorset Hill in North Yell. The return route then cuts back to the Herra and to West Sandwick either via the road or the hills through some of the finest cliff scenery in Yell.

From West Sandwick the road veers up, away from the sea and cuts through moorland to the south of the Hill of Bouster, descending towards the head of Whale Firth. Windhouse is now clearly silhouetted against the skyline and the road soon meets the Mid Yell junction. The Yell circuit is now complete, from both approaches.

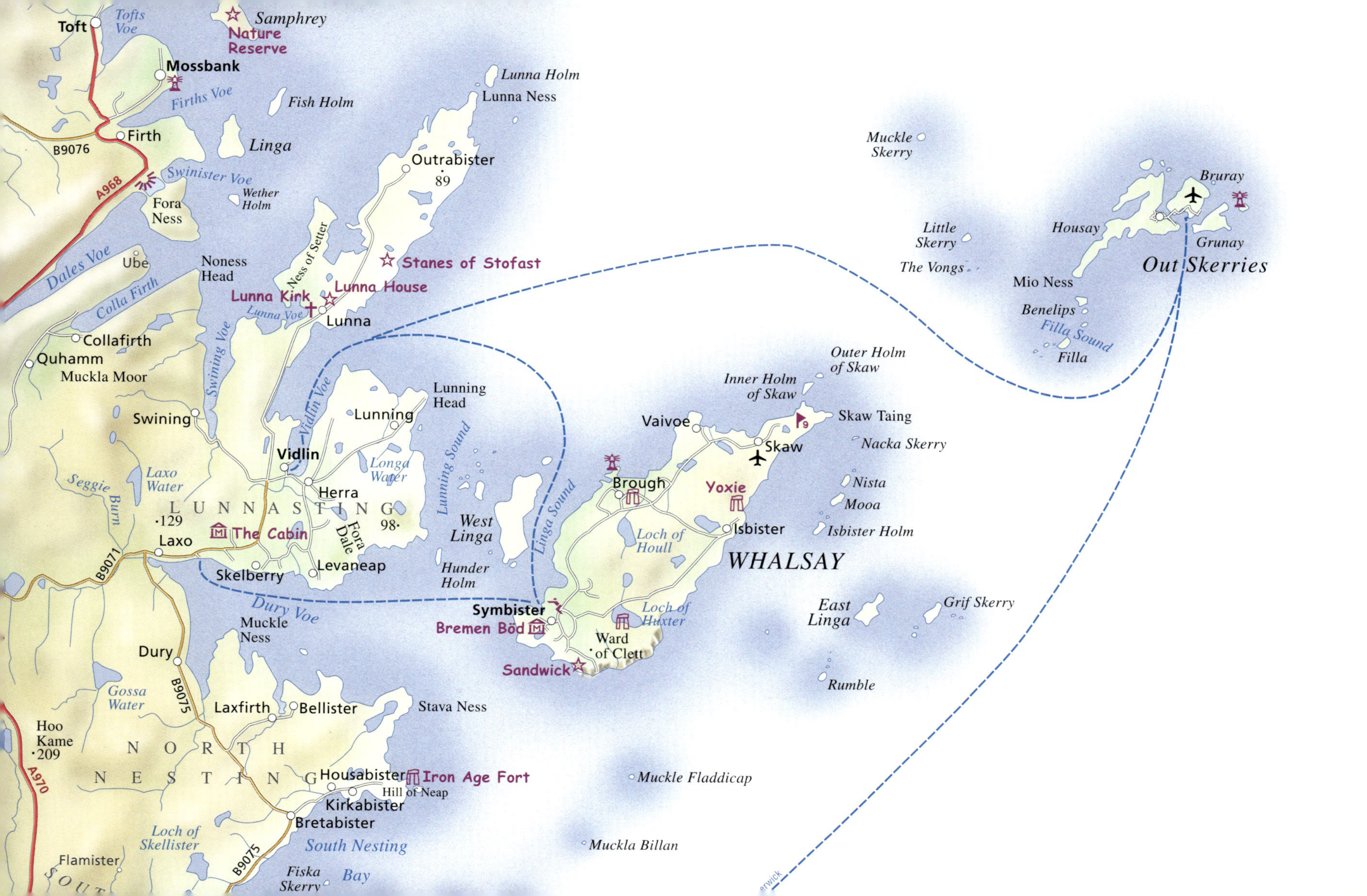
Toft
Tofts Voe
Samphrey
Nature Reserve
Mossbank
Lunna Holm
Lunna Ness
Fish Holm
Firths Voe
Firth
B9076
Linga
Outrabister
89
Muckle Skerry
Bruray
Housay
Grunay
Out Skerries
Little Skerry
The Vongs
Mio Ness
Benelips
Filla Sound
Filla
A968
Swinister Voe
Wether Holm
Fora Ness
Dales Voe
Ube
Noness Head
Ness of Setter
Stanes of Stofast
Lunna House
Lunna Kirk
Lunna Voe
Lunna
Colla Firth
Collafirth
Quhamm
Muckla Moor
Swining Voe
Vidlin Voe
Swining
Lunning
Lunning Head
Outer Holm of Skaw
Inner Holm of Skaw
Skaw Taing
Vaivoe
Skaw
Nacka Skerry
Vidlin
Longa Water
Lunning Sound
Laxo Water
Seggie Burn
Herra
LUNNASTING
·129
98·
The Cabin
Fora Dale
West Linga
Linga Sound
Brough
Yoxie
Nista
Mooa
Isbister
Isbister Holm
Loch of Houll
WHALSAY
Laxo
B9071
Skelberry
Levaneap
Hunder Holm
Dury Voe
Symbister
Bremen Böd
Loch of Huxter
Ward of Clett
East Linga
Grif Skerry
Muckle Ness
Dury
Sandwick
Rumble
Gossa Water
B9075
Laxfirth
Bellister
Stava Ness
Hoo Kame ·209
NORTH NESTING
Housabister
Iron Age Fort
Hill of Neap
Muckle Fladdicap
A970
Kirkabister
Bretabister
Loch of Skellister
South Nesting Bay
Muckla Billan
Flamister
Fiska Skerry

Whalsay and Out Skerries

WHALSAY

Whalsay, five and a half miles by two, with a population of just over a thousand, lies to the east of Shetland Mainland. The tiny Out Skerries lie to the north-east of Whalsay. The ferry to Whalsay usually leaves from Laxo but in certain windy conditions it goes from Vidlin. Signs at both ferry terminals always advise visitors when there is likely to be a change. The crossing, if conditions are reasonable, is one to enjoy, rather than to spend sitting in the car or the passenger lounge. You can sometimes see unusual migrant birds, rare divers and seabirds from the ferry and, unless the weather is poor, there are marvellous views of the eastern faces of Lunning and North Nesting and down as far as Bressay and Noss. In late spring, the small, uninhabited islands which you pass to the north – Hunder Holm, Bruse Holm and West Linga – are ablaze with sea pinks and thronged with birds. Whalsay's western face with its crofted landscape, clustered houses and backdrop of hills is a lovely sight as you approach Symbister and you can see why the nickname 'Da Bonnie Isle' has been applied to Whalsay for generations.

Most of Whalsay consists of ancient sedimentary rock, eroded from long-vanished mountains, buried hundreds of millions of years ago and altered by intense heat and pressure into the metamorphic schists and gneisses we see today. They have long since been forced above sea level into their present forms, along with slices and blocks of other rock masses, by earth movements. Through these layers of metamorphic rocks, jets of molten rock were forced in some places, ripping off jagged fragments of local rock, known as xenoliths, which can be found lying embedded in the solidified granite. Tourmaline and felspar crystals can grow very big in some rocks and beaches can prove wonderfully rewarding places to potter among. Fault lines run through parts of Whalsay where different rock types have slid against each other and there is a strip of limestone along a section of the east coast where Isbister has developed, its cultivation patterns marking the presence of more fertile, lime-rich soils. Wild flowers and seabirds dominate the coastline during spring and summer and sea asters grow on a few remote cliffs and small offshore islands.

The island is higher at the south, the Ward of Clett rising to 390 ft (119 m) and commanding splendid panoramas all round. At the summit are the remains of Second World War buildings, offering shelter from the wind, from whichever direction it comes. Sturdy cliffs gradually lose height as they run north, facing the eastern seascape with its scatter of uninhabited islands and skerries. There are a dozen or so good-sized freshwater lochs in Whalsay and four coastal settlements. You land in Symbister in the south-east corner, close to Sandwick which faces due south. A mile north of Symbister you reach Marrister, with Brough and Challister further north still. The old runrigs are still visible all round the houses and reaching up from the west-facing shore into the moorland behind. On the west side, at Kirk Ness, a sturdy church with a small belfry stands on the site of a much earlier church at the north end of a loch. In the summer, Tirricks (Arctic terns) often swirl around above the relatively sheltered shallows. The road rises further to the north as it crosses Challister Ness and swings into Skaw with its windswept airstrip and the most northerly golf course in Britain. Just north of Symbister, a branch road crosses the centre of the island to the east and drops down into picturesque Isbister.

Whalsay has more ancient prehistoric sites than might be imagined for its size. They tend to be well scattered through the landscape; house sites closer to cultivated land, burial sites higher up in the hills and there are the remains of a defensive site or blockhouse fort built out into the Loch of Huxter. North along the coast from here you come into the deserted settlement of Treawick, abandoned within living memory. On the southern coast of Whalsay, a remarkable number of ancient sites can be found all fairly close together at Sandwick, suggesting some intensive settlement at one time. There is a cup-marked stone near Brough, with 40 or so small bowl-shaped cavities cut from sheets of bedrock. But perhaps the best known of all Whalsay's prehistoric treasures is the Neolithic house site at Yoxie, north of Isbister on the east coast. The structure is impressive and, like the one at Stanydale on the west side of

Shetland, has been loosely called a 'temple', but many experts consider it more likely to have been a large house. It was excavated in the 1950s by archaeologist Charles Calder and a local historian, John Stewart.

Symbister House, once the seat of the Bruce family, is Shetland's most imposing Georgian building and towers above the village. The mansion, built in 1823 for the then massive cost of £30,000, is said virtually to have bankrupted the family, though one colourful account claims that this was in fact the intention, so as to deprive the descendants of their inheritance! As ever in Shetland, stories of oppression by the lairds abound and many present-day families can recount grim incidents from several generations back. Now the mansion, stripped bare of its interior finery, houses the island's secondary school. Among the many outbuildings are the office of Whalsay's local history society, one of Shetland's only two dovecots, and a three-seater toilet. There is a new primary school not far away and beside it, the local sports and leisure centre with its heated swimming pool. Not far from here, the Scottish poet Hugh MacDiarmid once lived with his wife and son in a cottage now converted into a camping böd. Fishing dominates island life more than anywhere else in Shetland save the Out Skerries and Burra Isle. Some of Shetland's biggest and most technologically advanced fishing boats can be seen in the main harbour which has been considerably enlarged and modernised. A fish-processing factory provides local employment. A range of smaller craft – dinghies, yachts and traditional 'Shetland model' rowing boats – lie moored in the inner harbour. The Pier House exhibition in Symbister is in a beautifully restored Hanseatic Booth, with excellent interpretive displays about the Hanseatic League and the merchants who lived here several hundred years ago – a trade which lasted for several centuries. Other historic buildings, docks and stone store houses and a man-made drying beach, indicate that the whole area must have been a hive of maritime and commercial activity. Stories of local fishermen's wealth, however apocryphal, abound. Whalsay today retains its strong individuality with its rich and distinctive local dialect and customs. Whalsay wedding celebrations can last as long as three days.

Hanseatic Booth, Symbister, Whalsay.

OUT SKERRIES

Looking east from Housay across South Mouth towards Grunay, Out Skerries.

Out Skerries, Shetland's and Scotland's easternmost landfall, is a cluster of small, rugged islands, roughly two and a half miles long by one and a half miles broad, 24 miles north-east of Lerwick. The islands make up tenfold in quality what they lack in quantity and a visit here adds something very special to a holiday in Shetland. The Skerries, as they are locally called, consist of heavily metamorphosed rocks with a band of limestone cutting through the centre of the group from east to west giving the soils added fertility. Although glaciation may have ground down the islands to some extent, it left a number of pockets of clay behind. The three main islands, Housay, Bruray (which are joined together by a bridge) and Grunay enclose a perfect natural harbour. The people of Out Skerries share with Whalsay folk the richest surviving form of Shetland dialect in the islands.

Settlers must have found the harbour several thousand years ago, as a number of prehistoric sites remain, among them a possible burial site on Mioness, two Neolithic house sites in Queyness and the remains of a probable broch on Grunay. Many other puzzling remains and stone features have survived the centuries, most famous of all being Skerries' Battle Pund. This curious stone circle (or rectangle) is said to have been an ancient site for solving disputes. Archaeology is not confined to the land; underwater exploration has revealed the locations of many shipwrecks. Artefacts retrieved by divers from the *Kennermerland* and other wrecks feature in the Shetland Museum.

Shipwrecks have decreased greatly since the building of the lighthouse on Grunay. A British plane crashed onto Grunay during the last war. An engraved wristwatch, found welded to some melted wreckage, enabled the pilot to be traced and eventually islanders joined his descendants in a special service of remembrance. A memorial has been erected on the site.

From the earliest times, the Skerries were extensively cultivated, but as in the rest of Shetland, much of this has now returned to the wild. The many acres of rough grassland now support magnificent displays of wild flowers from May into August. The scent on a still, warm summer's day is unforgettable. A particularly deep-red eyebright grows here and among the tormentil and lousewort keep an eye open for the tiny green frog orchid.

Those arriving by plane on the tiny airstrip miss the thrill of reaching the Skerries by ferry in rough seas. Cliffs seem to bar every approach, but at the last minute a channel appears and the ship is skilfully steered through into calm water and arrives at the large modern pier. Apart from the shop, church, village hall, post office, lighthouse and fish factory, the island has one of the smallest, most interesting schools in Britain. In this tiny nursery, primary and secondary school pupils enjoy a freedom of shared association and creative play, natural skills long since removed from the majority of school children by the separation of their schools and age-group segregation. I will never forget seeing the 'big ones' racing into the primary classroom to collect their younger brothers and sisters and taking them outside, lifting the tiniest and carrying them on their shoulders. When the end-of-play bell rang, back they all trooped, excited and breathless after their shared break.

Nowhere in Shetland, except perhaps Whalsay and Burra Isle, has been so dependent upon the fishing for its survival as the Out Skerries, right up until today. Salmon farms are the most recent chapter in the long, colourful history of fish. But there are many difficulties and risks in all branches of fisheries. Ingenuity, tenacity, dedication and teamwork of Skerries folk will be put to the test in the years ahead if the island community is to survive the coming decades.

Out Skerries by Joan Dey, a former head teacher, is well worth reading if you visit these islands. It is full of humour and history, stories of famous fights, shipwrecks, sailing tragedies and battles for survival.

Ramna Stacks
RSPB Reserve
Gruney
Point of Fethaland
Fishing Lodges
Fethaland
Uyea
Kame of Isbister
Sand Voe
Burrier Wick
Fugla Ness
Neolithic Axe Factory
Sandvoe
Isbister
Ness of Burravoe
Stourie
North Roe
Hevdadale Head
Egga Field
Moosa Water
Burn of Sandvoe
Burra Voe
Holm of West Sandwick
Muckle Holm
Lang Clodie Wick
Beorgs of Skelberry
·198
Ness of Houlland
Munga Skerries
Valla Kame
A970
Billia Field
Gruna Stack
Roer Water
Skelberry
Galti Stack
Turls Head
Sandy Water
Little Holm
The Faither
Muckle Ossa
Little Ossa
Lang Ayre
Giant's Grave
Long Taing
Ketligill Head
NORTHMAVINE
North Collafirth
Housetter
Yell
Ockran Head
Uyeascord
Mid Field
Ronas Hill
450
Collafirth Hill
Neap of Skea
Gossa Water
Tingon
Ronas Voe
Colla Firth
Collafirth
The Brough
The Villians of Hamnavoe
Quey Firth
Sound
Back of Ollaberry Fault
Feal
The Clift
Lamba
Brother Isle
Head of Stanshi
Johnnie Notions
Gluss Water
Heylor
·173
Ollaberry
Grind o da Navir
Hamnavoe
White Grunafirth
Bay of Ollaberry
Scarff
Art Gallery
Braehoulland
Assater
Holes of Scraada
Eela Water
East Hogaland
Little Roe
Mio Ness
Esha Ness
Calder's Geo
Urafirth
Gluss Voe
Skaw Taing
Burnside
Fiblister
Gluss Isle
63
Brei-wick
B9078
Seal Sanctuary
Turvister
Orka Voe
The Bruddans
Tangwick
A970
North Gluss
Bardister
Tangwick Haa
Heads of Grocken
Sand Wick
Ura Firth
Brei Wick
Isle of Stenness
Stenness
Hillswick
Orbister
Wester Water
Fishing Lodges
Hamar
Ness of Hillswick
Hillswick Booth
Sullom Voe Oil Terminal
Hill of Crooksetter
152·
Toft
Dore Holm
Hamar Voe
The Drongs
Punds Water
Dale Voe
Loch of Burraland
Fugla Ness
Baa Taing
Red Head
Enisfirth
The Houb
Scatsta Ness
Garths Voe
Gunnister
Isle of Gunnister
Sullom Voe
Voe of Scatsta
B9076
Sullom
A970
Isle of Nibon
Nibon
Laxobigging
Punds Lochs
Scatsta
Graven
·83
B9076
Loch of Lunnister
·121
Mill Geos
Mid Field
Mangaster
Trondavoe
Lang Head
Haggrister
St. Magnus Bay
Mangaster Voe
Outdoor Centre
Voxter
A968
Egilsay
Islesburgh
South Ness
Mavis Grind
Ell Wick
Brae
Dales Voe
Colla
Quhamr
Erne Stack
Skella Dale
Roe Sound
Swabi Stack
The Hams of Roe
Busta
Strom Ness
Weathersta
A970
Susetter
Roesound
South Ward
170
Busta Voe
MUCKLE ROE
Olna Firth
Old Whaling Station
Hamars
Grobs Ness
Tagon
Gillarona
Linga
Grobsness
Sneugie
·222
Murbie Stack
Loch of Gonfirth
Voe
North Ness
Swarbacks Head
Guns
Swarbacks Minn
Cole Ness
B9071
Setter
Gardie
PAPA STOUR
Papa Little
Gonfirth
A970
Vementry
Housa Voe
·91
Millburn
Gossa Water

Northmavine

The gazetteer now begins to unravel the corners of Mainland Shetland, from Northmavine southwards. In fact, returning from Unst and Yell, Toft and Mossbank are the first villages touched, but to simplify the progression, we begin with the furthest north.

One of Shetland's most popular walks is from Isbister to the most northerly point on Mainland Shetland, Fethaland, with its deserted fishing station, prehistoric sites and spectacular scenery. It is relatively straightforward, but fairly long, and can be gruelling in poor weather. A track leads from Isbister, the most northerly point of the A970, where the road ends, along past an old graveyard. There are interesting old wooden headstones here which are worth a detour from the path. Continue past crofthouses old and newly restored, northwards across the grassy moorland, until just before the land tapers away to a narrow point. In places along this route, purple mountain saxifrage, one of Shetland's botanical rarities, blooms in early spring.

Isle of Fethaland, Ramna Stacks and Gruney from Fethaland.

Gannet ('Solan').

Fethaland has beaches facing both east and west, making it an ideal site for a fishing station. During the days of the Haaf fishing, men would stay in small stone huts during the summer fishing season; between June and mid August, around 60 boats would have been in use. Over 20 buildings stood during its heyday in the late 1800s and just behind them is a prehistoric house site. Traces of old fish bones can sometimes be found in the upper beach strata, remaining from the split fish which were salted and laid out to dry. A prehistoric steatite quarry was once worked here. The marks of bowls and troughs can still be seen cut into the cliff face slightly north and east of the fishing station. A small modern lighthouse stands on the furthest point of the headland. The cliff tops are precipitous and indented here, so be very careful, especially if it is windy. There is a Pressgang cave in a cleft in the cliffs near here. The sea-lashed Ramna Stacks lie to the north and away to the east beyond them is the northwest coast of Yell, with the tip of Hermaness in Unst and Muckle Flugga far beyond.

There is an early Christian site on the inaccessible headland of the Kame of Isbister on the east coast, half a mile along the track north from Isbister. The best place to see the structures is from the high cliff-top of Virdifield to the south. A number of small square foundation outlines remain just visible, marking the locations of missionary cells on the level grass-covered summit. They stand directly opposite the monastic site at Birrier in West Yell. It is quite possible that they were contemporary and that there might have been some form of communication between them. Services were held near both sites in the summer of 2000, commemorating 2000 years of Christian worship in the islands.

The settlement of Sandvoe is about as remote from Lerwick as it is possible to get on Mainland Shetland. The Voe of Sandvoe itself is exquisite, especially when glimpsed for the first time from the North Roe to Isbister road. The sea reaches deep inland, round a curving inlet with great cliffs rising up on either side of it adding a majestic frame to the scene. The beautiful beach at the head of the voe is a particularly good place to spend a fine day when Shetland's prevailing strong south-westerly wind is blowing. In summer, meadow cranesbill grows in several places nearby, adding a rich purple-blue to the dazzling native flora.

Uyea is one of the most isolated corners of Shetland, a deserted settlement at the extreme north-western tip of the Mainland. You can walk along the coast from Sandvoe, but it is worth going on the peat track from the coastguard hut in North Roe. A Neolithic axe factory, old mills and the remains of a fishing station add to the interest. A sand causeway connects the island of Uyea itself to the mainland but is only crossable at certain times of the tide and even then, recent storms may have shifted the sands away, so access cannot be guaranteed. Even when the weather is fine, the ascent is awkward and in places very unsafe.

There is something of a magical quality to this tiny island, set among dramatic sea stacks. It has a lush growth of grass and a tiny flock of sheep are grazed on it each year. Grey seals give birth to pups among the boulders on the more inaccessible beaches here in October and you can sometimes see them from the cliffs above. The baby seals with their silver coats and enormous dark eyes are immensely appealing and it is easy to convince yourself that they are abandoned and need rescuing. But they are very closely supervised by their parents and are well adapted to their strange, harsh nursery. Take pictures if you wish, but don't approach too closely. The creatures can give ferocious bites and can move surprisingly fast. They often carry diseases, some of which can be contracted by humans. Mothers can be even more dangerous, so don't go anywhere near a mother with a young one nearby.

From Uyea you can walk southwards along the west-facing cliffs to the dramatic sea carved pool at Fugla Ness. Here, way out at the westernmost tip of the North Mainland, a small section of cliff has been eroded by winter seas to reveal rare secrets from the past. Under a thick layer of glacial till lies a narrow seam of fine, dark material. A small stream trickles down to the sea through a corner of the seam and in its bed are found remarkable fragments of Shetland's ancient, pre-human landscape. Tiny pieces of wood lie among peat particles and clay from the stream. These fragments are thought to be at least 40,000 years old. Pollen analysis indicates that at one time, there would have been open coniferous woodland here, with birch, oak and elm among other species and areas of heather and marsh nearby. The climate must have been far milder than

Uyea and Garmus Taing from Fethaland.

that of Shetland today. Evidence of oak, of Scots pine and even a Mediterranean species of heather has been found among samples taken by experts. None of these species remains in Shetland, nor do they appear in pollen found in soil core samples from prehistoric sites in the islands. Somehow, although the whole area must at one time have been covered with ice, tiny pockets of an earlier landscape have survived beneath the crushing weight and bulldozing action of the later glaciers. Only one or two other sites of pre-glacial peat, as this is called, are known in Shetland.

Retrace your steps to North Roe and begin the long, meadering route back to the south. Nestling under the lee of the massive Beorgs of Skelberry, the small hamlet of Skelberry has a busy, cheerful air. Beyond, close to the road are a standing stone, now fallen, and a prehistoric burial site known as the giant's grave. The Housetter road turns off left just south of the loch of the same name and continues to Lochend where a haa was built for the Nicolson family in the 1700s overlooking a long beach, with splendid views across the sea towards the east-facing cliffs of the Ness of Queyfirth.

The main road runs on south, bending sharply into the inlet of the Voe of the Brig, past the new Collafirth fishing pier, site of a former whaling station. The Burn of Roerwater runs out to sea here and the fit and adventurous can follow it up into the loch-scattered wilderness to the west where at the

Lang Ayre and Gruna Stacks to the north-west of Ronas Hill.

extremity, a waterfall cascades into Lang Clodie Wick. Several Neolithic house sites exist in the area.

Ronas Hill is Shetland's highest hill and is composed almost entirely of granite of about 355 million years of age. Frost and wind action have created a fragile ground cover of gravel and tiny plants, known as Fellfield habitat, over the upper slopes. Deep peat hags have formed lower down. From the top you can see from the Out Skerries to Foula and from Fair Isle to Muckle Flugga. The best approach is to take the steep access road from Collafirth to the former signal station and set off across the bouldery, heather moor to Mid Field, the smaller summit visible to the west. From there you descend a shallow valley and climb up to the top of Ronas Hill itself, which has a large and impressive chambered cairn at the top.

Across the boulder-strewn plateau to the west, the going can be dangerous, with deep crevices and crumbling edges to the massive, sheer cliffs. But many folk venture down the Burn of Monius to experience the grandeur of the Lang Ayre, with its mile-long shingle beach. Mountain azalea, bearberry, club moss and ferns survive in the harsh local conditions, amongst many

Male Eider Duck ('Dunter').

other species. Rare sea eagles have been seen here on occasions, and in summer the rocky slopes chime with the plaintive calls of golden plover. Anglers enjoy fishing among the remote lochs to the north and few other places in Shetland have the same freedom and wild spaces. To the south, the slopes intensify and certain parts are precipitous, so be really careful especially if the fog comes down. From Ronas Hill north, some of Shetland's wildest and least hospitable terrain can be found. There is no shelter and weather can change very quickly.

The A970 skirts Colla Firth, and passes a small community at the neck of Queyfirth. The main road forks just as Ronas Voe swings north-west, the right-hand branch leading to Heylor and the left towards Urafirth and Hillswick. But at this point, before following the route right into Hillswick, we take a detour into some of the settlements to the east. A side road branches to Leon and rises up the Hill of Ollaberry, and there are fine views over the Loch of Queyfirth with its shingle bar, before crossing over into the village of Ollaberry itself.

Ollaberry faces east across the sea towards Yell and clusters around an old centre close to the pier and beach. Some very old buildings have survived, as well as a primary school, shop, church and some more recent houses, producing an attractive blend of old and new. The Ollaberry Hall, one of the venues for the Northmavine Up Helly Aa, serves teas on some summer Sundays. A local crofter, John Williamson, was among the first to experiment with greenhouses and fruit cultivation. For many years his peaches, plums, apples and cherries were something of a legend, and at blossom time there was never a shortage of visitors.

North of Ollaberry the ground slopes up slightly, then levels off at a point where a shallow depression crosses the end of the rounded headland from east to west. This looks at first sight like an overgrown, deep drain, but it is in fact the line of a geological fault which is called locally the Back of Ollaberry

Fault. Geologists believe it is a continuation of the Great Glen Fault, which is exposed on the beach to the west. If you are agile and suitably clad for a rough, muddy adventure, follow the depression to the cliff-top and clamber down (with care) the gulley to the simitar-shaped beach. The tear fault forms the face of dark, hard rock to your right, which cuts clean across the beach like a great door. Exposed tear faults are rare features.

The B9079 winds south from Ollaberry over the moors and skirts Eela water, with its water treatment plant, and joins the main A970 from Collafirth, passing several branch roads which lead off to quiet, old settlements, each full of interest. Fiblister, lying to the east, comes first and is a particularly attractive farm with lovely views across to Gluss Isle. Next a road turns left for Gluss itself, and curves through a beautiful valley where Turvister, Nissetter, Bardister and South and North Gluss lie amid fenced and cultivated land. You can walk over to the gently domed Gluss Isle, with its long shingle tombolo and peaceful views west over the trim croftscapes. Seals and maybe otters, quietly murmuring eider ducks and scuttling waders will watch you should you spend time walking over to the isle. It is one of the best places from which to see the oil terminal across the sea to the east. Tankers slide slowly by, eased alongside the jetties by tugs. You can also walk south from here, round the Ness of Bardister, round Fugla Ness and the Houb, coming out into the village of Sullom.

Sullom is a quiet and peaceful village, facing south-east across the sea to the North Ward of Voxter. There has been a mine here, now a quarry, where magnetite was extracted. A super quarry was proposed for the Hill of Hagrister in the 1980s and though it hasn't come yet, many local people fear that the threat may return. Two roads leave the village, the south road joining the A970 at Islesburgh, near Brae, and the north leg joining the A970 at Johnnie Mann's Loch, almost opposite the Gunnister junction.

The Guide now returns to Ronas Voe, where the east coast communities were described, and takes you out to Hillswick and the north-west before returning to the A970 south and the settlements on the west side of the area.

Ronas Voe, Shetland's only true fjord, is very deep, and runs in under the southern lee of Ronas Hill. It is overlooked by the tiny settlement of Voe at its head. Along the shore can be found traces of the old whaling stations which once stood

Skeo Head, Ronas Voe, at dusk.

here. Further out along the south side of the voe, there is a fish factory. The north side of the voe is very beautiful and you can clamber along from the head of the voe, at least as far as the ruins of Feal where otters are sometimes seen. Ravens nest in early spring, relict trees and plants cling to the sheltered low cliffs. The road along the south shore swings south as the voe turns north, a branch leading on along the coast to Heylor.

A strenuous but superb walk begins here, following the massive headland past the empty crofts of Sannions and Sumra, right round to the point at The Faither and then south to the deserted township of Ockran, green amid the brown landscape. History records a sorry tale of local folk. The 1851 Census recorded 99 inhabitants in the ness in 14 separate crofts. Then in 1865 two locals, who had earned a fortune in the Australian gold mines, bought the tenancy from the landowner for twice its annual rental. They then evicted their own neighbours and families and built the big house of Newton which still stands at Tingon today, and introduced sheep, attempting to grow even richer. Many ruins remain as witness to this Clearance. The brothers eventually fell out with each other and went bankrupt.

The Isle of Westerhouse and The Drongs from Hillswick Ness, with Papa Stour and Foula in the distance.

The area is full of geological interest, as here the Ronas granite meets the Eshaness volcanics and there are superb exposures along the Villians of Hamnavoe. The village of Hamnavoe has a magnificent broch site and the camping böd known as Johnnie Notions. The settlement here overlooks the sheltered Hamna Voe, with Hoohivda on the far side. From here a road connects with the B9078 to Eshaness and back to Hillswick.

The road which curved left at the Heylor junction passes Assater and joins the A970 at Urafirth. Hillswick is situated a mile or so along to the right. The village was once the furthest north point on the Mainland for the West Side steamer, a ferry and cargo boat, which brought passengers from Leith. The St Magnus Hotel, built in 1900, dominates the village. The wooden construction material was imported from Norway. Nearer the shore and allegedly formerly the oldest pub in Shetland, *The Booth* is said to date back to 1684 when a Hamburg merchant, Adolf Westerman, is recorded as having had a booth in Hillswick. It was converted in the mid 1990s into a vegetarian restaurant. Behind it, there is the Hillswick wildlife sanctuary, where oil- or storm-affected seals and otters are sometimes brought and treated. This facility was set up with funds raised after the grounding of the oil tanker *Braer*.

The large church, built in 1733, had a gallery built in 1825 and the manse about 30 years later. A shop and post office and small garage facility add greatly to the village amenities.

Hillswick Ness must number among the best of places to walk in Shetland, with virtually no fences or barriers to speak of at the outer end. Nearer to the farm with its Blacksmiths Forge there are walls and access on the western side is difficult. The easiest place to start is just outside *The Booth* itself and follow the shore west. The flowers are wonderful in summer and for those interested in ancient sites, the ness is full of them, none instantly obvious, but all there for the sharp-eyed to spot and examine. The ground rises gently as you make your way out towards the end of the ness with its tiny lighthouse. Beaches on the eastern shore have some wonderful pebbles, but the western face of the ness is much higher with massive cliffs and stacks. There is superb cliff scenery, with wide panoramas across Shetland's western coast and islands.

A short way back out of Hillswick the road for Eshaness turns left just before the village hall. It cuts uphill, overlooking the beautiful beach of Sandwick with the Drongs, sea stacks shaped like dragons' teeth, beyond. The road crosses Watch Hill and suddenly the whole Eshaness plain comes dramatically into view; a small world of its own. The road is like a spine, winding out to the west, with small rib roads branching off in both directions to reach outlying settlements, Hamnavoe, Hoohivda, Cross-Voe-Sand, Braehoulland and Leascole among those to the right, and Breiwick, Tangwick, West Hogaland and Stenness to the left. To the south, the curiously shaped stack of Dore Holm, rather like a drinking dinosaur, stands out starkly against the sea.

Eshaness has to rank among the top ten of Shetland's beauty spots. The dramatic 150 foot high cliffs are wave cut through extrusive volcanic rock from the Middle Devonian period. Massive sea stacks rise up from turbulent water and seabirds wheel and call. Tour buses call here endlessly in the season and locals take their visitors and relations to the lighthouse and car park just to stand and soak up the scenery. The North Atlantic roars against the land here, exploding in white mountains of spray on a wild day in winter and bursting up like geysers through many blowholes, yet in spring there can be days of totally windless, warm silence, with the sea nudging the rocks like a seal pup its mother. Seabirds abound here and

Tangwick Haa, Eshaness.

seals spread themselves out to snooze on the rocks below the cliffs, turning their heads to gaze inquisitively up at you as you gaze down. But the cliffs are very high and often have dangerous overhangs.

Calder's Geo cuts inland in a deep slash in the cliffs, the edges of which are frequently crumbly. When the sea is high, unexpectedly fierce waves could break and, at the very least, soak you to the marrow with ice-cold salt water. At worst you could be knocked down or washed over. It is advisable to keep well back at all times.

On a fine day you can walk north, passing the gaping Holes of Scraada where two blow-holes at the head of a long sea cave collapsed, leaving a tunnel 100 yards long to the sea. A small stream runs down from the Loch of Houlland with its ancient broch and causeway, and three old ruined watermills are found alongside it. A number of other ancient sites have been found in the vicinity. You can walk right along to where the coast bends east towards Hamnavoe just beyond Da Grind o da Navir, a particularly dramatic chasm in the stark ignimbrite cliffs where the sea breaks through in wild weather, hurling great rocks through the gap onto a storm beach high above.

Stenness today is a cluster of houses above a large pebble beach, with some ruins ranged around the shore above it. Here in the 1800s, 40 to 50 open boats were worked, setting off for 'da far haaf' and bringing back their catches of cod and ling to be cured. The fish were split, salted and laid side by side on the pebbles and stacked when dry, ready to be transported for sale. It would have been a hive of activity, with boats, boys and men, fish drying, seagulls crying; now the waves lap the deserted shore, rattling the igneous, multicoloured pebbles against each other. Take care on the steep grassy slope as you walk down to the shore and contemplate the sheer grim determination, the desperate need, which must have driven those fishermen to row out up to 40 miles west to set their lines. The long, cold, wet wait, then the hauling, and the rowing back, reading the skies for signs of bad weather and the ever-present risk of disaster.

Dore Holm from near Stenness, Eshaness.

A visit to Tangwick Haa museum is a must during the summer months. Staffed and run by volunteers, the standard of display and interpretation is first class and each year features a newly researched topic of local history. The building which houses the museum has been sensitively restored, with particularly fine woodwork inside. Nearby are the remains of an excavated burnt mound. Here in the early 1990s, experiments were carried out to see just how these ancient burning sites may have functioned. Visitors brought eggs to be boiled and great fun was had by all. Much was learned but many questions still remain as to the exact purpose of burnt mounds.

Urafirth lies at the head of a peaceful voe, and has a fine new school. In February, the Northmavine Up Helly Aa procession starts in Hillswick and parades all the way from the Hillswick beach to the edge of Urafirth, where it stops for the burning. The torches flicker and flare, songs rise up to a dark sky and then waves of arrowing flames fly through the air into the old ship, which is launched and pushed out to drift away over the water, burning into its own reflection. On occasions, Caain whales have swum into the shallow and accidentally beached themselves.

Deep inlets, such as Hamar Voe, feature in several places around the western sea coast. Olnesfirth, Scarpy and North and

The battered cliffs of Eshaness – looking across Calder's Geo from South Head of Caldersgeo.

South Lees face the Hamar Voe where, apart from the sound of sheep and the odd car in the distance, you are undisturbed. But half a century ago the scene would have been very different. There was a constant flow of ships and small boats here during the herring boom. At the head of the voe, Orbister presents a quiet and peaceful face to today's visitor, but 100 years ago it was a place of hustle and bustle. You can walk out around the shore past Hamar to the south and find traces of the busy fishing stations and shop where at one time several hundred telegraph messages a day were sent and received. The main road south of the Orbister turn is joined by the B9079 from Ollaberry.

Several other settlements lie on this stretch of coast, their tiny roads threading west from the main road to Brae. Just south of Punds Water a road winds over to Enisfirth which overlooks Gunnister Voe. You can walk the circuit of the Ness of Hamar, which is rugged and dramatic, with Hillswick Ness visible across Ura Firth to the west. A mile or so further south along the A970 another road turns off west to Gunnister and Nibon beyond. Near the junction, among the peat banks, the body of a man was found in 1951, buried in peat. Known now as the Gunnister Man, this person was dressed in homespun garments and is thought to have been a rent collector who came to grief somehow during the late 1600s, judging by the coins found in his knitted purse.

The small, scattered hamlet of Gunnister at the head of Gunnister Voe is set among some of Shetland's loveliest scenery. A wide arm of sea reaches deep inland past several small islets. The tiny Gunnister hall used to resound with the noise and laughter of dances, concerts, sales and auctions. There is a remarkable degree of shelter in the valley here and some unusual garden plants grow surprisingly well despite the latitude and climate.

A favourite place for Shetlanders to go on a Sunday afternoon, Nibon is an exceptionally beautiful spot. Otters often appear here and seals will watch you from the shallows, following your progress along the shore. Only a handful of houses stand here, sheltered from south-easterly winds by the high moors and inland cliffs which stretch right over to Mangaster, and from the ravages of the sea by the Island of Nibon to the west. Beware, though, the long, winding, single-track road which has to be negotiated first, and if you come by car, drive slowly in order to avoid having to reverse considerable distances, maybe even up hill or round a bend or two to allow other vehicles past.

The next small road to the west goes to the croft of Mangaster, tucked into the lee of Gruna Vird and the solid mass of high, craggy moorland to the north. There is a challenging walk here round to Nibon and back along the road past Gunnister. You would need a good six hours and more, even on a fine day. In poor weather it is easy to get lost on the tops. Mangaster Voe, sheltered on both sides with Islesburgh Ness to the south, was found to be an ideal site for salmon farming and considerable development took place in the 1990s.

Islesburgh Ness is a headland a mile north of Brae, full of geological and botanical interest, with superb views from its irregular coastline. Islesburgh Community Centre and Islesburgh House with its youth hostel in Lerwick, owe their name to this little corner of Shetland. A Smith family who farmed at Islesburgh, owned the house in Lerwick which they named after the ness. Islesburgh Ness, which means 'isle's broch headland', is well endowed with prehistoric features. An Iron Age house was excavated some years ago and a fine chambered cairn and Neolithic house site stand not far away. Some intriguing circular features around a small loch have never yet been fully explained. When the farmhouse was built near the site of the broch, many prehistoric tools were unearthed. A Pictish symbol stone was found here some years ago by the farmer John Copland. He was determined that the stone should not leave the islands and it can still be seen in the Shetland Museum. The 'Islesburgh Eagle', as it is called, seems to depict an eagle in flight, with something in its claws. The image has since been adopted as the symbol of the Islesburgh Centre.

In the 1970s the farm at Islesburgh was renowned for exceptionally good quality seed of the Shetland cabbage, a larger, tougher variety of cabbage than the conventional variety. Shetland's first garden nursery was established next door to the farm in the 1970s by John Copland when he retired. People visited the beautiful garden first, deciding which of the superb flowering and foliage plants they wished to have in their gardens, then bought specimens from the sales beds. Later he wrote a very popular gardening book, *Hardy Plants of the North*, which sold out twice. The farm has received many agricultural awards in recent years and in the 1990s had the reputation of producing some of the finest wool from Shetland sheep.

Just south of Islesburgh, the road rises a little, then dips downhill and bends slowly round to the east. For a moment, the sea appears simultaneously both to the left and the right of the road. This point is known as Mavis Grind, or *Maeve Isthmus*, a narrow gateway. The whole of Northmavine here is almost severed from the rest of Mainland Shetland. A good over-arm bowler can hurl a pebble from the Atlantic Ocean to the North Sea just by throwing it across the road from one shore to the other! Great craggy cliffs rear up to the right, their unstable faces still shivering down quantities of loose stone several decades after they were blasted to provide road-building materials for the oil terminal. The road follows the line of sea below them as it heads south towards Brae and the turn-off towards Muckle Roe and Busta.

Muckle Roe is a particularly lovely corner of Shetland. A mass of granite, wild and beautiful on the west, fertile and settled on the east, it is connected to the Mainland by a bridge across a short sea sound. If you have plenty of time, you can enjoy long walks around the coast from Otter Ayre on the north-eastern corner southwards as far as the Hams of Roe, a well-loved area of quiet beaches and spectacular cliff scenery on the west where many Shetlanders make frequent summer trips.

Cormorant ('Muckle Scarf').

MAINLAND
MUCKLE ROE
PAPA STOUR
VAILA
BRESSAY
LUNNASTING
NORTH NESTING
SOUTH NESTING
AITHSTING
WEISDALE
WHITENESS
TINGWALL
LERWICK
Scalloway
Tagon
Voe
Aith
Twatt
Bixter
Walls
Kaliness
Sandness
Laxo
The Cabin
Skelberry
Levaneap
Fora Dale
Dury Voe
To Whalsey
Muckle Ness
Dury
Gossa Water
Laxfirth
Bellister
Housabister
Bretabister
South Nesting Bay
Fiska Skerry
Ness of Skellister
Skellister
Brough
Eswick
Vassa
Glet Ness
Gletness
South Isle of Gletness
Unicorn Rock
Cat Firth
Brunt Hamarsland
Loch of Girlsta
Girlsta Mill
Wadbister Voe
Wadbister
Lax Firth
Oiled Bird Unit
Breiwick
Houster
Kebister Ness
Dales Voe
Califf
To Out Skerries
Gunnista
Heogan
Gardie
Bressay Sound
Brei Wick
Sound
Loch of Clickimin
Sandy Loch
156
Ham
A970
B9073
B9071
B9075
A971
Law Ting Holm
Loch of Tingwall
Asta
Nesbister
Wormadale
Laxfirth
Vatster
Loch of Strom
Gillaburn
Hoo Kame 209
Flamister
Loch of Skellister
Burn of Catfirth
Burn of Quoys
Grobs Ness
Olna Firth
Grobsness
Sneugie 222
Loch of Gonfirth
Setter
Gonfirth
Millburn
Linga
Cole Ness
Busta Voe
South Ward 170
Gillarona
Murbie Stack
Swarbacks Head
Guns
Swarbacks Minn
Papa Little
Vementry
Burial Cairn
91
The Rona
Sound of Houbansetter
Aith Voe
West Kame
Valley of Kergor
Mid Kame
Petta Dale
Petta Water
East Burrafirth
Scalla Field 281
Waterfall
Burn of Lunklet
Moa Water
Sand Water
Kergord Forest
Marina
Loch of Vaara
Clousta
Noonsbroch
Brindister
West Burrafirth
Neeans
Isle of West Burrafirth
Snarra Ness
Voe of Snarrane
Holm of Melby
Sound of Papa
Melby
Norby
Click Mills
Huxter
Woollen Mill
Sandness Hill 250
Bay of Deepdale
Deep Dale
Weinnia Ness
Coppa Wick
Mu Ness
Dale of Walls
Stourbrough Hill 173
Voe of Dal
Watsness
Wats Ness
Mid Walls
Voe of Footabrough
Vesquoy
Braga Ness
Littlure
Burrastow
Stapness
Linga
Vaila Sound
Vaila Hall
80
Tower
Whites Ness
To Foula
Grunnavoe
Gruting Voe
Scord of Brouster
Bridge of Walls
Loch of Voxterby
Lunga Water
Burga Water
Sulma Water
Fogrigarth
Unifirth
The Vadils
Clings Water
Hulma Water
Parkhall
Effirth
Stanydale Temple
Sefster
Loch of Gruting
Gruting
Seli Voe
Hoga Ness
Semblister
133
Garderhouse
Hestinsetter
108
Gossa Water
Culswick
Culswick Broch
Easter Skeld
Wester Skeld
Wester Wick
Silwick
Skelda Voe
Sil Wick
Wester Wick
Skelda Ness
Roe Ness
Reawick
Rea Wick
Kirk Holm
Leeans
Sand
Innersand
Fora Ness
Sandsound Voe
Sandsound
The Firth
Tumblin
Tresta
Aamos Kirk
Cluniess
Ross's House
Cott
Weisdale Hill
Textile Art Gallery
Huxter
Russa Ness
Weisdale Voe
Haggersta
Flotta
Hoove
Strom Ness
Whiteness
Whiteness Voe
Ustaness
Hoy
North Havra
The Deeps
Hildasay
Historic Granite Quarry
Langa
Bur Wick
Lamba Ness
West Vo
Geo of Bordi
North Ness
Gardie
Housa Voe
Fogla Skerry
Aesha Head
Biggings
North House
Hamna Voe
Kirk Sand

West Mainland

The Guide now describes the route out west, starting at Weisdale at the head of Weisdale Voe.

Skirting the head of the Voe, the road begins to climb towards the *Norseman's Inn* and the end of the road into Cott. Down here you can find Clunies Ross's house, now completely ruined, but still imposing, as are the remains of the old harbour on the shore. Here John Clunies Ross was born to a wealthy couple, Elizabeth Ross and George Clunies. After a career in the Royal Navy, in 1827 he became governor of the Cocos Islands in the Indian Ocean. His enlightened improvements to economic and social conditions earned him the islanders' title of 'King of the Cocos'. Just near the old house is a graveyard, site of an old church known as 'Da Aamos Kirk'. Money or gifts were deposited here when someone hoped for a special prayer or wish to be granted. Despite official church disapproval, the tradition survived long after the original kirk was demolished. As recently as the 1940s Shetlanders *en route* for war service brought their *aamis* (money or gifts) here before they left the island, hoping that this would speed their safe return.

The Cott road ends just beyond this point but at one time the community was much larger and crofthouse ruins can be seen far down the length of the ness. You can walk right round the western headland and back on the other side into Sandsound. There are fine views across the sea to the Scalloway islands from the ridge above. If the weather is calm, a ridge walk can be marvellous, with extensive views both east across Weisdale and west over Tresta, Bixter and the Skeld hills.

The road to Tresta goes up the west side of the valley out of Weisdale. A layby near the top provides a safe stopping place from which you can see for 30 miles south towards Fitful Head, across a foreground of islands and hills. The road turns sharply west as it levels out and if you feel like stopping there is a track at this point up to the mast on top of the hill above. From the summit you can see almost the whole of Shetland and if the weather is fine, the panorama is unbeatable.

The road crosses Weisdale ridge and a whole new landscape comes into view. A great expanse of sheltered water reaches from Tresta Voe into the wide firth, narrowing to Bixter Voe and finally Effirth Voe with the hills of the 'west side' for a backdrop. The sea here enters through Sandsound, a relatively narrow gap between headlands, out of sight to the south.

Just over the brow of the hill, the winding Burn of Tactigill flows south under the road as it emerges from a beautiful gorge, hidden from view to the north. Clay similar in some of its properties to kaolin can be found here and a representative of Wedgewood's potteries is said to have surveyed the place with the idea of extraction. But the deposits are relatively small and so factories were never built and the gorge was left to its wildlife, sheep and walkers.

The road descends gently into Tresta with its old house and walled, wooded garden. Other houses have been built along the shore and under the lee of the lower hills to the north, their cultivable land raking down the slope towards the sea. During the 1980s Lea Gardens were established here around a small crofthouse and became one of Shetland's most interesting gardens with an extensive plant collection.

A single-track road turns off to the left in Tresta and winds south past Lung Ness above the sea to Sandsound. Houses, some old, some new, have been built along the face of the slope here, enjoying wonderful views to the west and south. A long, pleasant walk can be taken from the end of the road here right round Russa Ness and back over the ridge to Cott and Weisdale.

Just before Bixter, a road branches north, signed to Tumblin. A winding single-track road connects scattered houses and crofts, some placed at the end of further branched tracks, and eventually ends at a turning place. The whole road is untypical of Shetland, lying out of sight of the sea. Interesting valleys, their stream banks concealing in places half-buried remains of planticrubs and other stone structures. The name 'Tumblin' is said to originate from a local incident many years ago, when the tiny church roof tumbled in.

Bixter, a sizeable hamlet, with new houses scattered among older ones, well above the sea, has grown up at the junction between the main road link to the north and the road out west. The village has a veterinary practice, doctors' surgery, a shop, garage and public toilets.

This gazetteer now breaks off where the road forks from the road to the west and describes the route to Aith and Voe with its many fascinating side roads.

The hills are wide and curving as the B9701 rises north from Bixter. A side road turns west to the quiet crofting settlements of Twatt, Clousta and Noonsbrough. There is a lot to explore in this out-of-the-way corner of the 'West Side' and few visitors manage to penetrate its secret corners, with their archaeological sites and rich bird life. A large hotel, long since burned down, was built here in the nineteenth century to service the requirements of the holidaying sportsmen who came in droves to shoot waterfowl in the 'Vadils', a salt-marsh and muddy shingle area much frequented by waterfowl. This habitat has recently been awarded special European conservation status.

The road to Aith continues to the north, rising slightly then dropping down towards Aith Voe and its fringe of densely settled slopes. As it bends sharply to the right, there is a fork north to Vementry. This route makes a rewarding detour, with many miles of cliff and seashore scenery to enjoy. As you approach the farm of Vementry at the end of the road, look out for a small loch on the right with a rowan tree growing on a tiny island, and ivy and honeysuckle growing along a fenced embankment. A short sea sound lies between the mainland shore and Vementry itself, which has not been inhabited for many years.

The Island of Vementry, sometimes described as 'little Shetland', has a bit of almost everything that Shetland is well known for: glorious scenery, wild flowers, superb archaeological sites and even First World War features. At the top of the highest point stand Shetland's finest ancient burial cairns. Beyond, at Swarbacks Head overlooking the seaway westward, stands an enormous gun complex, quietly rusting away above a series of underground bunkers and shelters which were part of Shetland's coastal defence system during the First World War.

Redshank ('Ebb-Cock').

Aith, overlooking the sheltered waters of Aith Voe, is a large village with a junior high school, shop, garage and a sheepskin business. The village has a new leisure centre, marina and one of Shetland's two lifeboats is based here. Look out for activities based in the hall during the summer, where local folk set up a splendid catering venture during the late 1990s. One of the highlights of the Aith year is the regatta with its multitude of events.

The road continues north, then curves round towards East Burrafirth, crossing the Burn of Lunklet. A signed path here leads to Ramnageo, a spectacular gorge and waterfall. In summer, honeysuckle and wild roses bloom here in abundance among bell heather and a dozen other wild flowers. The scene is one of Shetland's most photographed and is well worth seeing.

East Burrafirth has grown up along the coast facing south-west across Aith Voe. Evenings can be lovely here, with sunsets tinting the water and night time bringing reflections of lights on the farther shore. It seems hard to believe that the side road which leads into the hamlet is one of the most recent features in the landscape. But the construction of the single-track link in the 1920s across the upper grazings of the seashore crofts is still remembered. The road men got 6d (2 1/2p) per hour and had to walk or cycle to the job and stay in an old house all week. The nearest shop was in Grobsness, several miles across the hills and back again, often walked by children carrying messages.

South Voxter, a mile or two further north, is signed off the main road to the left. The short road gives way to a track and forks, one branch leading over to the old settlements of Houbansetter, Ladie and Quiensetter on the western shore of the ness opposite the island of Papa Little. Here, many years ago, during a visit to Shetland by the Royal family, the young Princess Anne and Prince Charles were ferried with their escorts and spent a blissful day playing among the heather and along the shore while their parents went about their official business. Above South Voxter the ruined crofthouse of Moon stands starkly against the horizon, its empty windows gaping against the sky.

Grobsness, at the end of another short road to the left, overlooks a sheltered stretch of water where salmon farming was established in the 1990s. An old Haa house ruin stands a short distance down the slope from the road, facing old and

East Burra Firth and Aith Voe at dusk, with Aith Ness, Papa Little and Muckle Roe beyond.

new crofthouses. A shop and busy fishing station once stood here.There are fine views across the settlement of Gonfirth below and across Gon Firth itself towards South Voxter and Cole Ness. Views are even better half a mile further on, when the road curves round the face of the hill. It descends very steeply before ending in a large turning place, beyond which the access to the Grobsness settlement is gated. Linga and Muckle Roe and Wethersta fill the scene to the west and north, with Papa Little and Vementry to the south.

The road rising up to the Loch of Gonfirth is narrow and twisty, so take care and be prepared for oncoming traffic. There is a strangely remote and bleak feel to this loch, with its pewter-grey water and dark rock-strewn margins. A young girl once found a finely worked white quartz arrowhead here, a great rarity among Shetland's archeological treasures. The road levels out, following the curves of the shore, then drops steeply down towards Voe. You can glimpse long vistas to the south along the valley between West and Mid Kame before the road crosses a fast, full stream near a large old quarry and enters Voe itself.

The route north via Aith from the road out west, now meets the main north-south Voe to Lerwick road, which is covered in the North-East and Central Mainland chapter.

The Guide now returns to Bixter and continues west to Park Hall, where a small road leaves the A971 heading south to Effirth and Reawick, west to Skeld and eventually rejoins the main road shortly before the Bridge of Walls. Park Hall stands forlorn and shabby now, having been empty so long that all traces of former glory are lost. The big house was home to the Bowie family, from whose ranks came many notable scholars and enterprising Shetlanders over the years. In its heyday it was very grand with some unusual features and extensive gardens.

Effirth with its scatter of crofthouses overlooks the head of Effirth Voe below. The road skirts higher moorland to the west, through Semblister, where a small side road branches east to Sand. Notice the old, but well-preserved hill dyke to the right of the road as it rises up the hill towards Sandhoulland. The road forks here, the right fork leading to the imposing Haa of Sand, built in 1754 for Sir Andrew Mitchell of Westshore in Scalloway, which has windows allegedly taken originally from Scalloway Castle. The Haa overlooks Sand Voe, with its splendid beach sheltered by the narrow finger of Fora Ness beyond. Near the old pier and former fishing station is a cemetery and the complete chancel arch of St Mary's pre-Reformation church, which is linked with local legends concerning Spanish sailors shipwrecked here.

Experimental tree plantations and ponds were introduced into the old crofting landscape here during the 1990s. You can go as far as Inner Sand overlooking the narrow Sandsound Voe and the high bulk of Russa Ness beyond before returning to the B9071. Turn left, passing Garderhouse, which overlooks Seli Voe, with its salmon farm and the island of Kirk Holm on which ancient foundations remain. Reawick comes in sight, set above a

Surviving chancel arch of St Mary's Church, Sand.

lovely crescent of warm, russet sand fringing the shore here. A fine walk along the precipitous cliffs and round the headland, passes Deepdale and the Hill of Swartagill before leading you back to Easter Skeld.

Easter Skeld overlooks Skelda Voe and has a splendid modern hall, housing estates, a new school, Camping Bod and imaginatively sited sheltered housing with views across the sea for all the residents. The village was a hive of industry in the late 1800s as a centre for the dried salt fish trade, exporting to Spain. Remains of old buildings stand near the pier. Today the state-of-the-art Shetland Smokehouse produces fine salmon and other fish delicacies, sending them all round the world. A side road left goes to Scarvister where a scatter of houses face the early morning sun, above Tarasta Ayre. You can walk from here right round the dramatic headland of Skelda Ness with its magnificent sea stacks and geos. At the T-junction the road turns left to Wester Skeld and then divides.

Ignoring the right fork to Westerwick, you reach Silwick with its peat stacks, tiny fields and string of old crofthouses set above the shallow valley and shingle beach. Some of the most dramatic sea stacks in Shetland can be seen when walking out to the coast from here, one of which supports a cormorant colony. A truly splendid walk along the cliffs to the west takes you right round to Westerwick, guarded by a protective curve of scapolite-rich cliffs leaving wonderfully framed views out to sea. A handful of houses, marshy fields and the site of an old mill beside the burn grace this tiny valley. There is very little space for cars however, so ask and park sensitively if you come by vehicle and intend walking. A quiet hour spent on the beach here heals many a weary spirit. From here, if you feel like a longer walk, you can continue west to Culswick, or you can return to Wester Skeld.

From Wester Skeld the road now goes due north, meeting the one from Easter Skeld at Hestinsetter, meaning 'settlement of horses'. Turn left and after a mile, take the left fork into Culswick, one of Shetland's most attractive corners. It is an area of stunning cliff- and sea-scapes, seabird colonies and superb archaeology, set in an old crofting and grazing landscape under wide skies. There are some unusual wild flowers among the marshy fringes of the loch here and the small community cherishes the unspoilt, peaceful atmosphere which pervades the valley. A fine walk out to the west passes deserted, enchanting

Sandness Hill, Hill of Bousta and Snarra Ness across West Burra Firth.

Sotersta, and reaches Culswick Broch, still one of the largest broch remains despite considerable robbing of stonework. It has a doorway capped with a huge, triangular lintel stone. The area is among the finest for coastal walking with views across to Vaila, Whites Ness and Gruting. Retrace your route to the junction where the Culswick road turned off. You can now turn left and head north, cutting across bleak moors, past Ola's Voe and Hoga Ness where you may notice some remarkable old double dykes, stretching east across the hills in a die-straight, east-west line.

Keep an eye open for grouse as you descend towards Seli Voe with its fringe of habitation, old, deserted and new. The road curves up and round to a crossroads; go left for Gruting itself, straight ahead for West Houlland with its broch site and reach Bridge of Walls, or right for Stanydale.

Gruting is one of the richest areas in Shetland for Neolithic sites and has an air of antiquity with numerous settlement sites, ancient walls, burial sites and clearance cairns. If instead of turning left to Gruting you had turned right at the crossroads, you would have crossed a wide stretch of moorland, passing Loch of Gruting and the road to Sefster and Heathertown, and come to Stanydale.

You are signposted to the famous 'Stanydale Temple' site, the dramatic and massive stone Neolithic building which far exceeds the normal house size of this period. Stand within those sturdy walls and you are standing where some of the earliest settlers in the islands stood, over 5000 years before. A glance at the 1-50,000 Ordnance Survey map will show you several other sites nearby. The present landscape here is thought to have been influenced by Neolithic overfarming, which impoverished the land and led eventually to a period of depopulation.

The road continues north from here and rejoins the main A971, completing the loop begun at Park Hall.

Turn left at the A971 with Hulma Water lying below to the north. After a mile or so, a road is signed off right to the Papa Stour ferry. Papa Stour is described on page 161. This road threads its way through some of the most mysterious and varied scenery in Shetland, linking the scattered settlements of Unifirth, Brindister, West Burrafirth and Fogrigarth right out as far as Snarraness. Those who like really wild places will enjoy exploring the rugged headland of the Neans, with its scores of tiny lochs and craggy outcrops, which was home to the legendary 'Tief o' da Neeans', a thief who lived in a cave here long ago. There are great views north from here, of the West Burrafirth islands and Vementry as far as Hillswick and Stenness in the distance.

When the Papa Stour ferry point was moved to West Burrafirth from Sandness, it gave this corner of Shetland a new lease of life. There is a pier, carpark and toilets. The entrance to the sea is guarded by treacherous skerries and stacks and a safe passage past them has been secured with leading lights. You can see small, white huts in two places on the coast here, which, when viewed from out at sea, shine lights which change colour if the boat steers a fraction either side of the central beam, thus shining a perfect course. A ruined broch stands on a holm below Engamoor and few places are more peaceful. The rocks of the area have been heavily faulted; split and fused many times so that sandstones, breccias, conglomerates and metamorphic outcrops can be found alongside each other.

The narrow road winds on past West Burrafirth and peters

out above a shingle beach at Snarra Ness where the sea has almost cut right through, nearly turning Snarraness into an island. A fault cuts through the metamorphic rock where the land is narrowest. The Ness widens beyond into hilly terrain, forming an ideal bastion to the forces of wind and sea to the west. The old house has been beautifully restored and you could ask before leaving a vehicle, or walking further out. A glorious walk starts here which leads right round the Ness and back, with wonderful sea views and cliff and seashore scenery. The cliffs are sliced by geos and inlets, full of caves. At one point a series of massive rocks has tumbled from a high cliff face and among them nestles the Snarraness press-gang cave in which local men hid from the press gang during the Napoleonic Wars. From Snarraness there is an old way round the coast to Sandness, through the deserted township of Kellister.

Returning to the main A971, the road continues south for a mile, then curves west into Bridge of Walls overlooking the Voe of Browland, meeting the branch road from Skeld.

The Guide now follows the road south into Walls and the neighbouring settlements, before returning to this point and continuing to the west.

The old centre of the village of Walls, or Waas, as it is called in Shetland, still clusters round the pier and the old harbour and the old haa, with its charm intact despite many visual changes over the years. Walls is a lively community, with a school, swimming pool, and village hall. The Walls bakery has raised the status of traditional Shetland products, especially their oatcakes, in recent years. Walls is a great sailing centre with events and activities almost all year round. Sadly, the community has, like many others in Shetland, lost members to accidents at sea. The shop, garage, surgery, care centre and health centre café add to the convenience for locals, but country shops in Shetland suffer increasingly from the effects of big supermarkets in Lerwick and their futures are far from certain.

The road forks in Walls, the left branch crossing a bridge and leading south past the shop to Saltness, Grunnavoe and Vadlure to Whites Ness. The Whites Ness peninsula reaches south, almost touching Vaila. It divides Vaila Sound from Gruting Voe and is an excellent walking area. To the east lies the Ward of Culswick, high above its skirting fringe of moors and cliffs. You may be able to make out the broch on the right against the skyline. Look out for the tiny, enchanting house at

Point, set like a gem into a curve of the shoreline at the Stead of Whitesness.

Returning to Walls and turning left, there is a small loop road which branches right past the Loch of Kirkigarth and links the branching settlements of Bardister, Stennestwatt and Brunatwatt, curving finally north and connecting with the A971 again. Continuing through Walls, a road leads left past old council houses and a church, to the pier from which the boat to Foula leaves. An old manse near the junction has been converted into a camping booth and has an interesting garden. Stapness is signed left just beyond the village as you rise up the hill and houses here enjoy the finest views of Walls spread out below. Further out of Walls still, Burrastow is signed left leading past Riskaness, Lera Voe and the shore base for Vaila with its tiny broch-style oil store. This branch has a short loop back through Greenland and Burraland and a longer loop via Vesquoy, both of which rejoin the Walls road to Mid Walls and Dale of Walls. A new road was cut through the Dale of Walls, to Upper Dale and out to the Sandness road. The Guide now returns to Bridge of Walls.

From Bridge of Walls the road forks right for Sandness. The area to the north is full of large lochs, and at one time a hotel for anglers was built here. You can walk for miles along the silent loch shores and across the hills between them. This part of Shetland has many prehistoric sites and the Scord of Brouster, signed to the right just north of the fork to Sandness, has been excavated and interpreted for visitors with an information board explaining the features of the Neolithic village and the local vegetation and habitats from the period.

The road from Lerwick to Sandness still feels very long and tortuous. But compared with the journey only a few years ago, it is splendid. After you pass the junction to Dale of Walls, it is only a few miles to the green pastures and lovely coastline of this fertile and attractive corner of Shetland. A scatter of single houses, crofthouses and clusters of dwellings fills the landscape,

Haa House, Sand.

all lying in the lee of the massive bulk of Sandness Hill to the south. There is a school at Sandness, and the ferry to Papa Stour formerly plied from the pier at Melby just below the site of old Melby House, the seat of power in times long gone by.

The remarkable history of pure Shetland wool took a leap forward in recent years when the spinning mill was set up. The story of Shetland Woollen Mill is something of a recent legend. Peter Jamieson from Sandness conceived the idea of buying the machinery from a closed-down mill in England. He found one, dismantled and packed all the parts, took them back and re-constructed them in Sandness. The products now made here go straight to the top of the market and are sold in Harrods and other exclusive shops abroad. Staff at the mill welcome visitors.

Visit the glorious sandy beach at Norby and walk around the cliffs to Little Bousta, past rocky, sheltered coves and dramatic headlands. There are many prehistoric sites and some of Shetland's bonniest crofting landscapes. This is the western end of the old route to Kellister and Snarraness.

Huxter, at the far end of the road past Sandness, is the furthest settlement west in Mainland Shetland and has many features worth exploring. A broch site and several other prehistoric, smaller sites are found nearby, as well as a freshwater loch with marshy fringes rich in wild flowers each summer. The burn runs westwards into the sea, through a gulley where several old click mills once turned to grind the grain harvested from local fields. A great deal of restoration work has been done on the mills in recent years. This has halted the decay which would otherwise have rendered them little more than heaps of stone, like most of these mills. Fossil fish scales have been found in places along the rocky coast in this area.

Huxter is also a starting point for one of the loveliest and most dramatic walks in Shetland, along the cliff tops right round to the Dale of Walls. It passes above the magnificent Bay of Deepdale and is only a short way from the summit of Sandness Hill, from which views stretch almost the full length of the isles. Foula, when the sky is clear, dominates the seascape westwards and is seen from here at its most powerful and brooding. Seen from Foula, the rise of Sandness Hill is one of the clearest features along the Shetland profile. Once you get to the Dale of Walls, you will find one of the most beautiful burns in Shetland. The crofthouses here are trim and well tended, with a continuous flow of colour from garden

Cley Stacks across Coppa Wick near Dale on the far west coast of the Mainland, with Papa Stour beyond.

flowers to wild flowers along the burnside.

There is magnificent coastal walking all the way from Dale of Walls right round the coast to the south and east to Watsness, along the cliffs through some of the West side's most beautiful coastal scenery around Mid Walls. A number of lochs and crofting townships, some more recent houses and a string of ancient sites can be seen. Foula dominates the seascape to the west all the way along the coast here.

More dramatic sea- and landscapes and wildlife feature as the coast curves round towards Footabrough, at the head of Footabrough Voe, with its broch site overlooked by a number of houses and crofts. Springtime here is especially rich in wild flowers and bird life, as the land has been little changed and a number of deserted settlements in the area bear witness to a larger local population in earlier times. The coastal route leads along the southern shore of the voe, round wave-battered Braga Ness, across rock-strewn cliff tops to the south-east. Overlooked by the Hill of Scarvister, the scenery is craggy and exposed. A singularly lovely corner is the deserted township of Littleure nestling into the lee of The Peak, a protective arm of rock jutting out across a tiny natural harbour.

The island of Vaila to the east soon comes into view. A watch tower, hunched onto the cliff top of a precipitous headland, stands looking out to sea. Eventually the shoreline swings north hugging Vaila Sound, the higher mass of hill and moor above giving increasing shelter from westerly winds and soon Burrastow comes into view. Burrastow House dates from 1759 and is now run as a successful hotel, with a reputation for wonderful local food.

Vaila was inhabited from ancient times and a large number of prehistoric sites have been identified in the island. It is privately owned and can only be visited by arrangement. Vaila Hall stands today in a magnificent setting. From the 1580s its history is well documented, with the ownership changing roughly every hundred years. Cheyne, Mitchell and Scott, all key Shetland figures in their day, added in turn to its buildings and features. In the 1890s the island was bought by Yorkshire mill-owner Herbert Anderton. His descendant, Henry Anderton, laid on expensive but very popular banquets in the great hall in the 1970s. It was sold to Dorotta Rychlik in the 1990s. Vaila forms a particularly important link in the chain of events which have shaped Shetland's fishing history. It was here that Arthur Anderson first devised a scheme to revolutionise Shetland fishing management and the livelihoods and wellbeing of fishermen and their families. A painting by an unknown contemporary artist depicts Anderson's fishing business and the beach in Vaila (see page 84).

There are prehistoric sites in the island and sections of ancient boundary walls. Magnificent natural arches, sea cliffs, sea caves and stacks around the shores draw many a sailing boat in for a closer look during the summer. Wild flowers are prolific, especially since Vaila has become an organic farm, with reduced pressure on grazing. The great house and its gardens have been restored along with the reservoir, road and other buildings on the island. Vaila, like much of remote Shetland until recent times, has no mains electricity and uses generators. The oil tanks which hold the fuel for generators and boats are stored in a remarkable new building in the form of a small, perfectly built stone broch by the new service pier for Vaila, which screens beautifully the lurid but functional tanks from view. A second building, for use when rough sea delays crossings, has been constructed to resemble a small lighthouse.

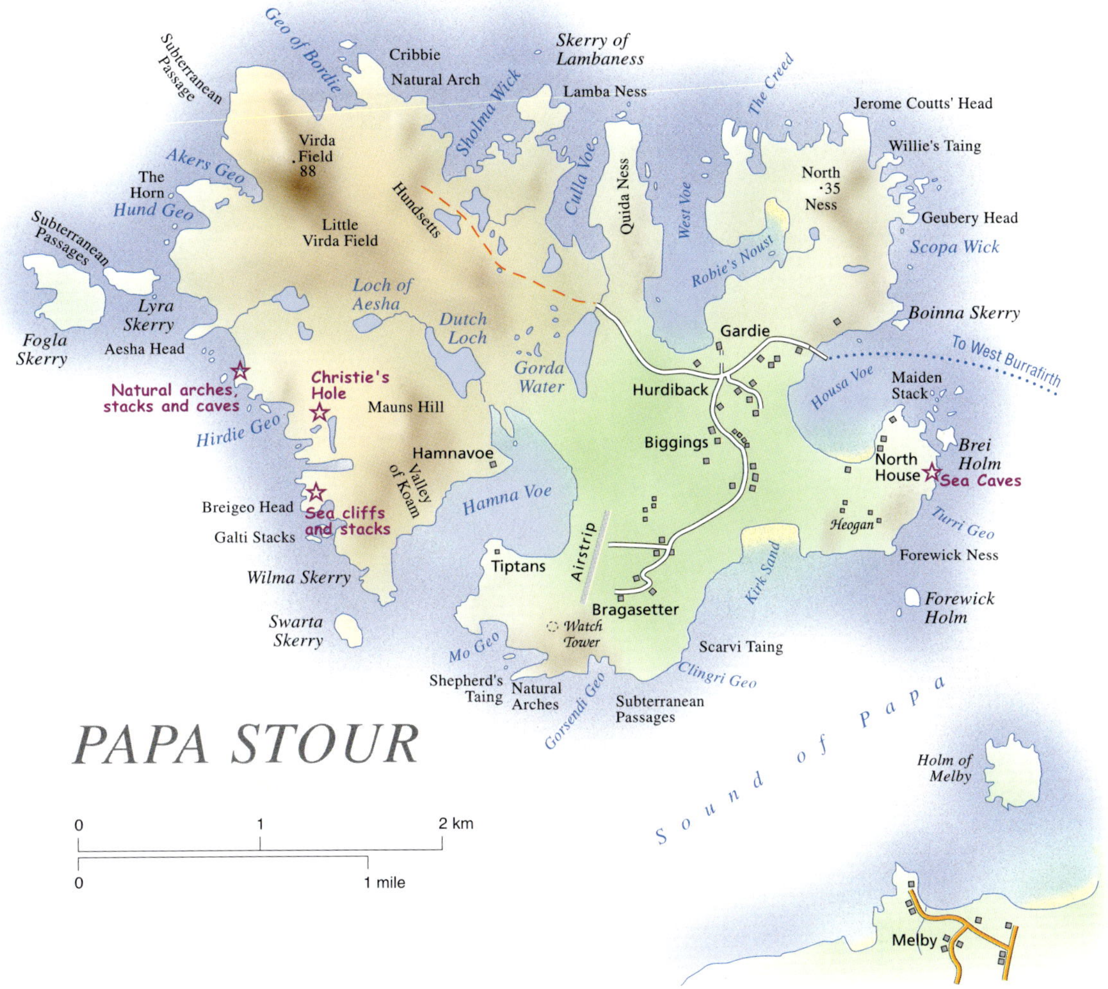

PAPA STOUR

Papa Stour, which means 'Great Island of the Priests', is one of the most magical of Shetland's smaller islands. Around the coast, the volcanic tuffs and lavas have been carved by the sea into a spectacular series of cliffs, stacks, blow holes and geos. Sea caves around and even under the island are among the finest in Europe and attract canoeists from all over the world. Many people have experienced particular feelings of peace and calm here, when walking through the island, whose scale accounts for some of its charm.

Here, more than perhaps anywhere else in Shetland, you can see the contrast between the inby (enclosed) and outby land. Generations of folk have taken turfs for animal bedding, soil improvement and roofing. The stripped ground to the west of the hill dykes has bright-green mounds remaining at intervals, created by the piling up of turfs for collecting and transporting back to the crofts. Each heap once belonged to a particular family or individual. To the east, just over the boundary wall, there is contrasting lush pasture and deep soil with fields knee-deep in flowers. The flowers in spring and summer have become well known as a result of their scent; a scent so strong that during summer fogs, or darkness, as the old fishermen's stories tell, men far out at sea, way out of sight of land, were able to guide themselves home by following the effects of both the drifting waves of perfume and the 'Möder Dy', a subtle current, almost a pulse of movement in the water, indicating the approach of land.

Stack alongside Lyra Skerry from Stourhund, to the far west of Papa Stour.

Tales that survive of Vikings, elopements and shipwrecks have enthralled listeners for generations. In the early 1800s, islander Gideon Henderson was paid to keep a young man in the island, ostensibly because he was 'insane'. His well-to-do family apparently found his eccentric temperament a major embarrassment. The Hon Edward Lindsay was a prisoner in the island for 26 years. After several attempts, he was finally helped to escape by a Quaker, Catherine Watson, who was convinced of his sanity; a conviction upheld by the subsequent declaration by the Vice Chancellor's Court in London. There is a spring in the island called 'Lindsay's Well' to this day.

The Papa Stour sword dance, a curious, traditional dance, with its medieval overtones was almost lost but is now saved for posterity. Archaeological sites abound all over the island. The most famous is Da Biggins, excavated by Dr Barbara Crawford during the 1970s and '80s, thought to be the site of the house of a Norseman of considerable importance. An interpretive panel has been erected on the site.

A modern day saga could be written about the 'hippies' of Papa Stour. As a result of population decline in the 1960s and 1970s, the school closed and some islanders feared that Papa

Looking west from a croft at Biggings, Papa Stour, towards Mauns Hill.

Stour would become yet another uninhabited island. One local man took the controversial step of advertising for new members of the community and a colourful procession of folk arrived over several years. Some stayed and others left, yet more stayed a short while and 'flit' or removed to other parts of Shetland. Several decades later many families still remain, some of whom have set up thriving businesses and contributed greatly to island life. There are still people who, hearing tales of wealth and housing, freedom and excitement, arrive in Shetland hoping for instant satisfaction of all their needs and finding life far harder than they expected.

To the north of Papa Stour lie a cluster of tiny islands called the Ve Skerries. In calm weather they are havens of tranquillity, where the silent sea rises and falls only inches, but in a storm, nowhere could be more dangerous. For centuries these were a menace to shipping and many lives were lost when wrecks struck the low, sea-obliterated rocks in bad weather. Particularly heartbreaking was the loss of the crew of the *Ben Doran* in 1930. A lighthouse was eventually erected in the 1980s. No lives have been lost here since. A memorial to the crew of the *Ben Doran* stands in Sandness churchyard.

Gaada Stack
Sheepie
Arva Skerry
The Ness
Hellibaas
Logat Head
Freyars
East Hoevdi
Strem Ness
Mucklegrind
Skeld
Soberlie Hill
Skiodar
Bloberg
Ruscar Head
North Bank
Codlafield
The Kame
Flick Lochs
Ruyhedlar Head
Rokna Skerries
Burns
Swaa Head
Heoag
Gossumeador
Bark Hill
Nebbifield
The Sneug 418
Overfandal Loch
Scrodhordins
Lioag
Taing Head
Hornalie
Hamnafield
Sloag
Ham
Pier
To Walls
Hamar
Ham Voe
Mill Loch
Mires
Wester Hoevdi
Tounafield
Baa Head
Mucklaberg
Little Ham
Durga Ness
Wick of Mucklaberg
Smallie
Shoabill
The Daal
South Wick
Broadfoot
Airstrip
The Noup
Naggards
Mid Hoevdi
Punds
Skirnawilse
Biggings
Helliberg's Wick
Boat Harbour
FOULA
South Ness
Hord Head
Rippack Stack
Doalie
Boniberg
0
1
2 km
0
1 mile

Foula

Curved aedge o da wirld
a conductor staands, makkin
symphonies o licht

From *Sunset Trowe Da Gaada Stack: A Response to a Photographic Image by Colin Baxter*, by Christine De Luca.

Foula is a massive natural fortress of Old Red Sandstone which guards Shetland's approaches from the west. The full power of its natural forms can only be experienced by walking among the peaks, or standing at their feet. The Sneug, the highest point, is some 1377 feet (420 m) high and the cliffs at the Kame are sheer, towering 1246 feet (380 m) above sea level, second only in the UK to those of St Kilda. The nearest Shetland coastline is 14 miles (22 km) away and is often barely visible.

Foula's sandstones are relieved by a metamorphic band on the east side. Tiny plant fossils can be found in a few places and rare trace fossils from early creatures. Many wild plants survive here, but the birds are Foula's most impressive wildlife and give the island its name: *Fugl-oy*, or 'bird island'. A large colony of great skuas or Bonxies breeds here, as well as Arctic skuas, kittiwakes, guillemots, puffins and fulmars. Islanders used to scale the cliffs to harvest eggs in spring. Shetland's most attractively coloured and patterned sheep are found here.

From Ristie in the north, with the dramatic natural arch of Gaada Stack offshore, south through Ham to South Ness is a walk of almost four miles, but on a fine day you can wander three times as far. From Shetland the striking profile of Foula dominates the scene to the west with the great hills of Hamnafield, the Sneug, the Kame, Soberlie, the wide glacial valley of the Daal and the lower hill of the Noup to the south. The locally famous 'Sneck o' da Smaalie' is a wickedly slippery scramble down a cleft to a cliff foot, not recommended without local guides and climbing equipment.

Often weather-bound, Foula demands extraordinary

The Noup, Smallie and Wick of Mucklabrek from Hamar, Foula.

qualities of toughness and independence among its human population. Lack of natural harbours puts fishermen at a disadvantage but few crofting communities have withstood the temptation to leave for softer, easier lives with such resilience. Families who have had to leave spend much of their spare time back 'in the isle', coming by ferry from Walls or by plane from Tingwall. Foula school, one of the smallest, but best-equipped in Britain, is used by the whole community. There is a unique multi-sourced electricity generating scheme. Wind, when it blows, generates power and surplus energy is used to pump water to a high loch, providing water power when the wind drops.

Archaeological and historical features exist, but many have been destroyed or lost. A broch was said to have stood at the north end, and a 'Picts' house at Crougar. These, plus a cairn at Harrier, have disappeared but traces of Neolithic houses, an ancient chapel and burial ground at Harrier remain, where, legend says, a monastery formerly existed. A possible Viking boat burial, a few burnt mounds and burial cists have been recorded and a 'bog' body was reportedly uncovered and immediately reburied during peat digging in 1883. Records of Norse history and folklore survive, including the legend of Queen Katherine of Foula and a ruin still bears her name. The old Norn speech survived longer here than in the rest of Shetland, as did the old Julian calendar, officially ended in 1752 in Britain. Old Yule is celebrated on 6 January and new year on the 13th.

A number of ships came to grief on Foula's shores in bad weather before the lighthouse was built. In 1948 a schooner

Gaada Stack just north of Ristie, Foula, at sunset.

struck Da Heed o da Hurd and her cargo of timber was lost. *The Oceanic*, sister ship to *The Titanic*, ran aground and sank off Foula during the First World War. There were other war-time casualties. A Whitley bomber crash-landed and despite a dramatic impact, all the crew climbed out alive. Carrier pigeons survived the crash too, and they were fitted with messages and released to summon aid. Foula folk recall the tragedy of a Canadian Catalina which crashed into Hamnafield in thick fog in the early 1940s. Seven men died but one survived, allegedly because he had been sitting in the look-out tower when the plane hit the ground. Foula folk erected a particularly fine war memorial here.

You can get no further west in Shetland. But, if you have the stamina and the weather is kind, climb the great hills and when you reach the top of the Sneug, gaze west and south, scanning the far horizon for the faint mark of Orkney which is just visible if the conditions are right. You may even see the mast on North Ronaldsay. During the era of the Haaf fishing, men, according to local stories, would 'row Foula doon' – row so far west that even Foula sank completely below the eastern horizon.

0
5 km
0
5 mi
Brei Wick
Brough
To Ulsta
Nature Reserve
Samphrey
Dale Voe
Sullom Voe Oil Terminal
Hill of Crooksetter 152
Toft
Tofts Voe
Loch of Burraland
Fugla Ness
The Houb
Mossbank
Lunna Holm
Lunna Ness
Sullom Voe
Voe of Scatsta
Garths Voe
Firths Voe
Fish Holm
Sullom
Scatsta Ness
B9076
Firth
Linga
Scatsta
Laxobigging
Graven
Swinister Voe
Wether Holm
Outrabister
89
Fora Ness
·83
B9076
Mid Field
Haggrister
Trondavoe
A968
Dales Voe
Ube
Noness Head
Ness of Setter
Stanes of Stofast
To Out Skerries
Outdoor Centre
Voxter
Colla Firth
Lunna Kirk
Lunna House
Lunna Voe
Lunna
South Ness
A970
Brae
Collafirth
Quhamm
Muckla Moor
Swining Voe
Vidlin Voe
Lunning Head
Outer of Skaw
Inner Holm of Skaw
Skella Dale
Swining
Lunning
Vaivoe
Busta Voe
Weathersta
Vidlin
Longa Water
Lunning Sound
Skaw
Nacks Skerry
A970
Susetter
Seggie Burn
Laxo Water
Herra
Brough
Yoxie
Nista
Hamars
·129
LUNNASTING
Fora Dale
98
West Linga
Linga Sound
Loch of Houll
Isbister
Olna Firth
Old Whaling Station
The Cabin
Grobs Ness
Tagon
B9071
Laxo
Hunder Holm
Isbister Holm
Linga
Grobsness
Sneugie ·222
Skelberry
Levaneap
Cole Ness
Loch of Gonfirth
B9071
Voe
Symbister
Loch of Huxter
East Linga
Setter
Dury Voe
Bremen Böd
Muckle Ness
Ward of Clett
WHALSAY
Gonfirth
Dury
Sandwick
Millburn
West Kame
B9075
Gossa Water
Laxfirth
Bellister
Stava Ness
Petta Water
Hoo Kame ·209
NORTH
Valley of Kergor
Mid Kame
A970
NESTING
Housabister
Iron Age Fort
Muckle Fladdicap
Aith Voe
East Burrafirth
Scalla Field ·281
Petta Dale
Hill of Neap
Kirkabister
B9071
Waterfall
Burn of Lunklet
Bretabister
Loch of Skellister
South Nesting
Muckla Billan
Flamister
Burn of Catfirth
Burn of Quoys
Fiska Skerry
Bay
Marina
Aith
SOUTH
Ness of Skellister
Climnie
Litla Billan
B9075
Skellister
Ling Ness
Haerie
Moa Water
Sand Water
B9075
Kergord Forest
NESTING
Brough
Eswick
Moul of Eswick
WEISDALE
Loch of Girlsta
Vassa
The Sneckan
Textile Art Gallery
Brunt
Hamarsland
Cat Firth
A971
Weisdale Hill
Glet Ness
Hoo Stack
Gillaburn
Gletness
Tresta
Huxter
Girlsta Mill
Wadbister Voe
Unicorn Rock
South Isle of Gletness
Aamos Kirk
Clunies Ross's House
Kaliness
Loch of Strom
Cott
Wadbister
Sandsound Voe
Sandsound
Vatster
Lax Firth
Weisdale Voe
Haggersta
WHITENESS
Innersand
Russa Ness
Oiled Bird Unit
Breiwick
Laxfirth
Houster
Kebister Ness
Wormadale
Fora Ness
Flotta
Strom Ness
Hoove
A971
Dales Voe
Califf
Score Head
Hoy
Whiteness
Voe
Nesbister
TINGWALL
Aith Ness
Law Ting Holm
Aith Voe
Voe of Cullingsburgh
Ustaness
Heogan
Gunnista
BRESSAY
North Havra
Whiteness
Loch of Tingwall
A970
Bressay
Gardie
Asta
LERWICK
Noss
Hildasay
Loch of Clickimin
Noss Sound
Visitor Centre
Historic Granite Quarry
Bur Wick
Sandy Loch
Brei Wick
Noss National Nature Reserve
Noss Head
Langa
A970
156
Sound
Pettyfirth
Noup of Noss
Linga
Scalloway
B9073
Ham
Scalloway
Wadbister
Cheynies
Ward of Bressay 226
Feadda Ness
Cradle Holm
Papa
Uradale
Gulberwick
Torshavn, Seydisfjördur, Bergen, Hantsholm (seasonal)
To Aberdeen & Kirkwall
Kirkabister

North-East and Central Mainland

Will you come oot fae da toon da-day
An we'll hear da laverick sing,
An waatch da stenshakker dart owerda broos
O da hills a Lunnasting.

From *Macarism* by Rhoda Bulter.

The Guide now returns to Brae in Delting and completes the route around the North-East Mainland before continuing south. One of Shetland's largest villages, Brae has grown rapidly during the past 20 years. It makes a good base to stay while exploring the North Mainland and Muckle Roe. The village's setting is very attractive, a scatter of buildings clustered around the head of Busta Voe where only a narrow strip of land divides it from the head of Sullom Voe to the north. Streams flow down from the high moorland to the east and there is rumoured to be gold among the fine shingle sand of the beach. But little shelters the village from bitter northerly winds in winter. Ancient prehistoric sites are found in the hills all round Brae and there must have been many more along the shoreline, long since lost under more recent building, but a broch site still survives at nearby Burravoe.

The oldest buildings are around the old pier, looking across the water to Busta House, one of Shetland's oldest buildings, now a fine hotel. There are legends and stories galore about this lovely old house and there are few more pleasant places to spend an evening in Shetland. A number of traditional crofthouses stand among more recently built houses along the main road and several housing estates present a rich variety of architectural styles. Brae is well served by its two garages, large shop, hotel, building centre, leisure centre, boating club and post office. There is an Indian take away, community office and a health centre with doctor and dental practice nearby and a residential

Busta House, Brae.

care centre for the elderly. Near the *Mid Brae Inn* there is one of Shetland's rare older tree plantations.

A junior high school has been built near the modern swimming pool, replacing an older one which has been imaginatively converted into the community hall. The former hall now looks incredibly small and inadequate, standing below the present-day road surface opposite the shop and the junction with the Sullom Voe turnoff. The tendency in Shetland to repair roads by simply adding layer upon layer of road-surfacing materials has resulted in many properties ending up below road level, and is only now beginning to be addressed. You can explore several small roads leading away from the main road through Brae, south to Burravoe, west to the white-painted, airy Church of Scotland or north for Northbrae and the chapel and east up into the hills, past the graveyard and the new all-weather sports pitch behind the school.

Brae had a lively role to play during the Second World War, with a sea plane base only a few miles up the road. Sullom Voe reaches right down to Northbrae and a small arm extends east into Voxter Voe just to the north. Here Valayre Burn races from its source in the hills above, down a spectacular gorge, into the sea below. Recently improved access, stiles and footpaths enables you to walk among the relict trees, some re-introduced roses and honeysuckle growing in places along its lower reaches. Voxter Outdoor Centre, a former manse, used during the last war as a small field hospital, stands at the voehead. It offers excellent residential and environmental study facilities to groups. There is a walled garden with apple and cherry trees. Trondavoe, a little to the north, once had an old smuggling hole, but it was filled in many years ago. Scatsta airport, a little further on, was constructed to service the sea plane base during the war and now serves the oil terminal, said to be the largest in Europe. It was from here that Shetland's excellent local weather forecasting service was produced; now sent up from Aberdeen, 200 miles away.

When T.M.Y. Manson wrote his *Guide to Shetland* in 1932, he said of this area, 'the principal feature of the panorama is the remarkable Sullom Voe, which winds for eight miles...its suitability for boating may here be emphasized and visitors at Brae will be able to enjoy it to the full'. What a contrast today! The oil terminal site dominates the area, especially at night, when it twinkles like a distant city, but by day little is seen that doesn't nestle into the low hills behind. The only real intrusion is the small cluster of flare stacks which burn by day and dominate the sky by night. A lurid, pulsing glow can often be seen over the area from quite distant parts of Shetland. But critics are often accused of ignoring the flares out in the oilfields beyond the horizon, where many more times the amount of gas is flared off and the energy waste is far higher.

It is hard to believe, coming fresh to Sullom Voe, what a remarkable alteration to the land and sea here was effected by the building of the terminal. Half of Orka Voe, a colossal area of sea, was filled in and built over, with enormous technical and engineering difficulties, subsidence, saturation, drainage and slippage. One oil worker told me that he left a lorry parked on a section of infilled land one night and that the next day it had sunk and vanished completely into the waterlogged depths. Yet the terminal stands and functions as if it was built entirely on terra firma. The seashore and seabed nearby are monitored regularly for pollution and so far, the results published have revealed remarkably clean beaches, compared with other oil terminals. Otters frequent the area and the road to the terminal has a hazard sign at one point which warns about otters crossing; and they frequently do.

East of the head of Garth's Voe, a small crofting settlement once flourished, but in the Second World War it was selected as the site for an RAF base. The picturesque township of Graven was 'swamped in a sea of concrete' as one local man put it. Sixty years later, much of the concrete is still there. The sizeable Burn of Laxobigging flows out to sea here, swollen by water drained from an immense area of hills and moorlands which stretch up as far as Crawsiller Knowe (*crawsiller* is the Shetland dialect word for mica) overlooking Dales Voe to the east.

From Sullom Voe the road crosses north of Graven to

Firths Voe on the east side of Shetland and meets the A968 road from Voe to Toft and the ferry to the Northern Isles. A huge construction camp was built here for the building of the terminal, now all demolished bar a sports centre. The village of Mossbank, beyond, was an important business centre in the north, visited every fortnight until the 1970s by the ferry, *Earl of Zetland* from Lerwick, and it was formerly the crossing point for the ferry to Yell. Several large, uninhabited islands lie in Yell Sound not far away. This community perhaps more than any other suffered from the 'oil invasion' as it came to be known. Masses of extra housing and facilities were built for the incoming oil workers and a huge new school replaced the older one. But as the oil pace slowed, employment was strategically reduced and the population fell, leaving empty dwellings, an altered landscape and an uneasy community which is slowly picking up the threads and gearing into a new identity and dynamism.

An interesting story is told of an old woman who lived in a crofthouse on the south side of the hill overlooking Firths Voe. Many years ago she began to behave in a very strange way, coming out of her house and shouting and screaming at some sort of invisible intruders. She railed at them for bringing their machines onto her land and ordered them off. Frantic with rage and wretchedness she bewailed the mess that they were making of her beautiful fields. It was assumed that she was losing her mind, and few paid any attention. But many years later, when an oil pipe was laid across that stretch of ground, with diggers churning up the ground for months as the work progressed, a few folk remembered her anguish and wondered whether the invisible machines she had 'seen' and screamed at, were some kind of premonition. The crofthouse where she lived became a ruin and the fields overgrown.

The new ferry service goes to Yell from Toft, another mile or two round to the north, and the road continues north to Brough beyond. Toft was once an old port for Leith traders and whalers; now a fine carpark, a waiting room with toilets and a telephone stand above the beach and queues form and manoeuvre into line for each ferry crossing. The hill to the west is oddly green; evidence of massive reseeding after the huge construction camp was demolished. Three disused sports centres were not demolished, however, and it may be some time before their unsightly bulk vanishes from the scene.

Looking north-east along Dales Voe towards Fora Ness.

Cars returning from Yell take the A968 south to Voe. The road follows Shetland's east coast here, climbs up the north face of the Hill of Swinister, then turns south at a sharp, dangerous bend overlooking dramatic Foraness, joined to the shore by a double tombolo. It runs under the steep shadowing bulk of Dales Lees to the west, alongside Dales Voe with its saltmarsh at the head and salmon cages offshore, sheltered from easterly storms by the narrow barrier of Easter Hill of Dale. From here it is only a few miles to Voe, past a scattered community of crofts, small farms and houses. Until the late 1990s the scene was dominated by the marvellous white blades of the Sussetter Hill aero generator. Technical problems curtailed its useful life however and after it was sold, despite rumours of it being shipped to the third world, in the end it was blown up.

The narrow road which leaves the A968 and leads north-east up Gardie Hill carries on and drops over into Collafirth, a tiny community still holding a marvellous air of old Shetland. Separated by the long heather-covered ridge of Garda Ness from the wide road through Dale, with the broad valley and expansive views, the area is like another world. The old croft of

Quhamm is now derelict, but until not long ago still bore the old thatched, or 'tek', roof, with its moulded chimney pot, and a well-tended kale yard. From just beyond the cluster of houses by the shingly and rocky shore you can walk right round the coastline into Swinning on the east side of the ness. The cliffs are steep in places but the seascapes and seabirds make for breathtaking views. Look out for otters and seals.

Having detoured north from Brae via Sullom Voe and Mossbank and down to Collafirth, the Guide now returns to Brae and describes the route to Voe from there. These routes, the A968 and the A970, meet at Tagon, just north of Voe.

A mile south of Brae on the way to Voe, a small road leads off west to Wethersta. Here farms and crofthouses stand looking out across Olnafirth and south-west towards Swarbacks Minn. A small industrial site here has seen many an enterprising business get started. A number of houses have been built in recent years and there are many fine gardens with some splendid newly constructed dry stone walls. Sadly not a trace remains of the old house built here in the 1600s, contemporary with the one at Jarlshof. There can be good walking around the coast here on a fine day, with wide sea views over to Muckle Roe and East Burrafirth.

The hills slope up steeply to the north and the ground to the south drops away from the road to Olna Firth. On the shore, below the road, is the site of one of Shetland's four whaling stations. A cluster of buildings remains where once there was a hive of activity; smoke, steam, smells and noise now only dim memories among a dwindling number of older Shetlanders. But you can still pick up the odd piece of whalebone washed up along the beaches nearby. In spring, the roadsides between Brae and Voe in places are golden with daffodils. Here and there short stretches of the former single-track road can still be seen. One loop near Voe has been signposted as a parking area and is a good place to stop so that you can admire the marvellous views. But exercise caution entering and leaving this lay-by, as traffic often roars past at dangerously high speeds.

The head of Olnafirth supports two settlements, Tagon on the northern slopes and Voe itself around the southern shore. Tagon has a pub in addition to the shop and church and there is a large house, set among trees, which was once a doctor's surgery. The A968 to Mossbank and the North Isles ferries branches off here. A short way north along it stand the local primary school and village hall. Here every August the Voe Agricultural Show is held. Marquees and stalls, cattle and produce competitions and a full programme of events, well supported by refreshments, make this a day worth planning for. Check the date in advance at the Shetland Tourist Office.

Heading south from Tagon, a right turn off the main road leads to Voe, one of Shetland's most attractive villages. The setting is very photogenic and the old buildings a delight, and full of history. The old weaving sheds, the truck system and trade are not so very long gone and the present bakery flourishes. The old post office and shop were altered into a restaurant in the 1990s and one of the weaving sheds was converted into a splendid and spacious camping böd. A number of new houses have been built, some with sizeable trees suggesting a favourable micro-climate. The big house stands squarely above the village among its own large trees, indicating the benefit of good shelter from the south-west.

The route from Voe through to Aith and Bixter, with many smaller settlements, has already been described more fully in the West Mainland chapter.

The Loch of Voe, which flows out into Olnafirth here, is thought to have been the site of Shetland's own ice cap during the last Ice Age. Many glacial features survive in the area and are well worth looking out for. Notice the very large glacial erratic behind the war memorial on the main road, just south of Tagon. There are more around the loch itself, especially on the north and eastern slopes above. A tree-planting project near the loch has created a shelter belt of fine young trees, so the appearance of the surroundings may alter considerably over the next few years.

The road to Laxo and Vidlin and to the ferry to Whalsay and the Skerries joins the main road just south of the Loch of Voe. There is often a cluster of cars parked near the junction. People frequently car-share, or make use of the main route buses, leaving cars at the nearest point for the drive home. You pass a couple of lochs on the south of the road, which from time to time have been visited by migrant birds. So if you are interested, pull off the road and scan the water and the marshy margins for waders. I once saw a purple heron here. Peat banks can be seen here and big, covered peat stacks are often built nearby and visited regularly by their owners for fresh stocks of fuel.

Looking north from near Neap, Kirkabister, towards Valla Ness and Stava Ness.

Heading east towards Laxo, just before you come to the sea, the road to North Nesting turns off south. You can take this route as a fascinating, though slower, alternative to the main road to Lerwick. Massive moorland expanses separate the communities of North and South Nesting. Kirkabister is well worth exploring and has some excellent coastal walking. The view south from almost any point on the Kirkabister road offers fine panoramas of the South Nesting skyline, with the Ward of Bressay and the Noup of Noss rearing dramatically up far behind to the south. A ruined manse dominates the skyline at Kirkabister and one of Shetland's Iron Age promontory forts is found nearer the cliff edge, facing a small island which was once joined to the mainland. Sturdy walkers can take to the coast here and walk right round to Billister. Beware of collapsing cliff edges here; keep well back.

Returning to the North Nesting junction at Laxo, the head of Laxo Voe is interesting, with a wide shingle bar almost sealing it off from the open sea; a stretch of muddy estuary and a prehistoric mound rather like a broch site on the overlooking slope to the west. The wide road to the ferry continues past the hamlet here and the Whalsay ferry pier, a carpark and toilets are off to the right. Watch out if you carry on towards Vidlin, as the new wide road ends abruptly, reverting to a narrow ribbon of single track. In spring and summer the verges of the old road are dazzling with wild flowers, especially orchids. The new roadsides boast little more than gravel and grass.

There is a peaceful quality about this corner of Shetland. The poet Rhoda Bulter was born in a crofthouse near the south-facing shore and gleaned much of her inspiration from the life and spirit of the area. There are a number of famous wreck stories from the wild coastline around it and tales too of smuggling. A road leads off to the hamlet of Skelberry to the right, but the main Vidlin road curves north and passes the loch of Kirkhouse, another good place to scan for birds, but avoid stopping in passing places, as it can disrupt local traffic. The roads to Lunna, Lunning, Swinning and Vidlin meet at a crossroads next to the shop and across the road stands the recently refurbished Vidlin Hall.

Going west past the shop at the crossroads, the road to Swinning climbs gently up and over a hill, dropping down into a broad, peaceful valley full of signs of former cultivation and settlement. Today only a handful of original houses remain, with a few recent additions and conversions. Salmon farming became a major new industry in the 1990s and this voe was ideal for cages. At the end of the road, well-established gardens have managed to support some sizeable trees, including fern elder, oak and beech, unusual species for Shetland. Here too can be seen glacial deposition features and a number of prehistoric sites have been identified nearby. For those with good heads for heights and sure feet, a fine walk can take you north round the coast from here to Collafirth. The slopes are steep and slippery and there are some awkward crossing places where streams cut deep channels as they run over the edge into the sea. The beautiful but deserted steading of Sannick still stands forlornly in a small valley about a mile north of Swinning. The old couple who lived here until recent years, were great local historians and welcomed visitors.

From the Vidlin crossroads continue north if you intend to explore the Lunna Ness road. The road is single-track all the way, with some blind bends and plenty of unrestricted sheep access, so be warned. At first you can see well out across Vidlin Voe, then the route deflects to the west and crosses the

Lunna Kirk, Vidlin.

watershed, dropping down to a sheltered sea, where otters are frequently seen. You get wide views here right across Yell Sound to Ronas Hill and Northmavine. Even the Ramna Stacks can be seen briefly against the sea and sky. As the road curves round into West Lunna Voe, you see a small tombolo and several houses and other buildings. Lunna House, built in the 1660s, dominates the scene and its windows stare out towards Lunna Kirk and the beautiful, sheltered area around it, with its curious scatter of historic ruins. Lunna House was the first base for the 'Shetland Bus', a secret resistance operation run by Shetland and Norway during the Second World War, before it moved to Scalloway, the headquarters being then at Kergord.

Two roads once ran down from Lunna House and both can still just be traced by the rise of an embankment and some stonework on the grassy slope to the north. One went down to the seashore and the other levelled out and followed the contour of the hill round to the east, where almost two centuries ago a beautiful garden was laid out. The terrain is ideally formed for a garden, with a gently sheltering curve of the hill enclosing an arena protected from all the worst angles of wind and facing a splendid view out to the islands across the sound. Now only grass, moss and heather survive.

Lunna Kirk is one of Shetland's oldest and most attractive, with many interesting features. A walled enclosure behind the kirk has some puzzling remains in it, consisting of mounds and banks, thought by some to have been an ancient ecclesiastical site. On the skyline to the south, there is a continuation of the wall, with a small folly at its highest point. Slightly to the north and down at the seashore is a one-time booth, or shop and trading station, above what would once have been a drying beach.

The Stanes of Stofast are worth a special visit by anyone with an interest in geology. High on a peat moor, east of the road a mile or so north of Lunna House, they stand where they once fell, released from the crushing grip of a vast glacier. From a distance they could be a ruined castle; close to, especially if viewed from the south, they resemble a giant sphinx, with a strangely beautiful profile, gazing sternly out to the eastern ocean.

Vidlin is the largest village in this corner of Shetland, with evidence of human settlement here going back many thousands of years. There is a considerable area of level land and the head of Vidlin Voe provides a good, sheltered harbour for boats. The community is a thriving and industrious one, with many successful entrepreneurs among its members. There is a newly built school and village hall and a well-stocked shop and garage. Salmon farming developed on a large scale in the late 1990s here and there are some sizeable farms and crofts. The ferry to Whalsay uses the ferry terminal in Vidlin when wind and sea conditions render the Laxo terminal unsafe.

To reach the tiny, very attractive settlement of Lunning, go right through Vidlin, bearing north where the road to Leveneap turns to the south, then, where the road follows parallel with the shore out to Kirkhouse, look for the sign to Lunning. The steep, single-track road winds up and over the heights here, past the loch of Gerda Water; the views from the top are marvellous, but if you are visiting by car, it makes more sense to stop on your return, when you will be facing the view as you descend. The terrain here is craggy and wild. Make sure you are safely off the road and not blocking entrances or passing places should you stop. A wide pull-off at the summit overlooks the dramatic loch of Longa Water which lies below, with Little Water beyond it, stretching out towards the south, surrounded by a kind of moon landscape of rocks and cliff faces, with the Noup of Noss seen far away in the distance across the sea. There is rough, but excellent walking in this area, which is full of prehistoric remains and ancient place names. The delights of the secret Fora Dale and the remote house of Bonidale are well worth exploring, particularly in good weather.

The road continues eastwards, dipping and twisting, past Gelins Water down into Lunning itself. There is only a small area of level land here and it has been cultivated for centuries. Two ruined mills can be found on the north-facing slopes of the hills to the south, leading up to Mill Loch. Here only a handful of houses and outbuildings stand today, looking east, out towards the west coastline of Whalsay spread out across a stretch of wide, exposed sea. Only a few decades ago, virtually every house here had a thatched roof. A standing stone can be seen here. There is a lovely panorama across the mass of small skerries and larger, uninhabited islands in Lunning Sound. Drivers should note that there is limited parking space. Ask, if you wish to go walking and leave a vehicle, and avoid obstructing local activity. There is no straightforward access to the sea and the coastline is wild and rocky.

This is as far as you can go to the east, so the text now returns to the point where the Vidlin road turned off the main road at the Loch of Voe and heads south through the 'Kames'.

The Kames, a series of long ridges and broad valleys, run almost due north-south down the central mass of Shetland. They were chosen as the best site for a huge wind farm in 2006. The road south from Voe runs between East and Mid Kame. Wide, peat-covered slopes rise up each side to high moors beyond. These heathery, peaty hills have been heavily glaciated and the massive ridges are smooth and steep. Their alignment reflects the underlying geology, revealing the heavily faulted bands of contrasting rock types lying close together like knives in a drawer. Each type has eroded differently, the most resistant remaining as high ridges, while the more easily worn rocks became the valleys in between. The Kames form the continuation of Shetland's 'backbone' of high ridges and moors. It is possible that prehistoric islanders may have retreated from seashore locations and survived in settlements in some of the deeper valleys when the first Norsemen arrived in Shetland. Evidence may lie in the place names such as Pettawater, or 'Loch of the Picts' in Norse terms.

The road into South Nesting turns east off the main A970 and branches south again at the Nesting shop. A small island just offshore to the south-west is connected to the mainland at low tide. This stretch of very sheltered sea is Catfirth and it provided a safe location for a number of naval bases during both world wars. Some of the remains of buildings, bunkers and other features can still be found nearby. There are beautiful sea- and island-scapes off Gletness, on Nesting's southernmost coastline. There is a seemingly unending variety of prehistoric sites and in spring and summer, wonderful wild flowers, especially in May, when primroses blanket the lime-rich fields and banks. The area has several

Looking south-east from near Gletness, South Nesting, towards Score Head and Score Hill on Bressay with Noss beyond.

lochs where unusual waterfowl often feed and a wonderful winding, enchanting coastline much frequented by otters.

South Nesting, with its limestone bands beneath the ground surface, is full of tiny valleys, gorges, peaks and hollows. Vivid green, fertile fields tuck themselves in between knolls and hummocks of limestone outcrops and a wealth of wild flowers gild the roadside verges in summer. Try to visit both South and North Nesting, which are quite different in character, but equally rewarding to the courteous explorer. The best visits can be made to coincide with days when local halls are open for teas and homebakes. As well as crofters and craftsmen, Nesting men were expert seafarers, voyaging around the world in fishing, whaling, trading, naval and merchant navy ventures throughout the centuries. Look out for local history exhibitions featuring some of the more famous characters while you are here.

Nesting is sheltered from the west by miles of high, wild moors and valleys, full of Shetland's marvellous moorland birdlife. But the eastern fringe is more populated and the ground more cultivated. There are some particularly dramatic corners, such as the Quoys Burn, a gorge and tiny melt-water channel which runs almost due north into the hills; Flamister in its high, remote hollow overlooking Catfirth; Gletness, with its dainty narrow headland and multitude of prehistoric sites, just peeping above ground level and Ling Ness, surely among the most exquisite corners of Shetland. The nature of the coastal territory is very special, but here more than in many other parts of the islands, private land ownership controls access. Most landowners are pleased to be asked for permission to walk across their areas, but there can be exceptions. Lambing time is the most likely to be awkward, so be considerate.

The road which links North and South Nesting hugs the low cliffs and skirts the hills to the west, passing beside many old and new dwellings, as well as prehistoric sites of various kinds. Stone walls, old signs of cultivation and drainage indicate times of much higher local populations and more intensive working of the land. At Skellister a side road cuts off to the east providing an interesting detour as it threads through South Nesting. The side road loops back to rejoin the main road at the shop. The Eastern slopes of the Hill of Skellister overlook the wide, sandy, pebbly Muckle Ayre at the head of the West Voe of Skellister. Much of the story of local geology can be told on this beach, where mica crystals sparkle in the edge of the sea and pegmatite, tourmaline and enormous felspar crystals flash among the schist and gneiss pebbles.

A series of headlands reaches out to the north: Tur Ness, Ness of Skellister, Ling Ness and the Moul of Eswick. On a fine day, away across a turquoise sea to the north, the clustered settlements of Housabister, Kirkabister and the dramatic profile of the Neap itself are clearly seen, with the higher Ward of Symbister in Whalsay rising behind them in the distance. In wild weather, the seas that hammer onto the beach can be enormous, as can be imagined from the smooth roundness of the pebbles. The beach at Housabister to the north is not as exposed and the pebbles there are far rougher by comparison.

Return to the junction with the main road in order to follow the guide south towards the Tingwall Valley. The Loch of Girlsta to the east is said to have been named after a Viking maiden who drowned in the loch. It is Shetland's deepest loch, and home to the extremely rare Arctic char, now protected, which are thought to have become established here as the ice retreated, over

10,000 years ago. At the southern end of the loch a narrow road forks east, signed for Brunt Hamarsland, 'brunt' meaning burnt, place-name evidence of the early practice of clearing woodland for use. The hamlet here lies out of sight over the skyline and commands marvellous views over Catfirth. Residents have had splendid sightings of killer whales in recent years.

Just south of the Brunt Hamarsland junction is the settlement of Girlsta with a number of houses scattered on either side of a crossroads. Here one road winds uphill to the west and drops down into Stromfirth and leads finally to Whiteness. To the east, a narrow road leads down towards the sea. The main road carries on south to Tingwall, with the tiny, picturesque croft of Linkster set like an ivory jewel in a green crown to the west, just before the airport runway comes into view. Tingwall airport serves the whole of Shetland as the base for the air ambulance. Scheduled flights also serve the Out Skerries, Fair Isle and Foula, and until 2001, Unst as well. The main road connects here at a large junction, with the road to Walls and the West Side, then curves east, past the Tingwall crossroad and rises up a long hill before descending to Dale and the golf course a mile to the south.

Returning to Girlsta, a short stretch of road leads to where a limestone kiln once operated; part of it can still be seen. Quantities of broken limestone would have been spread, alternating with layers of peat until the kiln was full. It would then have been fired and the resulting ash slaked with water and stored in barrels, ready for use. There are fine views east here across to Wadbister on the far shore, a scene which gradually filled with salmon farming activity in the 1990s. A well-established garden with trees lies at the end of the Wadbister road, which turns off east just past Girlsta. For many years, the owner allowed visits by wedding parties, who wished to be photographed in a colourful, gracious garden setting, a rarity at that time.

Another road turns east after the Wadbister junction. This is the northernmost access to the Tingwall valley and leads over the hill, past one of Shetland's biggest quarries. Laxfirth lies over the far side and as the narrow road bends south towards Strand, it passes by a curious little building with three pointed windows. This was once a school. The road now meets up with the other access road into Strand which left the main road just opposite the Linkster access. As you pass the northern end of the Strand Loch, look out for otters and seabirds in the shallow sea inlet to the left.

The road forks at Strand Loch and a branch forks left near a large number of houses which have been built recently and also passes an interesting building with a large car park. After the grounding of the *Braer* and subsequent oil spill, large sums of money were sent to Shetland by concerned people all over Britain and elsewhere. One initiative which followed was the setting up of an oiled bird unit which was built in Tingwall. The centre is run by an SSPCA officer and injured or oiled birds are taken here and treated. If they recover they are released into suitable habitats and in certain cases flown south to reserves or centres where their future recovery can be monitored in more suitable environments.

The road continues over the hill to the south-east, and down to a T junction with Breiwick signed left and Califf to the right. There are small hamlets and some large farms here overlooking the sea and the oil rig servicing base opposite, an archaeological dig on a prehistoric settlement to the west of the service base here uncovered valuable information about an early archdeacon of Shetland whose *teind*, or tithe barn, once stood here at Kebister.

Retrace your route, turning left at the road which passes between the loch and Tingwall school and hall. There are many lovely gardens in the area and you can often watch Shetland ponies in the fields near the farm, before you reach the junction with the main road to Lerwick. To enjoy the full length of the Tingwall Valley, cross over the main road and continue south towards Veensgarth and Herrislee. The Tingwall Agricultural Museum was established by Jean Sandison in the 1980s in her farm buildings at Veensgarth. The collection includes Shetland traditional furniture, household items, crofting and blacksmith tools, a forge, coopering and wheelwright tools and agricultural implements and machinery. The development of the museum saw a revival of interest in old ways and traditions, leading to a series of folklore evenings which became very popular. These in turn led to interest in reviving Shetland's traditional dances and their links with other Northern and Scandinavian traditions.

The old Tingwall primary school has been modernised and a new village hall built close by. In medieval times, Tingwall Church was the head church for the whole of Shetland. The

Weisdale Voe from Scord of Sound in April snow.

original church was built on a splendid site, on top of a rise in the land. It is thought to have been built around 1136 and dedicated to St Magnus. Like the churches at Ireland near Bigton and Papil in West Burra, it had a tall round tower. This church was replaced in about 1790 by the modern one. The churchyard has some elaborate old gravestones in a mausoleum and a stone sarcophagus. Just past the church there is a recently constructed garden and memorial to a pilot who was killed when an ambulance plane crashed a few years ago.

In Viking times, the Lawting, or parliament, met in Tingwall, giving it its name. The site still exists, though much altered in appearance from the original structure, at the northern end of Tingwall Loch. An interpretive display stands in the nearby car park. A modern entertaining version of the Ting, the 'Althing Debate', occurs regularly in winter, with a programme of topics debated before large, enthusiastic audiences in the local school.

From this point the Guide describes the route north to Weisdale and Kergord, before returning to Tingwall and proceeding to Scalloway and Lerwick.

From Tingwall, the road west passes the small airport and the Planticrub nursery. It rises and crosses a watershed before dropping past the Westing Hotel down into Wormadale with Nesbister below. A viewpoint here allows you to pull off and enjoy stunning views down Whiteness Voe and west across the White Ness and Strom Ness peninsulas, as far as Foula in the distance. Shortly after the Nesbister road turns off to the left, another road leads down into South Whiteness, which is one of the best otter-watching places in Shetland. There is a shop and an old schoolhouse near the junction. Some excellent walks can be enjoyed in the area and superb views can be found from the ridge tops, especially the Hill of Hellister, from which you can see the whole of the Whiteness peninsula.

Just past Whiteness Primary School, the road turns north into Stromfirth, a hidden valley, discreetly guarding many beautiful secrets. There is a route through to Girlsta and Wadbister from this point, skirting one of Shetland's most beautiful lochs, Strom, which is fed by a substantial stream. At the seaward end, it flows with such force out to sea at low tide and the sea enters with such power at high tide, that there has been talk of a tidal energy facility being built here. During the last World War, eggs were sent from Stromfirth, as they were from many other places, to the troops in Europe. One local lass wrote her name and address and a message on one egg. The soldier who received it came to Shetland after the war and met and eventually married her sister; a story still told and loved by her descendants.

There are lovely views south down the voes before the winding road arrives at Weisdale, with its shop, garage and fine jewellery workshop and showroom nearby.

The Weisdale valley is one of Shetland's longest and most magnificent, lying between two sheltering ridges, 800 feet (240 m) high to the west and 500 feet (150 m) to the east. The east-facing hill is scored by water channels and a small corrie can be seen. A spring near here produces water of bottling quality. The Weisdale Burn is almost a small river and it flows to the sea, which here reaches deep inland. You can watch seabirds or even otters, and small whales have been known to enter the shallows. At the head of the voe, the main road west crosses a bridge and continues up the hill. The guide detours here and takes a side road north along the valley floor past the church and manse towards Kergord.

A thriving community once lived along the valley; families tending their crofts, sharing labour and resources as demand dictated. Then the sheep invasion struck. Exceptionally grim accounts of evictions and cruelty in the Weisdale Clearances were described by John Graham, in his well-loved novel *Shadowed Valley*. Many people left the area, some walking over the ridge towards Aith. Bitter tales describe men being forced to demolish their own homes in 1855 and build the Weisdale Mill out of the stone. This building has been converted into the Bonhoga art gallery. The road carries on north past some large tree plantations, known loosely as Kergord Forest. One ruined cottage still stands, deep inside the Lindsay Lee plantation, with a tree growing out of the old hearth; a haunting sight. Originally a house called North House stood here. A new house, built for an incoming farm manager, was named Flemington after the Fleming family who lived there. This was changed to Kergord House later. In 1940, it was used as the headquarters of the Shetland Bus, the name given to the secret operation which ran supplies, agents and resistance workers between Norway and Britain during the Second World War. Guides and Scouts have a camp here and there is a tree nursery at Kergord where rare native species have been propagated with increasing success.

The Guide returns now to Tingwall and takes the road through the Tingwall valley, which runs south from the Herrislee crossroads to Scalloway, winding between broad fields and metamorphosed limestone outcrops to Asta. The narrow road has passing places and entrance ways. The Loch of Tingwall, beloved of anglers, is skirted by acres of marsh flowers in the spring and summer. Waterfowl and waders frequent the loch in spring and summer. Gardens attract migrants and birdwatchers saw an exceptionally rare blue-cheeked bee eater here one year. Loch of Asta, much used by Shetland model yacht racers, is partially bordered by the Asta Golf Course. The road emerges at the Scalloway junction, after passing a bus depot. Scalloway Scord quarry gapes wide to the left.

The limestone-rich, fertile valley of Tingwall has been settled since the earliest times. Ancient lands have been successively farmed and old house sites used for newer ones, each new structure obliterating the former one. On the site of one new house, built over the site where an earlier, traditional crofthouse stood, over 200 prehistoric artefacts were found. These consisted largely of stone tools, bone and pottery. An ancient standing stone, its origins long since lost and forgotten, stands close beside the road; a burial cist, uncovered by accident in a quarry, can be found not far away. Several ancient structures border Tingwall and Asta lochs and a large burnt mound stands opposite the bus depot close to the Scalloway junction. A broch was discovered relatively recently during house construction work in Scalloway itself.

Some think of Scalloway as the jewel in Shetland's crown. There can be few finer settings to any settlement than the marvellous backdrop of harbour and islands. The traditional approach to this large village, or small town as some prefer to see it, is from Lerwick, and down the Scord, the steep, winding descent from the ridge of hills between Shetland's east and west coasts. Buses and cars stop here so frequently for the stunning views that a layby and interpretive panel were eventually installed to accommodate them. Scalloway fringes the heads of two adjacent bays and the balance of land and water, influenced by the ever-changing skyscapes, is mesmerising. Islands lie scattered across a silvery expanse of water, boats and harbour features, buildings and farmland combine to set a splendid scene, crowned with the gaunt remains of its old castle.

Scalloway Castle, built by forced labour, was completed in 1600, and stories abound concerning Earl Patrick Stewart who lived here for a few turbulent years. The *Court Book of Shetland* 1615-29 has survived four centuries, recording civil and criminal trials which took place here. Theft, murder, assault and even alleged witchcraft featured among the crimes of the day. The Castle, though ruined, is accessible and has an excellent interpretive display on the ground floor. Originally four-storeyed, the castle has fine turrets with chequered corbelling, vaulted kitchens, sturdy cellars and a great hall which can all be explored. Fine views over Scalloway and the islands can be seen from the upper-storey windows.

A large, modern secondary school has been built beside the earlier one and the primary school shares the same site. The swimming pool and leisure facility alongside is open to the public at regular times and is a good place to repair to should the weather turn unfriendly. There are several shops, including the two main stores which open from early morning

Scalloway Castle.

until late at night and on Sundays too. There is what locals claim is Britain's best fish and chip shop as well as pubs, a hotel and several eating places. The recently built North Atlantic Fisheries College stands prominently across the bay at Port Arthur and apart from the study and training facilities, offers an accommodation block, restaurant and evening film and lecture facilities throughout the year. The former knitwear factory is the chosen site for Scalloway's new museum and Shetland Bus exhibition.

Scalloway Museum, established and run by volunteers, is well worth visiting. There is a range of interesting displays and exhibits, which are constantly being revised and improved. Most significant is the feature on the 'Shetland Bus'. Scalloway played a key role in the running of the operation. A total of 206 missions were carried out during the early 1940s, landing ammunition and secret agents by night in Norwegian fjords and bringing back refugees and resistance workers. Prince Olaf's slipway, not far from the Museum, commemorates this link between Shetland and Norway.

Spend time too, simply walking through Scalloway,

Da Bulwark House, Scalloway.

exploring the streets and houses. The Bulwark is a beautifully restored former booth hugging the very edge of the waterfront near the harbour. The old Scalloway Haa, built around 1750 for the Scott family, still stands imposingly within its walled and stepped surrounds. Stop to read the curious plaque on a house wall along the street nearby.

It is only seven miles from here across the hills east to the present-day capital, Lerwick.

TRONDRA AND BURRA ISLES

A slash of metamorphosed limestone slices right through the north-eastern corner of Trondra and outcrops here and there in other parts of the island. This creates fertile soils in some places, and a remarkable variety of wild flowers in spring and summer. The bridge from the Mainland to Trondra was built 30 years ago, close to the north-eastern corner of the isle. The population had begun to decline seriously and though there was divided opinion about the wisdom of a bridge, there is no going back now and the island is seeing an increase in housebuilding and people moving back again. There are some important local prehistoric sites and a vast heritage of local stories and memories from harder, more self-sufficient times gone by. A new public hall helped restore island confidence and many a fine night of music, dance and feasting has taken place there since it was built. Burland, with its imaginative and popular Crofting Trail, is one of Trondra's treasures. Shetland cattle, ponies and sheep graze close at hand and various poultry species including Shetland ducks, geese and hens range freely around the outbuildings. There is a fine traditional Shetland boat-building workshop and a restored mill here.

The twin bridged islands of East and West Burra lie to the south of Trondra. The rocks of the islands are heavily metamorphosed. Pebble beaches abound and here you may find examples of most of the local rock types, broken into small pieces and polished by the sea. Summer reveals the island in its most flamboyant flowering beauty; many birds nest along the shores and on the open ground, so watch where you walk and try not to disturb them. Shetland's oldest swimming pool, a natural rock pool extended years ago by concrete walling, still remains, where Shetland's first lifeguard kept watch in the summer and fishermen and their children learned to swim in safety; a skill which may have saved many lives over the succeeding years. Shetlanders love Burra especially for its wonderful beaches; Meal Sands and Minn at Papil attract large numbers of local people on hot, summer days and the swimming is exhilarating!

These islands were intensively settled over thousands of years. They have a strong fishing tradition and a large proportion of local families still live by fishing, salmon farming or fish processing. The islands are thought to have been chosen for early Christian settlements, judging by the number of early Christian carved stones which have been found. The most famous is the Monks' Stone, found in the churchyard in Papil. The original stone is now displayed in the Shetland Museum. There are several workshops and salmon and mussel farms, a garage, repair workshop and petrol station, as well as a large number of crofts.

Burra is gradually becoming a dormitory for Lerwick workers. Since the coming of the bridge in 1971, new waves of house building have swept through the scene. It is a place to walk, rather than drive, round. The Viking name of 'Hamnavoe', meaning sheltered harbour, makes it virtually certain that there was once a Norse farm, or more than one, nearby. But the remains of these probably lie buried beneath the walls of present-day crofthouses such as Branchiclett and Mail. The old fishing cottages of Roadside are especially attractive, with their wrought-iron fences and geranium- and begonia-filled porches. One tiny workshop is beautifully decorated with symmetrically arranged sea shells.

The old and new schools overlook the village. Hamnavoe itself has only made relatively recent concessions to cars and roads. Sheep ruled up to virtually every doorstep (they still sleep on some, as is evident on the morning after by the scatter of droppings, or 'sheep's pirls'!) and some houses still have no gardens at all; standing white-walled and trim surrounded on all four sides by grass right up to all four walls, like toy houses on green velvet cloth. A maze of tiny paths threads among the houses to this day and are still in regular use. Sadly the big new shops in Lerwick have taken their toll on local services and Hamnavoe has lost three shops in recent years, including an excellent local butcher's shop. The remaining shop and post office is well stocked and welcoming.

The village harbour is protected by a promontory terminating in Fugla Ness with its lighthouse. Walk out here on a summer's day, when the turf is blanketed with sea pinks, and imagine the same scene in winter when white seas rise like mountains and smash against this sheltering barrier, tossing huge rocks about like matchboxes. As you gaze back across the harbour at the clusters of houses old and new that glint in the sunlight, imagine the scene a hundred years ago, when no fewer than three fishing stations operated from here. There are traces of prehistoric settlements, several burnt mounds and also the site of a souterrain.

If you have time, explore more of Burra and contrast the bleak, windswept moors with the other settlements to the south of the island. There is a wide, open stretch of rocky moorland between Broch and Toogs, where Arctic terns nest in spring, so please give the birds a wide berth if you are here at nesting time. Broch, Toogs, Houss, Bridge End and Papil display a variety of houses, old and new, ranging from traditional crofthouses notably, the restored buildings of Easthouse and small bungalows to ostentatious villas, scattered across a truly beautiful landscape. Perfect views from here take in small hills, tiny valleys and hollows; a maze of islands and headlands, the massive bulk of the Clift Hills to the east and the open sea with the stark peaks of Foula in the centre of the western horizon. Fine walks can be had round Kettlaness and Symbister to the south and Brunaness to the north. Many a tiny track leads over to isolated dwellings and most of the shoreline is walkable, affording access to some of Burra's wilder, dramatic corners.

On a fine day, take the track south uphill from the road to Heogaland and stand by the underground reservoir on the summit. From here there are uninterrupted views across the tapering headlands of East and West Burra, over a pattern of islands as far as Fair Isle in the south, right round to Foula in the west and the whole face of West Mainland to Scalloway and the hills beyond to the north. To the east lies the

The Monks' Stone of Papil.

Fugla Stack and The Heugg to the south of West Burra.

massive southern backbone of Shetland, the Clift Hills, with the sheltered Clift Sound at their feet. The great steep slopes are uninhabited and raw in their wildness, only the wide Quarff valley breaking through their bulk a little to the north.

All the smaller islands are sadly no longer lived in. Hildasay, Oxna, Papa, South Havra, Linga and Langa – their names ring like faint bells, tolling the passing of a distant age, with all the history of centuries of family life and struggle, the fishing, the croft work and knowledge that went with it.

Retracing our steps to cross the Trondra bridge, we return to East Voe and the Shetland Mainland. A small side turning to the right leads to Uradale and the beautiful natural gorge and Burn of Sundibanks, immortalised in a lovely Shetland song and clad in a mass of primroses every spring. A fine walk begins from the shore here and leads along the ridge to the south into Wester Quarff, a route tramped regularly by the Quarff folk many years ago. High up on the horizon to the east, are the gaunt outlines of two buildings. These were built in 1938 to carry Shetland's first ultra short-wave telephone link with mainland Scotland.

LERWICK

The route from Scalloway to Lerwick offers you two choices. You can go the 'north route', turning right onto the main road at the Brig of Fitch, passing Dale golf course and Gremista farm. Or, after leaving Scalloway and passing the Scord Quarry, you can fork right just over the hill and take the old 'Black Gaet' route, the B9073, turning left for Lerwick at the 'sooth road' junction. The north route is about a mile longer, but if you enjoy golf, then a few hours on this course offers a real challenge. The green hillside here is sheltered from the prevailing southwesterlies, at least a little, and if you look closely, you can see the route of Lerwick's first 'meal road' north, faintly visible crossing the greens and rising to the brow of the hill to the left. But there are eyes watching you as you play. Birds, especially crows and occasionally seagulls, have taken to swooping down and snatching up golf balls, flying off with them and dropping them far away in the heather moors around!

Lerwick, Shetland's capital, grew because of the shelter provided by the island of Bressay against the wild winter seas and storm waves which lash the east coast during the year. Bressay Sound is a perfect natural harbour, valued by sailors for centuries for its shelter and accessibility from both north and south. To this day, incomers arriving to live in Shetland are called 'sooth moothers' in reference to their having arrived via the south mouth of the harbour.

Trading posts grew up where visiting ships could do business and as more and more buildings followed, the development towards a town became inevitable. Today giant cruise ships lie at anchor in Bressay Sound, where Viking adventurers, Dutch and German trading vessels and French men of war sheltered hundreds of years ago. Today, small boatloads of tourists are ferried ashore from the visiting floating hotels of cruise ships to sample the delights of the town and the best of Shetland's produce, contributing greatly to the islands' economy. The town is constantly evolving as businesses come, change and go, buildings are altered, and streets and harbours are transformed by modern facilities and features.

The town of Lerwick dominates life in Shetland, (according to many country folk, far more than it should!) and the steady 'drift to the toon' has swelled both the population and the proportion of resources which have to be spent on it. Yet the town is barely 300 years old, Scalloway, the historic

Lerwick and Bressay Sound from Ward of Bressay.

capital, having been gradually eclipsed as Lerwick's trade and population grew. Here, the Shetland Islands Council have their meetings and departments; the hospital, Shetland's largest secondary school, two large primary schools and Shetland College of Further Education all serve the island community.

If your time is limited, try to see the older parts of the town if you can. Visit the beautiful sea front with its wharves and slipways and tiny stone warehouses, known as 'the Lodberries'. Walk through the lanes with their stone houses, winding steps and alleyways. Some lucky folk live here, but others think them not so lucky, fearing damp and salt water seepage, battering from the east during storms and even, it is claimed, fish down the chimneys in exceptionally savage storms! The Lerwick lanes still hold echoes of the past and you can wander all day through the tiny narrow stone-bound ways between some of Lerwick's oldest houses, up and down the face of the once-long-ago sea cliff and hillside, from 'Hillhead' as it is still called, to the sea and back.

Explore Fort Charlotte, the Cromwellian star-shaped fort built in 1665 to subdue the Dutch, who burned it down in 1673. The fort was built on a high sea cliff, and would have dominated

Lerwick Town Hall, waterfront and the Bressay ferry from Victoria Pier.

the whole area as the tiny settlement of Lerwick clustered below and to the south, along the shore. The fort lay in ruins until 1782 when it was rebuilt and equipped with guns, parade ground and barracks. Shetland's first-ever 'proper' road, built as part of the fort's requirements, led from the fort up to the Knab overlooking the sea. The newly built Shetland Museum is a must for those who have several days to spend in Shetland. Here you can walk among state-of-the-art displays, look up at real boats, hung from the roof, see a reconstructed 'extinct' Shetland pig and a leatherback turtle; a working lighthouse and a thousand and one stunning exhibits set in the superbly designed new galleries. The Shetland Archives share the same site and have vastly more space and facilities than their earlier premises permitted. You can enjoy the art exhibition space and eat in the new restaurant overlooking the old dock, which has also been restored. Visit the Shetland library, which has a new Learning Centre with 16 computers as well as books of all kinds. You can make use of their Shetland room and research old newspapers on the microfiche equipment. There is also the Shetland Family History Society centre nearby where descendents of former Shetland families can spend time searching for information about their own family histories.

There is a beautifully restored and laid-out interpretive facility in the Böd of Gremista, birthplace of one of Shetland's famous sons, Arthur Anderson, founder of the P&O shipping

Bressay Sound and The Lodberries, Lerwick, at dusk.

company. The adjacent beach was once used for drying fish. Don't miss Lerwick's Clickimin Broch, a ruined prehistoric fort, at the seaward end of the loch, which you can get right inside. There is a footpath all round the loch, from which you can observe a remarkable range of visiting waterfowl and waders each year. Otters feed and play here too and, though shy, sightings are frequent, especially in the early morning and late evening. You can enjoy a swim if you feel inclined, or a fitness session at the Clickimin Leisure Centre and refreshments afterwards.

Shetland gears up for its visitors with a crammed programme of events, exhibitions and special displays in the summer months. The local museums open new displays and in Lerwick the Islesburgh Exhibition, held in the community centre, celebrates a glorified, simple, happy past. It features old open hearths, or the later 'Modern Mistress' or 'Victoress' iron ranges, the framed pictures of the *Gospel Ship* and wooden glove- and sock- stretchers. It was a life of few possessions, a life ruled by weather, seasons and animals, dependent on family members and good neighbours to cope with peak croftwork periods, help in emergencies and join in celebrations. The reality was probably considerably harder and more gruelling, but nevertheless many former crofters admit to missing many aspects of their previous lifestyles. Here you can watch spinning and Fair Isle and lace knitting, listen to local fiddlers and learn Shetland dances. Look for the spinning wheels with their different styles; the 'tushkar' which was used to cut peats and the 'kollie' lamp whose light illuminated the interiors of Shetland homes long before gas or electricity arrived.

In the summer there are often guided tours of the town which are very informative and often entertaining as well as interesting. Maps and guides to walks in Lerwick, plus advice on routes, are available from the Tourist Office. Always check here to find out what performances, local shows or special events are on during your stay. Free leaflets are produced about the different areas and island topics of interest.

Armed with the latest information on eating places and watering holes (for the refreshment scene in Shetland can change from year to year), explore passageways and arches, stopping now and then to refresh yourself in a café, coffee house or bar. Some of the latter, *The Lounge* in particular, are famed for their live, spontaneous music-making. You might hear an Irish whistle, a guitar, a Shetland fiddler or a visiting musician from far away, come to sample the magic of local music-making.

Shoppers can wander from the sublime to the ridiculous in terms of novelties, warm woollen underwear of the old style and wonderful hand knits. Shops selling Shetland lace scarves, fingerless gloves, locally made pottery and jewellery rub shoulders with others selling plain, practical supplies for all four seasons. Ships' chandlers, excellent charity shops and hardware stores make for even more exciting exploration.

The town was established during the days of fish trading and the industry is as alive today as it has ever been, but the technology has changed beyond all recognition. The seafront itself can be a wonderful place to walk, investigate or just sit and soak up the atmosphere. A marvellous variety of vessels passes through Lerwick during any one year and the Esplanade is a great place from which to observe and enjoy them. There are boats from every corner of the globe, whether oil-related, survey vessels, cruise ships or cargo ships. Fishing boats all bear the registration codes of their ports of origin: L.K. is Lerwick, B.F. is Banff in Scotland

Detail of fishing boat, Lerwick Harbour.

and any passing fisherman will cheerfully tell you the home port of other vessels. Look out for marine protection vessels in their pale grey-green paint; even the Greenpeace ship *Rainbow Warrior* visits occasionally. Yachts, speedboats, rowing boats and, grandest of all, the Bergen three-masted schooner *Statsraad Lehmkul*, are frequent sights.

There are few greater pleasures in Shetland's capital than an exploration of the waterfront, both old and new; from the small boat harbour where the splendid replica Viking galley *Dim Riv* and the beautiful *Swan*, a restored zulu fishing boat, as well as the lifeboat and a score of other craft are moored, to Holmsgarth where the big Aberdeen ferries anchor. For the uninitiated, fishing boats and boats of all kinds are an immensely exciting spectacle, not only by day, but at night as well. The traditional darkness of the sea at night is a thing of the past; now you look out not over the pitch black, moonlit or starlit sea, but over a dark expanse filled with shimmering reflections and a dazzling array of lights, warning buoys and coloured navigation lights, some flashing at different speeds.

Lerwick has expanded so far from its original seafront settlement that a number of crofting townships and farms have been engulfed with houses and other buildings. Sound, once a peaceful crofting settlement, where smoke drifted from a handful of small houses and cattle grazed between rigs of corn and kale, is now home to thousands of people who live in the housing estates of Nederdale, Sandveien and Ackrigarth and the private estates of Fogralea, Murrayston and Westerloch and the large villas crammed into the steeper slopes above. Shops, a garage, community centre and a large primary school cater for growing local needs. More expansion is likely in the years ahead. A glorious sandy beach, the Sands of Sound, still soaks up the sun to the east here and the flower-strewn grassy approaches are well used and much loved.

There is an enjoyable walk along the sea road here from the roundabout out to the Ness of Sound with good birdwatching and fine views across to Bressay. At the ness itself there are extensive wartime remains; old bunkers and crumbling concrete foundations can make for some hazardous but interesting exploration. The wide, sweeping fields and attractive tree-clustered farmhouse of Seafield add greatly to the graceful proportions of the scene but the threat of more housing developments is ever present.

ISLE OF NOSS
BRESSAY
TRONDRA
LERWICK
Scalloway
0
1
2 km
0
1 mile
Fora Ness
Kebister Ness
Stacks of Vatsland
Holms of Vatsland
Easter Rova Head
Holm of Beosetter
Outer Score
Inner Score
Score Head
Score Minni
Bars Geo
Blue Geo
Holm of Gunnista
Ness of Beosetter
Elvis Voe
66
Aith Ness
Minni of Aith
Aith Voe
Baa Berg
33
White Hill
Sweyn Ness
Sand Wick
Gunnista
Hill of Gunnista
Heogan
Bay of Heogan
Lochs of Beosetter
Globa
Loch of Aith
Bruntland
Voe of Cullingsburg
Bay of Cuppa
Loder Head
Rules Ness
Geo of Vatsie
To Out Skerries
Brugarth
Wormadale
A971
Hoove
Catwalls
Swinster
Laxfirth
Oiled Bird Unit
Houster
Dales Voe
116
Hill of Grimista
Loch of Kebister
Hill of Herrislee
135
Veensgarth
Strom Ness
Stromness Voe
White Ness
Whiteness Voe
Point of Nebister
Nesbister
Hill of Grista
Broo Loch
Loch of Grista
Grista
North Setter
Law Ting Holm
T I N G W A L L
Setter Hill
South Setter
Loch of Ustaness
Loch of Garth
Loch of Tingwall
Hill of Fitch
Hill of Dale
Böd of Gremista
A970
Gremista
Bressay
Bressay History Centre
Gardie Ho.
Maryfield
Hill of Setter
Setter
Everby
Loch of Setter
Ander Hill
Mansie's Berg
Papil Geo
Clingri Geo
Noss Sound
Visitor Centre
Gungstie
North Croo
Hill of Pundsgeo
The Cletters
107
Loch of Houlland
128
Loch of Asta
Asta
Neugles Water
Brig o' Fitch
Hill of Fitch
83
Loch of Clickimin
Fort Charlotte
A970
A969
Voe of Levaneo
Clodisdale
Hoyersta
Uphouse
Brough
Loch of Brough
Noss National Nature Reserve
Point of Heogatoug
180
The Rump
Noss Head
Noup of Noss
Rumble Wick
Nesta Vo
Voe of the Mels
Loch of Burwick
Houlland
Outnabreck
Mossy Hill
Gossa Water
Clickimin Broch
Brei Wick
The Knab
Sound
The Glebe
Hoove
Pettyfirth
Loch of Grimsetter
Hellia Cluve
Bur Wick
Berry
The Scord
Run Hill
Loch of Wick
Hill of Shurton
175
Sandy Loch
A970
Sound
Taing of Ham
Ham
Wart
Wadbister
Wadbister
Millburn Geo
Huster Roo
Barn Stane
Hill of Setter
Geordie's Holes
Holm of Ness
Geos of Hovie
Feadda Ness
Point of Hovie
North Atlantic Fisheries College
Scalloway
East Voe of Scalloway
B9073
Seafield
Loch of Trebister
Voe of Sound
Grey Head
Ward of Bressay
226
Loch of Seligeo
Seli Geo
Grut Wick
Green Head
Grostane
Bersa Hill
Garths of Sand
Gulberwick
Flossy Loch
Lang Lochs
Easterhoull
Uradale
Sundibanks
Ness of Trebister
Ness of Sound
Dainaberg
Hevdi
Lourie's Stane
Kirkabister Ness
Kirkabister
Ward Hill
Mossy Hill
Gulber Wick
Setter
The Nizz
Ovluss
Daal
B9074
Loch of Brindister
Hill of Brindister
Ness of Setter
75
Brindister
Sand Vatn
Round Point
Burland
Crofting Trails
Loch of Couster
165
The Ord
Hamar
Clift Sound
Hogaland
Scrae Field
Milla Geo
Maatrut
Geos of the Ven
Orkneyman's Cave
The Bard
81
Mid Dublin
Giants Leg
Natural Arch
Bard Head
Wester Quarff
Easter Quarff
Foulageo
East Voe of Quarff
To Aberdeen and Kirkwall
To Bergen, Torshaven, Hantsholm and Seydisfjördur (seasonal)

Bressay and Noss

BRESSAY

Without the island's sheltering bulk to the east, Lerwick and its excellent harbour would never have become established. The haven of Bressay Sound has seen ships drop anchor for several thousand years. Bressay should be experienced, if at all possible, from the sea as well as from the land. Enquire about local boat trips which enable you to appreciate the superb cliffs, underwater wildlife, deep sea caves and natural arches for which the island is famous.

Like much of Noss, Bressay is composed of ancient sandstones, with a small but spectacular volcanic vent and related geological intrusions and alterations nearby on its eastern face. Bressay sandstone made first-class building stone and quarries were worked until relatively recently. The stone dykes in Bressay reflect this and many a fine house in Lerwick was built from Bressay sandstone. Very fertile soils have formed over the sandstone, allowing for some crofts and a large farm to become well established. These are connected by attractive but very narrow roads, which require careful negotiating.

From Lerwick, a roll-on, roll-off ferry takes you to Bressay in just ten minutes. Once on the island, the road leads from the ferry point past the Bressay History Centre and Maryfield House (once home to an infamous factor, John Walker, and now run as a hotel) and then comes to a T-junction. A left turn takes you past the large farm and laird's house at Gardie, first built in 1724 and altered a number of times since. You can enjoy clear views of Lerwick's seafront as you approach the north-west corner, with its fishmeal factory, scattered settlements and beautiful coastline. The line of the bridge, or Tunnel was planned to go from here to Lerwick. To the right the road heads south, following the shore as far as the church, then it turns inland to the east. A side road leads north past the shop and the primary school and reaches a number of small crofting townships. You can walk out to Bressay's northern seashore here.

A road runs south opposite the shop, and winds between the higher and lower pastures with their crofts. The highest

Gardie House, Bressay, across Bressay Sound in the last light of a mid-winter afternoon.

point in Bressay is the 'Waart', or the Ward, a hill topped with TV and radio masts accessed by a track leading up opposite the Glebe. The views from the top are quite unbelievable. You can, on a clear day, see Foula to the west, Fair Isle to the south and Unst to the north, as well as many smaller islands and much of the Shetland Mainland besides. Closer to lie the streets and features of Lerwick, laid out like a map below you.

The road continues past Ham, one of the best sites for the tussock grass, or 'tushie girse', which was planted in the 1890s, and ends a mile or so further on at the Bressay Lighthouse. This was built by David and Thomas Stevenson in 1858 but it is no longer manned, and like all the other Shetland lighthouses, has been made automatic.

The remaining lighthouse buildings are to be used for tourist accommodation and the lighthouse interpretive display. On a fine day you can follow the cliff tops east from the lighthouse along as far as the Bard, where a massive First World War gun still stands on its mounting, pointing out to sea. Watch out for the steep cliffs and the collapsing dug-out shelters and bunkers nearby. Bressay had an important role during the

Everby and Ander Hill on the east side of Bressay.

Second World War, with anti-aircraft guns, heavy and light, operating. From here you can see Mousa and the whole east side of the South Mainland stretching away towards Sumburgh.

From the shop crossroads, a road heads due east across the island to Broch and the Noss ferry point. At various points along this narrow single track, access roads lead off to other small settlements. Marvellous walks can be enjoyed all round the island. Ander Hill in the east rises up like a bastion against the bitter easterlies that sometimes blast Shetland. A look-out tower, built by the Admiralty and now ruined, stands at the highest point. From the ridge you can look down on to Cullinsbroch with its collapsed broch, site of an ancient church and graveyard with a tombstone to a Dutch skipper erected in 1636.

It was here that the famous Bressay Stone, mentioned earlier, was found and its replica stands today where the original stood for centuries. The whole surrounding area is full of ancient remains and the ruined crofthouses may well have originally been built from stone taken from the broch and other prehistoric structures nearby.

Shortly before the road terminates at the Noss ferry car park, a track to the right leads to the deserted townships of Grimsetter and Gorie, the latter the site of one of Shetland's first exotic greenhouses, famous for its peaches, plums and grapes; and beyond, south to the ruined settlement of Wadbister. A prehistoric souterrain, or earth house, was discovered here. Excellent walking can be enjoyed among the old settlements and along the cliff approaches.

Look out for displays by the thriving Bressay history group which researches into local history and provides talks and holds exhibitions during the year in their small museum near the ferry pier.

NOSS

Noss, a small uninhabited island just east of Bressay, has some of the most spectacular seabird breeding colonies in Britain and is an essential place to visit. The whole island is now a designated National Nature Reserve and two wardens live here, and research and interpret the island for visitors every summer. There is a small interpretive centre in the restored pony pund behind the former farmhouse of Gungstie. The island is accessed by a small boat which you hail from the Bressay shore. Toilets are provided. Check before you visit, to make sure that you avoid the one day each week when the island is closed.

Composed largely of ancient sandstones and mudstone deposits, the strata is exposed along cliff faces. Weathering has eaten into the exposed rock, creating marvellous ledges and crevices for seabirds to nest in. From the rocks just above sea level, to the thick grassy sward at the top of the cliffs, a range of birds raise their young from spring to summer in a very special hierarchy of nest sites. In the basement of this ornithological 'high-rise block' are the shags and guillemots. Next, on first-floor level, come the razorbills. Higher still, fulmars have set up colonies and here and there are some kittiwakes. Going further up, gannets dominate, creating not only the bulk of the noise but the smell as well. At the top, nearest the edges, come puffins. Further back from the edge and right across the top of the grassy summits of the stacks are the greater and lesser black-backed gulls.

Today's seas break against high sandstone cliffs which were formed as sediments, settling on seabeds themselves beneath the ancient seas of 300 million years ago. Some layers in the

Noss Head across Rumble Wick, Isle of Noss.

sandstones are said to contain minute fossils of primitive creatures living at that time. The Noup of Noss, the highest point of the sheer eastern cliffs, stands 600 feet (180 m) above the sea below and is a landmark on the horizon from far away to the north, south and east. Over the whole island, a thick growth of grass, heather and wild flowers provides grazing for sheep, shelter for ground-nesting skuas, pipits, skylarks and other birds, as well as a wonderful backdrop for visitors. The ruins of long-derelict crofthouses can be seen on the south-facing levels above many acres of former runrigs.

There are ancient remains here too, albeit well buried by time, in particular those of one of Shetland's early Christian churches. There is usually one special open day each year with activities and refreshments. Allow at least three hours for a walk round the whole island, and four if you want to take time to draw, gaze out to sea or rest and enjoy the atmosphere. If you want to enjoy the seabird cliffs but not a long walk, opt for a short boat trip from Lerwick (weather permitting). The close-up spectacle of birds, caves and sealife makes these trips unforgettable. Tickets can be booked and times are posted in the tourist office.

Skelda Voe
Roe Ness
North Havra
Whiteness Voe
Loch of Tingwall
A970
LERWICK
Gardie
To Out Skerries
Bressay Sound
Skelda Ness
The Deeps
Historic Granite Quarry
Hildasay
Langa
Asta
Loch of Clickimin
Visitor Centre
Noss
Noss National Nature Reserve
Noss Sound
Bur Wick
Sandy Loch
156
Brei Wick
Sound
Pettyfirth
Scalloway
B9073
Linga
Scalloway
Ham
Wadbister
Cheynies
Ness of Sound
Voe of Sound
Gulberwick
Ward of Bressay
226
Feadda Ness
Cradle Holm
Papa
Uradale
Loch of Brindister
Kirkabister Ness
Kirkabister
Trondra
B9074
Gulber Wick
Trebister Ness
Oxna
Bruna Ness
Burland
Crofting Trails
Brindister
BRESSAY
Bard Head
Hogaland
Hamnavoe
Broch
Wester Quarff
Meal Sands
Easter Quarff
East Voe of Quarff
Lang Sound
WEST BURRA
Coall Head
Toogs
Clift Sound
Clift Hills
261
Lime Kilns
Bridge End
EAST BURRA
Fladdabister
Papil
A970
Duncansclett
Houss
Clift
Tow
Minn
Holm Field
Ward of Symbister
CUNNINGSBURGH
Aithsetter
Houss Ness
Greenmow
Kettla Ness
West Voe
Royl Field
293
North Voxter
Helli Ness
To Bergen and Hantsholm (seasonal)
Windmill site
South Voxter
South Havra
Hamari Field
Hill of Deepdale
171
256
Catpund
Little Havra
Deepdale
May Wick
Leebitton
Maywick
SANDWICK
Swinster
Sand Lodge
Mousa
RSPB
Ness of Ireland
Hoswick
Sandwick
Muckle Bard
Channerwick
Da Warp and Weft
Cullister
Broch of Mousa
Mousa Sound
Broch of Burraland
Ireland
Channer Wick
Hos Wick
Sand Wick
Bigton Wick
St. Ninian's Isle
Bigton
Levenwick
No Ness
St. Ninian's Chapel
Southpunds
St. Ninian's Bay
Levenwick Broch
B9122
Rerwick
263
Ward of Scousburgh
Colsay
Clumlie
DUNROSSNESS
Spiggie
Scousburgh
Troswickness
Loch of Spiggie
Noss
Skelberry
Dalsetter
Symblisetter
To Aberdeen & Kirkwall
Boddam
Wick of Shunni
Loch of Brow
Voe
Ringiesta
The Ords
283
Hillwell
Croft House Museum
Fitful Head
Quendale Mill
Garth
Bay of Quendale
Exnaboe
Siggar Ness
Toab
Point of Tangpool
Garths Ness
Scatness Excavation
Pool of Virkie
Grutness Voe
Grutness
Scatness
Lady's Holm
West Voe
Sumburgh
Jarlshof
79
Fort
Compass Head
To Torshavn and Seydisfjördur (seasonal)
Voe of Sumburgh
Horse Island
Sumburgh Head
0
5 km
0
5 miles
Sumburgh Roost
To Fair Isle

South Mainland

tawny-gold in Autumn sun, they lie
Like lions asleep.

From *The Clift Hills* by Christian Tait.

From Lerwick, the main road to the south leads to Quarff, Cunningsburgh and Sumburgh, and a host of beautiful places, large and small, on the way. Outside Lerwick you pass the reservoir of Sandy Loch on the right and the residential blocks of the Lerwick Observatory on the left, where weather data is gathered on every day of the year. You may even be lucky and see a weather balloon being released. Just south of the Observatory a narrow road branches left and crosses a stretch of moorland past small lochs. The road drops down towards Gulberwick, and there are marvellous views to the south along Shetland's eastern coastline.

Gulberwick is a scattered community that has grown relatively recently. Much of the scale of the old hamlet has been lost, but a new, more modern effect is now emerging as houses are built and changes made. Often in winter the waves funnel in so furiously that water breaks white far out to sea, giving the bay a wild, white splendour. In 1148, Earl Rognvald and his crew are said to have been driven ashore at Gullbervik and the *Orkneyinga Saga* records the hospitality he enjoyed at a local house and how he teased his hostess. Canoeists enjoy exploring the coastline round here and on calm summer evenings venture out round the headlands, which are full of sea caves and dramatic clefts and arches.

Quarff is the next village to the south after Gulberwick. Something strange has happened to the land here at some point far back in time. Where most of the valleys in Shetland cut north-south, the Quarff valley, or 'Quarff Gap' as it is often termed, cuts straight across the ridge east-west in a deep U shape. Some experts have suggested that the valley may be all that now remains of an ancient river which ran east towards long-vanished inland lakes draining some of the long-lost

The dawn silhouette of Noss and Bressay beyond Ward of Greenmow on the east coast of the South Mainland.

mountain ranges to the far west. A growing community here enjoys some fine views and particularly fine displays of wild flowers in summer. Some houses face the sea to the east at Easter Quarff, some, at the far end of the Quarff turn-off, face west at Wester Quarff and there is a scattering of dwellings alongside the road right through the valley between the two.

There is a fine walk from Wester Quarff north along the high ridge to Scalloway, a route much frequented in days gone by, when Scalloway was the capital and roads did not exist.

Fladdabister is one of Shetland's gems and deserves a special visit. Among a tangle of old cottages, many now derelict, down near the east-facing shore a few miles south of Quarff, wild flowers swarm each spring and summer. There are meadows between the road and the sea worthy of a visit in their own right. Drifts of primroses, celandine and king cups bloom in profusion and a tangle of ferns, bilberries and wild shrubs festoon the steep sides of a beautiful gorge which has been cut by a lively stream running east from the high slopes behind. The flowers are only part of the pride of Fladdabister though. Near to the shore, perched on a jutting rocky outcrop, are the remains of some lime kilns, witness to a thriving limestone-processing business which operated until the 1930s.

The beach here is renowned for the attractive calcite pebbles worn smooth by the sea from rocks torn from the cliffs nearby. In places the rock face by the beach has been smoothed into hollowed curves where the calcite banding is strikingly clear and bright. They lie among strands and bales of seaweed in a lovely curve, facing north-east towards Bressay and Noss. Seals often gather just offshore, watching your every move. You can enjoy coastal walks from here along the shore, both to the north and south. From Fladdabister you can continue south towards Cunningsburgh.

Just before you reach Cunningsburgh, a road turns left signed for Aithsetter. This is the first of several small, single-track roads which wind among the tangle of crofting communities between Cunningsburgh and the sea to the east. They are full of interest and character, as are the local folk, about whom George Lowe, writing in 1774, said, 'The people of this small spot, a stout, hardy race by all accounts the wildest in Shetland.' There is a primary school, an environmental glass recycling venture, garage and shop, and a splendid new village hall which hosts a series of teas and attractions through the summer. Try to find out what is on during your visit and if possible, aim to visit Cunningsburgh on its annual show day in August. Produce of all kinds, livestock, crafts and plants, refreshments and entertainment make the Cunningsburgh Show a great day out.

You could if you have the time spend several peaceful hours following the twists and turns of road and shore here exploring the hamlets of Aith, Gord, North and South Voxter, Aness and Greenmow. Old and new buildings, ancient and modern agricultural methods and techniques stand side by side. Electric cables swing from post to post over new gardens and

Lime kilns, Fladdabister.

rigs of Shetland oats and kale. Hybrid hens scratch alongside Shetland ducks and fast cars glide quietly past a field where you might see an old Ferguson tractor hard at work, its well-maintained engine belying its 60 years of age. But do explore here with consideration and courtesy, as folk are busy, proud of their traditions and wary in case people park their vehicles across passing places, field accesses and driveways.

On a fine day you could walk out to Helliness, a peninsula which reaches far out into the sea to the east. From the trig point on the hill at its tip there are magnificent views back to Shetland's east-facing coastline both to the north and south. A deserted nineteenth-century farm, along with some sturdy stone walls, stands among lush grazing below you to the west of the summit. Excellent views out to sea here cover everything appoaching Shetland from the east and south and Helliness would have been an important look-out point over the centuries.

To continue exploring the South Mainland, leave Cunningsburgh and head south along the A970. The road passes close to a shingle beach as you leave the village and the cliffs, hills rise steeply to the right. One of Shetland's most important

Looking south-east from Setter across Wick of Sandsayre towards Sand Lodge and Ward of Burraland.

archaeological sites lies here. The burn of Catpund courses through a narrow valley here and in its steatite bed lie the marks of ancient quarrying. Bowls and troughs were carved *in situ* and chipped out whole as finished vessels here in prehistoric and Norse times. You can still see the outlines of vessels cut into the rock. Large stone vessels, troughs and bowls of Catpund steatite have been found on archaeological sites far from Shetland.

The road to Sandwick turns left just south of Catpund. The land here sweeps down and opens out to the east below the broad moorland hills to the west. Sandwick itself is a tiny seashore-hugging hamlet of little more than half a dozen houses, but it has lent its name to a much bigger area, consisting of a series of hamlets and settlements, forming a sizeable community between the main road to Sumburgh here and the sea. Look out for the booklet *Footsteps through Sandwick* which was produced by local children and guides visitors through the area. There is a bakery, a shop and garage and a modern junior high school with public swimming pool nearby.

The Mousa ferry leaves from the newly built pier in north-facing Leebitton, with its picturesque miners' cottages, their gardens brimming with colour every summer. Look for seals along the rocky shore here at low tide and enjoy the interpretive exhibition and boat building displays in the building beside the car park. Toilets are available here and if you need refreshments for your visit to Mousa, the shop is only a mile away in Sandwick. The local sandstone can be seen in the many superb drystone walls in the area.

Just beyond the Mousa pier stands the sombre bulk of Sandlodge, one of the larger and longer-lasting lairds' houses, with outbuildings and a sizeable walled garden attached. Sandlodge is still lived in and its lovely garden is tended. Once a year it is opened to the public. The house and grounds are enclosed by splendid dry stone walls or 'dykes'. Beyond that again, is the site of the Sandlodge mine, opened in 1798, with a series of tunnels which ran out a considerable distance under the sea. A vein of rich copper-bearing rock runs close to the shore and under the sea here. Insufficient ore was found to make the mine financially viable, though the quality was said to be very good. A number of companies succeeded each other in attempts to make a decent profit from the ore. But extraction was tricky, costs proved too high and the mine closed. There were various attempts to reopen the mine between 1920 and 1922.

Norse steatite bowl carved into the rockface, Catpund.

Try not to miss a visit to the island of Mousa, now managed by the RSPB, famous for its Broch which is cared for by Historic Scotland. The boat crosses daily whenever the weather permits, during the summer tourist season. Fast walkers can cover the whole island in a couple of hours, but I prefer four in order to explore in comfort. The marvellous scenery, a mass of seabirds and carpet of summer wild flowers. You can often hear seals singing from the wide, shallow bay on the east side, swimming close in with their pups, to stare at you.

Mousa Broch is not only one of the seven wonders of Shetland, but probably of Scotland too, if not Britain. It is the biggest and the best-preserved broch in Britain and the drystone-walled, fortified tower house, built during the Iron Age, is still standing after 2000 years! The scale doesn't really hit you until you are inside it and it has to be seen and, if possible, climbed, in order to be believed. The entrance is narrow and the walls thick. Only one person could ever have entered at a time, allowing the inhabitants plenty of scope for vetting and dealing with intruders. Sit on a stone ledge inside and meditate for a while on the extraordinary skill of the folk who must have built the broch. Peer into the recessed rooms and the stone-lined wells and store chambers. If you do climb up the internal stairs, built between the outer wall layers, watch your step and take your time. This is definitely not an experience to be rushed.

The *Orkneyinga Saga* tells of Erlend the Young, who one spring abducted Earl Harald's mother Margaret from Orkney and fled to Mousa with her. They were there for several months, so there must have been reasonable comfort and provision at that time.

The most exciting time to visit Mousa is in the middle of the night in July. Storm petrels nest inside the stonework of the broch. During the day, the parent birds are out at sea, but they come ashore after dark to feed their young. Shetland summer nights are very light, so the best darkness falls after midnight. The experience of sitting huddled silently inside the broch in twilight and hearing the walls suddenly come alive with sounds is unforgettable. The tiny petrels skim past at high speeds and despite the darkness, and the watching strangers, find their way instantly to the right crack between two stones to locate their own chicks.

Mousa today is uninhabited, the last family having left in the nineteenth century. But when George Lowe visited in 1771 he found 11 families there and reported it as being 'tolerably well cultivated' and 'producing well'. Outside the broch little can be seen of the structures and defensive walls which once formed a crucial part of the whole complex. In Low's time, house foundations and the remains of a big wall were still standing. Today, only ruins remain of once well-kept farm buildings and grass covers the once productive acres. Beware the 'maalies', or fulmar petrels though, as they nest among the tumble of rocks along old stone walls and in old planticrubs. The fluffy chicks look adorable, but if you come too close, you are likely to get spat on and sprayed with foul-smelling, unwashoutable oil. This defence mechanism has been a factor in the successful spread of these birds. The oil, when sprayed onto other seabird species, clogs their feathers and they can suffer as a result. Look out for seals and seabirds on your way back to the Mainland.

If you wish to visit the Broch of Burraland, follow the cliff tops past Sandlodge and south along the cliffs. This broch stands opposite Mousa Broch and formed part of a network of Shetland brochs around 2000 years ago. If you have time, follow the cliffs round and walk out along the No Ness peninsula. There is a spectacular, cliff-hugging, narrow road which terminates at a small turning area. Here are marvellous views of the whole of Sandwick from the sea. A good time to see it is late on a summer's evening, when the hills stand out dark against a luminous sky, turning slowly through a soft version of all the colours in the rainbow as the light fades. Don't leave your car in any passing or turning places here; you could cause considerable inconvenience to farmers and crofters.

From the south-western corner of Sandwick a single-track road winds into the hamlet of Hoswick, clustered tightly above the sea. There is a pub, a knitwear factory and opposite, the Warp and Weft Museum with its excellent café and sales corner. This is a splendid place for a wet as well as a fine day out. The displays give you a real insight into local life in times past, especially about the weaving industry and also the history of the harvesting, or Caain, of pilot whales which stranded from time to time on local beaches. Read some of the copies of proceedings from the famous court case of 1890 where for the first time in Shetland's history, local people won the right to keep what they salvaged and not forfeit it to the laird. There are many old-fashioned machines on display and a large collection of old radios and signalling transmitters from fishing boats and local communications bases.

The great sweeping curve of sand and shingle here forms a popular beach in the summer. This beach was the site of a great 'whale caa' in September 1888, mentioned above. At one point outcropping rocks can be examined to find fool's gold, or iron pyrites, glinting out of them. From Hoswick you can see back across to Sandwick with the old and new schools, swimming pool and the spread of houses of many styles and sizes.

Shortly before the Sandwick road out of Hoswick rejoins the main road to Sumburgh, another small road leads left signed for Rompa. It winds up and over a broad hill and drops down to a tiny handful of houses, strung out along a south-facing slope immediately above Channerwick. The lines of scores of old rigs are clearly visible on the hillside, but none are now in cultivation. The bay here is exceptionally attractive with its massive shingle beach, burns and beautiful meadows. These are packed to the rims with a wealth of wild flowers in late spring and summer. There is a turning place above the houses. The return journey reveals magnificent views north across the whole of Sandwick, No Ness and Noss in the distance, and then drops down to rejoin the Sandwick road. Turn left onto the main Road heading south. As you approach the steep curving bends above Channerwick, you will see disturbed ground where in 2003, serious landslides in the area broke across the road after heavy rain. There was great damage to the roads and Hoswick Bridge and a house were destroyed.

Three separate ways lead down into Channerwick, or Chandrick, as local people call it, but they are narrow, steep and do not make for sensible turning or parking. The view is so splendid that it is tempting to stop, and there is a short section of old road where you can park and enjoy the view. The shingle beach is worth exploring for small specimens of local rock types and the whole area is of interest to geologists. As little as 50 years ago, there was a considerable population at Channerwick. Now many of the older houses are empty. Two particularly fine gorges have been cut by streams flowing down into the bay from the hills of Midfield and Roylfield to the west and north. The road goes south above Channerwick, takes a wide curve to the left in the crook of the valley, then straightens out for a short while. If you look across the bay to the north, the stark

Towards St Ninian's Isle across Bigton Wick, the tombolo and St Ninian's Bay.

slash of a deep geo makes for a striking cliff scene.

From here there are two routes to Sumburgh. This book follows the western route south first, then returns to this point to follow the eastern route south via Levenwick, through Clumlie, Dalsetter and Dunrossness to Sumburgh.

CHANNERWICK TO SUMBURGH VIA BIGTON

The main A970 swings round to the south above Channerwick in a wide bend. At its mid point, take the single-track road which branches off to the west. Passing places have been constructed at various points where road visibility is bad. The road winds and dips across moorland, descending along the side of a narrow valley where picturesque crofthouse ruins bear witness to a past age where every available acre of productive ground was worked. The road bends to the south and Bigton, St Ninian's Isle and the sea to the west come into view. Prepare to branch off into the village, as the road southwards continues well above the village down the 'long straight mile', a section of road as straight as a ruler which is bordered by marvellous flowers in summer.

Bigton is a large village, with a heart of traditional cottages and more recent buildings. The narrow lanes which twist and turn between the buildings are very attractive, each turn revealing a new angle of backdrop scenery: hills, islands and seascapes. Look out for local events advertised in the shop. Bigton has a shop, café and a lively and creative community and there is rarely a weekend without something 'on' in the village hall.

At the northern end of Bigton, a narrow lane runs out of the village and across to the straggle of houses on the south-facing hill ahead. This hamlet is Ireland, and boasts one of the most magnificent views in Shetland, out across St Ninian's Isle and the scatter of islets to the south, with Fitful Head as a stark and sheltering backdrop. There was once a towered church here, one of only three in Shetland. Today nothing remains of the site, and even the precise location of the building has been lost. Some moulded stones of Orkney Old Red Sandstone were found locally, which are thought to have originated as part of the fabric of the ancient church. One is in the Shetland Museum collection, which bears traces of carving and shaping; possibly as part of pillars or other elaborate features.

Maywick lies a mile or two north of Bigton and is beautifully situated and full of charm. A handful of houses cluster together above a north-facing beach, sheltered from the worst of the south-westerlies by higher ground. You can walk along the cliff tops all the way round to Bigton in fine weather, enjoying views which take in both the west side of Shetland and the whole of Clift Sound up to Scalloway. South Havra lies a few miles out to sea to the north-west, with its windmill tower silhouetted against the skyline. A new business started up in Maywick in 2000, producing fine oak-smoked fish. But as with all small, compact settlements, space, especially for parking, is at a premium and local people, their work and animals should come first. So once again, if you have a car ask locally for a suitable place to park, and make it clear you are aware of the problems. Your thoughtfulness will be much appreciated.

The beach itself is very attractive, with both sand and shingle, and is sheltered from the east, west and south, affording calm, peaceful beachcombing during weather in most of the prevailing wind directions. But it is not an ideal place to go during a good northerly blast! The cliff faces are loose and there are frequent small rockfalls. At first you may not see the access to the beach. Turn left between the cottages and look out for a 'sneck', a small gap between the first cottage on the right and the barn to its left. This narrow track leads to a series of boulder steps and the beach below. The access is not a good one for the less mobile and agile. If you are a long-distance walker and have a liking for longer, rougher routes, a beauty begins here and leads you north along the Clift Hills to

Brooch, St Ninian's Isle Treasure.

Quarff, some 15 miles away as the crow flies. It is not advisable to tackle this route alone, or if there is any risk of bad weather.

ST NINIAN'S ISLE

At the south-west corner of Bigton, a road to a large farm turns off at a right angle and crosses a cattle grid, where signs direct you right for St Ninian's Isle along a tiny single-track road. A picnic area and interpretive sign have been provided just behind the beach and there are good views of the island even if you are unable to walk to it. The exquisite sandy ayre with the island and its superb cliff scenery is one of the most famous Shetland scenes. Occasionally breached in winter, the narrow 'sand road' stretching out across the sea is a stunning spectacle. Tides and currents sweeping round the back of the island meet on either side of the ayre, constantly washing sand from the seabed up to form what is technically termed a 'tombolo', a feature of sinking coastlines.

You should allow at least 15 minutes to cross the ayre in reasonable comfort and a little longer back again. Soft sand makes for heavy going, but apart from that, the flat, gleaming silver pebbles of phyllitic schist are so exquisite that you may well lose time gathering them and skimming them over the sea. Turn the pebbles this way and that to see the crystal faces reflecting light differently at different angles, just like the silken weave of a damask table cloth. Allow longer if you wish to climb the sandy track up into the island to see the ancient, ruined chapel site of St Ninian. This lies on the east side of the isle, overlooking the beach, a short way to the north.

The hoard of elaborately chased bowls, spoons and other items since known as the St Ninian's Isle Treasure was found here. Replica pieces are on display in the Shetland Museum and islanders hope to see them restored to the islands, instead of being kept in Edinburgh.

Rabbits have drilled the island thoroughly with their burrows and sheep graze alongside them quite happily. Starlings nest among the chapel walls and all kinds of seabirds frequent the wilder, western cliffs. A walk right round the once inhabited island would take a good two hours or more, but beware dangerous cliff tops, especially in wet, misty or windy conditions.

From Bigton, head south along the "straight mile", past Geosetter with its burn and low trees, favoured by migrants and continue past Rerwick, set above its old rigs. A small sandy beach lies to the south and although (or maybe because) access is far from easy, the beach is one of the quietest and most peaceful in the South Mainland. Take your time as you pass along the road here, as the wild flowers can be particularly dazzling in summer.

Scousburgh with its cluster of dwellings and hotel, lies a few miles south of Rerwick and enjoys wide panoramas across Spiggie Loch and Dunrossness to the North Sea to the east and the Atlantic Ocean to the west. The former post office with its red telephone box stands virtually on top of a large broch site. Vanlop is signed left and the road rises up the hillside and skirts the rising moorland to the east. Fabulous views down over the whole of St Ninian's Isle from here are really worth seeing, especially during a fine sunset.

The road divides at Scousburgh, one branch heading east to Robin's Brae and the A970 to Sumburgh, while the western route goes steeply down towards the sea. A burn flows out from the north through a narrow valley and five ruined water-mills still stand in sequence along its course. A tangle of tiny hamlets lies between the west and east coasts here, connected by narrow lanes. Among them nestle traditional buildings, beautiful gardens and fine fields, concealing countless ancient sites beneath them. This area was densely populated in prehistoric times. The whole area is sheltered from the north by Ward of Scousburgh, a hill where a wonderful bronze Viking brooch was found, now on display in Shetland Museum.

Spiggie is a gem of a loch, well known for the many waterfowl which rest and feed here during the migration season. Swans overwinter on the loch, which has formed in relatively recent times. It is extensive and lies in a north-south curve across the floor of a shallow valley, surrounded by crofting settlements. Formerly it was an arm of the sea, a great storm built up sand into dunes, sealing the area off and it became a fresh-water body. The Peerie Voe, west-facing and petite, has been the subject of many a prize-winning picture in local photographic competitions. The view out to sea is exceptionally fine, framed either side by sea cliffs, with islands and stacks between. Here a large burn flows briskly out to sea from the loch. Look for the noosts in the

Loch of Spiggie from the north.

banks to the north of the beach here. You can gather a wealth of different seaweeds and you might be lucky enough to find a sea bean – a tropical drift seed from the West Indies, round, dark brown and polished – lying stranded by the tide after crossing half way round the world!

Noss cliffs can be seen stark and dramatic against the skyline to the south-west and they are almost too beautiful to be missed. The tiny hamlet of Noss itself lies at the end of a narrow road which cuts up west from the road around the south side of Spiggie Loch. Here you can walk for half an hour in a loop back round to Spiggie, taking in a section of some of Shetland's finest cliff scenery. Fulmars glide within feet of your head, making the best use of thermals. Puffins nest here too, as they do at Sumburgh Head, and the view across the sea to Foula makes it even more worth while.

Rising almost sheer from the sea, the massive bulk of Fitful Head can be seen from a considerable distance out at sea both from the south and the west. At night a warning light flashes rapidly from the summit.

If you have time, explore East Longland and Brow Loch and the many lanes and paths which criss-cross this corner of Shetland. Archaeological sites occur in many places and the local sandy soil produces wonderful fields of carrots and potatoes, while gardens are brimming with flowers and vegetables. As well as sheep, ponies and cattle graze here, and some real mixed farming can be found. There is excellent walking in the hills which rise to the north of the whole area.

Local farmers grow more crops than in much of the rest of Shetland, which can be vulnerable to damage, so be careful where you walk and ask permission before crossing fields and fences. Unimaginably violent storms lash the coast here from time to time and over the centuries sand has been driven further and further inland. Now a hummocky, grass-covered expanse of ground behind the sand dunes covers the sites of many buildings, including a church. The beach was once quarried for sand, but this was thankfully stopped before further damage was caused to the machair, as this habitat is called. The settlement of Brake lies nearby, famous for its Pictish symbol stone, the Brake Stone, found in 1998.

Quendale Mill.

Quendale has had a turbulent history and is well worth a visit. A large, restored water-mill at Quendale Farm is a must for visitors, with its shop, imaginatively designed interpretive displays and extensive range of old machinery. Garths Ness, where the *Braer* struck in 1993, was a place of disaster long ago. This area, together with much of the land to the south and west, was once home to many Shetlanders who, during the infamous Clearances, were deprived of their homes and crofts in singularly violent and objectionable fashion by the agents of the big landowners of the day. Ask at the mill for more information about this period.

The road from Quendale leads back past several houses and two churches to the main A970 beside a garage and several shops.

CHANNERWICK TO SUMBURGH VIA LEVENWICK

The road swings round a curve to the south, with Levenwick below to the left. There are two roads into this settlement, the first one turns off the main road soon after the bend, but if you can, stop for a while above the village to take in the whole panorama. Where the lower houses almost meet the sea, just above the beach, with its band of glowing sand and tiny sand dune fringe above, there is a graveyard built onto a large, symmetrical green mound. There are theories that beneath the mound may lie the remains of a Viking ship burial. A telephone box stands at the junction and you can walk or drive into the village from here. Once off the fast main road, you are back in a quieter Shetland again, with small, fenced fields, a scatter of old and less old houses and a curve of cliffs descending to a superb white sandy beach. Turn left again off the side road opposite a bus stop, following the sign for Netherton, a tiny cluster of houses near the shore. In summer verge sides and gardens down here are brilliant with red-hot pokers and meadow cranesbill, many of which have spilled over into ditches and banks. The road splits, one short leg carrying on to a turning point and the gated track to the cemetery, the other turning left for the beach. Here the tiny parking area with its picnic site is often packed with cars in the summer. This beach is glorious in all weathers, but is especially appreciated in days of southerly and westerly winds, when it is more sheltered than many.

Whales and dolphins can sometimes swim into the wide, sheltered bay and occasionally have difficulty getting out again. A minke whale stranded here in July 1997. There is a good walk around the cliffs from the eastern end of the beach. A little scrambling skill is required, but the views from the top are fabulous. A herring station once operated from the shore here and remains of old piers and an artificial drying beach can still be seen. Watch your feet as you pass by the extreme north-western corner of the cliff, as the 'beach' stones lie thick among the grass. Access-improved walking routes follow the dramatic coast here along to the broch.

Levenwick hall is often open for Sunday teas in the summer and there is a very modern care centre not far from the famous Levenwick shop, which for many years opened at any time of day or night, barring Sundays. For Clumlie, the next settlement along to the south, rejoin the main A970 and turn left as soon as you see the sign at the next turn-off.

Clumlie has some good, level acres of land and a large farm with a few other scattered crofts, many long since empty. One has within its boundary wall a sizeable broch, out of which much of the croft buildings were probably built. Above and behind to the west, the skyline was dominated for almost half a century by an early-warning station during the cold war. Communication masts and transmitter dishes, which transmitted and received signals and later directed messages across the sea to the oil rigs, stand silent and slightly menacing high up on the ridge. By the

Netherton and Leven Wick early in the morning on a calm spring day.

turn of the new century, mobile telephone masts were being constructed as yet another wave of technology began to rise alongside the older one. Arctic and common terns nested in the rocky wildness around them in their thousands until the later 1980s. Now only a handful of those numbers remains. From the Loch of Clumlie a burn pours down towards the shore at Trosswickness, passing the ruined remains of a long string of mills.

The lowermost of these mills, at Trosswick, is still in perfect working order and come February, if the loch is full enough, a sack of corn, oats or bere dried over many weeks beforehand in the farm kiln may be hefted to the mill and poured into the hopper. The stream may then be diverted through the mill lade to turn the horizontal wooden blades, or 'feathers', on the vertical tirl, or shaft, below the mill floor. The grindstone above is a hand-cut masterpiece of craftsmanship. Few sounds are more evocative of the hardier, simpler way of life in old Shetland than the sound of the water racing and roaring below your feet, the rapid, rhythmic clattering rattle of the mill gear, the clapper and shoe as they spin the stone and crush the grains. Flour and bran hiss softly as they spill into the circular well and mount up in a soft, pale, circular mound around the edges. The meal is raked into a heap, shovelled into a tray, sieved and bagged ready for baking. Remaining coarse fragments are set aside for the cows or kye.

The Clumlie and Trosswick road leads south over the hill and drops towards Dalsetter. In a stone dyke or wall alongside the road here, there is a huge, round boulder with a special history. It is a glacial erratic, of what has been identified as Tonsbergite (an unmistakable dark-pink crystalline rock from near Tonsberg in Norway). The exact course and sequence of glacial movement across Shetland during the ice age has been confusing and difficult to establish. The evidence provided by the Dalsetter Stone gave very precise indications of movements towards the end of the last ice age. The stone has, sadly, lost some of its grandeur because of the selfish hackings of greedy rock collectors, in their futile attempts to secure themselves a piece of the stone as a souvenir.

Dalsetter has a massive ruined broch site with defensive earthworks around it. Foundations of other buildings almost certainly lie beneath the ground. There is access through fields nearby, from the road, but take care to close all gates behind you if you find them closed and try not to damage stone walls. The precipitous cliff edge here comes quite close to the broch, so be very careful if you decide to explore the coastline. Four other broch sites can be seen from this point, some clearer than others, and a fine afternoon's walk can take in all of them.

A fish-curing station operated from Boddam in days long gone by and an old fishing booth still stands down by the shore. A little further south, a road turns left and winds between stone walls and flower-crammed verges and passes Boddam's star attraction, the Crofthouse Museum. The old crofthouse of Southvoe with its barn and byre, kiln and mill here were fully restored and equipped with all the tools, furniture and fittings typical of a traditional Shetland crofthouse of around 1870. Don't miss this experience, in particular because of the immensely knowledgeable and friendly local guides, who bring the place to life. There is always a fire burning in the hearth and sometimes the fiddle is brought down from the wall for an old Shetland tune. Ask to see the home-made mouse trap or 'moose faa'. The wooden box beds are of interest too; how on earth did so many folk sleep so crammed together and with so little room to stretch out?

The name 'Dunrossness' means 'headland of the roaring tideway' and refers to the almost constant din from the 'roost' or tidal currents just to the south. Here, currents from both sides of Shetland meet and tangle into some of Shetland's most feared seas. There has been considerable development in the area and many new houses and housing estates were built as oil- and airport-related employment rose. As the oil phase began to wind down the local population level dropped. The large modern Dunrossness primary school takes children from many villages where their schools were closed down.

Exnaboe stands opposite the airport with yet another broch at Eastshore at the end of the road, which is now actually slowly falling into the sea. A modern boating club stands nearby and on a rise of ground behind it are the ruins of some old croft buildings almost certainly partially built from the stones of the broch. Here the cottages overlooking the Pool of Virkie have some of the best birdwatching in Shetland, as many migrant waterfowl, seabirds and waders first alight in the shallows below them. Hot on the heels of the birds come the birdwatchers and locals can watch both!

Toab, to the right of the main road, has seen huge changes in the landscape, especially during the Second World War. There is a mixture of housing, old and new, as well as a shop, a hall and a broch site too. You can walk along the shore here to the wonderful Quendale Sands, where massive dunes have been known to lose thousands of tons of sand during gales and hurricane-force winds, burying fields and buildings behind them. The humps and hollows to the north of the beach cover landscapes of the past, home now to interesting grasses, sedges and rushes which enjoy the sandy habitat.

There are warning lights on the roadside as you approach the line of the airport's main east-west runway, which are red during landings and take-offs. A little beyond the lights lies the Scatness excavation. Here, many years ago, a broch site was breached during road building. In the last decade of the twentieth century, an archaeological dig began, which soon proved to be one of the most exciting in the country, revealing extensive Iron Age, Pictish and Viking remains. If you visit Shetland during July, you may be able to join guided tours around the site and examine the reconstructed Pictish and Iron Age buildings which have been built nearby. The team from the Living History TV programme came up for several

Puffin with a beak full of sandeels.

summers and researched the technology and craft skills of the different periods.

Sumburgh Head with its stark white lighthouse, built in 1820 by Robert Stevenson, stands guard high on the wild, tilted rock faces of Sumburgh Head, Shetland Mainland's southernmost tip. No longer manned, the lighthouse tower works automatically; the gleaming prisms still revolve and sweep their vital beams of light far out across the lethal currents of the roost to the south. Today the offices and rooms are home to the Shetland branch of the RSPB, a fabulous vantage-point for birdwatching headquarters, and SOTEAG, the Shetland Oil Terminal Environmental Advisory Group. There is also self-catering accommodation for visitors.

If you are lucky, you may glimpse humpback whales breaching in the sea around Sumburgh Head, especially in June. Every year now 'whale-watching' weekends are held and increasing numbers of locals and visitors flock to try their skill with telescopes and binoculars, summer sea-fog permitting. A massive prehistoric promontory fort stood here until it was largely destroyed by the lighthouse construction work, only a short section of rampart now remaining. But it is not human interest which draws hordes of people to this exposed site, but bird life. There are several interpretive panels and a sizeable car park provides a safe stopping point for thousands of visitors every year.

Some of the most spectacular island seabird colonies in Britain are found along these cliffs and the access and viewing points are constantly being improved. Puffins may potter and mutter within a few feet of you; gannets dive and bonxies harrass; guillemots whistle and eider ducks croon; kittiwakes cackle and the sea seldom ceases its assault and battery at the feet of the shelving rock faces. Sea pinks carpet the turf in spring and other wild flowers cram every nook and cranny of the cliff faces from May to September. At times the scent is almost overwhelming. Fine views can be enjoyed from the top of Sumburgh Head. Fair Isle lies away to the south, Noss is just visible to the north and east and below you to the west lie Sumburgh Hotel, the archaeological site of Jarlshof, Sumburgh Airport and the fertile fields of Dunrossness. The underlying beds of sandstone here provide wide, gentle slopes and fertile, even soils; as a result, farms are larger than in many other parts of Shetland.

The coastline today probably follows a very different course from that reached by the first settlers, allowing for a sinkage of about 16 feet (5 m) of vertical land during 6000 years. The original landfalls may lie beneath the present shallows of the surrounding sea, which batters the coast and in winter sends clouds of spray washing over the ancient ruins, which are now protected by tough sea defences. Only half of Jarlshof stands today, the rest having been swept away by several thousand years of storm seas, which still occasionally cast sea-worn artefacts onto the local beaches. It was just such a storm which revealed Jarlshof in the first place, in the early 1900s, uncovering masses of stonework and debris. The discovery led to the excavation and the present world-famous site becoming established as one of Shetland's major attractions; a layer-cake of cultures – Bronze Age, Iron Age, Viking, Medieval – all preserved one above the other. Take time to go round at your leisure, as the site is overwhelmingly complex.

The beaches are among Shetland's most splendid; long, wide stretches of pure white sand, deserted for much of the year and on sunny summer days, they come close to perfection. From whichever direction the wind comes, at least one sandy beach remains sheltered. You can walk north from Sumburgh Head, following the eastern cliff tops and drop down to the shore at the Lawards, where a massive storm beach was hurled up in the famous storm of 1900. Fish and plant fossils have been found among the rocks here and the boulders are a patchwork of beautiful patterns of lichens. You can also follow the west-facing cliffs and the shore along to Jarlshof as long as you can negotiate a few walls and fences with safety and without damaging them. Beware scattered rocks hidden among long grass as you approach Jarlshof itself. Keep an eye open for migrant birds among the bushes of the Sumburgh Hotel garden, one of the best places to spot newly arrived rarities.

Scatness to the west lies parallel with Sumburgh Head. The road into Scatness becomes a track as you head south beyond the houses. There are a number of small lochs and it is worth looking out for smaller migrant birds here, sheltering among the grassy hollows. The ness narrows towards its southern tip and to reach the prehistoric blockhouse fort of Ness of Burgi, you need to be able to scramble and clamber

Fitful Head, Scatness and West Voe of Sumburgh, from Sumburgh Head.

with some confidence. An excavation of the site in 1935 found traces of fireplaces and small amounts of bone and pottery. The fort has a central entrance door and thick-walled cells to either side and a third to the west, greatly damaged by erosion. A second fort site exists not far from this one, but with much less of its structure still visible.

This headland takes a ferocious battering from the full force of winter Atlantic rollers and the south westerly gales which can assault Shetland at any time of year. But the best time to visit is in late May and early June, when the sea pinks or thrift blanket every square inch of ground space across the ness and right onto the rocks at the sea's edge. It is a very different place today, from the scene which would have met your eyes during the last war. Bunkers, many of which can still be found, were constructed all over the area and thousands of servicemen with their camps, huts, gun emplacements and guard posts dominated Dunrossness for many years. Local people had to present passes to enter the Scatness area unless they were under 16, and the rattle of anti-aircraft fire shook the windows in local houses whenever enemy aircraft were sighted.

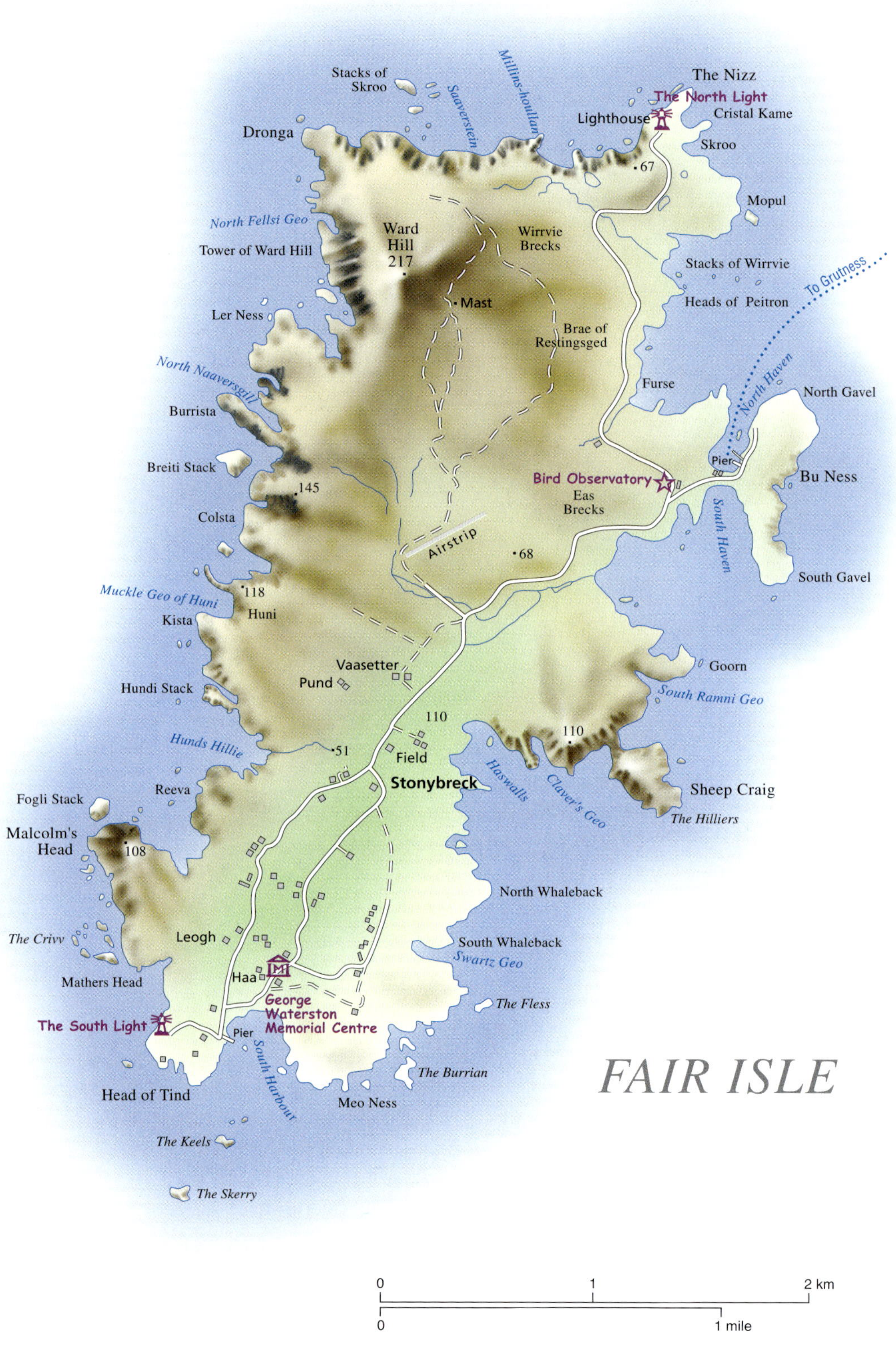

Stacks of Skroo
Millins-houllan
Saaverstein
The Nizz
The North Light
Lighthouse
Cristal Kame
Skroo
Dronga
67
Mopul
North Fellsi Geo
Ward Hill 217
Wirrvie Brecks
Tower of Ward Hill
Stacks of Wirrvie
To Grutness
Heads of Peitron
Mast
Ler Ness
Brae of Restingsged
North Naaversgill
Furse
North Haven
North Gavel
Burrista
Pier
Breiti Stack
Bird Observatory
Bu Ness
145
Eas Brecks
Colsta
South Haven
Airstrip
68
South Gavel
Muckle Geo of Huni
118
Huni
Kista
Goorn
Vaasetter
Hundi Stack
Pund
South Ramni Geo
110
110
Hunds Hillie
51
Field
Stonybreck
Haswalls
Claver's Geo
Sheep Craig
Reeva
Fogli Stack
The Hilliers
Malcolm's Head
108
North Whaleback
The Crivv
Leogh
South Whaleback
Swartz Geo
Haa
Mathers Head
George Waterston Memorial Centre
The Fless
The South Light
Pier
South Harbour
The Burrian
Head of Tind
Meo Ness
The Keels
The Skerry
FAIR ISLE
0
1
2 km
0
1 mile

Fair Isle

Whether you arrive in Fair Isle by air from Tingwall on Mainland Shetland, or by boat from Grutness near Sumburgh, the approaches are dramatic in the extreme. It is easy to see why so many people have been drawn to visit the island throughout the centuries. Fair Isle, which is now owned by the National Trust for Scotland, appears at first glance to be bare and exposed. But as you explore, it opens up into an endless delight of hidden corners, spectacular geos and cliffscapes.

A large number of archaeological sites have been identified here and several from different periods have been excavated in recent years. The present occupied buildings have been sensitively preserved and modernised, new ones built and old ones altered with great attention to overall impact and scale. Two graceful aero generators provide the electricity needs. But perhaps the most striking visual feature throughout the spring and summer are the wild flowers which grow from one end of the island to the other in glorious profusion. Orchids over a foot high can sometimes be found growing in the marshy areas in good years.

There is a thriving community in Fair Isle, the southernmost of the Shetland Islands. Its location in the sea makes it a frequent first landfall for exhausted migrant birds blown off course by storm winds on their annual flights between Scandinavia and southern Europe and beyond. An astonishing variety of species turns up each year, making it one of the best places in the world for seeing large numbers of different species of birds, including many rarities.

Facilities for visitors are well developed and there are few Shetland communities more welcoming, a quality for which the islanders have been well known throughout several centuries. The world-famous bird observatory and hostel are well worth a visit. Equipped for guest comfort as well as scientific study, the observatory plays an important part in monitoring and analysing migrant bird movement within a global network throughout the world.

Migrant Bluethroat.

Heligoland traps are set in key locations around the island and checked at regular intervals. Any birds caught are weighed, recorded and released. Storm petrels breed here in the summer. They are caught, weighed and ringed at night, attracted to the nets by spotlights, though it seldom gets very dark.

The western cliffs of Fair Isle – looking south from Ward Hill to the headlands of Ler Ness, Colsta, Kista and Reeva with Malcolm's Head in the distance.

Fair Isle lies in the middle of the fairway between Northern Europe and America and despite its relatively small size, many vessels have been wrecked here. On 23 May 1868 the 1800 ton *Lessing* from Bremen struck Clavers Geo in thick fog and by a miraculous combination of luck and skill, all the crew and the 465 German emigrants and crew, *en route* for New York, were rescued. In 1877 the full-rigged *Black Watch* from Nova Scotia, only four months old, was wrecked at Shalstane and 23 crew and passengers were saved. On 12 March 1915, the 4323 ton Danish steamer *Canadia* ran aground at Helli Stack.

Fair Isle's most famous wreck, the Spanish ship *El Gran Grifon*, went aground here in 1588. The crew were sheltered and fed by the islanders who were massively outnumbered. The famous patterned knitwear to which the island gives its name is believed to have been introduced by the Spaniards and is still

Looking across South Harbour from the sea towards Springfield, Vaasetter and Sheep Rock.

hand-knitted here; locally hand-made garments resting comfortably at the top end of the market for such goods. By the end of the 1990s, a number of other local crafts and skills had developed including traditional Shetland boat-building, fiddle- and spinning-wheel making, stained glass and hand-felting.

An excellent local museum is a must for every visitor and tells in more detail the history and traditions of this unique island community. The museum commemorates George Waterston, whose passion for birdwatching and love for the island helped keep him sane during long imprisonment in Germany during the Second World War. He spent his hours planning a birdwatching observatory for the island. After his release, at the first opportunity he bought the island and eventually realised the dream.

Island history is often sung here too and *Fridarey*, the Norse name for the island, is also the name of a local folk group. Two places of worship, the kirk and the Methodist Chapel, are used alternately on Sundays and visitors are made very welcome at both. In the kirk, a beautiful new stained-glass window is worth a visit in its own right.

Travel & Holiday Information

Every year the Shetland holiday-maker scene changes a little. Shetlanders are creative and enterprising, always coming up with new ideas, a new craft, eating place or interpretive facility, but the main attractions – the scenery, wildlife, traditions and welcome – never change. For up-to-the-minute information, make the Shetland Tourist Office your first port of call, or better still, write to or telephone them in advance. They will send you details of all the latest prices, travel options, transport within the islands, accommodation and activity possibilities, together with extra items to suit your own needs and interests. There will be leaflets on many Shetland topics and individual leaflets for each area of Shetland. Their telephone number is 01595 693434, or you can write to them at Market Cross, Lerwick, Shetland Islands.

During your stay, buy the local newspapers which have excellent advertisements for local events, auctions, sales etc. BBC Radio Shetland 92.7 FM, presents a half hour programme each weekday from 5.30 pm, with features and interviews often following the national 6 o'clock news. The islands also have locally owned SIBC 96.2 broadcasting 24 hours a day every day.

The *Shetland Times* comes out every Friday morning and the entertainments pages are well worth scanning for ideas. In addition there is a free magazine, *The Shetland Visitor*, published every year, which is packed with information for visitors and most shops and venues have stacks for the taking, so get hold of one as soon as you can and peruse it at your leisure. They also have a web site, www.visitshetland.com. Increasingly these days, local communities produce their own visitor information in the form of booklets or leaflets. Try to gather a selection of those you are likely to get to, as they will add greatly to your enjoyment.

Visitors are welcomed at all times of year. Every season has its own merits. Spring can be cool, but tends to have clearer weather than the summer, when heat is often followed by days of sea fogs. Autumn skies are stunning, with glorious sunsets and magnificent cloudscapes. Both autumn and winter can provide marvellous opportunities to watch the northern lights (aurora borealis, or 'Mirrie Dancers' as they are called in Shetland). Winter is the time for the famous fire festivals; the Up Helly Aa of Viking guisers with their flaming torches. But summer is the most popular time, when nesting birds, young lambs and ponies and acres of wild flowers enrich the landscapes.

CULTURE & LANGUAGE

Shetland's culture and language are constant sources of interest and study. Newcomers to Shetland will notice the Shetland dialect immediately, but some districts have stronger forms than others and Shetlanders could be said to be virtually bilingual. Islanders have a natural courtesy which requires them to modify their own way of speaking in order to be understood by strangers. But a chance hearing of two local folk chatting away can be a revelation. Whalsay and Skerries retain the richest and strongest form of Shetland dialect still to survive. Many years ago attempts were made in schools to stamp out dialect in children, 'for their own good'; the idea then prevailing that only English, spoken well, would secure them a good job and future prospects. Sadly this attitude, together with the arrival of television, resulted in the overall reduction and dilution of daily use of the dialect and the local education authority is now promoting dialect as an important element in the curriculum.

Food as a luxury item, or eating out as a leisure activity, are recent innovations. Traditional eating patterns remained much the same for years, as food was home grown or caught. But changes came in with supplies brought up during the War and even more so during the later oil 'invasion' when construction workers were fed like lords. Certain Shetland dishes retain their popularity, however, and no village function or wedding would be complete without cured and dried or 'reestit mutton', 'tattie soup' and 'bannocks' . Older generations speak wistfully of 'stap and crappin' a fish-liver and oatmeal dish, 'kirn milk', a unique curd made with untreated milk and 'sharp blaand', a tangy drink derived from the liquid remaining after butter is made. A number of delicious foods are now produced on a commercial scale and, through skilful marketing, are now on sale in a number of prestigious outlets in the UK and abroad. Tea and homebakes accompany many an entertainment and you can surprise your host by asking for a 'peerie scar' of milk or a 'peerie corn' of sugar; the dialect terms for 'a little bit' of liquid or food.

MUSEUMS, EXHIBITIONS & ARCHIVAL INFORMATION

Shetland gears up for its visitors with a crammed programme of events, exhibitions and special displays. The local museums open new displays and in Lerwick the Islesburgh Exhibition, held in the community, celebrates a slightly glorified, simple, happy past; a life of few possessions, a life ruled by weather, seasons and animals. The reality was probably considerably harder and more gruelling, but nevertheless, many former crofters admit to missing many aspects of their old lifestyles. Here you can watch spinning and Fair Isle and lace knitting, listen to local fiddlers and learn Shetland dances.

Visitors are welcome at the Shetland Library in Lerwick. After several decades in its purpose-built Hillhead home, it has moved to newly converted premises in an old church. The library service reaches every corner of Shetland with its two mobile library vans. Schools are well served through school libraries. Much of the published work on Shetland can be accessed through the Shetland Room. A large collection of literature is housed here, including many old and wonderful volumes, as well as microfiche records of newspapers and other literature. A number of well-known Shetlanders gifted their own collections of Shetland books to the library, so that they could be enjoyed by islanders in the future, and the collection is steadily added to as new works are published. Several computers add to the research and information facilities.

A priceless store of original texts, letters, diaries, articles and documents and a number of old books, reprints and recent anthologies are kept in the Shetland Archives. On a rainy afternoon, an hour spent here, reading some of the vivid accounts of life in Shetland several hundred years ago, can enrich a visit immensely. Whether visiting sea captains, travelling preachers or scientific researchers, all record memories and evidence of an island life long since vanished and forgotten. Some of the works of past writers on Shetland have become collectors' items and are eagerly sought after at the local Shetland book auctions. From time to time, new treasures turn up and it is tantalising to imagine what fresh revelations still survive, as yet undiscovered.

A growing number of visitors come to the islands to trace their ancestors who left Shetland during the past few centuries. The Shetland Family History Society has an office in and is eager to help with research.

Arts in Shetland are also well catered for, with an Arts Trust which supports travelling exhibitions, resident artists and sculptors, writers and drama and dance teachers. Concerts and theatre shows, a film club and bursaries for exhibitions and study trips all receive funds. Village halls and local hostelries host evenings of singing or musical entertainment, locally written plays and poetry readings. Traditional tales, legends and rich local folklore are enjoyed at story-telling evenings.

RELIGION

There is a remarkable variety of spiritual and religious groups in Shetland, with a wide range of places of worship. These include Salvation Army, Plymouth Brethren, Quakers, Buddhists, Baptists, Bahais, Methodists, Mormons and Jehovas Witnesses amongst others every week. Catholic, Episcopalian, Church of Scotland, Unitarian and Evangelical Christian denominations keep in touch through an active ecumenical trust and share in a number of joint events every year.

LEISURE & RECREATION

Leisure and recreation in Shetland is incredibly well provided for, with sports, swimming and fitness-suite facilities now available in all the main islands.There was a time, not long ago, when football was virtually the only competitive sport. Some badminton would be played in the halls, especially over the autumn and winter months, and Shetland model yacht racing had a great following.

Subsistence farming left little time for leisure. Now, not only is the range of sports and leisure pursuits astonishingly wide, but the standard of play has improved to the point where Shetland teams go to all the Inter-Island Games, returning with steadily increasing numbers of medals, and Shetland hosted the Games in 2005. It is not unusual to find Shetlanders playing in national teams including youngsters with many sports including table tennis being played to the highest standard in junior teams.

A recently revived sport is yoal racing, when special hand-built wooden boats of a traditional Norse design are raced by teams of men and women. Rowers practise hard every fine night around Burra, Scalloway, Aith and other villages where there are clubs. Few sights are more lovely than the slim profile of a beautiful yoal speeding silently in stark outline against the glare of the setting sun reflected in a silver-pink sea. A number of Shetland craftsmen have kept yoal-building skills alive and their workshops can sometimes be visited. A race on a different scale is the Bergen to Lerwick yacht race which creates excitement every summer, with concerts and parties to welcome the Scandinavian contestants.

Boat trips, which have facilities for the disabled, are available for visits around Noss and Bressay, and Foula, or out on sea-angling trips.

Cycling in Shetland can be wonderful, with good roads, minimal traffic and few serious gradients but on occasions the wind makes up for that! Bicycle-hire facilities are widely available.

Walking in Shetland is a liberating experience. Traditionally Shetlanders have walked the 'banks' of the shoreline, the hills and cliff tops and in most places walkers are welcome. It is always sensible to prepare for a change in the weather, though, and there are many ways in which you can increase the pleasure of your trip. The most important tip is to speak to local people. You can learn more in five minutes' conversation with a local resident than you can in weeks of reading guidebooks!

Shetland's Access programme is continually adding to improvements in stiles, gates and bridges to make walking easier. Enjoy walking in Shetland, while ensuring that your visit is welcomed by those who live and work there by following this advice:

SHETLAND WAY OF WALKING

CONSIDERATION FOR YOURSELF:

- If possible, walk with a companion and let someone know your intended route and anticipated time of return.
- Good maps of Shetland enhance every walk. The 1-25,000 Ordnance Survey maps are ideal for walkers. A compass is essential on moorlands if fog descends.
- Warm clothing and footwear with good gripping soles. Waterproof or breatheable outer clothing, an extra jumper, gloves and a hat, some food and drink; a basic first-aid kit.
- A camera, spare film and extra lenses. Take a plastic bag to protect them from salt-laden wind.

- Avoid cliff edges, boggy ground and slippery rocks.
- Keep away from aggressive nesting birds.

CONSIDERATION FOR OTHERS:

- Ask for permission before crossing fenced crofting areas or farmland and for advice about parking a vehicle if you have one.
- Avoid walking near sheep with lambs. Walk along the edges of fields of grass, or other crops, not across the middle. Never take dogs anywhere near livestock.
- Don't try to climb stone walls or barbed-wire fences. Use stiles wherever possible, but if you have to open a gate, always close it securely behind you.
- Never close a gate which has been secured in an open position.
- Keep water supplies clean, take all litter home and avoid risk of fire.
- Photograph wild flowers, don't pick them. Keep well away from nesting birds.

MUSIC & FESTIVALS

Shetland is extraordinarily rich in music. Traditional tunes are as popular today as they ever were. Traditional songs are less of a feature, though there are plenty of new songs written and annual competitions and events keep song-writing alive. The legendary Tom Anderson made Shetland fiddle music famous. He held annual summer schools in Stirling and spent much of his life saving and gathering old tunes and teaching them to young Shetland children; his 'Peerie Angels'. An annual music festival brings in hundreds of entrants and scores of performers, with great competition for the titles of Young Fiddler of the Year and Young Musician of the Year. The Shetland Folk Festival has become world famous and several other major musical events punctuate the calendar.

Shetland's most famous festival is Up Helly Aa, which takes place in Lerwick on the last Tuesday of January each year. Often assumed to be a relic of the Viking Ages, it is in fact a Victorian spectacular, based loosely round the ancient Viking ship burial tradition, but with a practical purpose at its heart. At one time, the ancient tradition of winter fire celebrations in Lerwick began to get a little out of hand. The streets were extremely narrow and the once popular local custom of tar-barrelling, common to many northern Scottish towns (and still celebrated in a few) left a trail of damage after the uproarious barrellers had passed by, scorching the doors of wealthy or powerful local individuals with their fiercely burning barrel as they passed by. A series of meetings in Lerwick created a new, colourful ceremony, redolent of Victorian Viking splendour, and with social order carefully observed.

The festival is designed to take place with proper attention to safety and little of the original wild abandon survives. All is strictly controlled by a committee and office bearers. A man has to serve for many years on the committee before being eligible for inclusion on the list of future Jarls. Men only are allowed to take part and the day itself is led by the Guizer Jarl and his henchmen, the Jarl Squad, consisting of male members of his family, relations and friends all dressed in Viking costume.

This group leads the processions during the day, making pre-arranged visits to schools and hospitals, and reading the elaborately designed, painted proclamation or 'Bill'. This text is erected in a central place and contains humorous, hidden references to individuals or incidents, which amuse passers-by.

Other squads follow the Jarl Squad, dressed in their own sets of costumes, which are hand made for the occasion, with much secrecy, until the night of the event itself, as the exact nature of the dress and the acts are revealed only to those taking part. The Jarl Squad escorts the dragon ship to the burning site, where the Guizer Jarl makes traditional speeches. Then, after the mass singing of three special songs and some rousing cheers, the torches fly through the darkness into the galley and flames rise into the sky. Fireworks often follow the burning. The crowd stays to watch until the dragon head on the prow collapses, then the streets begin to empty as people make their way to the many halls where acts will be performed all night long.

'The Bill' – Up Helly Aa proclamation at Market Cross, Lerwick.

After the burning, hundreds of strangely dressed men in teams, or 'squads', travel from hall to hall, performing at each venue a short dramatic presentation complete with costume and music, which usually features a topical incident or controversial item from local recent history. Performance quality varies a great

The Guizer Jarl and burning galley, Up Helly Aa festival.

deal from squad to squad, especially towards the end of the night! Each squad follows the others in carefully arranged succession, so that all halls see all acts. Each hall is organised by a group of Shetland ladies who provide food and soft drinks all through the night. Guests eat, drink, watch the acts and dance the night away. There is always a local holiday on the Wednesday, so that those who took part can sleep and recover from the after-effects! Each year hordes of visitors and foreign media flock to watch, film and report the spectacle.

Lerwick's Up Helly Aa has been lighting up the streets of the town every year (except for a brief interruption during the war) for well over a hundred years. Many other villages and communities have their own, less formal versions where women and girls take part in the procession, a few lucky lasses are seen, dressed as Viking princesses, in the jarl squad and men help to host and serve guests. In Hillswick, Scalloway and Brae the Viking ship burns as it sails in the sea, creating some wonderful images. Visitors can choose from many Up Helly Aas spanning some of the darkest months from January through to March.

Agricultural shows take place in the height of summer in Walls, Cunningsburgh, Voe and the North Isles, all hoping for better weather and more vistors than each other. The North Isles have shows too and there are few better times to visit than on their show days.They are well spaced out, so everyone in the islands who wishes can get to all of them. Look out for the programmes in the *Shetland Times* and in local shops. Traditional produce can be admired, such as Shetland tatties, Shetland kale and green eggs laid by the old variety of Shetland hens, the finest hand-knitting, Fair Isle patterns, Shetland lace, hand-spun wool and home baking. Superb displays of pot plants, exotic, greenhouse-grown fruit and local vegetables and arts and crafts compete for your attention with a programme of livestock parades, sports events and sheepdog handling.

Every Shetland district has its Community hall with a hall committee who programme each year with an astonishing variety of events, from wedding receptions, jumble sales and fund-raising functions to concerts and political meetings. There are a few tiny halls still in existence from the days 'before oil', which look impossibly small by comparison with the large, well-equipped buildings used today. Look out for posters and advertisments in the *Shetland Times* for hall teas, which are served in a selection of villages in rotation, on Sunday afternoons during the summer months. There are often craft stalls, exhibitions and sometimes music to enjoy, as well as teas with homebakes.

Entertainment comes in many forms and an unusual one to look out for is an auction; the sale rooms in Lerwick attract a colourful following. Displenishing sales are held to sell entire house contents, often at the house in question, or just outside it. Shetland pony sales are held in October, cattle marts are seasonal and fish markets take place regularly. For some, the regular book sales in Lerwick are a 'must' and books about Shetland sometimes fetch enormous prices.

Regattas feature regularly throughout the summer and local people attend in good numbers. There are races for different age groups, including children, teenagers and men and women. Fishing competitions, or Eelas, involve dozens of small boats heading out to sea at a given time and returning *en masse* to count and compare their catches. In the evenings the prizes are awarded in the local hall, and a Shetland supper of bannocks, tattie soup and reestit mutton, or maybe some fish, is served and a band plays for dancing.

Brae has its carnival day, with a grand parade of floats onto which money is thrown by the crowd, to be caught in buckets and given to charities afterwards. Aith has its Lifeboat Day and Scalloway has a Gala Week, with activities on every night. The Children in Need event has taken off in Shetland and each year fund-raising ideas vie with each other.

A Medieval festival, The Johnsmas Foy has been re-established in recent years and is becoming a very popular event in Lerwick. A continuous programme of events held in late June, celebrates Shetland's fishing heritage with live music, arts and food.

Festivals and celebrations, often with local variations, took place all year round until relatively recent times in Shetland. Special days, dates for certain tasks, some very ancient in origin, spanned the whole calendar. Bonfires at Christmas and New Year were common in Shetland and other Nordic countries at one time and some communities still carry this on today. Midsummer bonfires were also a great feature at one time, as they still are in many other Scandinavian countries, where the festivities follow patterns that go back over a thousand years. Those who are interested in this aspect of island history should read James R Nicolson's *Shetland Folklore* for a fuller account. A simplified calendar of traditional and ancient festivals follows.

APPENDIX

The Old Shetland Year

A calendar of traditional celebrations in a simplified, chronological order. A brief account of what took place is included, where it is known. Few are still remembered and sadly fewer still kept up.

5 Jan	Yule E'en	Old Christmas Eve. Guizers, or 'Skekklers', dressed in elaborate straw costumes, went round entertaining friends and neighbours. Dancing, music and a dram or two followed the guizers' arrival and much fun was had by all.
6 Jan	'Old' Yule	Old Christmas, still celebrated in Foula.
13 Jan	Old Ne'erday	Old New Year.
Late Jan	Uphalliday	Norse festival to celebrate the ending of winter. The original name for Up Helly Aa, the last day, or end of the Yule holiday period.
29 Jan	St Antony Day	
2 Feb	Candlemas day	Pre Reformation festival. Pigs said to be killed at this time and prepared for use later. Weather lore: 'If Candlemass day be bright and fair, Half of the winter's to come and mair If Candlemass day be wet and foul, The half of the year be gone at yule'.
22 Feb	Petermas Day	Feast of St Peter.
24 Feb	Løbers-mas	From Old Norse Leap Day. An old rhyme says: 'The lark will greet as long after Løbers-mas as it sang afore Candlemas'.
17 Mar	Bogel's Day or Marimass	Feast of St Mary. Start of a spell of bad weather. A tiny patch of corn was sown on this day, carefully monitored as the year went by and harvested to make Buggle cakes, which were eaten on the next year's Bogel's Day. The weather on the last three days of March was often wild. This spell was called the Bogel Ree.
25 Mar	Lady Day	Start of the crofting year. Last three days of March were called the 'Borrowing days'. Various versions; in one, the weather for the three summer months was predicted from these three days. 'The first of them was wind and wet, the second of them was snow and sleet, the third of them was such a freeze, it freezed the birds nebs to the trees.'
14 Apr	The 'Feast of Perpetua and Felicity'	Mentioned in a conveyance from Sandwick dated 1360.
16 Apr	Simmermill Day	Start of the summer half year. An old crofter commented: 'Certain things had to be planted by then, Shetland kale and corn as well. Tatties didn't matter so much'.
1 May	Maunsmas (St Magnus) and also Beltane	Bonfires were lit and danced around. Young folk competed to leap across the fires. This date marked the start of the Haaf fishing season. Beltane Ree was a three-day fishing festival, or foy, a surviving relic of sun-worship of the god Bael, with many rituals and ceremonies.

24 Jun	Johnsmas Simmermill Foy, or midsummer festival	Young girls would pluck Johnsmas (plantain) heads, pull out the stamens and bury, or hide, them. The next day they were examined and if more stamens had grown, a wedding was likely to follow. Some accounts refer to sleeping with them under their pillows to dream of future husbands. Dutch fishermen arrived and celebrated with festivities marking the start of their summer herring fishing season. More bonfires were lit.
4 Jul	Martin o' Bulliamas Day	If it rained that day, it would rain for 40 days. Likewise if fine, 40 fine days would follow.
1 Aug	Lammas	End of the year's Haaf fishing. 'Lammas speets' (heavy rain)
23 Aug	Laurencemas	Feast of St Lawrence.
21 Sept	Matjomas	Feast of St Matthew.
29 Sept	Michaelmas	Feast of St Michael. The end of the growing season.
14 Oct	Winter Day	Cattle brought in and tied in their stalls (and the first Saturday after Winter Day was called Winter Sunday Saturday).
1 Nov	The feist of Hallamas	A time for roofs to be repaired.
3 Nov	Soloman's E'en (originally Samhuinn)	
11 Nov	Martinmas	Feast of St Martin. Shetland leases traditionally began and ended on this date.
30 Nov	Andersmas	Feast of St Andrew.
4 Dec	Barbarasmas	Feast of St Barbara.
17 Dec	Sow Day	Seven nights before Christmas.
	Tulyas E'en	On Tulya's E'en two straws were laid in a cross shape at the entrance to the corn and hay yard, a hair from the tail of each cow was plaited and hung above the byre door and a glowing peat was carried through all outhouses to guard against Trows.
18 Dec	Helya's E'en	The night after Tulyas E'en. 'Milk-an-mell' was eaten and this rhyme was said, to protect children: Mary Midder, had de haund Roond aboot for sleepin' bound. Had the lass, and had the wife, Had the bairns au der life. Mary Midder, had de haund Roond da inants o' wir laund.
19 Dec	Byana's Sunday	Sunday before Christmas. Half a cow's head was boiled and eaten for supper. A candle was set into the eye socket of the cleaned skull and it was lit and carried through the house on Yule morning.
20 Dec	Tammasmas	Feast of St Thomas. No work or amusements were allowed after dusk. A rhyme says: 'The very babe unborn cries 'O dül, dül', For the brakkin o' Tammasmas Nicht Five Nichts afore Yule! Some records refer to Tunderman's nicht, possibly a relic of Norse worship of Thor.
25 Dec	Yule	

APPENDIX 3

Chronology

Dates BC are approximate   * = indicated from 20th century finds

BC	
110,000	Mediterranean plant and tree species growing in Shetland. (See Fugla Ness, Uyea)
10,000	The last Ice Age ends.
8000	Shetland hit by world's largest tidal wave from NE, triggered by vast submarine landslide.
4000	First traces of Neolithic settlers in Shetland.*
3500	Scord of Brouster first settled.. Jarlshof first settled.. Stanydale 'temple' built.
2500	Cache of barley laid down in a house at Ness of Gruting. *
2000	Blanket bog begins to form.
	Bronze smith working at Jarlshof.*
1500	Scord of Brouster abandoned.*
1000	Clickimin Broch settled.
500	Beginning of the Iron Age.*
100	Probable establishment of Picts as a distinct political grouping in Scotland.
40	Probable date of manufacture of a Roman pottery shard found in Clickimin Broch excavation.
AD	
80	Tacitus, the Roman historian, writes of maritime tribes in Northern Europe.
100	Mousa Broch built. *
	Clickimin abandoned.
98	(Nennius records) a Saxon attack on the Picts, which 'laid waste the Orkneys'.
300	Roughly the end of the Iron Age.
400	Approximate start of a colder, wetter period of weather lasting until about 800 AD.
500	Iona Christian centre founded. Monks begin to venture northwards to Orkney, Shetland, Faroe and Iceland.
550	Roughly agreed as the start of Pictish Shetland.
	Brake Stone carved.
563	First Christian missionaries thought to have arrived in Shetland.
600	Brude MacBile laid waste the Orkneys.
682	(Nennius states that) Vikings have overrun all the islands of Britain.
749	Christianity established in Shetland.
750	Bressay Stone erected.
800	First Viking settlements established in Shetland. St Ninian's Isle Treasure probably buried at about this time.
843	Kenneth Mac Alpine united the Scots and Picts in Scotland.
900	Roughly the start of the 'Little Climatic Optimum', a period of warmer, dryer weather lasting for 300 years.
910	Jarl 'Turf' Einar dies after a peaceful reign.
950	Rough date of an English coin found at Scatness.
995	Norway becomes officially Christian.
1000	Silver thistle-headed brooch lost in Gulberwick, found almost a thousand years later by a schoolboy.
1065	Approximate date of death of Earl Thorfinn the Mighty. Earldom split between sons Paul and Erlend.
1117	Magnus Erlendsson killed at Easter in Orkney. Cult of St Magnus begins.
1190	Document in which Earl Harald Maddadarson refers to himself as the Earl of Orkney.
1195	Shetland confiscated from Earls of Orkney by King of Norway.
1200	Serious deterioration in climate begins about now.
1231	Earl of Angus succeeds to Earldom and the Norse line becomes extinct.
1263	King Haakon with 200 war galleys, shelters in Bressay Sound, *en route* to try to defend the Hebrides.
1300	Poor climatic period comes to an end.
1302	Apostles Church built in Bergen, funded largely by rents from Shetland and Faroe.

1312	Raids by Scots on Shetland.
1321	Angus line ends and Strathearne line succeeds to Earldom.
1350	Black death.
1369	More Scottish raids on Shetland.
1379	Earldom of Orkney and Lordship of Shetland passed by marriage to St Clair of Roslin, until 1468.
1391	Probable date of the murder of Malise Sperra during a struggle for control of Shetland.
1397	Norway united with Denmark under Queen Margrethe, and ceases to exist as a separate kingdom.
1418	A Scot, William Tulloch, appointed Bishop of Orkney (and Shetland).
1469	On 28 May Shetland was pledged in pawn to Scotland for 8000 florins, to be redeemed in due course.
1471	The Lordship of Shetland was annexed to Scotland, with the Earldom of Orkney.
1500	Approx. beginning of a period of climatic deterioration lasting well over a century.
1560	Scottish Reformation. 'Kirkmen' began to arrive in the islands.
1562	Earl of Bothwell fled to Shetland after defeat of Mary Queen of Scots at Carberry Hill.
1565	Queen Mary gave Robert Stewart a grant of her lands of Orkney and Shetland.
1577	Evidence taken of complaints about Laurence Bruce of Unst.
1588	Spanish transport ship wrecked on Fair Isle.
1598	Muness Castle built in Unst for Lawrence Bruce.
1600	Scalloway Castle built for Earl Patrick.
1611	Privy Council Act abolishes Norse law in Scotland.
1615	Earl Patrick and son hanged in Edinburgh.
1616	Privy Council Act passed for the establishment of schools in every parish in Scotland.
1628	Date on Bressay tombstone of Agnes Gifferd 'ane vertuous and discreit gentlewoman.'
1629	Outbreak of plague.
1630s	Famine. Some lairds support Covenanters' cause.
1636	Captain Claes Jansen Bruyn of Durgendam dies after his ship reached Bressay Sound from Mozambique.
1640	Dutch warship and three armed vessels of the Dutch East India Company attacked by Spanish warship.
1653	English fleet of 94 ships capture 50 Dutch herring 'busses' in Bressay Sound.
1665	Fort construction begun, Lerwick.
1667	Commissioners of Supply established.
1670s	French and Dutch at war.
1673	Dutch burn Fort and part of Lerwick.
1677	More Dutch fishing boats burned.
1680s	Fisheries begin to decline.
1688	'9 years war' begins. Token storming of Scalloway Castle by Lerwick gentry.
1690s	Bad harvests and famine.
1696	Act passed for the Settling of Schools, to reinforce the legislation of 1616.
1700	Smallpox. John Brand visits Shetland.
1702	'3rd war of containment' of France begins.
1703	French burn 100 Dutch herring 'busses' in Lerwick harbour.
1707	Act of Union between Scotland and England. Shetland becomes politically part of Great Britain.
1713	Shetland's first official SSPCK school opens in Walls.
1721	John Buchan, minister of Northmavine, gets four schools established in his parish.
1730s	Greenland whaling begins. Potatoes introduced to Shetland.
1736	*Isabella* takes mail and general cargo to Aberdeen once a year.
1738	Charter granted initiating educational changes; allowing agriculture, trades, knitting etc. to be taught.
1740	Revd John Mill, minister of Dunrossness, starts his diary.
1750s	Greenland whaling peaks. Far haaf fish production increases greatly. Smallpox vaccinations reduce deaths.
1752	Gregorian calendar officially replaces Julian calendar. Many parts of Shetland continued to use the old one.
1755	Population at 15,000.
1760	Govt. subsidy awarded to a trading consortium in Leith to deliver mail to Lerwick five times a year.
1763	Bruce of Symbister pioneers new fish curing and drying methods.

APPENDIX

1770	Smallpox contained, allowing birth rate to rise and population level to increase. Lerwick grows rapidly.
1774	George Lowe visits Shetland. Happyhansel School opens in Walls.
1776	Flax spinning factory built at Catfirth.
1780s	Industrial Revolution begins in Shetland. Kelp production begins and Sandlodge copper mine opens.
1790s	The first *Statistical Account of Shetland* compiled by Sir John Sinclair. The start of 20 years of Press Gang operating round Shetland. There were 1100 Shetland men serving in the Navy in 1793 and 3000 in 1808.
1797	A road was built from Lerwick to Tingwall.
1803	Education Act passed, enabling teachers' salaries to be increased.
1809	Arthur Edmondston writes *View of ancient and present state of Zetland Islands*.
1813	*Doris* lost with all hands *en route* for Shetland.
1814	Several lodberries now in Lerwick.
1815	Greenland whaling in full swing.
1816	Lerwick's first Parochial School opens.
1820s	'Hay & Ogilvy' ship builders established. First big farms laid out at Sumburgh and Sandlodge. Faroe fishing starts.
1821	Shetland Bank starts; own notes printed.
1825	First steamer service to Shetland. Paddle steamer *Sovereign* runs between Aberdeen and Lerwick.
1830	Tingwall farms laid out. Tenants moved and runrigs ploughed over.
1832	Fishing disaster on east side of Shetland; over 100 men lost. Reform Bill passed, giving landowners and tenants the right to vote.
1834	Herring boom.
1836	Shetland's first newspaper, *The Shetland Journal*, is launched.
1839	Edward Standen visited Shetland; began to promote Shetland hosiery.
1841	*The New Statistical Account of Shetland* produced.
1842	Great herring crash; biggest ever financial disaster for Shetland.
1843	Poor Law enquiry commission.
1847	Arthur Anderson returned as MP for Orkney and Shetland.
1848	Potato blight strikes.
1849-51	Meal roads being constructed in various parts of Shetland.
1850	A road was blasted through Mavis Grind connecting Northmavine with the rest of Mainland.
1850s-70s	Weisdale Clearances.
1856	Gas lighting installed in Lerwick.
1859	50 Greenland whaling ships in Lerwick harbour on 9 March.
1861	Population at 31,670. Emigration increases.
1862	Anderson Education Institute gifted to Shetland by Arthur Anderson.
1867	*Diana* enters Ronas Voe after 6 months trapped in ice; 14 months at sea.
1868	First steamship service to N. Isles; *Chieftain's Bride*.
1871	First *St Magnus* sailed. Emigration surge; 4640 Shetlanders leave during next 10 years.
1872	Landmark Education Scotland Act passed to set up state schools. *Shetland Times* newspaper founded.
1874	Tar barrelling banned in Lerwick. John Brown installs steam-driven hammer in Freefield engineering shop.
1875	Herring fishing begins and Faroe fishing declines.
1877	Lerwick Harbour Trust founded and the *Earl of Zetland* begins her 68-year service.
1885	The *Shetland News* founded.
1886	Crofters' Holdings Act introduced. Victoria Pier opened in Lerwick. Betty Mouat, shipwreck survivor, drifts to Norway.
1888	Lerwick Fever Hospital built.
1889	Local Government (Scotland) Act. Zetland County Council set up.
1893	Dr Jakobsen begins his studies of Scandinavian words in use in Shetland.
1900	The 'Great Gale' strikes Shetland from the south-east.
1904	27 July German fleet anchored off the Knab.
1905	First motor boat, the *Napier Major*, visits Shetland.
1913	First cinema, the North Star, opens in Lerwick.

1914 First World War begins. Sea plane base at Catfirth. 10th Cruiser Squadron based at Swarbacks Minn.

1917 Lerwick becomes a convoy port.

1926 First seine nets introduced for inshore flatfish catching.

1932 Mains water and sewerage system and electricity supply connections begin in Lerwick.

1933 The first civil aeroplane lands in Shetland.

1934 Epidemic of typhoid; 243 cases recorded during the year.

1936 First scheduled air service established.

1939 Second World War begins. Sullom Voe becomes an RAF base. Over 20,000 military personnel arrive.

1943 America lends three submarine chaser boats to the 'Shetland Bus' operation.

1947 Town and Country Planning Act passed.
The *New Shetlander* is launched.

1950 Echo sounders and Decca navigation technology increase fishing efficiency.

1953 New power station opens at Gremista.

1955 Noss officially becomes a National Nature Reserve.

1960 Shetland's first fish-processing factory opens in Scalloway.

1961 The new Gilbert Bain Hospital opens.

1963 *Shetland News* ceases to be published.

1964 First oil-exploration licences released in Britain. Television arrives in Shetland.

1965 Highlands and Islands Development Board established. First Norwegian purse seiners arrive.

1966 Shetland Museum and Library open.
Highlands and Islands Development Board (HIDB) set up by Labour Govt.

1967 Snowy owls arrive in Shetland and breed in Fetlar.

1968 Shetland Archeological & Historical Society formed.

1970 Air service between Sumburgh and Baltasound, Unst, begins.

1971 Oil discovered in the 'Brent' field to the east of Shetland. Trondra and Burra sea bridges built.

1973 Oil rig servicing begins in Shetland.
Sandy Loch reservoir constructed near Lerwick.

1974 Ninian oil field discovered.
Zetland County Council Act passed.
Shetland Bird Club launched.

1975 Zetland County Council is replaced by the Shetland Islands Council.
In a referendum in the same year Shetland votes 'No' (56% against 'yes' 43%) to membership of the EEC.
Earl of Zetland ferry replaced by inter-island car ferries.

1976 Fishing Limits Act established securing 200 mile fishing zone.

1977 Radio Shetland first broadcast.
Herring fishing ban imposed.

1978 *Esso Bernicia* spills 1100 tonnes of heavy bunker oil.

1979 Drilling licences for oil are renewed.

1980 The first plans are debated by Trinity House which lead eventually to the automating of all Shetland's lighthouses and the loss of all remaining lighthouse keepers and their families from the communities.

1981 H.M. Queen Elizabeth and King Olaf of Norway open the Sullom Voe Oil Terminal.
First Shetland Folk Festival held.
Shetland Field Studies Group established.

1983 Shetland Knitwear Trades Association set up.

1985 Hamefarin in Shetland.

1991 HIDB restructured into Highlands and Islands Enterprise by Conservative Govt.
Shetland Enterprise formed.

1993 *Braer* oil tanker wrecked off Garth's Ness; 86,238 tonnes of oil spilled.

1995 Bonhoga Gallery opens.
Clickimin Centre opens.

1997 Scatness sees beginning of Viking/Pictish excavations.

1999 Lerwick and Shetland host the Cutty Sark Tall Ships Race.

2000 Waste to Energy plant comes on stream.
A new *Shetland News* periodical appears in colour.

2001 Shetland Aerogenerators install three wind turbines between Scalloway and Lerwick.

2002 P&O Ferries era ends. North Link takes over.
'Sting Ray' trial tidal generation project commences in Yell Sound.

APPENDIX

Historic Sites and Artefacts Checklist

Böd of Gremista, Lerwick
Böd of Nesbister, Wormadale
Booth of Ollaberry
Catpund Quarry, Cunningsburgh
Chancel arch, Sand
Clickimin Broch, Lerwick
Cullinsburgh cross slab, Bressay
Fladdabister kilns
Fort Charlotte, Lerwick
Haa of Burravoe, Yell
Haa of Sand
Hanseatic Booth, Symbister
Hjaltadans stone circle
Jarlshof, Sumburgh
Lerwick Lodberries
Loch of Huxter, Whalsay
Lunna Church
Lund Graveyard
Mousa
Muness Castle, Unst
Pier House, Whalsay
Quendale Mill, Dunrossness
Scalloway Castle
Scalloway eclipse stone
Scatness, Sumburgh
Scord of Brouster, Walls
St Ninian's Isle, Bigton
Standing stones, Busta
Stanydale, Gruting
Stenness fishing station, Eshaness
Strom Castle
Sumburgh Lighthouse
Tingwall Law, Ting Holm
Underhoull Broch, Unst
Uyeasound
Vementry chambered cairn
Vementry guns
White Lady of Queyon, Yell
Yoxie, Whalsay

MUSEUM ARTEFACT HIGHLIGHTS

Viking comb
Gulberwick brooch
Dutch coins
Kebister armorial plate
Shetland knives
St Ninian's Isle Treasure;
(replicas only in Shetland)
Papil Stone
Bellarmine jar
Model ships

Best Landscape Guide

BEST BEACH GUIDE

Shetland has over 200 sandy beaches at various points around its 3000 miles of coastline, many small and inaccessible, but all beautiful in different ways. Winter storms can often alter the appearance of a beach and the quantity of sand may vary from year to year. A small selection of my favourites is given here, with some notes for additional information. Details about sea shells are not included, because collection of shells is not recommended as it damages the habitat. Some beaches can provide shelter at both ends, hence several wind directions are listed in some cases. Bear in mind that strong winds can be turbulent and the degree of shelter in some conditions will be variable.

The symbols following each place name give rough indications of beach quality, accessibility, degree of shelter from the wind, provision of toilet, car parking facilities, etc., and other features as follows:

Star rating for sheer loveliness:
*good, **very good, ***beautiful, ****exquisite

N,S,W,E, and NE, NW, SE, SW; sheltered from the north, south, west and east, and from the north east, north west, south east, south west, etc.

A1 = easy access
A2 = access possible
A3 = some walking required
A4 = access more difficult
T = Toilets provided
CP = Car parking available
IP = improved facilities planned

Norwick, Unst ** S, SE,SW, A1, CP, IP.
Burrafirth, Unst ** W, E, S, SW, SE, A2.
Skaw, Unst ** SW, W, A1, CP.
Sandwick, Unst *** W, SW, NW, A3, IP
(Prehistoric and historic sites nearby).
Lunda Wick, Unst ** S, SW, E, NE, A1, CP, IP.

Tresta, Fetlar *** N, NE, NW, E, A1, CP, IP.

Breckon, Yell *** S, SE, SW, W, E, A4, IP.
West Sandwick, Yell *** E, SE, NE, N, A2, CP, IP.
Gossabrough, Yell ** S, SW, W, A1, CP.

Sandvoe, Northmavine *** E, W, A1, CP, IP,
(Ancient chapel nearby. Old Haa house not far away).

Norby, West Mainland ** S, SW, SE, E, A2, CP.
Melby, West Mainland ** S, SW, SE, A1, T, CP, IP.
Reawick, West Mainland ** N, NW, W, A2.
Banna Minn, Burra Isle ** E, SE, NE, A3, IP.
Sands of Meal, Burra Isle *** N, W, NW, NE, A4, T, CP, (Can be very crowded at times), IP.

Gulberwick S. of Lerwick, Central Mainland
* W, SW, NW, N, A2.
Sands of Sound, Lerwick, Central Mainland
** W, NW, N, A2,
(Can be busy during fine weather and holidays), IP.

Sand Garth, Bressay * SW, S, SE, A2.
White Ayre, Bressay ** S, A4.

Cumliewick, S. Mainland ** E, S, SE, NE, A3, IP.
Levenwick, S. Mainland *** S, SE, SW, W, A1, CP, IP.
Maywick, S. Mainland * S, SE, E, W, SW, A2, IP.
St Ninian's Isle, Bigton, S. Mainland
**** N, S, E, W, A3, IP,
(Tombolo beach link to island. Ancient remains).
Quendale, S. Mainland **** N, NE, NW, W, A3, IP.
Rerwick, S. Mainland ** N, W, NW, NE, E, SE, A4.
Scousburgh, S. Mainland *** S, SE, NE, A1
(Sand dunes behind beach.
Caravans nearby. Can be crowded).
West Voe of Sumburgh, S. Mainland
*** E, SE, NE, N, A2, T, CP, IP.
Grutness, S. Mainland
** S, SW, W, NW, N, A1, CP, IP.

BEST CLIFF SCENERY

Almost anywhere in Shetland can produce fabulous cliff scenery. Some of the best views anywhere can be had from the inter-island ferries, while crossing from one island to another.

DRAMATIC PHYSICAL FEATURE CHECKLIST

Aesha Head, Papa Stour
Back of Ollaberry Fault
Deepdale, Walls
Drongs Stacks, Hillswick
Eshaness cliffs
Gloup Voe, Yell
Grind of the Navir, Eshaness
Hams of Muckle Roe
Muckle Flugga
St Ninian's Isle tombolo
Sheep Rock, Fair Isle
Sneck O Da Smaalie, Foula
Stanes of Stofast, Lunna Ness
Villians of Hamnavoe, Northmavine
Ronas Hill, Northmavine
Clift Hills
Hermaness
Fitful Head
Foula

APPENDIX

Plant Checklist

This is a shortened list of Shetland's wild plants, which, apart from those listed as rarities, can be found with little difficulty during the spring or summer months. The habitats have been roughly divided into groups, as a number of plants can be found in more than one habitat; for example, dry banks and verges can often support plants commonly found on cliff faces. Underlying limestone or serpentine rock can alter the plant species' range considerably, and certain habitats, such as saltmarsh or fellfield, have very specialised plant communities. Mosses, sedges, rushes and shrubs follow the flowering plants in each habitat group. There are great differences between specimens of the same plant where one is found on grazed, or exposed ground, and another in sheltered, sheep-free areas. Spring squill can flower at ground level in grazed cliff-top pasture, yet just over the sea fence, it can reach eight inches in height.

The common English names of the plants are listed in alphabetical order, followed by the Shetland name in bold and lastly the Latin name in italics. Shetland plant names are gradually dying out, but a number are included here, though some names have been lost through time. Though only one dialect name per plant is used in the checklist, there is considerable variation in local names from place to place in Shetland and you may well come across different ones.

For those with a particular interest in botany, consult David Malcolm's *Shetland's Wild Flowers*, or *The flowering plants and ferns of the Shetland Islands*, by Walter Scott and Richard Palmer.

BANKS, VERGES & DRY GRASSLAND

Autumn hawkbit - *Leontodon autumnalis*
Bird's-foot trefoil **(Caticlews)**- *Lotus corniculatus*
Bush vetch - *Vicia sepium*
Common daisy **(Kokkiloorie)** - *Bellis perennis*
Dandelion **(Bitter aks)** - *Taraxacum officinale*
Fairy flax - *Linum catharticum*
Field gentian **(Deadman's mittens)** - *Gentianella campestris*
Frog orchid - *Coeloglossum viride*
Hogweed **(Keksie)** - *Heracleum sphondylium*
Kidney vetch - *Anthyllis vulnararia*
Lady's bedstraw **(Hunders)** - *Galium verum*
Meadow buttercup **(Kraa's taes)** - *Ranunculus acris*
Meadow vetchling - *Lathyrus pratensis*
Mountain everlasting - *Antennaria dioica*
Pignut **(Swine's murricks)** - *Conopodium majus*
Red clover - *Trifolium pratense*
Self heal - *Prunella vulgaris*
Slender St John's-wort - *Hypericum pulchrum*
Sneezewort **(Pepper girse)** - *Achillea ptarmica*
Spear thistle - *Cirsium vulgare*
Spring squill **(Grice's mooricks)** - *Scilla verna*
Tufted vetch **(Moose peas)** - *Vicia cracca*
White clover **(Smora)** - *Trifolium repens*
Yarrow - *Achillea millefolium*
Yellow rattle **(Fool's pennies)** - *Rhinanthus minor*

False oat-grass **(Ockrabung)** - *Arrhenatherum eliatus*

HILLS AND MOORS
Bell heather - *Erica cinerea*
Bilberry **(Blaeberry)** - *Vaccinium myrtillus*
Common dog violet **(Snori)** - *Viola riviniana*
Cross leaved heath - *Erica tetralix*
Crowberry **(Berry hedder)** - *Empetrum nigrum*
Eyebright **(Lammas flooer)** - *Euphrasia officinalis*
Heather **(Ling)** - *Calluna vulgaris*
Heath bedstraw - *Galium saxatile*
Heath milkwort - *Polygala serpyllifolia*
Heath speedwell - *Veronica officinalis*
Heath spotted-orchid **(Curly dodie)** - *Dactylorhiza maculata*
Lousewort **(Sookie flooer)** - *Pedicularis sylvatica*
Marsh violet - *Viola palustris*
Sheep's sorrel - *Rumex acetosella*
Tormentil **(Bark flooer)** - *Potentilla erecta*
Wild thyme - *Thymus praecox*

Cotton grass **(Luckaminnie's Oo)** - *Eriophorum angustifolium*
Hair moss - *Polytrichum commune*
Heath rush **(Burra)** - *Juncus squarrosus*
Mat grass - *Nardus stricta*
Purple moor grass - *Molinia caerulea*
Splendid moss - *Hylocomium splendens*
Vivaparous fescue - *Festuca vivipara*

MARSHES, BOGS, STREAMSIDES, DITCHES, LOCHS & WET GRASSLAND
Angelica **(Spootie trumps)** - *Angelica sylvestris*
Bog asphodel - *Narthecium ossifragum*
Bog pimpernel - *Anagallis tenellis*
Bogbean **(Jule girse)** - *Menyanthes trifoliata*
Common butterwort - *Pinguicula vulgaris*
Common marsh bedstraw - *Galium palustre*
Creeping forget-me-not - *Myosotis secunda*
Devil's bit scabious - *Succisa pratensis*
Double orange mimulus - *Mimulus x burnetii*
Early marsh orchid - *Dactylorhiza incarnata*
Grass of Parnassus **(White Kaitrins)** - *Parnassia palustris*
Lady's smock **(Moddoo dokkies)** - *Cardamine pratensis*
Lesser celandine - *Ranunculus ficaria*
Lesser spearwort - *Ranunculus flammula*
Marsh cinquefoil - *Potentilla palustris*
Marsh lousewort - *Pedicularis palustris*
Marsh marigold **(Blogga flooer)** - *Caltha palustris*
Marsh pennywort - *Hydrocotyle vulgaris*
Marsh ragwort **(Gowans)** - *Senecio aquaticus*
Marsh thistle - *Cirsium palustre*
Marsh willowherb - *Epilobium palustre*
Meadowsweet - *Filipendula ulmaria*
Monkey flower - *Mimulus guttatus*
Northern marsh-orchid **(Curly dodie)** - *Dactylorhiza majalis subsp. purpurella*
Primrose **(Mayflooer)** - *Primula vulgaris*
Ragged robin - *Lychnis flos-cuculi*
Round leaved sundew - *Drosera rotundifolia*
Water avens - *Geum rivale*
Water forget-me-not - *Myosotis scorpioides*
Water mint - *Mentha aquatica*
Yellow iris **(Seggie)** - *Iris pseudacorus*

Sphagnum moss - *Sphagnum (various)*
Water horsetail - *Equisetum fluviatile*

CLIFF FACES, ROCKY OUTCROPS & GORGES
Alpine meadow rue - *Thalictrum alpinum*
Birdsfoot trefoil **(Caticlews)** - *Lotus corniculatus*
Creeping willow - *Salix repens*
Dwarf juniper - *Juniperus communis*
Glaucous dog rose **(Klingra)** - *Rosa caesa subsp. glauca*
Golden rod - *Solidago virgaurea*
Honeysuckle - *Lonicera periclymenum*
Meadowsweet **(Julegirse)** - *Filipendula ulmaria*
Moss campion - *Silene acaulis*
Red campion **(Sweet willie)** - *Silene dioica*
Roseroot **(Lady's footstool)** - *Rhodiola rosea*
Scot's lovage - *Ligusticum scoticum*

Sea campion **(Bogiflooer)** - *Silene vulgaris subsp. maritima*
Sea mayweed **(Witchie flooers)** - *Matricaria maritima*
Sheepsbit - *Jasione montana*

Broad buckler fern - *Dryopteris dilatata*
Common polypody - *Polypodium vulgare*
Greater woodrush - *Luzula sylvatica*
Hard fern **(Trowie cairds)** - *Blechnum spicant*
Wavy hair grass - *Deschampsia flexuosa*

SEASHORES
Buckshorn plantain - *Plantago coronopus*
Common scurvygrass **(Sailors' hope)** - *Cochlearia officinalis*
Curled dock - *Rumex crispus*
Orache - *Atriplex subsp.*
Sea milkwort - *Glaux maritima*
Sea plantain - *Plantago maritima*
Sea rocket - *Cakile maritima*
Sea sandwort - *Honckenya peploides*
Silverweed **(Blue girse)** - *Potentilla anserina*
Thrift or Sea pinks **(Banks flooer)** - *Armeria maritima*

Lyme grass - *Elymus arenarius*
Marram grass - *Ammophila arenaria*
Yellow-orange lichen - *Xanthoria parietina*

ARABLE LAND
Bugloss - *Anchusa arvensis*
Changing forget-me-not - *Myosotis discolor*
Chickweed - *Stellaria media*
Common hemp nettle - *Galeopsis tetrahit*
Common nettle - *Urtica dioica*
Corn spurrey **(Meldie)** - *Spergula arvensis*
Creeping buttercup - *Ranunculus acris*
Field forget-me-not - *Myosotis arvensis*
Fumitory - *Fumaria officinalis*
Groundsel - *Senecio vulgaris*
Northern dead nettle - *Lamium moluccellifolium*
Northern knot grass - *Polygonum boreale*
Red dead nettle - *Lamium purpureum*
Ribwort plantain **(Johnsmas flooer)** - *Plantago lanceolata*

GARDEN ESCAPES / INTRODUCTIONS
Bluebell - *Hyacinthoides hispanica x H. non-scripta*
Double green daffodil - *Narcissus various*
Magellan ragwort **(New Zealand daisy)** - *Senecio smithii*
Meadow cranesbill - *Geranium pratense*
Montbretia - *Tritonia x crocosmiflora*
Pheasants eye narcissus **(Grave flooer)** - *Narcissus poeticus*
Pink purslane - *Montia sibirica*

Quaking grass - *Briza media*
Tussock grass **(Tussie girse)** - *Poa flabellata*

RARITIES AND PLANTS LESS COMMONLY SEEN
Alpine Lady's mantle - *Alchemilla alpina*
Autumn gentian - *Gentianella amarella*
Birch - *Betula pubescens*
Dwarf cornel - *Cornus suecica*
Edmondston's Chickweed **(Shetland Mouse-ear)** - *Cerastium nigrescens*
English stonecrop - *Sedum anglicum*
Germander speedwell - *Veronica chamaedrys*
Long-headed poppy - *Papaver dubium*
Northern rock-cress - *Cardaminopsis petraea*
Norwegian sandwort - *Arenaria norvegica* subsp. *norvegica*
Oyster plant - *Mertensia maritima*
Purple saxifrage - *Saxifraga oppositifolia*
Rowan - *Sorbus aucuparia*
Sea aster - *Aster tripolium*
Trailing azalea - *Loiseleuria procumbens*
Tway-blade - *Listera cordata*
Water lily - *Nymphaea alba*

Adders tongue - *Ophioglossum azoricum*
Moonwort - *Botrychium lunaria*
Royal fern - *Osmunda regalis*
Wilson's filmy fern - *Hymenophyllum wilsonii*

Bird Checklist

This list is not definitive and more species could easily be seen by an observant visitor. In addition, especially after a spell of south-easterly winds, many other species may turn up. A simplified breeding habitat key is given below. Bear in mind that birds may be seen in very different habitats from time to time. The local Shetland name is given in brackets.

Bird nesting habitats.
1) Coast
2) Sea cliffs
3) Hills and heather moorland
4) Loch and stream sides
5) Gardens and trees
6) Croft and pasture land

4	Red-throated diver (Raingoose) *Gavia stellata*
1,2	Great black-backed gull (Swaabie) *Larus marinus*
1,2,3	Fulmar (Maalie) *Fulmarus glacialis*
3,6	Common gull (Tina maa) *Larua canus*
1,2	Storm petrel (Aalamootie) *Hydrobates pelagicus*
1,2	Lesser black-backed gull (Peerie swaabie) *Larus fuscus*
2	Gannet (Solan) *Sula bassana*
1, 2	Herring gull (Maa) *Larus argentatus*
2	Shag (Scarf) *Phalacrocorax aristotelis*
2	Kittiwake (Rippack maa) *Rissa tridactyla*
2	Cormorant (Muckle scarf) *Phalacrocorax carbo*
1	Common tern (Tirrick) *Sterna hirundo*
4	Mute swan *Cygnus olor*
1,3	Arctic tern (Tirrick) *Sterna paradisœa*
1	Shelduck (Links goose) *Tadorna tadorna*
2	Guillemot (Lungwie) *Uria aalge*
4	Teal *Anas crecca*
2	Razorbill (Sea craa) *Alca torda*
4	Mallard (Stock deuk) *Anas platyrynchos*
2	Black guillemot (Tystie) *Cepphus grylle*
4	Tufted duck *Aythya fuligula*
2	Puffin (Tammie norie) *Fratercula arctica*
1,3	Eider (Dunter) *Somateria mollissima*
2	Rock dove (Wild doo) *Columba livia*
4	Red-breasted merganser *Melanitta serrator*
5	Wood pigeon *Columba palambus*
3	Merlin (Peerie hawk) *Falco columbarius*
6	Collared dove *Streptopelia decaocta*
3	Red grouse *Lagopus lagopus*
3,6	Skylark (Laverock) *Alauda arvensis*
1,3	Oystercatcher (Shalder) *Haematopus ostralegus*
6	Swallow *Hirundo rustica*
1	Ringed plover (Saandy loo) *Charadrius hiaticula*
3,6	Meadow pipit (Teetick) *Anthus pratensis*
3	Golden plover (Plivver) *Pluvialis apricarius*
1	Rock pipit (Banks sparrow) *Anthus petrosus*
6	Lapwing (Tieves nacket) *Vanellus vanellus*
1,5	Wren (Robbie cuddie) *Troglodytes troglodytes*
3	Dunlin (Plivver's page) *Calidris alpina*
3,6	Wheatear (Staneshakker) *Oenanthe oenanthe*
4	Snipe (Snippick) *Gallinago gallinago*
5	Blackbird (Blackie) *Turdus merula*
3	Whimbrel (Peerie whaap) *Numenius phaeopus*
5	Rook (Craa) *Corvus frugilegus*
3,6	Curlew (Whaap) *Numenius arquata*
2,3	Hooded crow (Craa) *Corvus corone*
6	Redshank (Ebb-cock) *Tringa totanus*
2	Raven (Corbie) *Corvus corax*
4	Common sandpiper *Actitis hypoleucus*
2,3,5,6	Starling (Stari) *Sturnus vulgaris*
4	Red-necked phalarope *Phalaropus lobatus*
5,6	House sparrow (Sporrow) *Passer domesticus*
3	Arctic skua (Skootie aalun) *Stercorarius parasiticus*
1,3	Twite (Lintie) *Carduelis flavirostris*
3	Great skua (Bonxie) *Stercorarius skua*
4	Reed bunting *Emberiza schoeniclus*
4,6	Black-headed gull (Heedie maa) *Larus ridibundus*

Try to visit the RSPB reserves of Sumburgh Head, Spiggie and Fetlar if at all possible. For keen birdwatchers, a stay in Fair Isle at the famous bird observatory is strongly recommended.

Bibliography

Airfield Focus Peter Ward, GMS Enterprises 1994.

Ancient Shetland Val Turner, Batsford 1998.

Bobby Tulloch's Shetland
Bobby Tulloch, Shetland Times 1993.

The Bod of Gremista
Bod of Gremista Management Committee 1989.

Bressay
Jonathan Wills, Bressay History Group 1991.

The Collected Poems of Vagaland
Shetland Times 1975.

Court Book of Shetland 1615-1629
Gordon Donaldson, Shetland Library 1991.

Diarist in an Age of Social Change
Ronald Sandison, Shetland Times 1997.

Drifting Alone to Norway
TMY Manson, Shetland Publishing Co 1986.

An Etymological Dictionary of the Norn Language in Shetland Jakob Jakobsen, Shetland Folk Society 1985 reprint.

Exploring Scotland's Heritage
Anna Ritchie, Royal Commission on Ancient Monuments 1985.

Fair Isle, an Island Saga
Valerie Thom, Edinburgh 1989.

The flowering plants and ferns of the Shetland Islands Walter Scott and Richard Palmer.

The Geology of Western Shetland W Mykura and J Phemister, Her Majesty's Stationery Office 1976.

Grammar and Usage of the Shetland Dialect
T A Robertson and J J Graham, Shetland Times 1991.

A Guide to Prehistoric Shetland
Noel Fojut, Shetland Times 1981 and 1986.

Guide to Dunrossness and Fair Isle
Peter Gray, Shetland Times 1992.

A Guide to Shetland's Birds Bobby Tulloch and Fred Hunter, Shetland Times 1970.

A Guide to Shetland's Mammals
Bobby Tulloch, Shetland Times 1978.

Innocent Passage J Wills and K Warner, Mainstream Publishing 1993.

Island Futures Roy Gronneberg and M Magnuson, Thuleprint 1978.

The Islands of Scotland
Hugh MacDiarmid, Batsford 1939.

Kebister Olwyn Owen and Christopher Lowe, Sutton Publishing 1999.

Lerwick Harbour
J R Nicolson, Shetland Times 1987.

Link Stanes Rhoda Bulter, Shetland Times 1980.

Love's Laebrack Sang
Lollie Graham, Shetland Library 2000.

Manson's Guide to Shetland T M Y Manson 1932.

The Natural History of Shetland
R J Berry and J L Johnson, Collins 1986.

A Naturalist's Shetland J Laughton and T Johnston, A D Poyser Natural History 1999.

A New Description of Orkney, Shetland etc, John Brand, Edinburgh and London 1703.

The Northern Isles
Alexander Fenton, Tuckwell Press 1997.

Northern Lights J J Graham and T A Robertson, Education Committee 1964.

North Sea Oil and the Environment Ed. WJ Cairns, Elsevier Science Publishers Ltd. 1992.

Orkney and Shetland Archaeological Guide
Lloyd Laing, David and Charles 1974.

Orkney and Shetland
Eric Linklater, Robert Hale 1965.

Orkney and Schetland 1771 George Lowe, Melven Press 1978 (reprint).

Orkneyinga Saga: The History of the Earls of Orkney Palsson and Edwards, Hogarth Press London 1978.

Otters Bobby Tulloch, Colin Baxter 1994.

The Place Names of Shetland Jakob Jakobsen, David Nutt 1936; reprinted 1993.

The Pictish Trail
Anthony Jackson, Orkney Press 1989.

The Ponies of Shetland
Maurice Cox, Shetland Times 1876.

Ports and Harbours Shetland Islands Council 1998/99.

The Quaternary of Shetland
J Birnie, J Gordon, K Bennett and A Hall 1993.

Rural Life in Shetland
Ian Tait, Shetland Museum 2000.

The Sail Fishermen of Shetland
A Halcrow, Shetland Times 1994.

Scord of Brouster Alasdair Whittle, Oxford University Committee for Archaeology 1986.

Sea Change Reginald Byron, Institute of Social and Economic Research 1986.

The Shaping of Shetland Val Turner, Shetland Times 1998.

Shetland Val Turner, Batsford 1998.

Shetland. An Illustrated Architectural Guide Mike Finnie, Mainstream 1990.

Shetland Animal Studies Rod Thorne, Shetland Times 1983.

A Shetland Anthology J J Graham and L I Graham, Shetland Publishing Company 1998.

Shetland and Oil J R Nicolson, William Luscombe 1975.

Shetland and the Outside World 1469-1969 Donald Withrington, O.U.P. 1983.

Shetland Archaeology Brian Smith, Shetland Times 1985.

Shetland Bird Reports, Shetland Bird Club.

The Shetland Book Zetland Education Committee 1967.

Shetland Cattle Stanley Bowie 1995.

Shetland Coastline Nature Conservancy Council 1980.

The Shetland Dictionary John J Graham, Shetland Times 1993.

Shetland Documents 1580-1611 and *Shetland Documents 1195-1579* Ed John H Ballantyne & Brian Smith, Shetland Islands Council and Shetland Times 1994 and 1999.

Shetland Field Studies Group archive, 1981 onwards.

Shetland Fishing Saga C A Goodlad, Shetland Times 1971.

Shetland Folk Books Shetland Folk Society.

Shetland Folklore J R Nicolson, Robert Hale 1981.

Shetland Geology and Geomorphology Nature Conservancy Council 1976.

Shetland in Statistics 2001, 1999, 1998, 1972 Shetland Islands Council.

The Shetland Isles Andrew T Cluness, Hale 1951.

Shetland: The Isles of Nightless Summer William Moffatt, Heath Cranton 1934.

Shetland Interpretive Plan Shetland Islands Council 1999.

Shetland Life magazines.

Shetland Life under Earl Patrick Gordon Donaldson, Oliver and Boyd 1958

Shetland's Living Landscape David Spence, Thule Press 1979.

Shetland Place-names John Stewart, Shetland Library and Museum 1987.

Shetland Lace Gladys Amedro, Shetland Times 1993.

Shetland's Northern Links, Language and History D Waugh, Scottish Society for Northern Studies 1996.

Shetland Proverbs and Sayings Bertie Deyell, Shetland Folk Society 1993.

The Shetland Report The Nevis Institute 1978.

Shetland Sandy Beach Audit G Macleod, Shetland Amenity Trust 1999.

The Shetland Sheepdog Mary Davis, Ringpress 1994.

The Shetland Sheepdog Margaret Osborne, Popular Dogs Publishing Co 1970.

The Shetland Story Liv Schei and Gunnie Moberg, Batsford 1988.

Shetland Traditional Lore Jessie Saxby, London 1932.

The Shetland Way of Oil John Button, Thule Print 1976.

Shetland's Wild Flowers D Malcolm, Shetland Times 1992.

Shetland Wool Stanley Bowie 1994.

Studies in the Vegetational History of the Faroe and Shetland Islands Johanes Johansen, Foroya Frodskaparfelag 1985.

The Third Statistical Account of Scotland: Shetland James R Coull, Scottish Academic Press 1985.

Toons and Tenants Brian Smith, Shetland Times 2000.

Traditional Life in Shetland James R Nicolson, Hale 1978.

Travellers in a Bygone Shetland Derek Flinn, Scottish Academic Press 1989.

The True Romance of Busta Frances Scott, Nelson Smith 1996.

A Vehement Thirst after Knowledge J J Graham, Shetland Times 1998.

Viking Scotland Anna Ritchie, Batsford 1993.

Walking the Coastline of Shetland nos.1-6 Peter Guy, Shetland Times.

The Windswept Isles Elizabeth Balneaves, Butler and Tanner 1977.

With Naught but Kin Behind Them Norah Kendall, Melbourne 1998.

Wrestlers with the Troubled Sea Louis Johnson, Nelson Smith 1994.

Glossary

Aets: Shetland oats, a tall, strong-stemmed variety.
Ayre: A bar or spit of sand.
Bairns: Children.
Bannocks: Flat scones
Ben: Bedroom end of a traditional crofthouse
Bere: An old variety of barley
Blaand: drink made from the residue of butter churning
Böd: merchant's trading booth circa 17-1800s
Burn: Stream
But: Living, kitchen end of a traditional crofthouse
Byre: Cowshed
Caain: A driving, or gathering of sheep or whales
Caain whale: Pilot whale
Darkening: Dusk
Dratsie: Otter
Dyke: Wall or boundary barrier
Ebb: Low tide
Essie cairt: Rubbish lorry
Fael: Turf
Foude: A judge during Norse rule
Fourareen: A four-oared open boat
Gaet: Small path or way
Geo: Steep-sided cleft or inlet in coastal cliffs
Gimmer: 1-2-year-old Shetland ewe (no lamb yet)
Grind: Gate, or gateway
Guizer: Disguised person, vistor to a party
Haaf: The deep sea
Hairst: Autumn
Hentilagets: Fragments of wool caught on the ground
Holm: Very small island off shore or in a loch
Inby land: Ground enclosed by a hill dyke
Jarl: Chief Viking
Kale: Cabbage
Kirn: Churn for butter making
Kirn milk: Whey
Kishie: Basket
Lallies: Toys, traditionally hand made
Lawthing: Norse law court
Lodberry: Store built out into the sea for unloading cargo
Lum: Chimney, or hole in a roof to let smoke out
Merk: Productive unit of land, in Norse times
Merrie Dancers: Northern Lights
Moorit: Natural warm brown shade of wool
Ness: A headland
Njugle: Mythical, wicked creature
Noost: Boat sized hollow in upper shore
Oily Muggie: Nickname for Northmavine folk
Ollick: Ling
Ootby land: Land outside a hill dyke
Orca: Killer whale
Park: Enclosed grassland
Peerie: Small
Peerie corn: A small quantity of food
Peerie scar: A small quantity of liquid, i.e milk or tea
Piltock: A young saithe
Planticrub: Small drystone enclosure, usually circular, built to protect plants.
Pone: A long turf cut to lay on a turf roof
Punt: A small dinghy
Quern: Stone for grinding corn by hand
Ranselman: Norse equivalent of a policeman
Reestit mutton: Cured mutton, very delicious!
Rigga rendal: A shared cultivation strip system
Rivlin: Viking shoes
Rooin: Wool-plucking method
Roost: Very noisy, turbulent tidal stream
Scattald: Common grazing area
Selkie: Wild seal
Shaela: A natural grey shade of wool
Sheep's pearls: Sheep's droppings
Sillock: Slightly younger piltock
Simmer Dim: Midsummer twilight
Sixereen: Six-oared boat for deep-sea fishing
Skat: Norse land tax
Skeo: Openwork store for drying meat and fish.
Skerry: Small rock, or islet in the sea
Spoots: Razor shells
Spootie Ebb: An exceptionally low tide
Stack: Large, free-standing sheer crag offshore
Stane: Stone
Stap and crappin: Traditional fish liver dish
Teind: Tithes
Taing: Seaweed
Ting: Norse parliament
Trow: Troll, or goblin-like person
Tup: Ram
Tushkar: Tool for cutting peats
Udal law: Norse legal system
Up Helly Aa: Victorian 'Viking' fire festival
Voar: Spring
Voe: Long sea inlet
Waar: Seaweed
Ward or Wart: Highest point of a hill
Wick: Beach
Yard: Vegetable plot, as in 'kale yard'
Yoal: A Shetland clinker-built boat
Zulu: Fishing boat

Index of Places

(**Bold** type indicates map)

INDEX

Jill Slee Blackadder lives in Shetland where she is a school teacher, and founder of the Shetland Field Studies Group. She writes regularly for *Shetland Life* magazine and a weekly column for the *Shetland Times*.

YOU'LL BE A TEACHER OVER MY DEAD BODY

BY

CLIVE WILLIAMS OBE

Author and Publisher: Clive Williams OBE MA LLB (Cantab) -

Honeycroft House, Pangbourne Road, Upper Basildon, Berks RG8 8LP
Tel 01491-671631 or 07974-314929
E-Mail clivewilliams@gmx.co.uk

This Book is dedicated to my colleagues in the County Secretariat of the former Berkshire County Council, who were and are a wonderful group of people. They were hard working, efficient and gave me unstinting support throughout my tenure as their 'Boss'. There were occasional tough times but we enjoyed life to the full and had many a laugh. The fact that almost 30 years have passed since I hung up my Shire hall boots, but we are still in touch, says it all. I hope these Memoirs kindle happy memories for them.

'What's he ever done? Has he ever done a day's work in his life? What great cause is he identified with? He is identified .... with the great cause of cheering us all up.'

Arnold Bennett – The Card (1911)

Overheard by Christina at the start of a Basildon Primary school historical walk, led by Clive

1st little boy – That's Clive Williams – he's famous
2nd little boy – Oh yeah – what's he famous for?
1st little boy – I dunno, but he's famous.

Printed by Lamport Gilbert Ltd, Reading, Berks, RG2 0TB
ISBN: 978-1-9999792-2-5

CONTENTS

BOB GASH & REORGANIZATION

COUNTY SECRETARY & COUNTY SOLICITOR

PREFACE

I come from a teaching family. My father was a teacher – his mother who died in the Spanish flu epidemic of 1919 was a teacher and my maternal grandfather, who actually knew Lloyd George, was also a teacher. My mother had one sister and she too married a teacher. So a teacher I was destined to be and I like to think I would have been a good one.

But it was not to be. I still remember my mother saying to me in 1945, when I was just 7, '*You'll be a teacher over my dead body*', and what my mother said in our household went. The phrase has stuck and I have used it as the title of this book. She actively discouraged me and my younger brother Paul from becoming teachers and as a result we both ended up as solicitors. Her reasoning was understandable. When my father went into teaching in 1926, he landed a well-paid job at Cardiff High School. You don't get 350 applicants nowadays applying for a junior teaching post but that was the position in Wales in 1926. He married my mother in 1932 and they had a very good standard of living – car, holidays abroad, even help in the house, while my mother never had a paid job.

That all changed with the 2nd World War and by 1945 the good times for my parents were over. The car had gone and holidays were a fortnight in Tenby or Newquay, Cardiganshire. Nor did they improve much during my father's lifetime. When I became an Assistant Clerk at Berkshire County Council in 1969, I was earning 20% more than my father, who was then Deputy Head at Cardiff High School, arguably the leading State school in Wales. My mother called this '*a disgrace*' and who can argue with her?

So these Memoirs mainly relate to my local government career of 28 years, most of which was spent with the former Berkshire County Council, that was abolished in 1998. For the first few years I was accommodated in the old Shire Hall in the Forbury in Reading. Later I was based at the grandly named Abbot's House, which was no more than a two-storey terrapin, next to Shire Hall. Then at the end of 1980 the whole Council moved to a purpose built HQ in south Reading, which was known as Shinfield Park. I was based there until 1989, when I took early retirement from the County Council at the age of 52.

It was no accident that I came to work in Berkshire as an Articled Clerk. I have set out the full story in Chapter 1, so I will not repeat it here. But in so far that I was in a sense family, I was very close to my Principal, Ellis Roger Davies (ERD), who was Clerk of the County Council from 1952-1972. There was very little as regards the goings-on in Berkshire that he kept from me and as the saying goes : 'he knew where the bodies were buried'. So when he retired he was prevailed upon to write a History of the First County Council (1888-1974). I was appointed as his Literary Editor and awaited with eager anticipation the exhumation of the bodies. ERD toiled mightily but what resulted was the most boring of books – a summary of 90 years of Committee meetings. I was not alone in being disappointed and ERD was urged to say something about the characters he had worked with. So he added a chapter on the Chairmen of the County Council and that brought the book to life. Even so he left out the juicier bits in deference to the living. But as 40 years have passed I have included them in these Memoirs and have written about many more with which I have had personal experience.

However it is not the scandals but the humour that I look back on with fondness. There was something to make one laugh at least once a week and it came from many sources and in many guises. When something tickled my fancy, I made a copy and slung it in a large box and the box, which is now full, has been my archive for these Memoirs. I don't know what possessed Mr & Mrs Duck to call their son Donald but why did he then have to go and live in 'The Old Swan'. The Councillors could be a hoot as well – the Hon Elizabeth Samuel's comment on her Labour opponent *'Don't you think Cliff Rayner is rather sexy in an earthy sort of way'* heard by everyone at the Property Committee was a classic. Some correspondents went to great trouble to write in verse and it seemed only polite to reply in like measure. The eccentrics and awkward squad took up an awful lot of my time but I could dish it out as well as receive it, as witness my letter which appeared in the Peter Simple column in the Daily Telegraph. When I used to be involved in Quarter Sessions work, you could almost guarantee that his Honour Judge Claude Duveen or Edward Terrell, the Recorder of Newbury, would say or do something outrageous or funny. My favourite letter was from a Mr Alan Hardy of Slough, which I have reproduced in full. What really amused me was that having dipped his pen in vitriol, Mr Hardy ended it *'Yours sincerely.'*

see colour page XVIII

The good times at the County Council changed for the worse for me in 1983, when my first wife Liz was diagnosed with terminal ovarian cancer and given 12 months to live. Our daughter, Rebecca was then 8 and her brother, Robert just 6. In fact Liz lived another 3 years and eventually died on April 1st 1986. ERD had died in February 1986 but he was aged 80 and for someone who was short and rotund and never took any exercise, that was a good life-span. But the real shock was the unexpected death of ERD's successor, Bob Gash, on April 19th 1986, aged just 60.

His successor as Chief Executive, Tony Allen, was a very different character from Bob and had a very different method of working. I had been indispensable to Bob Gash but that was not the case with Tony.

At the same time the Council intensified its cost saving attempts. Cost centre management was introduced and specialist units were created to monitor the spending Departments. The County Quantity Surveyor, previously a third tier officer in the County Architect's Department was made a Chief Officer in his own right and given a wide-ranging brief to comment on property savings. He was a bright young man but there were then some rare old battles between him and the County Architect and County Property Officer, who bitterly resented what they saw as his interference. The County Council decided to embrace the computer age and a Director of Information Systems was appointed to oversee the project. He had no time for County Supplies and more battles ensued between the Computer Department and County Supplies. Cost centre management certainly buttoned down expenditure but it meant that each of the 400 cost centres jealously protected its own patch and there are times when progress can only be made by joint working. I have kept 10 clips of paper regarding these various disputes but re-reading them after 30 years, they struck me as rather pathetic, so I have spared the reader the gory details and have just alluded to them.

The atmosphere at Shinfield Park undoubtedly soured following Tony Allen's appointment. The entire blame can not be placed at his door but his style of management undoubtedly contributed. You don't get a satirical magazine called 'Managers Health and (In)efficiency' doing the rounds in a happy organisation. Relationships at Councillor level also soured and party point scoring became the order of the day. This culminated in the disastrous County Council meeting of May 1988, which led me to conclude that my local government career had run its course.

The irony is that Tony Allen's vision of Berkshire as a Unitary County, which is now the case in many Counties, translated itself into the Conservative and Labour Groups (three-quarters of the Council) supporting Unitary government but based on Districts. Only the Liberal-Democrat Group were consistently in favour of retaining the County Council. I understood why the Labour Group were in favour as they rightly foresaw being able to gain power in Reading and Slough. But I could never understand the initial Conservative Group attitude, as expounded quite forcefully by Tony Wiseman (then Chairman) to Christina at the time of my departure. Later the Conservative Group changed its mind when it realized that Berkshire would be the only historic County Council to disappear, but by then it was too late. In my view dividing Berkshire into six Unitaries has not worked; they are too small and most are struggling.

Here I want to pay a tribute to my second wife Christina. I first met her when she was Research Director with Keep Britain Tidy and used to visit for Keep

Berkshire Tidy meetings. She was very supportive after Liz's death and eventually moved to Berkshire and helped me bring up Rebecca and Robert. We have been married now for almost 10 years.

Having read a first draft of these Memoirs, which ended in 1989, Christina felt I needed a more upbeat ending. So I have written about what I and Christina have been up to in the last 29 years and as a result these Memoirs have been extended by a third, as neither of us has been idle. The undoubted highlight of this period was Christina's Shrieval year from April 2009 - March 2010. The High Sheriff has no powers per se but has the ability to go anywhere in the County and to work with a wide range of Groups and Charities. A visit to Broadmoor was particularly interesting and we enjoyed organizing 9 days of 'Beating-the-Bounds of Berkshire' charity walks in May 2009.

I sometimes ruefully reflect that I appear to be working as hard as I ever did at Shire Hall; the only difference being that I no longer get paid. But I won't claim that as it will only encourage Joey Rowe to maintain that that is quite easy, as I never did a day's work at Shire Hall anyway. But joking apart, I am particularly pleased with what has been achieved at Watlington House in Reading and the Old Bluecoat School in Thatcham. Both buildings were on their knees when I first became involved but thanks to 10 years hard work, both buildings are now thriving community centres.

For those insider readers, who either worked at Shire Hall or Shinfield Park or served as a Councillor, I hope these Memoirs bring back on the whole pleasant memories. For those non-insider readers you may be surprised to find out what really went on at Shire Hall and Shinfield Park. You will also find out that it is no good getting ratty with local government officers – they respond far better to humour. Not so sure though that this also applies to Civil Servants.

Clive Williams OBE – February 2018

YOU'LL BE A TEACHER OVER MY DEAD BODY

ARTICLED CLERK

1

THE CLYDACH CONNECTION

I was born on the 16th June 1938 and on the 21st June 1938, Ellis Roger Davies (ERD), then Deputy Clerk of Berkshire County Council wrote on Shire Hall headed notepaper to my father, who lived in Cardiff, saying that he would be honoured to become my god-father, and how much he was looking forward to '*meeting the little fellow*'. I still have the letter.

ERD and my father were both born in Clydach-on-Tawe, an industrial village 7 miles from Swansea. My father was born in 1903; ERD in 1906 and they were very close, because my grandmother died in the Spanish flu epidemic of 1919 and ERD's mother was one of a group of her friends, who rallied round to help bring up my father and his younger brother Harry. When my father married my mother in 1932, ERD was his best man.

ERD's father was a mining engineer, who spent some time in South Africa. When ERD left school it was to go down a mine, as his father wanted him to follow him in his career. But mining was not for ERD and his father then managed to get him articled to the Town Clerk of Swansea. This was a colourful character who had a passion for hunting. He would spend the morning at Town Hall in Swansea and the afternoon hunting, to be followed by a spell in a local hostelry. His Chief Clerk would then arrive with the outgoing post for signature.

After completing articles and qualifying as a Solicitor, ERD landed a plum job as Prosecuting Solicitor for Manchester Corporation. Then in 1935 aged just 29, he was appointed Deputy Clerk of Berkshire County Council. He succeeded Mr Neobard as Clerk in 1951, and remained Clerk until 1972. He died in 1986 aged 80, only months before his successor, Bob Gash, also died unexpectedly. ERD and his wife Gwen are buried in Swallowfield Cemetery.

Meanwhile my father was appointed as a Master at Cardiff High School in 1926 and he remained at the school for 42 years, the last 15 as Deputy Head.

Probably his most famous pupil was John Humphrys of the 'Today' programme, who hated the school and left at 15. But I once met John Humphrys and mentioned my father had taught him. He became very excited, shouted out to colleagues –' *this young man's father taught me*' (I am 5 years older than him) and went on to say that he hated the school (which I knew already) but that he had had a lot of time for my father. I asked him why had had hated the school and he replied that the school was only interested in academic and rugby football results (which was true) and he hated sports and was not academic. I ventured to suggest that a man who wrote a book on grammar can hardly claim not to be academic and then the conference resumed and we spoke no more. But a week later he wrote a piece in the Sunday paper he was writing for at the time, clearly referring to our conversation. He never mentioned the name of our school but then he set down the reasons why he hated a school that he admitted most parents would do their damndest to get their children into. He is a complicated man with many hang-ups. I have seen him claim that he came from Splott in Cardiff, which is the most working-class part of the City. But attending the funeral of Billy Jerrett, my erst-while next door neighbour in Rumney, I was talking to his cousin Joan, who mentioned that she used to wheel young John round in a pram, as she used to baby-sit for his parents. '*I didn't realize you came from Splott*', I said. '*I didn't*', replied Joan, '*I lived in Roath and so did John*'. Roath is divided from Splott by the railway and is regarded as a lower middle-class area.

Both I and my younger brother Paul also went to Cardiff HS and after National Service I went on to study law at Queens' College, Cambridge. The school was very successful at sending students to Oxbridge. There were 35 of us from the school at Oxbridge during my 3 years. We used to hold an annual dinner alternating between Oxford and Cambridge. In 1960 when I was in my second year at Cambridge, ERD got in touch and invited me down to Reading with a view to becoming articled to him, once I had successfully graduated.

2
ARTICLED CLERK

So it was August 1960 when I first mounted the steps of the old Shire Hall in the Forbury, Reading.

In those days Universities and the professions were the preserve of the well-to-do. My father had just his teacher's income but my mother's family had come up in the world – her grandfather, William Morgan, had started with nothing but had risen to the position of Chief Engineer of the Llanelli Steel Works Company. Some of the Morgan money had been inherited by my mother, which meant that my parents were in a position to support me in gaining a professional qualification.

Without parental support one could forget about the professions as a career. Even as late as 1960 it was not the practice to pay articled clerks – in fact the position was even worse as one's parents were required to pay the Principal a premium, - in the case of the legal profession normally 100gns, around £2000 in today's money, though in my case ERD said '*Seeing as you are family, boy, I won't be charging your father*'. I was always 'Boy' to ERD in the early days. But he went on to offer a glimmer of hope. Apparently the Law Society was urging the legal profession to start paying articled clerks and ERD eventually persuaded the notoriously tight-fisted Finance & General Purposes Committee to put the articled clerk post on the bottom of the lowest scale – Clerical General Division 1 –which came to £10 a week (£8 after tax).

But back in 1960 when I first visited Shire Hall the financial position was such that it was not so much my seeking articles as ERD trying to sell me the concept. A short rotund individual, he was an excellent advocate and scarcely had I walked up the steps of Shire Hall, when I found myself sitting beside him in his Rover car, with the County Architect, Mr J T Castle, sitting in the back, being conducted on a whirlwind tour of Berkshire. I thought this was a considerable honour but quickly came to realize that being driven anywhere by ERD was an honour that every member of staff eagerly sought to avoid, such was his reputation for terrible driving. He loved talking and when he talked he always addressed the person he was talking to. When they cried out '*Watch out*' he would look back at the road ahead, swerve back to his side of the road, narrowly avoid the oncoming traffic, and then re-commence talking.

What saved him was the fact that he always drove exceedingly slowly. One of the Committee Clerks, Sam Saunders, later told me that he was cycling along the Bath Road by Maidenhead Thicket one Sunday afternoon, on the way to see a girl friend, when ERD's car overtook him. It was going so slowly that Sam speeded up, overtook ERD's car and as he went by said *'Good Afternoon, Mr Davies'*. On another famous occasion in 1967, ERD drove Freddy Jones, a senior Committee Clerk, to the Thames Valley Police Amalgamation Inquiry at County Hall, Oxford. The journey up was so horrendous that Freddy refused to return with ERD and caught the train instead. However, I was blissfully unaware of ERD's reputation at the time and there were no incidents on this inaugural trip around Berkshire. We first proceeded down the Bath Road (A4) from Reading to Newbury, where the County Council were building a combined Police Station and Magistrates Court at Mill Lane: in 2015 I was invited to the closing ceremony for the Magistrates Court. We had a look around the site and then travelled up the A34 to Didcot, where the County Council were building another similar scheme. It was that drive up the A34, which I still vividly recall, which sold Berkshire to me. It was a beautiful sunny August day. There was very little traffic around in 1960 and either side of the road as far as the eye could see you had extensive fields of golden wheat glinting in the sunshine. Dotted around were the traditional Berkshire farmhouses and barns with their red brick and mostly red tiled roofs. The wheat fields were interspersed with clumps of green copses and the landscape was pleasantly rolling to give added interest. The overall impression was one of space and tranquillity, light and air. I was bowled over and decided there and then that I wanted to come and work in Berkshire. I stuck to that decision. It was the practice then for potential articled clerks to be interviewed by a Committee in Bell Court Yard near the Law Courts in London, to see if they were fit and proper persons. When I told the Interviewing Panel that I was going to do my articles in local government they thought I was mad and did their best to talk me out of it, but I stuck to my guns.

Those who knew ERD will recall that he was a trencher man par excellence. His love of food started at a very early age. One day my father and a cousin wanted to cycle from Clydach to the Gower but had only one bike. ERD had a bike and was prepared to lend it but for the princely sum of 6d. which was duly paid. In those days you could get an ice-cream for one halfpenny and when my father and his cousin returned from the Gower, they found ERD exiting the village shop having made his twelfth ice-cream purchase of the day!

ERD was allowed to travel 1st class on the train on official business and this privilege was extended to staff who had to accompany him. So on a few occasions I accompanied him to London. I admired his technique. The train journey from Paddington to Reading in those days took 45 minutes and ERD always timed it so that on the way back he could down a full cream tea of several courses between Paddington and Reading.

In fact the only time I ever recalled ERD becoming really agitated was at one Annual Budget meeting. As these took place on Tuesdays the Council would provide a buffet spread for lunch – you got nothing, not even a cup of tea on normal Saturday Council meetings. On this particular occasion, the budget meeting finished only 20 minutes before ERD had to catch a train to London. The thought of leaving all this lovely food untouched was too much for ERD. '*Saunders*' he yelled '*get me a paper bag*'. Somehow Sam Saunders magicked a paper bag seemingly out of thin air and ERD literally ran round the buffet table cramming food into his paper bag. He then departed as fast as he could, bowler hat askew, with his brief case in one hand and his paper bag in the other, to catch his train.

Then there was the story of the hot cross buns as related to me by David Over. It was also witnessed by my successor as articled clerk, Bill Goyder, so at the time I was working in Oxfordshire. The best baker in Reading was E. J Scholes & Son, based at 18, Duke Street. A Mr Scotford ran the business and he and his family lived over the shop. One of his sons, John, eventually ended up as County Treasurer of Hampshire County Council – I played Rugby with him for Shire Hall. His younger brother Garth became the Berkshire Chief Fire Officer and he then succeeded Tony Allen in 1993 as Chief Executive.

ERD always got his buns from Scholes – but on the occasion in question something went wrong. Maybe his secretary was on leave and he had a temp in, who did not know the ropes. Anyway one morning he bit into his bun and there was a great roar. ERD knew his buns and this specimen was not from Scholes. The minion who had purchased the bun was summoned. '*Where did you get this bun*? demanded ERD. '*Parslows*' said the minion. '*Parslows*' exploded ERD – '*Parslows*' he roared in a voice that carried round the whole Clerk's Department '*Say not Parslows*!'

ERD had a younger brother, Trevor Owen Davies, known as TOD, who also qualified as a solicitor and went into local government. He was less successful than his elder brother and was languishing as Clerk to the Brixham Urban District Council when ERD secured him an interview for the post of Chief Legal Officer to the newly formed Bracknell Development Corporation. He was successful and in 1952 he moved to Berkshire.

In September 1961, I ascended the steps of Shire Hall in the Forbury for the second time to start my career as an articled clerk. The Forbury looked much the same in 1961 as it did in the 1912 photo on the front of this book. The Tudor Forbury House (nearside) and Suttons Seeds Warehouse were still standing but it was not long before the view I then saw changed forever and very much for the worse. In the 1960's Reading County Borough Council was hell bent on building office blocks and new roads and came up with a plan to build a new IDR (Inner Distribution Road) circling the town. Half of it was built but had the original plan come to fruition then it would have gone through the Forbury. But in preparation for their IDR, Reading Council allowed the historic Forbury House and Sutton's Seed Warehouse to be demolished and then allowed a hideous office block to be built on stilts on the site for the Prudential – the stilts were to allow the IDR to pass under the building. The Prudential office block has now been demolished and replaced by something a bit better, while the old Shire Hall has become the Forbury Hotel. It is an improvement on what there was but nothing will ever wholly correct the vandalism that was inflicted on Reading in the 60's by its Council. I have included in the illustrations pages, photographs and sketches to show the changes that have taken place since 1888.

3
ACCOMMODATION IN READING IN THE 1960s

On arriving in Reading my first task was to find somewhere to live on £8 a week. I quickly discovered that lodgings were in very short supply. Someone suggested that I approach the University of Reading and ask them to suggest the names of some private landlords. On their list were Pete and Desi Sheldon-Battle, who owned a large Victorian villa at 98, Kendrick Road, Reading, just south of London Road and within easy walking distance of Shire Hall. When I went to see them, they told me that they had decided to switch from male to female undergraduates, apart from one two-bedded room, where they already had an Indian student. I could have the room, and breakfast and dinner for £4. Done! and that was how I came to meet someone who has become one of my closest friends. Professor Dwarka Nath Bose, or Tutu, as he is known to family and friends, was only seven days younger than me but was already studying for a Doctorate in Physics. Now Reading has closed its Physics department but in 1961 it had a Faculty of Physics that was internationally recognized and attracted the brightest graduates from all round the world.

Tutu is the nephew of the famous Bengali Indian nationalist leader, Subhas Chandra Bose, commemorated by statues all over Bengal. Fed up with British prevarication over granting independence during the 1920s and 30s, when the 2nd World War broke, out Subhas Chandra Bose threw in his lot with the Japanese. The British Indian Army was vast and in the early days of their campaign in South-East Asia, the Japanese took 250,000 Indian POW's. Bose went among them and recruited about 70,000 to fight under his command against the British – the other 180,000 remained loyal to the British cause. Paul Scott's 'Raj Quartet' brilliantly captures those times and the tensions that arose. At one stage Bose went by submarine from Tokyo to Berlin via Africa and Murmansk to meet Hitler. He eventually disappeared, shot down it is thought over the jungles of Burma in 1944. He has a dedicated museum in Calcutta (Kolkota).

After Reading University his nephew Tutu returned to India and became a Professor of Physics at the Indian Institute of Science at Kharagpur in Bengal. So there we were at 98, Kendrick Road – two 23 year olds – co-habiting with a house full of 18 year old girl undergraduates. It obviously affected Tutu deeply, because he has since written a playlet about the experience, though a Welshman called Dave seems to feature rather more in the action than the writer. The truth is that the 18 year olds regarded us as elder brothers. They would wander into our bedroom in various states of undress, pour out their hearts regarding their problems with their boy-friends and ask us for our advice.

Generally though it was Tutu's advice that they sought, as he used to dress it up with Eastern mysticism, while sitting cross-legged. I was sure it was all hocus pocus but Tutu could always keep a straight face. After 6 months Tutu obtained his own flat and I then had another room-mate, who was mad about ballroom dancing. He would then spend what was left of his leisure hours scraping the wax off his dancing shoes. I took this for a fortnight and then I found myself a room of my own with a Mrs Gawthorne at 40, Western Elms Avenue, off the Oxford Road.

No 40, Western Elms Avenue was just like being back in the Army. Indeed Mrs Gawthorne would have put many a sergeant major to shame. Your room had to be immaculate and no smoking was allowed, not that that bothered me as I have never been a smoker. Mrs Gawthorne told us that she used to have students, until one blotted his copybook. She fed us well and we received a full English breakfast each morning complete with a fried egg. The one rule was that you ate everything put in front of you. Apparently one student hated fried eggs but he was so terrified of Mrs Gawthorne that he couldn't summon up the nerve to tell her. As a way of overcoming his dilemma he took to smuggling the fried egg up to his bedroom. But rather than then take it out of the house and dispose of it elsewhere, he simply left the fried egg in a drawer and did the same on each succeeding day. Come half term the problem had all become too much and he went home leaving behind 20 congealed fried eggs in the drawer in his room, which Mrs Gawthorne, with her acute sense of smell, soon discovered. No more students!

Mrs Gawthorne was also a member of the Reading Writers' Circle and she used to give lectures. On one occasion she was due to give a lecture to the WI in a Hampshire Village Hall. Her husband was a pleasant but very quiet man, who drove for a taxi firm. He was going to drive her down but she wanted to play her audience a record and had no record player. I had an old Dansette player and agreed she could borrow it. When I next saw her I asked how she had got on. Apparently the talk had been a disaster. She had gone to put on the record player and had blown all the lights in the Hall. Lady so and so, who was the WI Chairman then commandeered the caretaker's bungalow next to the Hall – the caretaker's wife was doing her ironing and had to stop to allow the record player extension lead to be plugged in. The record player was then switched on again and promptly blew all the lights in the bungalow! I said I didn't understand what was going on and then plugged the record player in and blew all the lights in No. 40, Western Elms Avenue! Fortunately another lodger came in at that stage and I asked him to pop down to mend the fuse, which was located in the coal cellar, while I beat a hasty retreat. Later I found two touching wires, where I had added an extension lead.

One phenomenon we don't suffer from nowadays, fortunately, is smog – a combination of smoke formed from coal fires and fog. We had one real pea - souper, while I was staying at 40, Western Elms Avenue. You really could not see more than a few feet in front of your face. It is surprising how quickly one then becomes disorientated. I remember groping my way from Shire Hall down Friar Street, running my hand along the shop windows to make sure I was going in the right direction and not round in circles. It took me over an hour to find my way back to my lodgings, which were only 1 ½ miles away from Shire Hall.

From Western Elms Avenue I moved up the accommodation ladder to a flat at 2, Derby Road, Caversham. It was owned by Queen Anne's School and has since been demolished to make way for a school extension. I shared with John Banks, who worked for the Milk Marketing Board, Rod Brayshaw, who was ex-Army and Willie Harrell, who was a student. I am still in touch with all three. Willie was a popular lad with the ladies and having no transport of his own had an encyclopaedic knowledge of the Reading Corporation bus timetable, which enabled him to date two or three young ladies on the same evening. He has also reminded me that the two of us opened the dancing at one Shire Hall Rugby Club festive occasion. I had obliterated the experience from my mind but it obviously made a deep impression on Willie. I don't know if that is the same occasion when Joey Rowe, Colin Wood and I streaked through the Calcot Hotel. Little did I know then that one day I would roll up every Monday at the same hotel to attend my Rotary Club.

I was at 2, Derby Road during the winter of 1963. I have never been so cold in all my life. The only way I could get warm was to put my sleeping bag inside my bed and get inside it. If you left a glass of water in the bedroom it was solid ice in the morning. The Thames froze over. At Windsor the Guards marched across the river. At Reading they were skating at Piper's Island. But when I tried to walk across the Thames at Reading Bridge, I had only gone out 6 feet or so, when the ice cracked and I beat a hasty retreat. But I watched a cat walk from one bank to the other.

My final accommodation during my articles was at Broadwater Cottage between Godalming and Guildford in Surrey. I teamed up with an old friend from Queens' called John Labrum and we shared a room, while we were cramming for our final exams at the College of Law in Guildford. The cottage was owned by the Guildford Corporation, who later built a crematorium at its rear. In the meanwhile it was let to a primary school Head master, Brian Bampton. His wife Joan was an alcoholic – a very sad case. They also had an au pair to help with their children. This was a very charming and attractive Austro/Italian girl, called Luisa (Lella) Re, who came from Milan. Her father was Italian, but had died and her mother was Austrian. We became very close and I spent several holidays with her in Italy after I qualified. I even learned some Italian, though I used to reduce Lella to tears of laughter as I often ended up speaking Latin. It appeared de rigueur to have an au pair in Guildford. Through Lella I met several and often it was a pure façade. One family used to spend all their money entertaining lavishly on a Saturday night, only to be reduced to eating baked beans for the rest of the week as they were so broke. Another au pair told me that she only had half a sheet to sleep on – her hosts couldn't afford to buy a complete set of sheets. As the old Welsh joke goes – 'I was so poor as a child that my parents couldn't afford to buy me a suit. But they bought me a top hat so that I could look out of the window'.

4
LIFE AT SHIRE HALL IN THE 1960s

At Shire Hall ERD was a very good boss and I learnt a great deal from him. He once said to me '*You may think I am paid a great deal of money*'. I did – his salary was £9K and mine was £500. '*Well,*' he said, '*I am paid £3K for the work I do; £3K for making sure you all do the work you are supposed to do and £3K for having my bottom kicked when things go wrong.*' Which is how it ought to be, except that too many bosses in my view forget the last bit and try to blame others when things go wrong.

ERD insisted that I spend some time in every section of the Clerk's department, starting with filing. In those pre-computer days, the filing department was the nerve centre of the Department and the two filing clerks, Len Seeley and Jack Lovegrove had an uncanny knack of being able to find any file. One day out of idle curiosity I was looking at some Education files and came across a request from a Lambourn couple to allow their son to leave school early in 1949 aged 14, to become an apprentice jockey. Berkshire has always been a big racing County with 3 nationally known racecourses at Newbury, Ascot and Windsor. The request was approved by the Education Sub-Committee and Mr and Mrs Piggott's son, Lester, went on to do great things on the racecourse. Some say he was the greatest jockey ever with 5,300 winners including 9 Derbys. But it has not all been success. In 1987 he was jailed for 3 years for tax evasion and in 2012 he left his wife of many years for a 55 year old filly.

I quickly realized that the County Council did not believe in spending money unless it had to. I came across another file in which the Clerk had had to obtain the agreement of the Finance and General Purposes Committee to purchase a replacement typewriter for his Secretary, Mrs Ann Whittall ! I realized then that ERD must have used all his oratorical arts to persuade the same Committee to start paying me. In fact the Council took a positive pride in being frugal. I came across a rhyme that had been written regarding a previous Chairman, Thomas Skurray, who had been Chairman of the Council from 1930-1938. He was a successful Brewer and according to ERD a ruthless individual, whose motto was 'we will do what we must; we will leave alone what we may'.

see colour page VII

Supreme he sits in Council Hall
Keeping a ceaseless watch o'er all
Untiring in his chosen work
Refusing any task to shirk
Resolved is County's rate shall be
A thing too small for eye to see

Yea, verily, a King is he!

The frugality permeated Shire Hall. The entrance hall started off by having a marble floor but the rest of the building was linoleum. The Council had carried out a cost evaluation exercise, weighing up the relative merits and costs of carpet and linoleum and had come down in favour of the latter. Office furniture was another area of saving. Although I was paid, there was no money to buy me a desk and chair. For most of my articles I had to hot desk, and when I could not find anywhere at all I used to retreat to the Electoral Registration room, where Harry Gould presided on his own in a large room with two enormous tables. He was always delighted to see me as he then had someone to talk to.

In some cases the savings verged on the farcical. When I left the Filing basement after a few months – it is now the very smart Cerise Restaurant and Bar – I joined Freddy Jones and Terry Lloyd in the Parliamentary and Common Law section. There were no desks at all in that section. Instead someone had fixed a large plank to the wall and the three of us sat in a row along the plank. Freddy was ERD's right hand man and was a fellow Welshman from mid-Wales. Terry was English albeit with Welsh roots. The section was not over busy and very formal. A letter would arrive. Freddy would read it and would then say in his mid- Wales lilt '*Here's an interesting letter, Mr Lloyd – perhaps you would like to draft a reply*'. Terry would then take the letter, give it to me and say. '*Draft something, Clive*'. I would then draft something and give it to Terry, who would alter it and then get Mrs Whittall to type up his draft. This would then go to Freddy, who would alter it again. Mrs Whittall would then retype it and Freddy would then carefully check the top copy against the carbon and eventually the masterpiece would be signed and sent off. The turnaround period normally took three days.

There would have been no need for such a section, had the Chairman of the Council been anyone other than Sir George Robert Mowbray 5th Bt (1899-1969). Sir George lived in Mortimer and was the son of Sir Robert Mowbray Bt, who was Chairman of the County Council from 1911-1916. Like his father he had a brilliant mind but ERD once complained to me that Sir George was like someone, who goes to buy a Persian carpet and spots a loose thread, which he pulls to remove. This only dislodges another thread and in the end if you continue pulling you end up with a pile of wool. Sir George was like that. He was always tinkering with the Council's Standing Orders, which generated work for Freddy and Terry but was really a waste of everyone's time in the greater order of things.

see colour page VIII

It also became apparent to me early on that Sir George loathed ERD and the feeling was mutual. Sir George was a tall English patrician while ERD was a short rotund Welshman. But it probably went deeper than that. Sir George was used to getting his own way and as far as his fellow Councillors were concerned, there were not many prepared to stand up to him. ERD was one such individual and moreover ERD could not be sacked without the agreement of the Minister of Housing and Local Government. Unless he committed a crime ERD was fireproof and this was anathema to Sir George.

Their mutual animosity was such that you could guarantee that whatever was suggested by the one would be opposed by the other. Not long after I had arrived at Shire Hall, the County Council were given the opportunity to buy a large area of land at Maiden Erlegh, in Earley Parish on the outskirts of Reading. ERD urged the Council to buy and suggested that the Council should consider moving their HQ there as even by 1961, the only Departments housed in Shire Hall were the Clerk's and Treasurer's departments. All the other Departments – Education, Social Services as it became, Planning, Surveyor's, Architect's and Property were scattered around Reading in rented office blocks. Maiden Erlegh had the added attraction that it was in the County. In Reading, which was then a County Borough Council, Reading were the planning authority.

Sir George, needless to say, was strongly opposed to the Clerk's suggestion. He made his views clear but even so ERD managed to get his suggestion through the Finance & General Purposes Committee, so that the proposal eventually went to full Council with a recommendation from that Committee that the Maiden Erlegh land be bought. Before the full Council meeting began you had the extraordinary sight of Sir George, the County Council Chairman, standing at the entrance to the Council chamber, lobbying everyone who went in to oppose the proposal. But when it came to the vote the motion to acquire the land was carried by just one vote. Whereupon Sir George said '*One vote is not enough*' and moved next business. And that was that. Incredibly no-one challenged him and Shire Hall remained in Reading until 20 years later it relocated to Shinfield Park to the south of Reading.

However there was a darker side to Sir George. He was married and there were children of the marriage but he clearly had homosexual leanings. There was a Committee Clerk in the Clerk's Department, one Tony Moffat, for whom Sir George had a soft spot. Moffat was hetero-sexual and found Sir George's attentions intensely embarrassing. The County Council used to have an Annual Sports Day and at one of these Moffat dropped his biro and was looking for it, when Sir George chanced by. The upshot was that Sir George stopped the Games and had us all crawling around on hands and knees looking for Moffat's biro. Meanwhile Moffat was begging Sir George to forget the wretched thing. It wasn't long after that that Moffat found himself another job in West Cornwall, about as far away from Berkshire and Sir George as it was possible to get.

It was no surprise, therefore, to learn that Sir George had once been convicted of importuning in the public toilets in Piccadilly Circus. He appealed successfully, being represented by Raymond Evershed (1899-1966), a brilliant lawyer, who became Master of the Rolls and a Law Lord. It was the aftermath of this case, which was interesting and a reflection on the way society operated in those days. According to ERD, the Lord Lieutenant of Berkshire, Sir Henry Benyon (1884-1959), who was also Chairman of the County Council for 1946-1947, and the Chairman of Berkshire Quarter Sessions, Sir Malcolm Hilbery (1883-1965), decided to carry out their own investigation into the matter. They got in touch with the Commissioner of the Metropolitan Police and after they had dined at Sir Harry's seat at Englefield, the officers in the case, who had apprehended Sir George in the Piccadilly toilets, were brought in, gave their evidence and were subjected to questioning. According to ERD, Benyon and Hilbery came to the view that Sir George had been a lucky man to have got off. But thereafter Berkshire Society was split more or less equally into two camps – those who were pro Sir George and those who were anti. It meant that on any major issue, such as the Maiden Erlegh land purchase, you had no idea what the eventual result would be. This of course did not make for smooth administration.

see colour page VIII

Sir Malcolm Hilbery had the reputation of being a stiff sentencer. On one occasion he sentenced an old lag to 10 years. '*But, my Lord*', spluttered the old lag from the dock '*I am an old man and not in good health. If I go down for 10 years I shall die in prison*'. '*Never mind, just try and do as much as you can*' replied the kindly Sir Malcolm.

In my perambulation around the Clerk's Department, I spent a few months in John Killick's Highways section. John spent most of his working life in that section and was the fount of all knowledge on the County's highways. He may even have been there when the Chairman of the Highways Committee was a Major Rhodes (sic). This was almost as good as the Treasurer's department, which had just two secretaries to look after the entire department. One was a Mrs Thrift and the other a Miss Needy. Meanwhile down at the Reading Registrar's Office of Births, Deaths and Marriage, the Superintendent Registrar was Mr Church; his Deputy was Mr Record and the Registrar of Births and Deaths was Mrs Tombs. But as previously mentioned my favourite of all was the letter I received from a Mr Donald Duck, and this is gospel – his address was the Old Swan!

In John Killick's Section I was given the task of preparing Section 40 agreements –agreements under the then Highways Act of 1959, whereby the County Council agreed to adopt a newly built road and maintain it in future as a public highway, if the developer built it according to the County's

Surveyor's specification. The Parishes of Earley and Woodley to the east of Reading and Tilehurst to the west saw an enormous amount of housing development in the 1960's. I had several dozen Section 40 agreements on the go at any one time for these Parishes. For each agreement the County Surveyor's plan drawing section would let us have 6 beautifully prepared plans. I would use 4 of them and have 2 left over. After this had gone on for a couple of months I was running out of space to store the superfluous plans. So I bundled them up and staggered over to the County Surveyor's Department to return them. The look on Bob Arnott's face was quite something, when he realized how much time he had wasted drawing plans that were not needed. Even in frugal Berkshire, there were savings to be had.

Another illustration of waste arose at the first Council meeting I attended. As already stated, these were held on Saturdays except for the Budget meeting, which was on a Tuesday. Apparently, when the County Council was first established in 1888, many of the Councillors were farmers or landowners and were in the habit of attending Reading Mart on Saturday morning. So they arranged for Council business to be transacted once the Mart had finished and they would then repair to the Athenaeum Club for lunch before returning home. Farmers and landowners were still strongly represented on the County Council in 1961, though no longer a majority, but the practice of holding Council meetings on Saturdays had stuck.

At my first budget meeting in 1962, I recall John Cumber Junior, the Chairman of the Finance and General Purposes Committee saying '*The next item on the agenda is the purchase of a computer for £250K. I have no idea what a computer is but the Treasurer (Mr Hardacre) tells me that we must have one. So I move*'. The Councillors thought the world of Mr Hardacre and so without anyone else speaking, the motion was carried. Later on the same agenda there was an item to install the first Pelican beacon crossing in Thatcham. Virtually everyone on the Council spoke and the discussion went on for over an hour. I thought then – the Council's entire budget is only £30M and they have just spent £250K (£2.5m in today's money) on buying something they don't even know what it is. Yet as regards something straightforward such as putting in a new crossing – where a simple yes was all that was needed - I have had to listen to over an hour of repetition. But t'were ever thus. The French Bull computer that was bought in 1962 took over the whole of the top floor of Shire Hall. It had an airlock and the operators had to be specially trained and paid a bit extra. And yet 50 years on the I-phone that you can buy for a few hundred pounds has more computing power.

Walter Simpson Hardacre was appointed County Treasurer in 1948. He was always Mr Hardacre to his staff and had some quirky habits. Tony Rayner, a long-time member of the Treasurer's Department told me that on gaining his accountancy qualification, one of his tasks was to spend half the morning sorting the post into the pigeon-holes of the various sections. The County Treasurer had his own pigeon-hole nearest the door and his job was to place anything of interest in Mr Hardacre's pigeon-hole. Sometime during the morning a crack would appear in the door and an arm would emerge through the crack to grab whatever was in the nearest pigeon-hole. This was all that Tony Rayner would see of Mr Hardacre for days, though when he found out that Tony took the Guardian, he would often 'borrow' it, without always returning it.

Hardacre retired around 1970 and was replaced by Michael Beasley, who was of the same ilk as Hardacre, though he did have his moments. He worked at Glamorgan County Council before coming to Berkshire – he met his wife Jean there - and what he told me about that Council has triggered off the next chapter.

5

NOT ALL COUNCILS WERE AS FRUGAL AS BERKSHIRE

Glamorgan had the normal quarterly Council meetings, plus a Budget day but they also had to convene Council meetings on Saturdays when Wales were playing Rugby at home, so that the Councillors could come to Cardiff and claim expenses, and then go on to see the game. The problem then was finding enough business to justify a meeting.

There was a different problem at normal Council meetings, which took place on week-days, in that the Council made sure its Councillors were well fed and watered. But as the refreshments included alcohol, the councillors then descended on the typing pool to try their luck. It got so bad that the typists had to be locked in for their own safety.

Then there was the nepotism problem. When I was at Cambridge in my third year, my uncle Tom, who taught in Port Talbot, asked me to befriend the Heycock's son, who was at Cambridge in his first year. Alderman, later Lord Heycock, was Chairman of Glamorgan County Council and a power in the land. I did my best but young Heycock was hard going – no spark or charisma. When he eventually graduated they created a Bursar post at a Port Talbot comprehensive – where my uncle taught – on a salary almost as high as the Head's. Young Heycock applied and was duly appointed by a Panel, which it being Wales, was of course chaired by his mother. He ended up as Deputy Director of Education of Glamorgan. He would have been the Chief if he had shown any spark of leadership but even in Wales nepotism has its limits.

Rodney Davis came from Durham County Council. He was appointed as Assistant Clerk the same time as myself and eventually left local government for a successful career at leading law firm Coward, later Clifford Chance. At Durham he clerked the Fire Brigade Committee, which had a whopping membership of 51. When it came to the purchase of fire appliances, in Berkshire once the money had been voted it was left to the Chief Fire Officer to get on with it. Not in Durham. They had a Fire Brigade Acquisitions Sub-Committee just for the purchase of equipment and all 51 members of the main Committee also sat on the Sub-Committee. They then decided to go en masse to London to inspect a possible future acquisition. Rodney tried to reduce the number travelling but had no success. So to cover himself and his Council he wrote to the Ministry of Housing and Local Government asking for a dispensation to take 51 members of the Fire Brigade Acquisitions Sub-Committee on a site visit. The civil servant who dealt with his letter phoned him up *'I say old boy – you've made a bit of a mistake haven't you – ha, ha, ha. You asked for a dispensation for 51 – you must surely mean 15 ?'* Surprisingly he got his dispensation. London does not like to upset the North.

Alan Dick, County Personnel Officer had a somewhat similar story to tell as regards his former Council, South Tyneside Metropolitan Borough. When he arrived he found it was his job to organize the Council's annual visit to inspect its outdoor education centre in the Lake District. The whole Council went on this, so he had to hire a very large coach. Copious quantities of beer had to be installed for consumption there and back and sarnies had to be provided. All was in place but he then found his Council refused to board the coach. No-one had told him about the sweets. Apparently it was the practice to give each councillor a bag of sweets before they boarded. So Alan had to go down to the market to purchase 50 bags of sweets. Then armed with their sweets the Council set forth.

Once on a visit to Rhos-y Gwaliau – the outdoor centre in Bala, North Wales, which was supported by Berkshire County Council for a number of years but is now independent - I stayed in a hotel, where a fellow guest was crying into his beer. It transpired he was a pilot, who had a vision of creating the first Welsh airline. He had obtained a meeting with Cardigan (Ceredigion) County Council to try and drum up support. He knew the Council made frequent trips to Brussels to seek EU aid and his pitch was that instead of spending 3 days making the trip he could get them there and back in a day. This went down like a lead balloon. What he was offering was one day's expenses instead of three. Wales is still waiting for its airline.

AROUND THE COURTS
6
THE SOLICITORS' SECTION

I eventually worked my way to the solicitors' section. In those days the County solicitors not only handled all the County Council's legal work but also acted for the Berkshire Constabulary and the Clerk also acted as Clerk to Quarter Sessions, which as their name suggests met quarterly to deal with more serious criminal cases than the Magistrates Courts. The most serious cases – murders and the like – were dealt with at the travelling Assizes, when a Red Judge sat. Berkshire was on the Oxford circuit which extended as far as Herefordshire and the Assizes in Reading were the first port of call. The County Council even owned a house in Christchurch Gardens, Reading, which was made available for the Red Judge and to the best of my knowledge remained empty for the rest of the year. On my first day in the Solicitors' Section, I was asked to go into Assizes and 'hold the hand' of a very experienced barrister, Mr Michael Talbot, who was Prosecuting Counsel in the case of R-v-Castro. I was then the only one left in the office but normally 'holding the hand' was a sinecure – you just sat there and made a note of any key events and/or liaised with any witnesses.

Mr Michael Talbot was a very experienced Counsel, who later became a Judge himself. He was a member of the Talbot family (Earls of Shrewsbury) - originally Bretons who came over with William the Conqueror and because they spoke Breton, akin to Welsh, were rewarded by being made Marcher Lords. The Red Judge was Mr Justice Sachs, who looked quite terrifying. The case of R-v-Castro involved a young Portuguese barber, who had eloped with his 17 yr old girl-friend to Gretna Green. But they were caught before they made it to Gretna, albeit too late to prevent a consummation of their relationship. The parents were furious and wanted Castro punished. So Castro was charged with taking away a girl under the age of 18 from her parents, with intent to have unlawful sexual intercourse. The case had not long started when Sachs J turned to Michael Talbot and said '*Mr Talbo*t – *it seems to me that the evidence suggests that the primary reason the defendant ran away with this young lady was to get married and that is not an offence.*' It was a pretty obvious point but Michael Talbot, experienced as he was, had failed to spot it. So he did what all barristers do when in a hole and needing time to think. He said '*I will take instructions on the point, my Lord*' and then turned to me and said '*What does Instructing Solicitor advise?*'. So I had a quick consultation with the Detective Constable, whose case it was, and we agreed that the Judge had a point. End of prosecution and quite a baptism of fire.

I had some of the happiest times of my career in that legal section. The Junior Assistant Solicitors were Roger Forshaw, who went on to become County Secretary and Solicitor of North Yorkshire County Council, and George Matthews, who eventually went back to his native Herefordshire, where he set up his own practice. Both sadly are now deceased. George was a polymath – he spoke fluent Russian, was an excellent pianist and was highly knowledgeable about antiques. He was also a very bright and sharp lawyer as was Roger. George's father was a farmer; his mother came from an academic family and as a boy George was torn between academia and following his father into farming. At Oxford his tutor was a notorious Scottish eccentric called MacTaggart. The story is told that one student went to see MacTaggart with his weekly essay but there was no sign of him. Then a voice came from an adjoining cubicle '*Push the essay under the door*'. The student did so. He waited and then there was a rustle of paper and a flushing of water and MacTaggart emerged from the cubicle but no sign of any essay. In George's case his first essay was handed back by MacTaggart with the sole comment '*Have you ever considered taking up farming*?' Given the fact that that is precisely what George had considered before opting for academia, it was probably the cruellest thing MacTaggart could have said, though one hopes it was unintentional.

see colour page XVII

Senior to George and Roger were John Kellett and Robert Adcock. Both came from local government families. Robert eventually ended up as Chief Executive of Essex County Council and was knighted. He was short and rotund like ERD and had boundless charm. He was always a perfect gentleman and I never saw him lose his cool in any way or ever become flustered. I assisted him in the Burfitt caravan appeal at Hurley, which went on for 9 days and which the County Council eventually lost. The opposing solicitor was a Scotsman called Gordon McMurtie, who was a partner at Tozers in Devon, who acted for the Caravan Council. Over 9 days we became quite pally with Gordon, and he eventually admitted to us that he hated caravans and had never put his foot inside one. He also kept telling us some very funny jokes, which can not be repeated.

see colour page XVI

John Kellett came from Cheshire, where his father was Director of Education. He eventually returned to Cheshire as County Secretary & Solicitor. Both Robert and John were married – Robert and his wife Valerie had twins, while John had married Sheila and honoured me by asking me to become godfather to their first born son John. Eventually John Senior and Sheila had four sons and a daughter. Sadly both John and Sheila died at a comparatively early age but we remain in touch with the family and try to meet up as often as possible. John Kellett senior was extremely hard working and very conscientious. He used to work late and then take work home. I reported to him in the office hierarchy and I suppose some of his conscientiousness rubbed off on me.

But when John had departed for Cheshire he was replaced by Robert Gray, whose mother had been the village schoolmistress of Checkendon School in Oxfordshire. Robert and his mother lived in Whitchurch-on-Thames; his father had been a military man but had died. I think there were 7 children in all and the family could claim Thomas Gray, the poet, as an ancestor. Robert was one of the most brilliant men I have ever encountered. He had a razor sharp brain and could see very quickly to the heart of any problem, no matter how complex. He was also a brilliant linguist. Like George Matthews he had learned Russian during National Service but he was also fluent in French and German and his Spanish was also reasonable. The three of us used to go out to lunch together and George and Robert would chat away very loudly in Russian, which attracted some interested looks. Occasionally they would refer to '*Nya Gloop Williams*'. I don't know much Russian but I do now know the Russian word for stupid. After a while Robert simply got bored with local government and went to the Bar. He became a QC (Queen's Counsel) in double quick time and specialized in planning law. He rented a flat in Lincoln's Inn and once a year, George Matthews, myself and Ted Andrews (who started life as a Committee Clerk and later qualified as a barrister) used to have dinner with him at Lincoln's Inn and then stay the night in the Inn's guest accommodation. But sadly Robert was struck down by cancer and eventually died at the age of 60. After his death I discovered that he was actually two years older than me, though he always claimed he was younger! Judging also by the number of sorrowful young men, who were present at his funeral, he was, as we had always suspected, gay.

see colour page XVII

Finally I should mention the Deputy Clerk at that time – John Keyworth Boynton (JKB). Tall, suave, well spoken with a good brain, he looked and acted as the Clerk and indeed when in the company of the short rotund ERD, those who did not know, always assumed that JKB was the Clerk and ERD his Deputy. John Boynton had won the MC in the War and was cool under fire. Terry Lloyd tells the story that one day he was in JKB's office having a draft report approved when Sir George Mowbray barged in without knocking and shouted '*Where's Davies?*'. Without even looking up, JKB replied '*I don't know where he is – ask his secretary*'. And the bully Sir George exited, having met his match.

But John Boynton also had a reputation for being parsimonious and he never seemed to have any money on his person. On one occasion, Sam Saunders, the Personnel Committee Clerk, told me that he went with Boynton to a meeting in Wokingham. They had lunch there and Saunders had to pay for it. On the way back, Boynton said '*Saunders, we need some money for petrol, can you lend me two quid i.e £2?*' '*I'm cleaned out, paying for lunch*', replied Saunders.' '*All I have*

SHIRE HALL (1961-1988)

SHIRE HALL (now the FORBURY HOTEL) 2018

ABBOT'S HOUSE – THE FORBURY – READING - 2018.

It replaced the two-storey terrapin formerly occupied by the County Secretariat.
The glass office block replaced the former White Lion pub.

SALE OF SHIRE HALL
31ST MARCH 1988
FOR £1.5m to GROSVENOR ESTATES

CENTRE
Gareth Gimblett Esq CBE DL
(Chairman of County Council)

RIGHT
Howard Waters
(Project Manager, Grosvenor Developments)

LEFT
The Author

ELLIS ROGER DAVIES DL ((ERD)
(1906-1986); Deputy Clerk (1935-1951)
Clerk (1952-1972)

ROBERT WALKER (BOB) GASH
(1926-1986)
Clerk (1972-1974)
Chief Executive (1974-1986)

ERD and BOB socializing at the Author's home in Upper Basildon - 1977

JOHN THORNHILL MORLAND
Clerk – (1889-1923)

Born in 1842 he came from the well-known Abingdon brewing and legal family. Cambridge cox in 1859 & 1860. He was Clerk of the Peace when the new County Council was formed in 1889 and he was persuaded to become its part-time Clerk. He was 81 when he finally stepped down!

He commuted by train from Abingdon to Reading, frequently ending up in Bristol on the return trip in latter years, as he was fast asleep by Didcot, where he was meant to change trains.

HAROLD HATTON UNDERHILL THORNE
Deputy Clerk (1910-1914)

Another solicitor, he joined up at the outbreak of the First World War, as did the 2 assistant solicitors – E Holcroft and R Attride, leaving 72 yr old Morland to soldier on alone. Commissioned, Thorne was a Lt Col with the Royal Scots, when he was killed on 9th April 1917, the first day of the First Battle of Arras – the third battle of Arras, fought later in 1917 is known as Passchaendale.

Holcroft survived but Captain Raymond Attride, aged 26, of the Royal Berkshires was killed on the Somme in August 1916.

CAPTAIN J. FREDERICK HAWKINS
County Surveyor (1904-1946)

Born in 1870, he was 34 when appointed County Surveyor. Very popular, the County Council reluctantly allowed him to join the Engineers on Gen Gibbons' staff in the Dardanelles in 1915. But he fell seriously ill and was operated on for appendicitis, under canvas in the Dardanelles. He nearly died and was invalided out of the Army. But he then resumed his position as County Surveyor and had served 42 years when he finally retired at the age of 76!

THE TWO COLONEL FREDS IN ACTION REMOVING SUTTON COURTENAY TOLL BRIDGE IN 1939

Col Fred Barker (Ch of Highways) No 1 on photo, observed by Col Fred Hawkins (Cty Surveyor) (No 3 on photo) about to chuck the toll Bridge in the Thames. The Thames Conservancy then had to fish it out and Berks and Oxon had to pay their very large bill!

(No 2 on the photo is the Ch of Oxon Highways).

ALDERMAN THOMAS SKURRAY
CHAIRMAN OF COUNTY COUNCIL (1930-1938)

The ruthless Abingdon Brewer, whose motto was:
'We will do what we must and leave aside what we may'

HENRY ARTHUR BENYON
Chairman of County Council (1946-47)
Lord Lieutenant (1945-1959) Bt 1958

He & Sir Malcolm Hilbery (Ch of Quarter Sessions) carried out their own investigation into Sir George Mowbray's brush with the law. They concluded Sir George was a lucky man to have got off.

SIR GEORGE MOWBRAY Bt
Chairman of County Council
(1944-46) & (1960-65)

'One is not enough' uttered when he refused to accept the decision of the County Council to purchase the Maiden Erlegh site, as he opposed the motion. No-one challenged him.

In spite of his brush with the law, Sir George went on to serve a second term as Chairman.

7
BRACKNELL NEW TOWN AND JOE BRANT

There was a notorious character in Berkshire at that time called Joe Brant. He was a big, burly, bruiser of a man, who had served in the Palestine Police, where I am sure he would have been very effective. On his retirement to the UK he bought a small-holding close to the centre of Bracknell, then a small market town. But in 1952 Bracknell was designated as the site of a New Town. According to ERD one day he was telephoned by Dame Evelyn Sharp, a terrifying lady who was the only female Permanent Secretary - in her case to the Ministry of Housing and Local Government. *'Mr Davies, the Cabinet met this morning to consider New Towns. There will be 6 and one of these will be in Berkshire. We would like your Council to tell us where to build it'*. So ERD phoned Tommy Houghton, the County Planning Officer, explained the position and a few days later the two of them toured East Berkshire, had a good lunch, and decided to recommend the County Council to settle for Bracknell. And so it came to pass. Nowadays consultants would be commissioned; large sums of money would be spent; numerous reports would be written, two years would elapse and you would end up with the same decision.

New Towns had to have Development Corporations and as previously mentioned ERD's brother, Trevor Owen Davies, was then appointed as Legal Adviser to the newly created Bracknell Development Corporation. Both the Development Corporation and the County Council then started acquiring land compulsorily to create the New Town and provide its public services. In consequence, Joe Brant's quiet retirement was rudely interrupted as various pieces of his land were appropriated by either the County Council or Development Corporation and he ended up with a visceral hatred for the Davies brothers. We once had to turf him out of Shire Hall, when he arrived unannounced, barged his way into ERD's office and started throwing ink wells and the like at ERD.

On one occasion the County Council wanted some more land from Joe to widen a highway. '*Leave it to me*' said the patrician Boynton but his suave charm got absolutely nowhere with Joe. So eventually ERD took over the negotiation and I went along with him as a witness and bodyguard. *'Now, Mr, Brant'* said ERD, '*We need this bit of your land. How much do you want for it'*. Joe named an outrageously high price. *'Done'*, said ERD. '*Now what else do you want*?' Joe asked for this and that and every time ERD said *'Done, what else*?' Eventually Joe said '*Bugger, you*' and stormed off. By capitulating ERD had taken all the fun out of Joe's baiting of the County Council. Joe refused to engage further so eventually we took the land and widened the road, without paying him anything. There was a sequel. Many years later after Joe had died and ERD had retired, I received a letter from solicitors acting for Joe's widow. They stated that she was in straitened circumstances and they believed that Joe's estate might be owed some money for land taken for a road widening scheme back in the 60's. I had the greatest pleasure in writing back, enclosing a cheque for the original sum that had been agreed, together with 20 years' interest. ERD once said to me that to succeed as a Clerk you needed some ability but an awful lot of low cunning. He had that all right!

8
SAVING WALLINGFORD HOUSE

see colour page XII

In those days the County Council would give its staff leave for Christmas Eve. You would then have Christmas Day and Boxing Day off and one more day. If you wanted any more time off you had to use your annual leave entitlement, which I think was 21 days. So on the 23rd December 1962 at 3.0pm I was just tidying up prior to returning to my digs to pack up for the Xmas break, when the phone rang. It was Jenny Carpenter, a planning officer in the Planning Department. The Planning Department were obviously having a Xmas party – they were always a lot livelier and fuller of 'joie de vivre' than the sober Clerk's Department. Apparently a builder owned a handsome building in Wallingford and having been refused planning consent for some development or other, he had got into a real strop and had informed Jenny that he was going to knock the building down over Christmas. She was in a bit of a panic and pleaded with me to do something. I needed this like a hole in the head but I said '*OK Jenny – leave it with me – I will see what I can do*'. I first phoned Col Richard Norman, Chairman of our Planning Committee, who was a keen conservationist. Fortunately he was in, so I was able to explain the position and obtain his approval to make a Building Preservation Order (BPO). I then went to the Planning Section and found that Hilda Hoskins, the Assistant Planning Committee Clerk was still there. She knew where the printed BPO forms were kept and she then typed up three copies for me. I then went down to see ERD, who I knew would still be working away. So I explained the position and he unlocked the Council seal; I wrote the details in the Sealing Book and I then had 3 sealed copies of the required Building Preservation Notice – one to be fixed to the building: one to be served on the owner and one for us.

By this time I had a car – a Ford Escort, which I parked at Shire Hall. I then drove back to my digs at 40, Western Elms Avenue, collected my things for the Christmas break and borrowed a hammer and nails from my landlord Mr Cawthorne. I then drove to Wallingford and a bit like Luther and his Articles, nailed a copy of the Notice to the front door of Wallingford House. I then had to find the owner who lived in a bungalow somewhere in Benson. In those pre satnav days this was no easy task, particularly in the dark but I eventually tracked him down. By now it was 9.0pm. I knocked on his door, got him to say who he was and I then served him with the notice and wished him Merry Christmas, adding that if he now knocked the building down we would have his guts for garters. I never saw a man look more surprised in my life! I am pleased to say that the building is still there – it is now known as Wallingford House, High Street, Wallingford and stands next to the Kinecroft. I very much doubt if any local authority would be able to act as swiftly nowadays – too many procedures and processes have to be followed.

9
ASSIZES AND QUARTER SESSIONS AND HIS HONOUR JUDGE CLAUDE DUVEEN

I always used to enjoy Assizes and Quarter Sessions. You never quite knew what was going to happen and there were plenty of laughs. When I first started at Shire Hall in 1961 the Chairman of Quarter Sessions was Sir Malcolm Hilbery, who was then succeeded by Sir Laurence Dunne MC, who was also the Chief Metropolitan Stipendiary Magistrate. Like Sir Malcolm he had a well-deserved reputation as a hard sentencer. I remember a man who ran a post office in Kintbury, who had got into financial difficulties and had 'borrowed' a comparatively small sum of money from the Post Office. He had a distinguished war record, as of course had Sir Laurence, but it counted for nothing – the post office worker went down for 3 years. The prisoners who had been sentenced used to provide a written appraisal of Sir Laurence's sentencing approach on the walls of the cells beneath Shire Hall. We all used to troop down there after Quarter Sessions had ended to read their appraisals and have a good laugh. Then the appraisals were painted over in readiness for the next Sessions. It was the only part of the Council's building stock that was regularly maintained.

There were fewer laughs at Assizes and I recall being in Court to watch this man being sentenced to death. We all knew that he would be reprieved but even so a certain frisson ran through the Court as the Judge placed the black cap – in effect a large black handkerchief – on his head. In the C19th an attempt had been made to dig a tunnel from Shire Hall to Reading prison but only half the tunnel was completed. Apparently rather than waste it, if anyone were sentenced to death, they would be left in darkness in the tunnel until the end of the day's proceedings, when they would be taken out and escorted to the prison. Just before Shire Hall was sold in 1988, I went with Harry Finch, the County Property Officer, into the basement of Shire Hall and we discovered the entrance to the tunnel, though it did not go far before being blocked by sewage pipes and the like. So the story was probably true.

On another occasion at Assizes a volunteer fireman from Hungerford had been arrested for arson. This is more common than you may think. Firemen enjoy putting out fires and can get bored if there aren't any to extinguish. Sometimes you get someone going round starting fires just for the buzz of putting them out. The gentleman in this case was only caught because he was always the first to turn up at the station, after the alarm had been sounded. In mitigation his barrister said that all was now well as his client had given up firefighting. The

Red Judge leant forward in his seat. '*That's all very well, Mr Snodgrass – but what if your client now developed an interest in the St John's Ambulance Brigade? – 3 years!*' Sir Laurence Dunne was succeeded as Chairman of Quarter Sessions by his Honour Judge Claude Duveen, who was also the County Court Judge. His father had been Joseph Duveen, a well-known art dealer, who had made a fortune 'discovering' grand masters and gaining healthy commissions selling them to wealthy Americans. Claude was Jewish and was also an Old Etonian. He was a man of very strong likes and dislikes. His likes numbered cricket, roses and the British working-man; his dislikes included lady barristers, the County Council and judging by one case I witnessed, his co- religionists.

On one occasion I was in Court when a barrister was about to start his final speech. '*I need to look something up*', said Claude – there was a retiring room next to the Bench, where he had a small library – '*but you carry on – I will keep the door open and I will be able to hear everything you say*'. Whereupon he disappeared into his retiring room. At that point a friend of the barrister who was on his feet, entered the Court room and became alarmed to find his friend in full flow, apparently addressing an empty Court. He thought his friend was having a nervous break-down and hurried off to get medical help. We had to rush off after him to explain the circumstances.

One of my cases before Claude involved Mr Ben Lloyd. Ben Lloyd was a brilliant stone mason but mad as a hatter. He had been convicted of speeding along the newly opened East Ilsley by-pass and had appealed against conviction. I kept a copy of his grounds of appeal, embellished with drawings of the stonework in Shire Hall, to which were attributed various sexual connotations. The basis of Ben's case was that he could not be convicted, as he was above the law. A splendid sergeant of what was then the Berkshire Constabulary gave evidence in a rich Berkshire dialect. '*I stopped the defendant's car and asked him what his name was. He replied that he was the Supreme Cypher, the Supreme Being and the Master of the Universe but subsequent inquiries revealed that he was Mr Benjamin Lloyd of Great Bedwyn.*' This was said with a dead pan face but the Court, apart from Claude, was by now convulsed in suppressed mirth. Claude, however, was furious and Ben Lloyd's appeal was dismissed in double-quick time.

In another case a Jewish gentleman called Mr Bloom, had appealed against a conviction for careless driving. One had to have some sympathy with him. He was driving his son back to school at Carmel College, when he was followed by a motorist, who was frustrated at being unable to overtake him. After being tailgated for several miles he stopped off at a police station to report the tailgater, only to find himself being charged rather than the tailgater. One might have supposed that Claude would have been sympathetic. Not a bit of it. He gave Mr Bloom a really hard time. The trouble was that Mr. Bloom could have been cast as Fagin in Oliver Twist. '*There I vos – drrriving along, ven thees man comes behind me and there he vos, hooting and blowing, blowing and hooting*'. Claude, the suave, very English Old Etonian, was incensed at this and Mr Bloom lost his appeal.

Then there was one of George Matthews' cases, which ended up before Claude. There had been floods in the Burghfield area. The Burghfield road acted as a dam for a time but eventually someone opened the blocked gullies and let the water flow across the road and onto the adjoining fields. The owner of the fields lost his crops in consequence and brought an action against the County Council, as it is an offence under the Highways Act for a highway authority to discharge substances from a highway onto adjoining property and cause damage. As previously mentioned Claude had no time for the County Council and the case was going very badly, until George Matthews arranged for the barrister acting for us to call the lengthsman as his witness. In those days the County Council appointed lengthsmen to look after the County roads. Each man had several miles of road to look after – keeping gullies open, cutting back hedges, cutting the grass on verges and taking away litter. When you look at the state of Berkshire's roads and grass verges nowadays, bring back the lengthsmen! Although Claude had no time for the County Council, he thought the British working man was the salt of the earth and George had prepared his witness carefully. There he was in his best blue serge suit; his hair brilliantined; tanned and with a strong Berkshire dialect – a genuine Berkshire working man. The County Council barrister put the following question to our witness: *'Did you clean out the gullies to let the water flow down the valley?'* Our witness replied *'No, sir I never went near that stretch of road – it was too dangerous.'* Counsel for the other side then got up to ask a question. He only managed about two words before Claude cut him dead with '*Stop bullying the witness*'. Game set and match to the County Council.

Another Claude story was told to me by Sgt Brian Mott of the Berkshire Police. He was on duty in Maidenhead Police Station when the owner of a Rolls-Royce called in to make a complaint, as his car had been damaged by a cricket ball, when he had been watching a game on Holyport Green. He said the umpire had been rude to him and insisted that Brian Mott do something. So Brian got in his police van and drove out to Holyport followed by the Roller. The game was still in progress and Brian could see that one of the umpires was Claude. He marched out to talk to Claude. '*Tell him to bugger off*', said Claude. *'He hasn't got a leg to stand on. The cases are against him and if he does go to court he will only appear before me!'* Life was different then.

Telling that story reminds me of another one that was told to me by ERD. When Col Fred Barker was Chairman of the Highways Committee, once a

see colour page VI

week he and the County Surveyor, Col Fred Hawkins, used to drive round the County inspecting the roads. On one occasion they came across a hole in the road and nearby was a workman leaning on his shovel and smoking a pipe. Col Barker had an abhorrence of smoking, so he got Col Hawkins to stop the car. '*My man*' said Col Barker '*You are smoking*'. The workman agreed that he was. Col Barker continued, '*I insist you put out your pipe. If you don't I will instruct Col Hawkins, the County Surveyor, to give you your cards*'. To which the workman replied; '*I don't give a bugger who you are. I work for the Post Office*'!

Col Barker was a real character. During his time in 1939 the Oxfordshire and Berkshire County Councils bought out the Sutton Courtenay toll-bridge, so that motorists no longer had to pay tolls. There is a picture in ERD's book, showing Col Barker and other members of the Highway Committee, along with their Oxfordshire colleagues, triumphantly removing the bridge. But led by the exuberant Col Barker, their next action was to chuck the bridge in the Thames, where it became an obstruction to boats. So the Thames Conservancy had to fish it out and the two County Councils had to pay their very large bill,

My final Claude story involves Joe Brant of Bracknell, of whom mention has already been made. Joe was opposed to anyone in authority and spent most of his time looking for fights with local Councils. On one occasion there was a suggestion that someone had been buried in the wrong grave in Bracknell's cemetery. This was nothing to do with Joe directly but as a ratepayer of Bracknell Parish and Easthampstead Rural District Council he decided to get involved. In those days it was open to any ratepayer to inspect the Council minutes of proceedings on payment of 1 shilling (now 5p). Joe duly arrived at the Council offices and demanded to see the minutes in question. But Joe being Joe then refused to pay his shilling. So the Clerk's Secretary, Miss Ward, refused to let him see the Minute book. Joe's reaction was to just grab the book out of her arms. But this was one spirited young lady and in spite of a serious mismatch in size, and no help from her boss, a timid man called Saunders, Miss Ward hung on to Joe as he sought to leave the building, clutching the minute book. Such was her tenacity that Joe eventually had to exit through a window and ended up leaving minus one shoe, left in the secretary's hand. The police were phoned.To reach home Joe had to pass the police station and soon a figure came into view hopping down the High Street with the Minute book under his arm. The Police then retrieved the Minute book and arrested Joe for breach of the peace and assault. He was convicted by the Forest Magistrates, who took a dim view of his actions and sent him to Quarter Sessions for sentencing, no doubt anticipating a sentence in excess of the 6 months they could have imposed. But Claude had no time for local authorities in general and Joe escaped with no more than being bound over to keep the peace.

Prosecuting Counsel was John Murchie, later Judge Murchie, who became a good friend. Both John Murchie and I used to amuse ourselves and each other by writing doggerel on the cases we were involved in. I am not sure if John wrote anything on this occasion – if he did I have lost it – but my own effort has survived.

ODE TO A FIREBRAND

I tell the tale of Joseph Brant,
A man much given to rave and rant
Enough to say that once he took
The Bracknell Parish Minute book

Joe asked if he could have a look
At Bracknell's Parish Minute Book;
His interest later it transpired
Was o'er a lady who'd expired

And buried once was disinterred,
This naturally Joe's wrath incurred-
Joe's rather sore that what he saves
Just goes in rates to dig up graves

Accounts of bodies moved from graves
The Bracknell Parish Clerk engraves
Within the Bracknell Minute book
So ghouls like Joe can have a look.

So every rate-payer like our Joe
Need only pay a bob and go
To have a long and lingering look
At Bracknell's Parish Minute Book

Joe thinks alas, he knows his rights;
Has ended up in numerous fights –
He said he would not pay a sou
And asked the Clerk what he would do

The Bracknell Parish Council Clerk
Not noted as the liveliest spark
He called a silly little man
And then a mighty fight began

The Clerk was vexed and said 'Tut,Tut'
Some even say he added 'Phhtt'
The Clerk's a man who takes great care
That no-one ever makes him swear.

Joe grabbed the book, said 'That's mine
Your Council's clerks will face a fine
Should you attempt to take this book
Before I've had my rate-payer's look.

The Clerk's a man who's long resolved
To never get himself involved
And that is why he could afford
To leave the fighting to Miss Ward

They locked the door and thus our Joe
Clean through the window had to go
There wasn't much Miss Ward could do
When all she had was Joe's old shoe

At Berkshire Quarter Sessions though
The Law caught up with poor old Joe
Joe stated he had been at fault
And pleaded guilty to assault

Before His Honour Judge Duveen
Was British Justice truly seen
The Bench's anger Joe incurs
And gets bound o-er for 2 whole years

10
EDWARD TERRELL - NEWBURY QUARTER SESSIONS

There was another eccentric Judge, in addition to Claude Duveen, sitting in Berkshire during my time working in the courts. This was Edward Terrell (1902-1979), the Recorder of Newbury. He was appointed Recorder of Newbury in 1935, when only 33 - a very early age for such appointments. It is said that his father, an eminent QC of the same name, was meant to be appointed but inconveniently died between the issue of the warrant of appointment and its arrival at the Terrell home. So it is claimed Edward Terrell Junior accepted an appointment meant for Edward Terrell senior. There may be truth in this. Edward Terrell was undoubtedly a very clever man. He had several patents registered by the outbreak of war and was then selected for a key operational unit in the Royal Navy, where he rose to Commodore, coming up with several more key inventions both to protect our ships by diverting torpedoes and also destroying enemy shipping. He also wrote the leading work on Patents. But Recorders are appointed to try criminal not civil cases and Edward Terrell was hopeless as a criminal Judge. Criminal judges have to deal with juries and Berkshire juries tended to be independent, some might say bloody minded. If not carefully handled they can well do the opposite of what they are directed to do. Edward Terrell failed to recognize this and as a result many a prosecution in his court went awry. It got so bad that in the end we sent as little work as possible to Newbury. This meant that every solicitor from Shire Hall attending Newbury Quarter Sessions got an ear-bashing from the Recorder, complaining about the paucity of work. But that was preferable to seeing one's hard work on a case going down the proverbial Swannee, because of the Recorder's inadequacies.

There was one case in particular that I remember. An Irish commercial traveller was driving down the A4 in Newbury in thick fog. He must have had a skinful and a half, because he managed to leave the A4 and drive into an adjoining Council estate. This estate is full of cul-de-sac roads and eventually he reached the end of one of these cul-de-sacs. Instead of turning around, he turned right, which took him up to the garage of one of the houses. He then turned right again and ended up on the lawn at the front of the house. Our intrepid traveller then drove on and after 20 feet or so reached a dividing hedge. He then turned right again and after another 20 feet reached the hedge at the front of the garden. Most normal people would have given up at this point but the Irishman continued to drive his car round and round the lawn until it was turned into a quagmire. Eventually the car's wheels could no longer get a grip for the mud and the car stopped. While all this was going on the noise awoke the occupants of the house, who looked out of their bedroom window in horror to see their lawn being demolished. They called the police. By the time the police arrived the Irishman had abandoned his car and was dancing an Irish jig on the lawn. The Irishman was duly charged with driving whilst under the influence of alcohol and much to my surprise he elected for trial at Quarter Sessions. I couldn't see what possible defence he could have and of course he didn't have one, other than to say it was foggy and he had got confused. Fortunately for him and unfortunately for the prosecution, he was tried at Newbury Quarter Sessions. Edward Terrell, the Recorder, could not let the facts speak for themselves. He kept interrupting the defendant's counsel and made a series of sarcastic comments about the Defendant's admittedly weak defence. In his summing up he demanded that the Jury convict and, of course, being a Berkshire jury they gave the Recorder a metaphorical V sign and acquitted.

The Recorder of Newbury was also very conscious of the dignity of his Court. On one occasion we had a case involving another Irishman, called Patrick O'Murphy, who had pleaded guilty to theft. He had a string of previous convictions, which the Clerk to Newbury Quarter Sessions – Leslie Southern, who was also the Town Clerk of Newbury - had to read out. On about page 3 Mr O'Murphy queried a couple of the entries on the register. Whether you had 48 or 50 previous convictions, struck me as immaterial but the Recorder took a different view. '*Mr Southern, this is a Court of Record – we must get these things correct. Could you and Prosecuting Solicitor* –looking at me - *find out what the correct position is. I will adjourn the Court'*. I got on very well with Leslie, who was a lovely Lancastrian, and in a back office we had a cup of tea and decided to contact the Garda Siochana in Dublin. ' *Hello, is that the Garda Siochana.?We are phoning from Newbury'. 'Where, Newry ?' 'No, Newbury, in England'. 'Oh sure that's a nice part of the world. I've got an auntie who lives in Marlborough. What's the weather like with you?' ' Very nice. Look we are at Newbury Court and we have got a Patrick O' Murphy here'. 'What only one? – we have got 20,000 over here'*. At this point Leslie and I decided not to waste any more of Newbury's ratepayers' money on phone calls to Eire. We went back to the Court and assured the Recorder that the two entries on the register, which Mr O'Murphy had queried, could be deleted from the record.

My final Edward Terrell story concerns the time when the Greenham Airbase was still an operational US Air Force base. The Court was sitting and then a B2 bomber passed overhead on its way to land at Greenham. The noise drowned out everything for several minutes. The Recorder became very angry. *'Mr Southern, we can't have the proceedings of my Court interrupted by US aircraft.*

This is a Court of Record. Please lodge a protest.' The Court carried on with its business while Leslie went off to make a phone call to the base. About 40 minutes later we heard a siren and then a crowd of top American brass from Greenham burst into the Court room. Obviously the news that they had upset a Limey Judge had been taken very seriously. But the change in the Recorder was dramatic. From fulminating about the Americans he started eulogizing them. '*What a pleasure to see our gallant American allies in this historic Court of Record.*' In a thrice he had a bemused American Commander sitting beside him on the Bench, and there the poor chap had to stay until the day's business was finished.

11
WINDSOR QUARTER SESSIONS

I have one other Quarter sessions story to tell and that was in Windsor, not Newbury. The Royal Borough of New Windsor had its own Quarter Sessions and there the problem was not the Recorder but the Clerk to the Court, who was a Windsor Solicitor – a partner in the firm of Lovegrove & Durant. A Clifford Larke was an amiable cove – I never knew what the A stood for – but he worked in a state of total chaos and I really mean chaos. I once went to see him on some business or other. I was shown into his very large office and there he sat at his desk at the other end of the room. The problem was that I couldn't work out how to reach his desk. He operated on the heap system of filing. Everything he dealt with was placed in a heap until it became unstable around the 4/5ft mark, when he started another heap. On the occasion of my visit the room was filled with many such heaps with just narrow corridors between. I had to zig-zag my way between the heaps to reach his desk. Most of the heaps comprised untaxed Barristers' briefs. As Clerk to Quarter Sessions, A Clifford Larke was supposed to tax them, so that they could be paid out of public funds but he never got round to the task, so anyone appearing at Windsor Quarter Sessions, knew that it would be years before they saw any money. As a means of reducing public expenditure it worked a treat, but I was surprised that the barristers tolerated his inertia for so long.

On another occasion at Windsor, a trial I was involved in had to be stopped when A. Clifford Larke announced that he had lost the Indictment. We spent half an hour searching all round the Court until A. Clifford Larke discovered that he had been sitting on it all along! He used to sit on a cushion and had shoved the Indictment under the cushion for safekeeping but had then forgotten where he had put it. It was that kind of Court.

The end for A. Clifford Larke eventually came when a case had to be adjourned again and again, as each time he kept forgetting one of the basics, such as convening a jury or asking the prison authorities to produce the prisoner! When the case eventually got to trial the jury disagreed and the case had to be re-tried. At the re-trial the Recorder Frank Blennerhassett QC, a very patient man, went through the check list with A. Clifford Larke and then buried his head in his hands in open court when told that A. Clifford Larke had convened the same jury as had failed to reach agreement ' to save time'. Yet another adjournment – the seventh. After that fiasco, he was persuaded to resign, to be replaced by a solicitor called Beer. Unfortunately Beer went ski-ing, broke both legs and at the next Quarter Sessions there was A. Clifford Larke back again, and saying how delighted he was to be there, to Frank Blennerhassett's considerable consternation.

But the case at Windsor which is etched in my memory had for once nothing to do with A. Clifford Larke's failings. It concerned a retired RAF Wing Commander Bamber, who lived in Buckinghamshire and had attended a mess reunion somewhere in Surrey. Mess reunions tend to be bibulous affairs and this one certainly was. At the end of the evening, just as he was about to leave, the Wing Commander got thrown into the fountain by his colleagues. It was a warm June evening and the WingCo's answer to his problem was to divest himself of all his clothes and to then drive home starkers, though he was in no fit state to drive anywhere, given the amount of alcohol that had been imbibed. His route home took him through Windsor where he encountered road works and a road reduced to one lane. Ignoring the red signal he kept driving until he met the traffic coming in the opposite direction. Unfortunately for him the car behind him was being driven by an off-duty Berkshire Constabulary Sergeant, who then arrested him and later at Windsor Police Station he was charged with both driving under the influence and with careless driving.

Now, however, his luck changed. The Police Surgeons were in dispute with the County Council over pay and were in a bloody-minded mood – employees in dispute with their employers over pay was a not uncommon state of affairs in the 60s and 70s. This was before the days of breathalysers and one of the tests to establish if you were under the influence or not was to walk a white line. Drunk as he was the WingCo accomplished this in good military fashion and then quite disgracefully, the Police Surgeon pronounced him fit to drive. That left the careless driving charge, which went to Windsor Quarter Sessions. At committal proceedings in the Magistrates Court, the WingCo's defending solicitor argued successfully that as he was not being charged with drunken driving but only careless driving, it would be prejudicial to his case to reveal to the jury that he had not had a stitch on when arrested. So the Jury were only told a third of the tale but even so they smelt a rat. At the end of the trial they deliberated for hours and eventually failed to reach a verdict. So the WingCo was tried again and the second time round he was acquitted. It was cases such as this and the one at Newbury involving the Irish travelling salesman, which convinced the authorities that they had to do something and the result was the introduction of breathalysers, blood tests and the like.

I myself used to prosecute in the County's Magistrates' Courts. One evening just as I was leaving Shire Hall I was contacted by Bracknell Police. The Inspector who normally prosecuted traffic cases had gone down sick, so could I step into the breach and take over the next day's prosecutions? As a result the next day I arrived at Bracknell Magistrates' Court to find that I had to prosecute 8 careless driving cases, and in each case the defendant was pleading 'not guilty'. However, in those days it was rare for defendants to have professional representation and all 8 defendants were representing themselves. Nevertheless it was a difficult day as I had not had time to read any of the files. I managed to read the first one before we started and then as I was prosecuting that case, I had at the same time to read up the next one and so on. But at the end of the day we had 7 convictions and 1 acquittal, which was a fair and just result, completely unachievable time wise nowadays.

The other thing I recall about my time in the Magistrates' Courts, was travelling time. If I needed to be prosecuting in Newbury Magistrates' Court at 10.0am, I used to leave Shire Hall, where I parked my car, at 9.30am. I needed 20 minutes to drive the 17 miles to Newbury and 10 minutes to sort out my papers. There were no traffic lights or roundabouts on the Bath Road between Reading and Newbury and not that much traffic, so there was nothing to hold you up. Nowadays, if you wanted to drive from the old Shire Hall to Newbury, after 20 minutes you would still be in Reading.

OXFORDSHIRE INTERLUDE

12

OXFORDSHIRE COUNTY COUNCIL (1966-1969)

In mid 1966 I moved to Oxfordshire County Council. I was still an Assistant Solicitor but my salary increased to £1800 pa from £1200 pa with Berkshire. As in the case of Berkshire, the County town, Oxford, was a County Borough and therefore of equal status to the County Council. Although similar in area then to Berkshire, Oxfordshire County's population was less than 400,000, whereas Berkshire's had been approaching 600,000.

The County Council HQ was a castellated Victorian Gothic building sited within the curtilage of the Castle, close to the Castle mound and to Oxford Gaol, which was then a working prison – now it is the very smart Malmaison Hotel. Most of the Clerk's department, including myself, were housed in a two-storey terrapin building standing between the HQ and Castle mound. It was not good accommodation - freezing cold in winter and stultifying in the summer.

The Clerk, Gerald Burkitt, was old school – very much the gentleman. He had photos of himself in his office riding to hounds and portraying him show jumping. He was a very modest, self-effacing man but as he had been awarded the Military Cross, he had obviously served with distinction in the 2nd World War. If anything Oxfordshire was even more parsimonious than Berkshire. This manifested itself by getting officers to double up on jobs but be paid one salary. Hugh Walton, the 2nd Deputy Clerk, was interested in history and ancient documents and so when the County Archivist retired he took over as County Archivist, while remaining 2nd Deputy Clerk. When the County Welfare Services Officer retired the Clerk was persuaded to take over the post. This worked to the advantage of me and the other Assistant Solicitor, as we ended up undertaking interesting, albeit non-legal, work.

I recall on one occasion I was sent to administer the estate of an old lady, who had lived in an ancient farm-house in Horton-cum-Studley, a hamlet about 6 miles from Oxford and backing onto Otmoor. The hamlet and the farmhouse were used as the setting for the filming of 'A Man for All Seasons' – the story of Sir Thomas More. Otmoor is now farmland but until the C18th it was a marsh, where the local inhabitants used to walk around on stilts. The lady in question had become incapable of managing her affairs and as her two sons had fallen out, the Court of Protection had stepped in and made an order for her supervision, which then became the responsibility of County Welfare Services and hence the Clerk. When I went to the farm-house it was like entering a time capsule. She must have been born around 1875 and had lived in the farm-house all her life. She had kept everything, - clothes and even all her Xmas cards. I contacted a local auctioneer and managed to get one of the two sons to accompany me as we toured the house and the auctioneer offered us a price on every article. The kitchen table, which had a C17th base went for £5. From what I now know, the estate was ripped off in a grand manner. You would have to pay several pounds nowadays for a genuine Victorian Xmas card and the old lady had left hundreds, which the auctioneer just took without paying anything. However the son seemed satisfied, so that was good enough for me. After the son had departed the auctioneer stated that he would like to make me a gift. I declined and I realized then that he had made a killing. However he persisted and eventually I accepted a leather Gladstone bag – the kind that doctors used to use. I still have it.

As part of my normal legal duties I was also given the task of registering Oxfordshire's commons, pursuant to the passing of the Commons Registration Act 1965. Under the Act, common land was defined as either village green, land subject to rights of common or manorial waste. The owners of common land or those enjoying rights of common had to register their interest or lose it. All manner of oddities emerged as registration proceeded. The lot meadows lying between Oxford and Yarnton were the most interesting. There had been three such meadows at one time, called Pixhey Mead, Oxhey Mead and West or Yarnton Mead. However, both Pixhey Mead and Oxhey Mead had succumbed to the Oxford By-pass and had ceased to be common land. But West or Yarnton Mead remained as common land and needed to be registered. It amounted to about 100 acres and was theoretically divided into 3 rows, each of 13 strips. There were 13 cherry wood balls, each with a name – Watery Molly was one such name as I recall - and the commoners could own a ball or part of one. Once a year the commoners would draw lots to decide which strips they would farm for the ensuing year. Eventually individual farming ceased and the grass from the meadow was auctioned off. But the commoners and bidders would still meet at the Grapes Inn in Yarnton and a pin would be stuck in a lighted candle. Bidders would then bid for the crop until the pin fell out of the candle. By 1966 the candle ceremony had become purely ceremonial but I do recall being shown Watery Molly by the owners of Woodstock Manor, who casually mentioned that the Black Prince had been born in their house. This was Edward of Woodstock, Prince of Wales, eldest son of Edward III (1330-1376) and the father of Richard II (1367-1399).

I also recall registering Nuffield Common. The registration was submitted by the owners, who are the Huntercombe Golf Club. The Common is subject to a scheme made by the former Henley Rural District Council under the Open Spaces Act of 1906, permitting the residents of Henley Rural District to play lawful games on the Common. I phoned up the Secretary of the Golf Club, who was a Scotsman, and drew his attention to the Scheme, pointing out that golf was a game and the existence of the scheme meant that anyone living within Henley Rural District was legally entitled to play golf on Nuffield Common. I was pretty miffed to then be patronized. *'Och, laddie, dinna fret yrself – there's nae problem. Just gae ahead and register'*. *'On your head be it'* thought I and went ahead and completed the registration. 23 years later I left local government and went to work for Field Seymour Parkes, a firm of solicitors in Reading. On my very first day in the office, the then senior partner, John Kirk, asked me if I knew anything about Commons. *'Actually, I do'* I replied. *'Well'*, said John ' *We act for the Huntercombe Golf Club and we have got a bit of a problem'*. *'I know'* said I and they still do. John Kirk then showed me a copy of the Oxfordshire County Council file, where there were copies of several letters and memos written by yours truly, all of which I am glad to say still held true.

I was also responsible for giving legal advice to the Weights and Measures Committee and this involved on occasions prosecuting the vendors of defective products, in particular items containing foreign bodies. Normally the Committee would authorize a caution for a first offence but sometimes first offences would be prosecuted if sufficiently serious. On one occasion we had a complaint that a lady living in Witney had found a sliver of glass in a bottle of milk, sold by Stokes Dairy, who were based just outside Witney. This was very serious and I obtained consent to prosecute the Company in Witney Magistrates Court. The Company were well established in Witney and very apologetic – never happened before etc etc. They then pleaded guilty and were fined just £5. Even in 1967 this was a derisory sum. But only a fortnight later we had another complaint of glass in a bottle of Stokes' milk. So back to Witney Magistrates Court, another guilty plea and this time the fine was £10.Then a few weeks later the same thing again. This time I thought the Bench will throw the book at Stokes but no – the third time the fine was just £15! I was shell-shocked and said to my witness - Mr Bartram, the County Health Inspector – that I could not understand what was going on. He gave me a funny look and I was then enlightened as to the fact that Stokes and the Bench were all in the same Masonic Lodge. So Bartram and I then carried out a formal inspection of Stokes' Dairy. It was unbelievable. Nearly all his staff were inmates at an adjoining asylum and they were running the plant after a fashion with minimal supervision. Even as we walked round the bottling plant, there was a broken bottle rattling around the filling head and no-one was taking the trouble to remove it. But the County Council did not have the power to shut down the dairy. So I asked Bartram if the next Bench to Witney – Chipping Norton – were also Masons but he thought not. So I said we would wait until we got a complaint from someone living within Chipping Norton's jurisdiction. We had several more complaints from Witney residents, which we ignored, and then eventually I was able to get before the Chipping Norton Bench, who fined Stokes so heavily that they put him out of business. I have several good friends who are Masons and those to whom I have related this story are as horrified as I was. So I think today's Masons have cleaned up their act. But when I was subsequently sounded out about becoming a Mason, I politely declined.

The planning system in Oxfordshire was an oddity, though this worked to my advantage. For 30 years the Chairman of the County Council had been the Earl of Macclesfield. By all accounts he had been an autocrat and you crossed him at your peril. But he had retired by the time I arrived at the County Council and had been succeeded by his daughter-in-law, Lady Parker, a very able and pleasant lady. But the Earl missed the County Council so much that he used to call in at the Clerk's office on a regular basis. He would sit in a chair in the General Office and talk to anyone passing. So it was difficult to relate this amiable old buffer to the stories of the autocrat that abounded. The County Planning Adviser was one Maurice Robinson. He had once been the County Planning Officer but he was one of those who had fallen foul of the Earl and had been demoted. At the same time the Planning Solicitor, Larry Hill, had been promoted to equal status and pay to the County Planning Adviser. It was a recipe for disaster. The two men hated each other and would only communicate in writing. But both would talk to me and I became a kind of go-between. In Berkshire most planning was handled by the District Councils and the County Council concentrated on structure planning, minerals and listed buildings. In Oxfordshire, however, there were joint County/ District Planning Committees, serviced by County Officers, dealing with all planning applications. As a result I became the legal adviser to the Chipping Norton/Woodstock Planning Committee. It met monthly, alternating between Woodstock and Chipping Norton. I would draft planning conditions, issue enforcement notices and I handled the occasional planning appeal. There were not many appeals, as the Committee invariably granted consent to whatever was submitted, provided it was being built in Cotswold stone or its concrete equivalent. But it was a great experience travelling around a beautiful part of the country, looking at sites and then advising the Committee.

13
FORMATION OF THAMES VALLEY POLICE AUTHORITY

It was during my time at Oxfordshire County Council that the Thames Valley Police Authority was formed on 1st April 1968. Prior to that the three Counties of Berkshire, Buckinghamshire and Oxfordshire and the two County Boroughs of Reading and Oxford had each had their own Police Force. The driving force for amalgamation was Roy Jenkins, the Home Secretary, who lived in East Hendred, in what was then Berkshire, but later became Oxfordshire. But first there had to be an Inquiry and Mr Mars-Jones QC was appointed to hold it. The Inquiry was held in County Hall, Oxford and Gerald Burkitt, our Clerk asked me to act as the Inspector's gopher. So for 3 days I ran the occasional errand for Mr Mars-Jones but mostly sat beside him, while the 5 Police Authorities argued strenuously against amalgamation. They were wasting their time. Mr Mars-Jones duly wrote his report, recommending proceeding with amalgamation and eventually took his reward with a seat in the High Court. Once it became clear that Thames Valley Police Authority was on its way in, the three Counties carved up the jobs. Buckinghamshire as the most populous County – they had no County Borough – provided the Chief Constable and Clerk; Berkshire the Treasurer and Oxfordshire provided the HQ at Kidlington and the Authority's Architect. Little did I think at the time that I would eventually become the third Clerk of the Thames Valley Police Authority from 1986-1995.

14
THE NALGO STAG EVENT

During my time at Oxfordshire I retained close links with Berkshire. For example I was still playing Rugby for the Berkshire Shire Hall RUFC each Saturday. My successor as Articled Clerk at Berkshire County Council was Bill Goyder, who lived with his parents at Pindars, Rotherfield Greys. His girlfriend, Belinda Todd, whom he later married, was the articled clerk at the Oxford solicitors' firm of Darby & Son. It was at a party at Pindars in 1967 that I first met my future first wife, Elizabeth (Liz) Peebles. She was a legal secretary at Darby & Son and was a close friend of Belinda's. We eventually married on the 5th September 1969, the same month that we bought a house at Blewbury, then in Berkshire, now in Oxfordshire and I moved back to Berkshire County Council to take up a position as 2nd Assistant Clerk (Planning & Highways).

I held my stag night at the County Council's Sonning Sports Club House. As a member of the NALGO Union (National Association of Local Government Officers) I approached the Oxfordshire Branch and suggested that we should further good relations between ourselves and neighbouring Branches and I volunteered to arrange a joint social with the Berkshire Branch if the Oxfordshire Branch would stump up the cost of hiring a coach. I must confess that nothing was said about my pending nuptials. To my surprise the Branch agreed. So I rounded up all my Oxford mates (very few of whom were members of NALGO) and we hastened down to join up with all my Berkshire mates at Sonning for what proved to be a somewhat riotous stag evening. At some stage I ended up in the Club House plunge pool and my trousers ended up on the Council's flag mast, where they got stuck and could not be retrieved for several days. My last memory of the evening is trouserless dancing a Scottish jig in front of Oxford County Hall, accompanied by the Oxfordshire County Council's Scottish caretaker, to the tune of 'Donald where's your troosers?'

ASSISTANT CLERK

15

2ND ASSISTANT CLERK (HIGHWAYS AND PLANNING) (1969-1973)

I had not thought when I moved to Oxfordshire that I would return to Berkshire. It was considered and was probably correct that the more authorities you could show on your CV the better your chances of further promotion. But having waited 6 months without a sniff of a job elsewhere, a suitable post came up in my old County. I applied and was appointed but it was no walkover. One of the other applicants, Rodney Davis from Co Durham, was so impressive that a 3rd Assistant Clerk post was created for him and he joined the Department shortly after me.

In my new post I had responsibility for all clerking and legal matters to do with highways and planning. I had a succession of assistant solicitors to help me and was blessed with two very experienced Committee clerks running my two sections. I have already referred to John Killick as Mr Berkshire Highways, who was always very supportive and had no problem in welcoming as a boss someone to whom he had once had to teach the ropes.

John was also superb with the County Councillors. They liked him, which was important but they also respected his knowledge and took his advice. Even Norman Stanley Furness Douglass was putty in his hands. N S F Douglass (he was a member of the Furness shipping family and was independently wealthy) was one of the many characters on the County Council. He had read for the Bar but some doubted he had ever been admitted. There were also suggestions that he had once fallen off his horse – he was a very keen huntsman – and that the fall had left him with a minor brain injury. Be that as it may, he knew enough law to cause me problems from time to time and he used to delight in turning up at Committee meetings with a copy of Pratt & Mackenzie's treatise on the Law of Highways, which he then used to try to raise legal points to debate with whoever was the Clerk's representative. Fortunately the remainder of the Committee used to treat him as a bit of a joke, so that he never got anywhere with his points, even when he was probably right. I remember on one occasion he asked the Chairman of the Highways Committee if the Clerk could rule on the legality of the AA stationing their boxes at crossroads – this used to be the practice around the country at that time. They probably were illegal obstructions but they served a useful purpose and no-one apart from N S F Douglass was fussed. In fact he wasn't fussed either – he just wanted to score a legal point with the Clerk but the Committee Chairman suggested that the Clerk's representative could investigate Mr Douglass's point out of Committee and swiftly moved on to next business.

There are two other Norman Douglass stories worth recounting. One foggy autumn day, I had to go to a village in the heart of the Vale of White Horse in North Berkshire, to serve a document. I was looking around in the mist for the house, when I was almost run down by a large horse, on the back of which sat Mr Douglass. '*Oh hello Williams*' said Mr Douglass '*Have you seen a fox*?' When confessing I had not, Mr Douglas disappeared into the mist up a nearby driveway.

The other Norman Douglass story was told to me by David Over, an Assistant Solicitor at this time, who later succeeded me as County Solicitor, jointly with Ralph Garbett. David was at the White Horse, Uffington with the County Council Countryside Committee on a site inspection, when they were joined by Mr Douglass. He then spotted two Ordnance Survey (OS) employees nearby engaged on a survey. Marching up to them Mr Douglass enquired if they had been tested. Taken aback the OS employees admitted they had no idea what testing Mr Douglass was referring to. '*Brucellosis*' replied Mr. Douglass '*I'm a member of the Berkshire County Council and can't have townies like you invading the countryside and infecting our cattle. You go and get yourselves tested*'. Whereupon the OS employees beat a hasty retreat. Mr Douglass then took the Sub-Committee to a nearby hostelry and demanded that the landlady serve the party tea or coffee. The landlady was not kitted out to do teas and coffees but such was Mr. Douglass's air of command that she ended up serving the party using her best china.

There were however, sometimes more serious matters afoot in relation to highways. The Government were building the M4 through Berkshire and Edward Davies, the County Surveyor, persuaded the County Council in 1967 that a connection ought to be built from the M4 to serve East Reading and then by means of a 3rd bridge across the Thames to link up with Caversham. The result was the A329 (M) which runs from Bracknell, then past a junction with the M4 at Winnersh, through Woodley and Earley to meet the A4. However, the 3rd bridge never materialized as Oxfordshire County Council and South Oxfordshire District Council have always withheld consent, fearing that major development would follow in the path of a 3rd bridge.

The route selected for the A329M followed the railway line but Earley had been developed up to the railway and initially the selected route required the demolition of around 150 homes in Mays Lane and Anderson Avenue. There was an unholy row about this and the Clerk's Department were in the thick of it as we were involved in acquiring the land needed for the road through compulsory purchase.

Eventually the Council retreated and halved the number of homes to be demolished. But this meant leaving many houses with virtually no back garden whatsoever and a 20 foot drop down to the road. However, over 40 years have passed and the houses are still there and occupied and the substantial retaining wall is still standing.

The retaining wall was built by one of the Assistant County Surveyors - Gethin Griffiths, a fellow Welshman and yet another Shire Hall character. He married ERD's secretary, Jeanne Smith as was, who later went into local government on her own account and became Chair of South Oxfordshire District Council. Their son Richard Griffiths DL became a very well known Reading Solicitor, for many years the senior partner of Blandy's, Berkshire oldest legal firm and Under Sheriff to the Berkshire Shrievalty.

16
MISS JOAN ABERY

Gethin Griffiths was very proud of the fact that he had constructed the first dual carriageway in Berkshire at Knowl Hill and that he had achieved this feat by taking a line from a load of railway sleepers. I think that highway engineers use computers nowadays. On one occasion Gethin was implementing the Long Lane,Tilehurst improvement scheme and I got an agitated phone call from him to the effect that Miss Abery was lying down in the road in front of his bulldozer and what action should he take? Miss Abery was one of a number of Berkshire eccentrics, whose paths crossed those of the County Council at not infrequent intervals. She was something of a woman of mystery, and by all accounts a very sad case. It was believed that she had been a pharmacist but that an unhappy love affair had tipped her over the edge. She wore rags, literally, and painted her face with white powder, so that she looked just like the portrayal of Miss Havisham in David Lean's film of Charles Dickens' 'Great Expectations'. She never cut the hedges around her bungalow in Long Lane and eventually the bungalow and its entrance disappeared from sight. Miss Abery would then pop out through a hole in the hedge. No-one was quite sure how she managed to sustain herself but she obtained her milk by going round her neighbours' houses just after the milkman had called, helping herself to a pint or two. But as for food I had myself seen her scavenging her way through the bins along Oxford Road.

Now as luck would have it, the County Council had made a CPO (compulsory purchase order) to acquire the land needed to widen Long Lane and Miss Abery was one of the landowners affected. There followed a game of cat and mouse. Having persuaded Gethin not to run his bulldozer over her, a tactical approach was adopted. Whenever Miss Abery lay down in front of the bulldozer, Gethin and his merry men went off to work elsewhere on their scheme and then when Miss Abery grew tired of lying in the road and popped back through the hole in her hedge, work resumed. She was a very fit lady and would walk for miles. About a year after the Long Lane incident I was walking through a wood in Upper Basildon, when whom should I see but Miss Abery. '*Hello, Miss Abery*' said I, '*How are you*?' She literally jumped in the air in fright. 'How *do you know my name?*' '*Oh, you are famous, Miss Abery*' said I and we went our separate ways. I never saw or heard of her again until I read an account of her sad demise in the local newspaper. Apparently she had died in her bungalow, but because it was sealed from the world no-one knew and it was weeks before the police went investigating. She used to feed the local foxes each evening and there was not much of her left to bury after the foxes continued their dining.

17
THE PLANNING SECTION

The other half of my section was involved with Planning. Reporting to me was another able Committee Clerk called Howard Budden. In two – tier government, most day to day planning matters are handled by District Councils. But the County Council retained responsibility for Structure planning, listed buildings and mineral extraction. The County Structure Plan was an important document as it determined how many houses would be built in the County. When Berkshire County Council was first created in 1888, Berkshire had a population of just 175,000 and Reading County Borough was 100,000. Berkshire had grown to 400,000 by the time I arrived in 1961, an increase of 131% in 73 years. The population of today's Berkshire is 850,000. It has lost North Berkshire but gained Reading and Slough, Eton, Datchet, Horton and Wraysbury, so to compare apples with apples, since 1961, Berkshire's population has increased from 500,000 to 850,000, an increase of 70% in 57 years.

One of the areas to be developed during this stage of my career was Lower Earley. The County Panning Committee wanted to see a comprehensive development and hired a leading firm of planning consultants, called Shankland Cox to draw up a Master Plan. They then thought quite rightly that the best chance of seeing the Master Plan implemented would be to engage with just one developer. At the time one of the country's leading developers was Wates. They had a good reputation and I was deputed to visit them to see if they might be interested. So I trekked up to their national HQ in South London and met their senior men. They were very apologetic. They would have loved to have carried out the development but said it was just too large a project for their firm to take on single handed.

It was left to an astute architect planner called Peter Barton and an estate agent called Felix Pole to form a consortium of developers to carry out the development. A number of developers were involved - though not Wates – and each was given a separate part of Lower Earley to develop. As each developer had its own building style, the overall comprehensive look sought by Shankland Cox was lost. In addition a war of attrition took place with the planning authority to relocate as much green space as possible from the heart of the development to the flood plain. It would be unfair to say that the end result was a disaster – Lower Earley remains a popular development where houses sell quickly, but it is not the model development envisaged by the County Council and Shankland Cox. You need New Town Commissions to achieve comprehensive development, but you only have to look at Bracknell New Town to see that New Town Commissions are not necessarily the answer either.

18
THE LAMB HOTEL, WALLINGFORD

see colour page XII

I have already mentioned my part in saving one listed building in Wallingford, when I was an articled clerk. Now as an Assistant Clerk I became involved in the fight to preserve another listed building in the town – the Lamb Hotel. It had been the leading hotel in Wallingford, but had fallen on hard times. It was owned by Usher's Brewery but they had given up on it and simply wanted to demolish and develop the site. Col Richard Norman of Milton Manor was still the Chairman of the County Planning Committee and remained a staunch conservationist. He wanted to save the Lamb as did the Deputy County Planning Officer, Pierre Porri and myself. The remainder of the Committee felt the preservation case had been lost. Wallingford was then a Borough Council, with a Borough Surveyor, who could have put a closure order on the building to protect the public, given the danger of passers-by from falling tiles. A closure order would have meant the end of the Lamb, so we constantly pleaded with the Borough Surveyor to hold his hand, to give us a bit more time to play Mr Micawber. But the reality was that there was nothing we could come up with to give the building a new lease of life. The County Council did have powers but there was no budget provision. So the Lamb looked doomed.

Then the news reached us that a consortium of local businessmen had been formed to buy the Lamb and turn it into an Antiques Emporium. And as they say the rest is history. Forty five years later the Lamb is still going strong under its new lease of life and remains one of the landmark buildings of Wallingford. I believe the consortium was formed by members of the Bosher family of Cholsey, well-known local builders. But to the amazement of everyone at Shire Hall another member of the Consortium was Charlie Elderfield, head of the County Treasurer's debt collection section. It later transpired that Charlie had been hiding his light under a bushel as he had had an incredible career. During the War he was a member of the SOE (Special Operations Executive) and had been parachuted into the Balkans to act as a British liaison officer with the Communists, under the leadership of Josip Broz Tito. He hit it off with Tito to such an extent that when Tito became President of Yugoslavia, Charlie was given a flat in Belgrade as a thank-you gift. After the end of the War and back in England, Charlie went into business and developed a successful chain of sports shops, which he eventually sold for a good price. Then although he did not need to work. he became bored and it was at this point that he applied for and was appointed to the middle-tier position of Head of Debt collection for the County Council.

ENCOUNTERS WITH THE FAMOUS

19

RETURNING OFFICER – AIREY NEAVE MP

We were sometimes called on to perform other tasks. The Clerk of the County Council was the Returning Officer for County Council elections, naturally, but also for General Elections. The Clerk also had the right to appoint Deputies to act on his behalf at those elections which he was not conducting personally, and thus it came about that at the General Election of 1970, which Ted Heath won for the Conservatives against the odds, I was the Returning Officer for the Abingdon constituency. The sitting Member was a Conservative, Airey Neave DSC OBE MC TD. He was a well-known war hero, who had managed to escape from the Nazis' Colditz prison in Germany and made it back home. An Old Etonian, he went to the Bar and then won Abingdon at a by-election in 1953. A popular MP, his majority was over 13,000 when I declared him elected at the 1970 election. He later became very close to Margaret Thatcher and that made him a marked man by the IRA. They managed to plant a bomb under his car and then blew him up and killed him as he was driving out of the House of Commons car park. That was on 30th March 1979. A few months later on August 27th 1979, the IRA assassinated Lord Mountbatten, the Queen's cousin and they narrowly missed assassinating Margaret Thatcher herself at the Grand Hotel, Brighton on 12th October 1984. Ian Gow, another close associate of Margaret Thatcher was assassinated by the IRA on 30th July 1990.

20

PRIME MINISTER MARGARET THATCHER AND THE PRINCESS ROYAL

see colour page XXVII

I was once introduced to Margaret Thatcher and have the photo to prove it. It was in 1987 when she was invited to speak to the Thames Valley Police at their annual social do. The then Chief Constable, Colin Smith, had been Head of Diplomatic and Royal Protection at the Met, which gave him an entree. I had been appointed Clerk of the Thames Valley Police Authority in 1986 on the death of Bob Gash, which is why I was there. It was so dangerous then that Maggie and Dennis Thatcher had to be flown by helicopter to Sulhampstead – they couldn't be driven by car. Maggie gave her 'the police are wonderful' speech, which, not surprisingly, went down very well. But it was the behaviour of Dennis Thatcher, which amused us most. On arrival he went straight to the drinks table and helped himself to a large gin and tonic. Then on entering the dining room, he crawled down the centre sprig so that he could shake hands with all the attractive Lady Superintendents and Inspectors that Colin Smith had cunningly grouped together right opposite the centre of the top table. In conversation he came over as very bright and well informed, so in reality he was not a million miles away from his characterisation in the 'Dear Bill' column of Private Eye. The following year, Colin Smith managed to obtain the Princess Royal as a speaker, and very good she was. Her speech was clearly her own work, as I could see it was literally written on the back of an envelope. But it was thoughtful and far from a hagiography.

21

AIR MARSHALL DOWDING

Air Chief Marshall Sir Hugh Dowding GCO GCVO CME was Head of the RAF during the Battle of Britain, which was fought over southern England during July-October 1940. By October Hitler abandoned Operation Sea Lion and Britain was saved from German invasion. Dowding died in February 1970, and shortly before he died I received a letter from him, asking if the County Council had any surplus milestones, we could sell him. I politely replied that we regarded our milestones as historic objects, not for sale and that was that. Dowding lived in Kent, so why on earth he wanted to purchase a Berkshire milestone or indeed any milestone, we shall never know

22
SIR DOUGLAS BADER

In 1981, by which time I had been appointed County Secretary and Solicitor, I was at my desk one day when the Shire Hall switchboard put through a call from Australia. '*Is that Williams?*' '*Yes, Williams speaking*'. '*Bader here*'. The only Bader I had heard of was the famous Airman, Group Captain Sir Douglas Bader CBE DSO DFC, who had lost both his legs in a flying accident at Woodley aerodrome in 1931. With tin legs he learned to fly again and through sheer bloody mindedness, at which by all accounts he excelled, he had rejoined the RAF and took an active part in the 2nd World War, including the Battle of Britain. '*Well, Sir Douglas,*' says I ' *What can I do for you?*' '*That bloody traffic order, you've made in Woodley. It is causing Lady Bader great personal inconvenience*'.' *I'll look into it personally, Sir Douglas*'. '*See that you do*'. End of conversation. Of course I had no knowledge of any traffic order in Woodley or anywhere else for that matter. But my name was like a corporate name and it appeared on all orders made by the County Council. I later found out that Sir Douglas and Lady Bader were divorced but Lady Bader still lived in Woodley. A parking restriction order had been made relating to a road in Woodley, where Lady Bader was accustomed to park. She objected to the order and she had contacted her ex-husband, by then in Australia, and had asked him to intervene. Needless to say the Order stayed in place.

I recently related this tale to my Rotarian friend, Richard Anderson, and he told me that he too had met Sir Douglas Bader. Apparently Bader was great friends with his former Head Master and once visited his school. The Head asked Richard to look after Bader for a while and Richard says he found him hard work and very objectionable. According to Richard the Lady Bader, who objected to our traffic order, had a drink problem and took to selling off her possessions to raise money. Richard knew the dealer who bought her things and acquired some of them from the dealer.

BOB GASH & REORGANIZATION

23

ROBERT WALKER (BOB) GASH

During the late 60's, Liz's younger brother Richard (Dick) Peebles had been appointed Head of Research at British Nuclear Fuels, based at Sellafield. He was not only a very clever lad, who went to Cambridge but he was also an excellent rugby player, who had played for the University but just missed out on a Blue. Liz and I went up to Cumbria to visit him one summer. Dick was living in digs and Liz and I camped in a field in Eskdale. The Bower House Inn was not far away and as the weather was not very kind we spent much of the week-end in the pub. There was a family staying in the pub – husband, wife and two sons - and they seemed to spend as much time in the bar as we did. I am not sure why it is but one local government officer can always spot another, so on one occasion when we were both lining up the drinks, I said to the unknown gent, '*I bet you work in local government*' and he admitted he did.

It turned out that his name was Robert (Bob) Gash and that he was the Deputy Clerk at Northamptonshire County Council. But he was mightily down in the dumps, because he had just missed out on being appointed Clerk at Suffolk County Council, although he was the favourite. He felt that his career was over. '*Why don't you have a go at Berkshire?*' said I, knowing that ERD had announced his retirement. '*No, point – you have a sitting Deputy*'. This was true, we had a well-established Deputy, Hartley Bramwell. '*Well*" said I ' *Hartley will obviously go for the job but I am not so sure that he* will *land it*'. Then we parted.

see colour page IV

Shortly afterwards in June 1971 I was sent on the 4 month senior management course at INLOGOV (the Institute of Local Government Studies), at the University of Birmingham. This was run by Professor John Stewart. We had a break after 2 months and I popped back into Shire Hall to say hello. '*Oh, by the way*' says I '*have they replaced ERD yet?*' '*Yes, some guy no-one has ever heard of called Bob Gash*'. So when Bob Gash took over from ERD I was the only person he knew in Berkshire. We became very close. You could say I became his right hand man.

It is interesting what you pick up on these management courses. Chatting to the Deputy Surveyor of Bradford in the bar one evening, I asked him what he did for holidays. '*Oh each year we hire a boat and cruise the Thames. It is so beautiful*'. By this time I had spent over 10 years in Thames Valley and had never once set foot in a boat on the Thames. I resolved to repair that omission as soon as I could, as indeed I have on a number of occasions –I celebrated my

75th birthday by treating my family and Rotary Club to a four hour cruise from Henley on one of Hobbs' vessels - and the Deputy Surveyor was quite correct – it is a wonderful experience.

Another course member at Inlogov was the Deputy Clerk of Londonderry or Derry. He explained how the Protestants controlled the City, even though in a minority, population- wise. Historically the City had been divided into 5 wards each with the same number of Council seats. But all the Catholics were concentrated in two of the wards, - while the Protestants lived in the other three, thereby ensuring that 3/5th of the Council was Protestant and 2/5th Catholic. To maintain that position new Council building was controlled to ensure that only Protestants were allocated houses in the three Protestant wards. Catholic tenants had to look to be housed in the two Catholic wards. In 2013 my wife, Christina, and I spent a week on Belle Isle near Enniskillen and we visited Derry one day and walked round the walls. On the west side you look down on the Bogside, where one of the end houses is still painted 'You are entering Free Derry'. On the east side you pass what is obviously one of the Protestant neighbourhoods, given that a large sign has been erected giving its name and bearing the inscription 'No Surrender'. Derry was founded in the time of King James 1, when the London Guilds were given land, dispossessed from Catholic chieftains, and encouraged to settle the area. So settlers and apprentices arrived to build a new settlement and develop new trades – a Protestant enclave within a Catholic hinterland, which maintained its political hold on the town through various gerry mandering techniques, including restricting the franchise to house owners, which favoured the protestants. No wonder we had 'the Troubles'.

24
THE BREAKING OF BERKSHIRE

1971 was a momentous year for Berkshire. In 1970 Ted Heath won the election at a time when local government reform was a hot political topic. The previous Labour administration were in favour of abolishing Counties and Districts and replacing them by a single Unitary Council. The Conservatives wanted to maintain the two tier arrangement but in a White Paper issued in early 1971 it was made clear to County Councils that they must review their boundaries having regard to 'the administrative convenience of their ratepayers', failing which the Government would undertake the task for them.

At the same time this communiqué was received, there was a crucial contest for the position of Vice-Chairman at the Berkshire County Council's Annual Meeting of 1971. Alderman Richard Seymour had been returned unopposed as Chairman. He was a Reading solicitor, who had his own firm, Richard Seymour, Aram & Co, which later merged with two other firms to form Field Seymour & Parkes. I later became a consultant with FSP and worked with them for 20 years. Richard Seymour was old school – very much an officer and gentleman, straight as a die, who was always immaculately groomed and always kept his cool. He was very well liked by all at Shire Hall. He had been awarded the Military Cross and had survived several years captivity at the hands of the Japanese. In fact there were a number of County Councillors, who had fought in the 2nd Word War but they never spoke about it. I did find out that one County Councillor, Captain John McCubbin, who represented Hungerford, had been a tea planter in Ceylon, as it used to be called, and had fought against the Japanese at the decisive battle of Kohima, when the Japanese advance was stopped. He had received a severe head wound and had a large metal plate fitted in his skull as a result. In the early 70's candidates for election were for the first time allowed to state their political allegiance on their nomination form. John McCubbin had obviously misunderstood what was intended, because in the appropriate column he entered not Conservative (which he was) but Captain. He was duly elected as the only member of the Captain party on the County Council.

The 1971 contest for the position of Vice-Chairman involved two very strong characters, Frederick (Derick) Derwent Pickering and Richard West. Both had had careers in the Colonial Service – I know Derick Pickering had been in Sudan, where his responsibilities included running the Sudan Railway. I think Richard West had worked further east.

Richard West settled in Dry Sandford in North Berkshire and was passionate about environmental matters. He succeeded Col Richard Norman as Chairman

ANNUAL MEETING OF COUNTY COUNCIL – MAY 1971

1. G Ellis – Dep Treasurer
2. H Stelling – Sen Asst Cerk
3. Lt Col Watt – Ch of Highways
4. Ald F D Pickering – Vice Ch
5. Hartley Bramwell –Dep Clerk
6. E R Davies – Clerk
7. Ald R Seymour – Chairman
8. Ald D Hartley Russell
9. M Beasley – Treasurer
10. Dr D Cullington – County Medical Officer
11. R Frank – Dir Social Services
12. R Stoddart – County Planning Officer
13. D Bailey – County Valuer
14. Chaplain
15. Maj Fairfax Harvey – Chairman Health Committee
16. Ald Mrs E Sheasby – Chairman Social Services
17. Col R Norman – Ch Planning
18. H G Critchell – Ch Clerk-Ed
19. T Elliott – Articled Clerk
20. F E Jones – Ch Legal Clerk
21. J Tainsh – Dep Cty Architect
22. T Saunders – Cttee Clerk
23. W Goodson – Ch Cttee Clk
24. A R Kimber – Asst Clerk
25. D C H Williams – Asst Clerk
26. A V Lewis – Asst Solicitor
27. R C Davis – Asst Clerk
28. D K Over – Asst Solicitor
29. D Johns – Cty Road Safety
30. A R Ealey – Ch Inspector Consumer Protection
31. R S Gibbs – County Supplies Officer
32. V Jennings – Cty Librarian
33. J D Killick – Cttee Clerk
34. G B Warner (Windsor)
35. Ald Salter Chalker
36. Ald Sir William Mount
37. E V Marshall (Sandhurst)
38. Maj H W Gray (Thatcham)
39. J Dawkins (Woodley)
40. D G Smith (Sonning)
41. Ald Sir Louis Dickens
42. Ald W J Cumber (Senior)
43.
44. Mrs M Long (Binfield)
45. T Lloyd – Cttee Clerk
46. Ald Col W Barroll
47. R E Moore(Newbury)
48. F J Pratt (Cookham)
49. A E Penn (Cumnor
50. D Mettrick (Abingdon)
51. J N S Brogden (Hinksey)
52. W A Wiseman (Bray)
53. F Reynolds (Old Windsor)
54. Cap C W Mayne (Harwell)
55. C J Cross (Moreton)
56. H J Benedictus (Maidenhead)
57. R H Duggan (Didcot)
58. L G Hitchcock (Didcot)
59. J Stewart Cook (Windsor)

LAST MEETING OF FIRST COUNTY COUNCIL
30th March 1974

Front Row: left to right: Air Commodore Sir Louis Dickens: J Stewart Cook: Frank Butters: Bob Gash: Richard Seymour (Ch) : Derick Pickering (Vice Ch): Sir William Mount Bt: Derek Hartley-Russell: John Cumber (Jr)

FIRST MEETING OF NEW COUNTY COUNCIL – 1st MAY 1974

1. K A Darvall
2. J Adams
3. W N J Huntley
4. The Hon Geoffrey Somerset
5. K W Johnson
6. D C B Pilkington
7. C D Merrills
8. W A Gilbey
9. W B Cranston
10. J T Clarke
11. N W Hopkins
12. D Tunnicliffe
13. R J Clibbon
14. G C H Slater
15. W A Wiseman
16. N E McBrien
17. B W Gardner
18. D G Smith
19. K G Baxter
20. W J Park
21. I T Coulson
22. A E Furley
23. J K Pocknee
24. R Armstrong
25. P S Cross
26. N W Rapinet
27. W L Stansfeld-Taylor
28. L D Moss
29. E G F Brown
30. G D Salisbury
31. F Lewis
32. W W E Badnall
33. V S Stoner
34. F S C Room
35. J Rigby
36. Capt J Mc Cubbin
37. Sq Ldr H R Walton
38. H G Wheeler
39. F L Roberts
40. R J Simmonds
41. A R Goodman
42. Rr Admiral H R Tribe
43. R E Shaw
44. G A Hughes
45. R A Willis
46. W F Brown
47. C J Thake
48. Air Commodore Sir Louis Dickens
49. C A Harrop
50. N E Avens
51. G F Sage
52. R M Bristow
53. T J Brown
54. H F Gater
55. G A Rush
56. Mrs M C Long
57. H J Benedictus
58. Mrs B L Whiteley
59. The Hon Mrs E A Samuel
60. Mrs K A Cheyne
61. Mrs N C L Robinson
62. Mrs F T Day
63. Mrs R Jones
64. Mrs V R Merrills
65. The Hon Mrs D Maclay
66. Mrs M Fergusson Kelly
67. Mrs R M Crichton
68. Mrs M E Funnell
69. P M Jones
70. Mrs K L Sage
71. A Alexander
72. Mrs N M S Maclean
73. P R Burrall
74. Air Commodore H G Blair
75. J S Cook
76. F A Butters
77. R H C Seymour
78. F D Pickering
79. R W Gash
80. Col R J Watt
81. R J Day
82. F W Dixon
83. Canon F J R Britnell

WALLINGFORD HOUSE

THE LAMB, WALLINGFORD

LEFT
Pierre Porri Esq
(Deputy Planning Officer)

CENTRE
Col Richard Norman (former Chairman of County Planning Committee)

RIGHT
The Author

CIVIC AWARDS CEREMONY
1980

CHAMBER OF COMMERCE FUNCTION

Author standing between Geoff Potter (County Surveyor) and Bob Stoddart (County Planning Officer) – Bert Ealey (County Weights & Measures Officer) to right of Bob Stoddart. The author attended Bob Stoddart's funeral in 2017 – he was 90.

MR MORLEY'S CARD INQUIRING ABOUT PROGRESS IN THE BERKSHIRE STRUCTURE PLAN!

MAJOR BRIAN SHONE
AND HIS BERKSHIRE
BOYS CHORISTERS

THE THEN LORD LIEUTENANT, SIR GORDON PALMER, BEING HERALDED BY THE BERKSHIRE BOYS CHORISTERS ON HIS WAY TO OPEN THE SPURIOUS ST OSWALD'S WELL IN FINCHAMPSTEAD

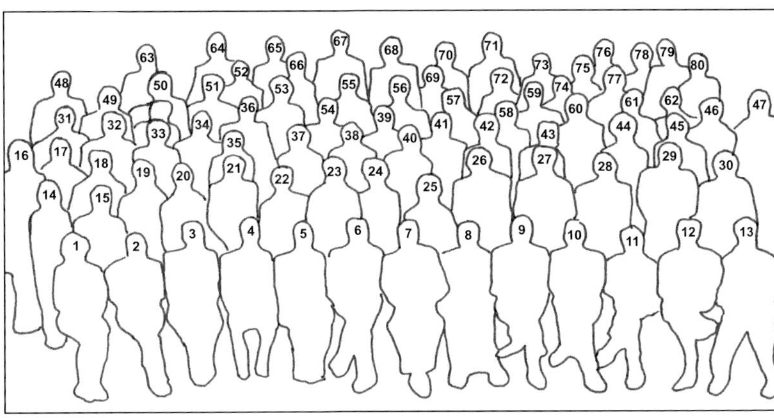

ANNUAL MEETING OF COUNTY COUNCIL - 1977

1.Rosemary Crichton
2.Richard Simmonds
3.Christopher Ward
4.Alan Furley
5.Derick Pickering
6.Bob Gash
7.Richard Watt
8.Gordon Slater
9.Lewis Moss
10.Jim Day
11.Lecky Stansfeld-Taylor
12.Tony Wiseman
13.Air Commodore Sir Louis Dickens
14.Naomi Robinson
15.Peter Jones
16.Yvonne Manisier
17.
18.Jean Gardner
19. Mrs V Merrills
20.
21. Elizabeth Samuel
22. M's V Osmond
23. Marion Fergusson Kelly
24.
25. Mrs M Funnell
26.Henry Benedictus
27. Dick Shaw
28. Bob Cox
29. P.Renton
30.
31. Trevor Timperley
32. David Smith
33.
34. Neville Auton
35.
36. Norman Hopkins
37. David Pilkington
38.
39. A Bristow
40.Air Commodore Gordon Blair
41. John Lawford
42. Ron Jewitt
43. Dr.Laurence Silverman
44. Kevin Boyle
45. Gerald Hughes
46.C D Merrills
47. Godfrey Odds
48.
49. Ron Dyason
50.
51. Neil Rowberry
52. Norman Pearson
53. Joe Slater
54. Ian Morgan
55.
56. Trevor Brown
57. Mike Orton
58. John McCubbin
59.
60.
61.F W Dixon
62.
63. John Gauld
64. Jamie Gladstone
65. Steve Norris
66. Charles Sage
67. J. Goodman
68. Frank Butters
69.
70.Paul Burrall
71. Frank Lewis
72.Paddy Day
73.W F Brown
74.
75. Brian Smith
76. Dr. Don McWilliams
77. Pete Ruhemann
78. Hamish Macbeth
79.
80. John Trimming

With Liz, Rebecca and Robert, meeting John & Sheila Kellett in Cheshire – summer 1980. John & Sheila had one daughter and four sons – John (the author's godson); Peter, Robin and Ted. John, the eldest is now 52.

Liz with Rebecca and Robert in the garden of Honeycroft House – Spring 1980

of the County's Planning Committee, which by this time had became the Environment Committee. Derick Pickering settled in Sunningdale in East Berkshire and interested himself in financial matters. He was also very political and almost singlehanded converted Berkshire from a Council run by independent Conservatives into one run by a Conservative Group, of which he became the de facto Leader. He also became active in local government affairs nationally, where he was regarded as a leading light.

When Derick Pickering first returned to England from the Sudan, he worked as a salesman for Glossops - a highways construction and maintenance company, the Vice-Chairman of which just happened to be my father-in-law, Harry Peebles. Harry and my mother-in-law Nora lived in York and it was a northern firm, though it had a southern base. Then the Company parted company with Derick Pickering but I always retained a good relationship with him, and when he retired to North Yorkshire to live near his son, who was Headmaster of Pocklington School, I visited him on several occasions, during our trips to York to visit the in-laws. He was always delighted to see me and we used to sink a glass of gin and tonic or two, reminiscing about the old times.

When it came to the vote for Vice-Chairmanship it was no contest. Derick Pickering won by a mile - only the North Berkshire Councillors voting for Richard West. But I have always believed that if that vote had gone the other way, the events that followed would have had a very different outcome.

When in response to the Government directive, Berkshire County Council met Oxfordshire County Council to talk about boundaries and administrative convenience it was very quickly agreed that North Berkshire should be handed over to Oxfordshire and the Henleys from Oxfordshire to Berkshire. I thought then and still think that it was a terrible deal. North Berkshire was the historic heart of Berkshire. Wantage was the birthplace of King Alfred the Great. Wallingford, the first County town had at one stage been the second most important town in the whole of the Kingdom of Wessex. It had then given way to Abingdon, which in turn had been succeeded by Reading. Apart from Wantage, Abingdon, Wantage and Wallingford, North Berkshire also included another historic town in Faringdon. The County was even handing over the White Horse of Uffington, which was the County symbol. Nor did it dawn on the negotiators that Berkshire County Council were also handing over major development investment areas at Faringdon, Grove near Wantage and Didcot, where development was by and large welcomed. All this was to be transferred in exchange for just Henley Borough and Henley Rural District Council, where any development is fought tooth and nail. But by this time, having lost the Vice-Chairmanship, Richard West was all for the deal, as it is my belief that by then he saw his future local government career in Oxfordshire not Berkshire. Moreover with his strong personality, he was able to take the North Berkshire Councillors with him. Maybe also Derick Pickering was not too unhappy about seeing the back of a political rival.

Berkshire also had a boundary along the Thames with Buckinghamshire. Relations between Buckinghamshire County Council and Slough Borough Council had deteriorated to the point that Slough would have gone to Timbuktu to get away from Buckinghamshire County Council. So Slough flung itself into Derick Pickering's arms and with Slough came the Parishes of Dorney, Horton, Datchet, Wraysbury and the Urban District of Eton.

Dorney soon went back to Buckinghamshire. Its Member of Parliament was Sir Ronald Bell QC, who was an old boy of Cardiff High School. Born in 1914 he would have been 12 when my father started teaching there in 1926, so my father may well have taught him English at some stage. Bell was a right wing Tory, a member of the Monday Club and an arch euro-sceptic. As a lawyer he was articulate and likely to prove a thorn in Edward Heath's side as he tried to take the country into Europe. It is said that Bell did a deal with Ted Heath – he would abstain on the Europe vote, in return for Dorney being put back in Buckinghamshire.

So when the White Paper was published at the end of 1971, the new County of Berkshire was to be shorn of North Berkshire, but it would acquire Henley Borough and RDC; Reading (no longer a County Borough), Slough Borough and the Parishes of Horton, Datchet and Wraysbury and the Urban District of Eton. When, however, the Local Government Bill was published a few months later there was a palpable feeling of shock in Shire Hall as Henley Borough and Henley RDC remained in Oxfordshire. In other words as far as the Berkshire/Oxfordshire deal was concerned, new Berkshire would be handing over one-third of the County to Oxfordshire in exchange for the Caversham Park Estate. Even Dunsden Parish, which as the crow Flies is only ½ mile from the centre of Reading, remained in Oxfordshire. So much for administrative convenience. I remember Dick Seymour touring Shire Hall pleading with senior staff not to be too hard on Derick Pickering, who had led the negotiations that had resulted in such a disastrous outcome.

The word on the street was that when they heard about the proposed land-swap senior Henleyites were furious, as they rightly foresaw that once part of Berkshire, a third Reading bridge would be built and development north of the Thames would likely follow. They must have put pressure on their Member of Parliament to do something and clearly his representations were successful. The Minister responsible for the Bill was Michael Heseltine, now Lord Heseltine, who later in 1974 became Member of Parliament for Henley. But Lord Heseltine has replied to the author to say that he played no part in the decision to leave the Henleys in Oxfordshire. So it is not clear who exactly took the decision. But if the powers that be felt it necessary to humour Henley, the fairer and more reasonable approach would have been to refer the whole case back to the two County Councils for further consideration. What happened appears indefensible and as more and more development is now crammed into an increasingly urbanized Berkshire, the loss of North Berkshire and its development areas at Faringdon, Grove and Didcot, is felt ever more acutely.

The shock at Shire Hall over the decision was replicated around the County. Residents were particularly incensed that they were going to lose the White Horse, the county symbol. A petition of 2,000 names was quickly signed – there were many letters of complaint to the papers - but it was to no avail. Even 40 years later, many residents of what was North Berkshire still refer to their patch as 'occupied Berkshire'. Some time later I was responsible for preparing the draft design for the new Berkshire's Coat of Arms for submission to the College of Heralds. The pre 1974 County Council had had a Coat of Arms with a shield flanked by a Unicorn and a White Horse. The new Coat of Arms, which I and my team designed, also had a Unicorn and a Horse, but this Horse was in black, as it was mourning the loss of North Berkshire! Somewhat to my surprise the design was approved by the College of Heralds.

Protests over the loss of the White Horse continued for years, and when he became Chairman in 1980 Lewis Moss had a go at resolving them. The County boundary between Berkshire and Oxfordshire had become a higgledy-piggledy affair as it followed Parish Boundaries rather than the actual Ridgeway. So the Ridgeway would be a more sensible boundary. But there was one problem with putting this forward as a solution – the White Horse lies to the north of the Ridgeway, so even if the Ridgeway had become the County boundary, the White Horse would have remained in Oxfordshire. There was then a discussion with the Vale of White Horse District Council. Their view was that they would be delighted to see the White Horse back in Berkshire but only if the whole District went with it. Their transfer to Oxfordshire had taken place without any consultation with them; they had been happy in Berkshire; were not very happy in Oxfordshire; but it was all or nothing. I was for continuing the fight but Lewis Moss over-ruled me and the initiative was abandoned.

25
REORGANISATION

The Local Government Act was passed in 1972 and the reorganised Counties and Districts were due to come into existence on 1st April 1974. This gave the outgoing Councils a chance to plan for the transition. Oxfordshire County, Oxford City and Berkshire County set up one Joint Committee to plan for life under a new Oxfordshire County, incorporating North Berkshire and Oxford City while Berkshire County, Reading County Borough and Buckinghamshire County set up a Joint Committee to plan for a new Berkshire, minus North Berkshire but incorporating Reading County Borough, Caversham Park, Slough Borough, Eton Urban District, and the parishes of Datchet, Horton and Wraysbury.

It was known that most staff would automatically transfer to the new Councils but it was also known that there would be competition for senior posts. Hartley Bramwell, the Berkshire Deputy, who had lost out to Bob Gash in Berkshire when ERD retired, set his sights on Oxfordshire County and took a personal interest in the Oxfordshire, Oxford City & Berkshire Joint Committee. It was known that the Clerk to Oxfordshire County Council would be retiring at reorganisation but in the event Hartley lost out again to Alan Brown, the Town Clerk of Oxford City, who became the first Chief Executive of the new Oxfordshire County Council. Instead Hartley became County Secretary & Solicitor of the new Berkshire County Council, but then retired from local government in 1977, at which point I succeeded him.

Not surprisingly Bob Gash concentrated his energies on the Berkshire, Buckinghamshire and Reading Joint Committee, where his chief contender at the new County for what were now being called Chief Executive posts, would be William Henry Tee, the Town Clerk of Reading County Borough. Harry Tee was very much the blunt northerner, who had his own inimitable style of management. He once got a phone call at home at 2.00am from a Reading resident complaining about a noise nuisance. Harry looked into the matter and sorted it. Then a few days later he phoned the resident back, also at 2.00am. *'That noise problem. Has it stopped?'*

The Joint Committee needed a small secretariat to service it and I was seconded by Bob Gash to head it. I had three staff to help me. Ted Andrews and Ray Druce came from the Clerk's department and Howard Davies from the County Treasurer's. Ted started life as a Committee Clerk but then read for the Bar and was admitted as a Barrister. In 1973 he became Deputy Clerk of Thames Valley Police Authority and his final move in 1979 was to

Runnymede District Council in Surrey, when appointed their Chief Executive. Howard was a qualified accountant, but he never returned to the Treasurer's Department. He remained working for Bob Gash and his successors and eventually became Assistant Chief Executive. Ray remained with me and we both eventually returned to the Clerk's department, though it was by then known as the County Secretariat.

The four of us were given just one room to accommodate us. It was chaotic but highly efficient as we were so cramped that everyone knew what everyone else was up to. So when people phoned up, there was always someone present to give them some kind of answer. The work entailed examining everything that a County Council did; looking at how it was handled in Berks, Reading County Borough and Bucks and then coming up with what appeared to us as best practice. The 18 months that our section existed just flew by.

26
POST RE-ORGANISATION

Come reorganisation day on the 1st April 1974, the new Berkshire County Council came into existence with Derick Pickering later elected as its first Chairman. Bob Gash and Harry Tee applied to become Chief Executive and Bob Gash was appointed. Harry Tee then retired from local government but died not long afterwards, a comparatively young man. In late 2017 I visited Joey Rowe in his new flat in Emmer Green and he took me to meet his near neighbour, Barbara Tee, widow of Harry. She was delighted to see us and we had a pleasant hour or so reminiscing about the old times.

Leading up to the creation of the new County, I personally had the offer of three jobs. Bob Gash asked me to continue with my team and in effect become Bob Gash's Personal Assistant or Assistant to the Chief Executive. I would have preferred the title Assistant Chief Executive but senior Chief Officers were strongly opposed and the suggestion was not pursued. The second job offer came from Richard West, by now Chairman of the Vale of White Horse District Council. He wanted me to apply to become their Chief Executive. I thought hard about this but decided in the end that the post would be insufficiently challenging. The third offer came from Hartley Bramwell to become his Deputy. After much deliberation I opted to stay on with Bob Gash, though I do recall suggesting that I would be happy to double up as Assistant to the Chief Executive and Deputy County Secretary. But that suggestion was rejected by both Bob and Hartley as each wanted his own man. So I joined Bob as Assistant to the Chief Executive and Hartley appointed John Downs as his Deputy.

Bob Gash in many respects had a similar background to myself. We were both sons of Grammar School teachers – in his case his father had been Head of Carlisle Grammar School; mine had been Deputy Head of Cardiff High School. National Service followed for both of us, though in Bob Gash's case his name was drawn out of the hat and he became a Bevin Boy and went to work in a mine, though at the surface rather than hewing coal underground. We were both Exhibitioners at Oxbridge Colleges - I at Queens' Cambridge; Bob at Christ Church College, Oxford and we both ended up in local government. We also had a similar sense of humour. But for Bob local government was a third choice of career. Blessed with height, considerable presence, a beautifully modulated voice and a good brain, he would have loved to have gone on the Stage and failing that to the Bar. Had he done so then I am sure he would have carved out a successful career in either. He knew all the works of Gilbert and Sullivan by heart and could sing every part in his very pleasant baritone voice. He also had the barrister's knack of being able to memorize a brief very quickly and then recall the salient points when needed. But events conspired against him. His father died while he was at Oxford and while there he met and fell in love with a Somerville undergraduate called Rosamond Brown. Wanting to get married, he needed paid employment. The precarious nature of careers at both the Stage and the Bar ruled them out and he settled for articles with the Clerk of Cumberland County Council.

Bob told me how in articles at Cumberland he once played a joke on his boss, which almost got him the sack. There was an Awards Ceremony, at which the Chairman of the Council was due to present a bronze medallion. The medallion was similar in size and colour to one of those Wagon Wheel chocolates covered in gold foil that you can buy in any sweet shop. The medallion and its ribbon was contained inside a smart presentation case and when at the Awards Ceremony the Clerk opened the case to hand the medallion to the Chairman he found he was handing over a chocolate, covered in gold foil, to be hung round the Award Winner's neck.

Inspired by this I once decided to play my own practical joke on Bob. A couple of times a month he used to sally forth from Shire Hall to visit a County Council establishment. Normally one of his section accompanied him and when it was my turn I found that he was very well received by the staff. It put a human face on what were seen and perceived by many as faceless bureaucrats at Shire Hall. It was also useful for us to see what the County Council was getting up to at the chalk face. However on one occasion he visited a secondary school and after his visit he was bearded in the staff-room by a vociferous and very left wing West Indian teacher, who was very critical of the County Council and what he saw as its failings in education. Ray Druce accompanied Bob on that visit and later told me that as they were walking back across the playground to Bob's car, Bob remarked in choice language that if working for Berkshire County Council was so horrendous, maybe the individual in question might like to return to his native island in the West Indies. It so happened that not long after this incident a letter arrived in the office from the Commission for Racial Equality (CRE). It gave me an idea and I got Steve Gillham in the Reprographics Unit to mock me up a blank sheet of paper with the CRE logo and heading. Then on 31st March I sent Bob a letter supposedly from the CRE, though it was signed by Mr Lirpa Loof, which I thought would be a dead giveaway, informing him that the CRE had received a complaint from a teacher at such and such a school that on a recent visit he had referred to the teacher in derogatory terms. The letter went on to say that the CRE liked to resolve these matters amicably and if Bob would sign the apology at the foot of the letter that would resolve the complaint. I then added a draft apology – *'I R... W... Gash do most humbly and sincerely apologize to Mr Gambo Mutumbiyu for calling him a b....... b........ and undertake never to use such language again'*. Some years previously I had had to look after 3 Nigerian local government officers and one was called Gambo Mutumbiyu. I thought the name had a certain ring to it. I had tipped off Bob's Secretary, Janet Skedgel, to expect an interesting letter on April 1st. She eventually emerged from her office doubled up with laughter. Apparently Bob had fallen for the letter hook, line and sinker and was walking up and down his room muttering *'I am not going to sign; I am not going to sign'*. So putting on the best Indian accent I could muster I got Janet to put me through to Bob. *'Oh Mr Gash, I am Mr Lirpa Loof. I understand that some joker has been sending letters from the CRE to distinguished persons in the County'. 'Yes, Yes'* said Bob *'I've received one'*. He still hadn't twigged but then I couldn't contain myself any more and my Indian accent started slipping. Finally he twigged *'You b.... Williams'* he said and fortunately started laughing.

It is perhaps appropriate to mention at this point one subsequent occasion when I had recourse to a spoof letter with dramatic results. It was in 1990 by which time I had left the County Council and had joined Field Seymour Parkes (FSP). The County Council were contracting out many of its services including highways maintenance and most of the former Surveyor's Department, including their Chief Officer, Bob Clarke, had gone to work for a firm called Babtie. Potholes abounded – they still do - but in the Parish of Basildon, where I have now lived for over 40 years, someone went round the Parish painting a white line around every pothole and giving each one a number. It seemed a curious thing to do but we reasoned that the County and Babtie had probably agreed a price to repair each pothole. However nothing happened following the painting of the white circles. The potholes remained and as the months passed were joined by baby potholes. As luck would have it a letter from Babtie then arrived at FSP, so I mocked up a Babtie letterhead. I then wrote ostensibly from Bob Clarke, the Head of Babtie, to the then Editor of the Country Neighbour, Basildon's parish magazine. The letter drew attention to the numerous potholes in Basildon and expressed embarrassment that there was insufficient money to repair them all. It then went on to say that Babtie would like to try a new initiative and invite local residents to sponsor a pothole. For a donation of £5 a little plaque would be placed in the road beside each pothole bearing the donor's initials.

The letter was obviously a spoof but the Editor of the Country Neighbour at that time was a very serious person and my spies at Babtie told me that the Editor had actually phoned Bob Clarke and asked him if his letter were a spoof. I had counted on his so doing. Bob Clarke, of course, had no idea what he was talking about, but the upshot was that a copy of my spoof letter went to Babtie and my Babtie spies told me, that on arrival there was panic, while they tried to find the author. But one of the lessons of life you learn in local government is that abuse per se has very little effect. Local government officers expect abuse and learn to live with it. But ridicule is another matter. No local government officer likes being laughed at and regarded as a joke. Within 24 hours of my letter reaching Babtie, lorries descended on Basildon from all directions and within 48 hours there wasn't a pothole to be seen.

Ray Druce told me the following story. One day he went to see Bob Gash and then the Wokingham Councillor, Mrs Marion Fergusson-Kelly, phoned. She could talk for England and it was impossible to get a word in edgeways, once she had started. So Bob sat there for several minutes listening to her and making the odd comment '*Yes, Really, Yes.*' Then he put the phone in his desk drawer and continued with Ray where he had left off before the phone call. Every few minutes he would take out the phone out of his desk, utter a few more '*Yes, Really, Yes*' comments and then put the phone back in the desk. He was still doing this when Ray completed his business and left the room.

Bob once took me to the Henley Management College to hear the Chief Executive of Sunderland lecture on modern management. His name was Kershaw and he had a national reputation as a guru in the subject. Also at the Seminar was the County Surveyor of West Riding, who knew Bob and also as it happened my father-in-law, Harry Peebles. He also knew Kershaw and introduced us to him after the Seminar. After a few remarks Bob dropped himself deep in the mire. He said to Kershaw '*Whatever happened to that Articled Clerk at Hartlepool Council, who went down for killing the Mayor's daughter?*' – '*He became the Chief Executive of Sunderland*' replied Kershaw. I didn't often see Bob Gash lost for words but that was one occasion.

The County Surveyor of West Riding knew the whole story. Kershaw had indeed killed the Mayor of Hartlepool's daughter - in love-play - in the Council chamber after some function. Rose Heilbron QC had managed to get the charge reduced to manslaughter and after he came out of prison, Sunderland took pity on him and allowed him to work with them as a legal clerk. A few years down the line the Law Society allowed him to sit the exams and become a solicitor. Come reorganisation Sunderland appointed 3 Chief Executives, each one of whom subsequently turned down the job. So after 3 rejections the Council had turned to Kershaw.

27
THE COLEBROOKE HOUSING AFFAIR AND LIFE IN THE NEW COUNTY COUNCIL (1973-1977)

What became known as the Colebrooke Housing Affair started in 1975 and was not resolved until 1980. It ruined the career of Frank Butters, a leading Conservative member of the County Council and cost him his knighthood.

Frank Butters supposedly earned a living in Public Relations, though he was so involved in local government, which paid only expenses in those days, that he had precious little time left to earn a living. I think that was the root problem – lack of cash. He lived in Bray and had a particular interest in policing matters, serving in 1975 as Chairman of the Thames Valley Police Authority and Chairman of the Association of County Councils' (ACC) Police Committee. The latter appointment involved him in national policing matters, including pay negotiations and it was the practice in those days to reward long-serving Chairmen of the ACC Police Committee with a knighthood. He was also Vice-Chairman of the County Council.

In July 1975 Frank Butters declared a pecuniary interest as he had been appointed as a public relations consultant by the Colebrooke Housing Association. He then asked me to set up a meeting between senior County officers and a Mr Barney, the Housing Association's representative, to discuss how the County Council and Colebrooke could help each other. He even arranged for Lt Col Richard Watt, the Leader of the Council, to attend the meeting, though in the event Richard Watt never appeared.

It was surprising that such a long-serving member of the County Council (he had served 20 years by 1975) did not really understand that it was impossible for a local authority to set up a one-to-one relationship with a housing association or indeed anyone else. Had the County Council wanted to start building staff accommodation – it had set aside no money to do so – then a number of bids would have had to be obtained from interested Housing Associations, not just the Colebrooke Housing Association. Likewise if the County Council had had any surplus land, it would have had to tender it and take the highest bid. All this was politely explained to Mr Barney at the meeting and you could see it gradually dawning on him that he had wasted his time in trekking over from Croydon.

That should have been the end of the matter but Frank Butters then set about destroying his own career in spectacular fashion. Having realized that in signing up Mr Butters as a consultant he had effectively been sold a pup, Mr Barney refused to pay Frank Butters his consultancy fee. Like an idiot Frank Butters then sued the Colebrooke Housing Association and in retaliation Mr Barney reported Mr Butters to Scotland Yard, alleging corruption. I ended up giving statements to the police, given my role at the centre of the affair. No action was eventually taken but while the affair was rumbling on, Bob Gash received a call from the Honours Committee, saying that Frank Butters was being put up for a knighthood as a result of his ACC Police Committee work and they were just doing a final check to ensure that everything in Berkshire was tickety-boo. So Frank remained plain Mr Butters. I felt very sad for him as he was a good member and had given his all for local government over many years.

28
LT-COL RICHARD WATT

One of Richard Watt's initiatives as Leader was to get my Section to service his group meetings, and to ensure open handedness we provided the same service to the Labour and Liberal Groups. It was an extraordinary arrangement and probably unique to Berkshire but it did mean that my section had an intimate knowledge of the workings of the three political groups. So we were able to warn colleagues in other departments of looming political problems and this gave them time to come up with solutions. What we had to avoid at all costs was being seen as the tools of a particular political group and in this I like to think we were successful, as we retained good relations with all three groups.

Richard Watt also went out of his way to forge good relations with the new Districts, particularly Slough and Reading. One of William Henry Tee's bright young men at Reading was a Mike Bichard – a young solicitor who had undergone management training. He was appointed to the newly created senior post of County Liaison Officer and worked hard to ensure that the new County Council worked amicably and effectively with the six new District Councils – the Borough Councils of Reading & Slough; the Royal Borough Council of Windsor & Maidenhead and the District Councils of Bracknell, Wokingham and West Berkshire. In subsequent years both Bracknell and Wokingham adopted Borough status, while Bracknell changed its name to Bracknell Forest Borough Council. There were joint working parties and joint dinners. I attended a few of these dinners. At Slough on one occasion consommé soup was served and the Slough Mayor (Labour) called over the waiter to complain that his soup was cold. Those County Conservatives and Liberals present politely said nothing but the County Labour Leader let rip *'You stupid twit – it's meant to be cold'*. So much for comradely solidarity!

Mike Bichard left the Liaison post after a few years and went on to have a glittering career; first in Lambeth; then as Chief Executive at Gloucestershire. He then became Permanent Secretary at the Department of Social Security and was eventually ennobled. Not bad for the son of a Southampton docker, though he did once tell me that his father had views to the right of Alf Garnett, which he as a good socialist found totally objectionable. So to teach his father a lesson he had once mocked up a requisition order and served it on his dad informing him that the Government were going to take over his garage to house some immigrants. He regretted doing this as the shock almost killed his father.

It was from Mike Bichard that I learnt why so many reorganizations do not work. They are concerned with structure rather than process. In his view, with which I agree, how people work together is more important than how they are organized. But improving processes is very hard and success is difficult to measure – it is far easier just to change the structure. It looks good but the reality is that it achieves little. There used to be one civil servant, whose job it was to handle gypsy and traveller affairs. I had a few dealings with him over the years and every time he was in a different Department. Same man doing the same job but moved from department to department as a result of incessant reorganizations.

Richard Watt also set up regular meetings with the County's MP's. Not all attended – I don't recall John Redwood ever coming - but those that did found them very useful. Unfortunately they lapsed after a few years and the County's MP's ended up identifying more with their local District Council than with the County Council. If the meetings had continued who knows what would have happened when Unitary Government featured on the agenda 15 years later? Just possibly the County would have stayed and the Districts would have been abolished.

Richard Watt lived in a large house in Hurst, which I think had Elizabethan roots. On one occasion he was approached by the representatives of a Hindu Swami, who wanted to rent his house for the whole of August. They were offering an eye-watering rental of £10,000. There was just one catch – there were only 2 phones at Hurst House – this was before the days of mobile phones - and the Swami and his followers wanted 10. This was the only reason why we found out about this letting. British Telecom used to take weeks to install new phone lines and Richard Watt wanted Bob to use his contacts with the BT Manager to jump the queue.

So the queue was jumped; the phones were installed and Richard Watt and his family left for a month's holiday in California. The Swami and his entourage then flew into Hurst House in a fleet of helicopters. They commandeered the local taxi firm and armed guards were seen patrolling the grounds of Hurst House. Then after a month they flew away and Richard Watt returned. They hadn't told him that the Swami had his own personal zoo, which had been accommodated within the house. The Swami had also left no forwarding address and had neglected to pay any of the numerous local tradespeople who had kept his entourage fed, watered and transported around – thousands were owed. It was a disaster and took Richard Watt months and much money to sort out.

Richard Watt was also Secretary of the Guards Polo Club in Windsor Great Park, when it was decided to build a new Club house. The Architect for the scheme - a Mr Simons -used to live in my village and he told me that he went down to the site one morning to find a load of squaddies digging the footings. Without saying anything to the Architect, Richard Watt, who was ex-Welsh Guards, had gone down to the Guards Barracks in Windsor and hired a squad of Guardsmen to work for him in return for payment of a few bob and a pint of beer. To make matters worse they had then failed to dig the footings in accordance with the plans. Then when it came to settling the Architect's account, Richard Watt tried to knock a bit off in return for arranging for the Architect to meet the Queen. He was like that.

As a result of our involvement with the inner workings of the Council's political groups, I became aware that the Conservative Group had requested Frank Butters to stand down as Vice-Chairman of the County Council, while his involvement with the Colebrooke Housing Association case was under investigation. He refused, considering he had done no wrong, at which point the Group in effect disowned him and he was replaced as their nominee for Chairman by Richard Watt.

Having been duly elected as Chairman in 1977, Richard Watt then did an extraordinary thing. He persuaded the Council to appoint a senior County Councillor, Gordon Slater, a retired diplomat, to investigate a possible breach of the Council's Code of Conduct by Frank Butters. It was a classic case of scoring an own goal as in his defence Frank Butters revealed that the moment he had established a relationship with Colebrooke, he had mentioned it to Richard Watt at lunch one day and Richard Watt's reply had been '*Thank you Frank. We can make a lot of money out of this*'. It was Richard Watt who had advised Frank Butters to set up the meeting between Mr Barney of the Colebrooke Housing Association and County officers, which he would attend. So it was a classic case of joint enterprise but with Frank Butters ending up the fall-guy and Richard Watt marching over his corpse. As mentioned Richard Watt had served in the Welsh Guards and attained the rank of Lt Colonel. He could claim descent from the brother of the famous James Watt and he had a cousin who was the Secretary of State for Wales. When he left the Army he had set up a building Company, called Tanglewood Enterprises. It had a turnover of £600K in the early 70's and much of its work was related to County Council school projects. The County Architect, Dick Paul, and his staff, used to tear their hair out over Tanglewood Enterprises. In contrast, Richard Watt's successor as first Leader and then Chairman - Lewis Moss - although also a property man, refused to undertake any work in Berkshire to avoid any suggestion of favouritism or impropriety. The Hon Elizabeth Samuel, one of the sharpest, brightest and most outspoken of the Councillors (of whom more anon) once said to me '*Of course Richard is a rogue, but we need a rogue to lead us at the present time*'.

This was rather harsh but she was alluding not just to Richard Watt's property exploits but also to the political cunning that Richard Watt was showing as Leader of the Council at a time – 1974-1977 - when his Conservative Group could only win votes on the Chairman's casting vote, as the combined strength of the Labour and Liberal Groups equalled that of the Conservatives. The Labour Group was led by two very bright and likeable individuals. Their Leader Alan Alexander was a Scot and later became the Professor of Politics at Strathclyde University. Alan had a great sense of humour and once told me that his father had been called Alexander Alexander. Apparently his grandfather had been sent by his grandmother to get the baby (his father) registered but made the mistake of calling in at numerous drinking establishments en route to wet the baby's head. By the time he arrived at the Registry Office he was so drunk that when asked what he was calling the baby all he could get out was Alexander Alexander Alexander. Alan's Deputy was the equally bright Dennis Tunnicliffe (now Lord Tunnicliffe). He had started life as a pilot and later went to run London Underground. He is now a Member of the House of Lords and I occasionally meet him at social gatherings.

The Liberals were also led by two very bright individuals in John Leston and Paul Hannon. Facing such talent it would seem improbable that a retired Army Colonel could hold his own but Richard Watt proved he was up to the task. I think his initiative in getting my section to service all the political groups helped. It helped to humanize the politics. The politics were still there but at that stage basically good natured and there were laughs a plenty. In fact I think working for the first Council during the period 1973-1977 was the most satisfying for me personally.

For a start the Council was pretty well off. With the acquisition of the substantial commercial rateable value in Slough and Reading, 80% of the County Council's money came from domestic and commercial rates and only 20% from Government grants. It was more or less financial master in its own house. If it wanted to build a road, it could find the money to go ahead. This gave a real purpose to its deliberations and led to many a lively debate. Of course it could not last. The Government eventually pooled commercial rates and took over distribution, with the result that the South-East now subsidizes Scotland, the North, Wales and Northern Ireland. No potholes there- if you want to see real potholes visit West Berkshire!

29
MRS PEARL SLATTER

The Conservatives secured a largish majority from 1977-1981 but they lost it for a time in 1981, when the Council became hung, or if you were a Liberal-Democrat, balanced. Then a bye-election took place in Theale in 1982 and the Conservative, Mrs Pearl Slatter, defeated the incumbent Liberal-Democrat Councillor. It meant that the Conservative Group again had a majority but only of one. Pearl then went on to hold Theale right up to the dissolution of the Council in 1998.

see colour page XIX

Unfortunately Pearl then slipped on some oil on the pavement outside the former Maggs' garage in Pangbourne and shattered her right arm, which remains incapacitated to this day. She was still in hospital being treated when the next Budget day approached. Her vote was needed and Pearl being Pearl she insisted on attending the meeting. I had to hire a private ambulance to get her there and she was then wheeled into the Council chamber on a trolley wearing a fetching blue nightie. As she already had one arm in the air, when the time came to take the vote she had to raise her other arm. And then when it came to vote against the motion, the Opposition argued that she was voting with them as she still had one arm in the air! Terry Mills, the ebullient Northern Irishman, remarked that she was only following the standard Irish practice of voting with both arms.

30
THE KNITTERS

Pearl was one of the Conservative Group of lady members. In addition to Pearl there were Ann Hilliard, Naomi Robinson, Sarah Palmer, Elizabeth Still and Elizabeth Samuel - all formidable in their different ways - who used to sit together in the back row of the Council Chamber during Council meetings and then take out their knitting. They were just like 'Les Tricoteuses ' during the French Revolution and it must have been quite unnerving for Opposition speakers, especially when the ladies made not too sotto voce remarks about the quality of the speeches they were listening too. Only Pearl is still living – sadly Naomi died in March 2018 aged 98. Pearl lives on her own in a cottage in High Street, Whitchurch, while Naomi used to reside in a residential home in Shinfield Green. I am still in touch with Pearl and Christina and I used to visit Naomi at Shinfield Green. In fact it was through Naomi that Christina and I first met.

I attended the funerals of both Elizabeth Still and Sarah Palmer – (the Hon Sarah). It is surprising what you learn at a funeral. Elizabeth Still was Jewish and had fled Germany before the War. During the War she served with the RAF as an air controller and as she spoke fluent German, she once conned a German Messerschmidt pilot with engine trouble into landing in England rather than Holland. Sarah had a way with the gentlemen and her conquests included the previous Duke of Wellington and a Red Judge.

31
STEVE NORRIS

On one budget day, the opposition moved that the rates be raised by 1p – the resultant £250K to be used to introduce pre-school education into Berkshire. The Conservatives were opposed to this but when the vote came the Conservatives lost by 1 vote. There was consternation among the ranks of the Conservatives as to who had gone missing. It turned out to be Steve Norris, who later went to Westminster and was Minister of Transport for a time. He claimed that he had been attending an urgent call of nature at the time the vote was called. I and my colleagues were pretty sure that Steve secretly supported the Opposition motion and that his hiding in the toilets was his way of expressing that support but as one Conservative wag stated '*His was the most expensive (1p) pee in history*'. We also had to fit a division bell in the toilets to avoid another such occurrence.

Steve, however, has a ready wit and when at the next Council meeting, he had to propose a controversial motion as Chairman of Property, he brought the house down with his opening remarks, ' *Mr Chairman, this is not the first time recently that I find myself rising from a hot seat with a piece of paper in my hand.*'

Steve has written his autobiography 'Changing trains' and I get a mention. When he was first thinking of standing for the County Council he phoned me up for a chat as to what would be involved and how much time he would have to devote to Council business, if elected. I could tell immediately he was a very bright individual, would very likely rise through the ranks of the Conservative Group, if elected, and in all probability would spend a great deal of time on Council business. But I realized to tell him that might put him off standing and the Council needed bright Councillors. So I was, to use the phrase, 'economical with the truth'.

Steve writes in his autobiography as follows: *The next morning I thought I might as well find out what being a candidate involved and rang the County Secretary at Shire Hall in Reading. 'Oh not much'* he said *'a council meeting once a quarter, a major committee meeting once a quarter. And a sub-committee on the same routine. That's just about it.' 'So that works out at one meeting a month?'* I asked. *'Yes, that's the formal commitment '*, Clive Williams asserted. *' Best of luck and perhaps we will see you soon'*.....The election in 1977 was a doddle....I was elected with a majority of over 1000. My political career had begun. *'Shortly thereafter I discovered that I could probably have sued Clive Williams for gross misrepresentation. The notion of one meeting a month was a far cry from reality.....In practice I found that every major committee generated its own working parties, ad hoc sub-*

committees, ex-officio appointments to boards and other committees and so on. Within two or three months my commitment was not one meeting a month but more like four a week. Most days I was in Shire Hall for one reason or another but more to the point loving every minute of it as I found out firstly just how much the Council was actually spending (in the case of Berkshire in the early 70's well over £500million a year) and the huge responsibility we had in areas like education, social services and structure planning. Within 6 months I was even given my first Committee – the Waste Disposal Committee.'

Later Steve was appointed Chairman of the Council's Property Committee.

Steve was one of the best mixers I ever met. He could mix with any group and was a great favourite with my staff, with whom he was on Christian name terms. He was also a notorious ladies' man, with a string of conquests to his name. For a time, when he was Minister for Transport in Maggie Thatcher's Government and later when a contender for the London Mayoralty, his name and his love life featured frequently in the gossip columns of the tabloids. On one occasion I was with Christina at Phyllis Court and spotted Steve Norris in another group. I mentioned this to Christina and she immediately asked me to introduce her to him. *'No way'* I replied. *'Oh go on'* she said. *'I am not going to introduce you to that man'* I repeated and to the best of my knowledge she has never met him, but given Steve's reputation, who knows!

COUNTY SECRETARY & COUNTY SOLICITOR

32

APPOINTMENT AS COUNTY SECRETARY & SOLICITOR

By 1977 I had decided that it was time to look for another post away from Berkshire, so I started applying for jobs. Then Hartley Bramwell, the County Secretary & Solicitor announced that he was leaving for a teaching post at Hong Kong University, having been granted early retirement. Hartley had an able deputy, John Downs, who was younger than me and was an obvious contender to succeed him. But I thought I would put my hat in the ring anyway. I then heard that I had been short listed for the post of National Park Officer with the Lake District National Park Authority. This interview preceded the County Secretary interview, which was the right way round from my point of view.

Bob Gash was one of my referees and must have mentioned my pending interview in Carlisle to Richard Watt, who when he heard the news immediately brought forward the date for interviews for the post of County Secretary to precede the Carlisle interview. I was then interviewed and offered the job of County Secretary & Solicitor. It was the classic case of having to choose between a bird in the hand or two in the bush. By now I had a young family – my daughter Rebecca was born in 1975 and my son Robert in 1977 – the year of the Interview - so I felt I had to play safe and accepted the post of County Secretary and County Solicitor. But I have always wondered what might have been had I rejected Berkshire and carried on with the Lake District National Park interview. If successful it would not have been a bed of roses. It was clear that some intensive battles were being fought between the various competing sporting interests and then there were the conflicting planning and environmental problems. But if I have any talent, I think I am quite good at conflict resolution. The job appeared tailor made for me but it was not to be.

I was due to take over the Secretariat in September 1977 but far from a smooth handover from Hartley Bramwell, I inherited a furore. In August the Reading Chronicle devoted the whole of their front page to an interview with Hartley. Hartley always came across as a very mild individual but notwithstanding the fact he had been granted the benefits of early retirement, in this interview he let rip at the Conservative ruling group, accusing them of being cliquey, ignoring officers' advice and in consequence wasting large amounts of public money. As one of the examples of wasting public money he cited my appointment, saying that his Deputy, John Downs, could have been appointed and the deputy post need not then have been filled, saving £9K. This was a bit rich on Hartley's part as back in 1973, as already mentioned, he had offered me his deputy post and I had suggested to Bob and Hartley that I could deputize for both of them. But my offer was refused by both. Each wanted his own man.

The Conservative Group did not take the Bramwell attack lying down. Derick Pickering was particularly savage, making it clear that in his view Hartley had contributed little during his time at Berkshire and the County were well shot of him. August is, of course, the silly season for news but we were all astounded when the two Reading Conservative MP's, Sir Gerry Vaughan and Sir Tony Durant, entered the fray and called for a public inquiry. This led to some of the nationals carrying the story.

I tried to keep a low profile but later that month I was interviewed by the Reading Chronicle and was quoted as saying that I would be 'more dynamic'. However the affair rumbled on in the local government press. On 4th August 1978 I was phoned by John Wardle in the County Surveyor's Department and he sent me a copy of 'The Surveyor', which had run the following article on 3rd August:

'*Something seems to be fundamentally wrong at Berkshire – or perhaps it is merely that the press has exaggerated the differences which exist or are suspected to exist. Credence is given to the whole business by the fact, not disputed, that the County Secretary left the county council's service some months ago because, he alleged, a clique of councillors were making 'wrong decisions' through ignoring officer advice.*

A difficult matter this. It is the right of councillors to act contrary to the advice of officers if they think fit. It is not for the officers to complain merely because the decisions which the council makes are not ones the officers would like to see. Equally it is the right of the officers to provide advice – and their right,too, it is submitted, to be heard even if councillors find the advice unpalatable. It is,however, not the job of officers to make value judgements about the decisions of their political masters or purport to be better interpreters of electoral will than the elected representatives.

Yet this might seem to be what Berkshire chief officers have come perilously near doing – for it is reported that they have said publicly that if the council continue to make cuts in services there will be a backlash of hostility from the electorate.'

I wrote to 'the Surveyor' on 9th August 1978, defending Berkshire's Chief Officers against the charge that we had overstepped the mark. My letter must have done the rounds because on 2nd September 1978 the Local Government Review carried the following 'Notes of the Week'.

NOTES OF THE WEEK

THINGS ARE NOT ALWAYS WHAT THEY ARE THOUGHT TO BE

If things are not what they used to be, they are not always what they are thought to be.

A few weeks ago, in a leading Note of the Week, we expressed a sadness that there seemed to be evidence of a deteriorating relationship between councillors and chief officers. We referred to press reports that in Berkshire chief officers had publicly disassociated themselves from the policies of the county council because the policies would, in the chief officers' view, adversely affect council services. We said then – which seems to have been the case – that journalists may well have exaggerated in giving a newsworthy slant to the affair when all that the Berkshire officers were doing was very properly to alert their political masters to the implications and consequences of the policies they were intending to pursue.

There has been no comeback from Berkshire to what we said – which may mean that our comments were accepted as fair and justified. But our attention has been drawn to a response by the County Secretary, Mr D.C.H. Williams to a rather more strident report in a contemporary journal of what may have been happening in that delightful county of Berkshire.

Mr Williams makes the point that the chief officers have been acting in a way that can not be faulted – and that does not surprise us one jot because we never suspected that they had. What has happened evidently is that the chief officers were asked by the majority group to give their comments on a nil growth budget – a budget incidentally, which had been prepared by the majority group after chief officer advice and taken straight to council!

As we understand it the chief officers argued that in Berkshire, with its growing population, a growth of at least 1% would be justified. Even a 1% growth, Mr Williams has pointed out, can only be achieved by making significant cuts in a number of areas. The upshot was that the council eventually approved a ½ % growth rate.

Mr Williams' own words 'Now that Council has made this decision my colleagues and I will, of course, do our best to carry it out with minimum disruption to services.' And he goes on, 'I do not think, therefore, that Berkshire Chief Officers can be faulted in the way they have approached this problem. Indeed I think we would have been open to justifiable criticism if we had backed off commenting for fear of offending the majority group'.

But what about the widely reported comments of Mr Williams' predecessor that a small clique of councillors were responsible for 'hundreds of bad decisions' by ignoring the advice of officers? Mr. Williams, if we may put it with respect, is at his best. In referring to his predecessor's 'Parthian shots of a year ago', he says: 'Like many local government officers used to the traditional system, he disliked the present political set-up. In publicizing his remarks, however, he was very much acting in a personal capacity. I am sure he would not expect his views and their public expression to become the basis of a charge that in some way Berkshire is different from any other authority in this country, which operates along political lines'.

.........There are no doubt many officers who are not enamoured of the intrusion of party politics into local government. .....One of the many virtues of the local government service is that an officer who feels ill at ease in its employment can seek another job elsewhere within local government...That is not only for the benefit of the officer but good for the health of local government.

Eventually life resumed its normal course. Hartley apologized to me for what had happened and once he left Berkshire I never saw him again. But in 2014 a fellow usher at the Reading Crown Court service told me that he and Hartley always went each year to the same hotel in Cyprus. Apparently Hartley, now well into his 80's, is living in a village in North Yorkshire and had sent his regards.

33
THE COUNTY SECRETARIAT

The two main functions of the Secretariat were to run the Council's administration and provide legal services. But it was also something of a conglomerate, including a disparate range of functions. The County Record Office was part of the Secretariat but it was really a department within a department and under the County Archivist ran itself. This was very different from Oxfordshire County Council, which as previously mentioned had a Deputy Clerk, called Hugh Walton, who was interested in archives and was duly appointed County Archivist!

The County Secretariat also had responsibility for Electoral Registration; Births, Deaths & Marriages; Diseases of Animals; Licensing Sports Grounds; the Rent Service; Management Services; Catering; Gypsies and even the Greenham Peace Women.

The Department had a large legal department - 10 solicitors and a number of legal executives, though some of the solicitors such as myself spent very little time on legal matters. Most of the legal work arose in connection with social services care cases. I recall one occasion when in order to save money I had issued an edict that no legal work was to be put out to barristers unless I had given my consent. I was then approached one day and told that a child care case was coming up and not one of our five solicitors was available, so could I authorize instructing a barrister. I looked in my diary – saw that it was clear that day – and told the inquirer that I would do the case. There was a stunned silence but the more I thought about it the more I warmed to the idea of appearing again in court, even though by this time my knowledge of child care law was pretty hazy. About a fortnight later one of the child care solicitors popped their head round the door and said that they were now free to take the case if I wished. I politely declined the offer. Then a second offered and a third. When the fourth offer came I bowed to the inevitable. My lads and lasses were obviously petrified that their boss would go into court and make a total idiot of himself.

My only other foray into the legal realm arose in connection with a child care case that went all the way to the House of Lords. The case of 'In re 'O' –v- Berkshire County Council' has established the principle that a Care Authority can take a child into care even before the child is born. In the case in question, a known drug addict was pregnant and from an earlier experience it was known that her unborn child would have absorbed her drugs and his or her life would be in danger unless he or she received immediate treatment after birth.

However, this was a new principle of law and the 'Guardian ad Litem' who represented the unborn child felt obliged to challenge it. The Council won at the Divisional Court, lost at the Court of Appeal and then won at the House of Lords.

When the case was heard by the House of Lords I attended in person with the Divisional Director of Social Services for Reading. There were five judges hearing the case, all wearing suits and sitting at a semi-circular table. However the table was partitioned into five separate carousels and each judge sat in his carousel surrounded by stacks of law books. Our Counsel was Mr Thomas Scott-Baker. In 1988 he was made a High Court Judge and in 2002 a Lord Justice of Appeal. He retired in 2017. He stood at a dais in the centre of the room facing the five judges. We sat behind him.

The judges then started asking our Counsel questions and it soon became clear that they had very little knowledge of child care law! The Divisional Director became quite agitated and concerned but I calmed her down. But gradually the judges worked their way into the subject; the questions started coming thick and fast and they then started picking holes in the replies they were receiving from Scott-Baker. Faced by five of the sharpest legal brains in the country, in no time our Counsel, although a very experienced barrister, was floundering and sank lower and lower. Having reduced him to a virtual gibbering wreck, they then gently built him up again so that he could leave the room with his head held high. It was a fascinating spectacle. And of course we won.

34
RUSSELL FRANK

Prior to reorganisation, the County Council had two Chief Officer posts of Children's Officer and Welfare Services Officer – though referring again to Oxfordshire, in that County, the Clerk had taken over the Welfare Services Officer role. Post reorganization all these services were brought together and County Councils appointed Directors of Social Services.

The former Berkshire Children's Officer retired at reorganization and there were no internal shoe-in applicants for the new post. But there were many external applicants, including Russell Frank, who was Chief Executive of the Jewish Welfare Board. There was just one problem – he was not a qualified social worker, which was a requirement of the job. In spite of that he was interviewed and made such an impression on the Interview Panel that they offered him the job. They then approached the Department of Health and were so determined that eventually the Department gave their consent to his appointment.

Russell was outstandingly good. In spite of not being a professionally qualified social worker he quickly won over all his staff. He was completely at home with departmental budgets and could argue his Department's case for resources on equal footing with the County Treasurer. He could also relate to the councillors, no matter what political persuasion they were. Because the work his Department undertook was so high profile and sensitive, when cuts were on the agenda, which was most of the time, social services were the last port of call. It was the support departments such as the Secretariat, which were visited first. But when fighting the seemingly interminable battles against yet more cuts, alone among what were called 'the spending departments', it was Russell who sprang to my defence. He had served in the RAF and often referred to the fact that for every Spitfire pilot who fought in the Battle of Britain, there were another 8 aircraft-men on the ground and without those 8 support staff, there would have been no Spitfire in the air, let alone one capable of fighting.

His argument was that you had to look at spending and support departments in the round and if substantial savings were required then you ought to cut activities, i.e both front-line and support staff. It was not a message the politicians wanted to hear but he was so right. When he retired he was succeeded by Mrs Ann Parker but sadly he then died not long after retiring.

35

THE WORK OF THE COUNTY SECRETARY

Most of my time as County Secretary was taken up with running the department, liaising with the Councillors, the Chief Executive and fellow Chief Officers and dealing with Berkshire's eccentrics. I don't know if we had more eccentrics in Berkshire than other Counties but it seemed like it. Moreover, most of them were highly intelligent, albeit obsessive. But I will start with the Councillors.

36

THE HON MRS ELIZABETH SAMUEL

Of the Councillors, I thought the Hon Mrs Elizabeth Samuel was one remarkable lady. She was wonderful. She was the daughter of Lionel Cohen (1888-1973), a Privy Councillor and Lord of Appeal. She married Peter Samuel (1911-1996) later the 4th Viscount Bearsted, one of the wealthiest Britons and they lived at Farley Hill, south of Reading.

Although a member of the Conservative Group, she was an independent at heart and had no hesitation in saying exactly what was on her mind. She was also very clever, and could be very cunning when needed. I have already referred to her comment about Richard Watt. On another occasion as mentioned in the preface she was at a Property Committee meeting, sitting next to Steve Norris and facing Cliff Rayner, a Labour Councillor. Elizabeth had a voice that carried and all of a sudden, a propos of nothing, she said to Steve Norris, in a voice that everyone in the room heard - ' *Don't you think Cliff Rayner is rather sexy – in an earthy kind of way*'. It was the only time I ever saw Cliff Rayner blush.

On another occasion I was with her at a meeting of the Thames Valley Police Complaints Committee, which she had chaired – I was the Deputy Clerk of the Authority at the time. I was with Elizabeth and Leslie Emment, the Deputy Chief Constable, at the end of the meeting, when the following conversation took place.

Elizabeth – '*Aren't these meetings a waste of time. There was no substance to the complaints we have just considered*'

Leslie Emment – '*I quite agree M'am*'

Elizabeth – '*Mind you there was one occasion when I almost lodged a complaint*'

Leslie Emment – '*When was that M'am?*' (encouraging Elizabeth was a big mistake but Leslie didn't know Elizabeth as well as I did. Had he known her better he would have changed the subject)

Elizabeth – '*Well I was driving my Capri down the fast lane of the M4* (although Elizabeth was a wealthy lady in her own right and could have bought whatever car she wanted, she had this yellow Ford Capri sports car, which she loved. It was, however, known in the lingua of the day as the Ford crappy, on account of its unreliability), *when I heard a knocking under the bonnet and the car stopped. I was sitting there in the fast lane, wondering what to dooooo, when this police car drew alongside and a bobby hopped out. I wound down my window and he said 'What the f——- h—- do you think you are doing you silly c—-. I thought that was a bit awf'.*

By this time I was creasing myself but all Leslie could say was '*I hope it wasn't one of ours, M'am'*.

Another Elizabeth story was told me by Ray Druce, who used to clerk the County Planning Committee, which was yet another committee that Elizabeth chaired at one stage. On this occasion she had decided to hold the meeting at her home at Farley Hill and Ray Druce went early to get the room ready. Shown into the room Ray saw the walls were lined with French Impressionist paintings, and thinking he was on his own, he said out loud '*Boy those would be worth a bob or two if they were originals*'. But unbeknownst to Ray, Elizabeth had returned to the room and heard his remark.

'*Young man*', she said '*I have never been so insulted in my life – of course they are originals*!' Which, of course they were. She and her husband, Viscount Bearsted, must have had one of the finest collections of French Impressionist paintings in private hands. There was a very pretty Renoir as I recall, several Toulouse-Lautrecs, assorted Manets and Monets, a Degas – maybe 20 in total. There were even several grand masters hanging in the toilet. Over the years I managed to wangle three visits to Farley Hall, just to see the paintings.

During Lewis Moss's time as Chairman (1980-82) Liz and I were invited to a luncheon at his imposing residence 'Queensmere' in Lower Wokingham. Liz was placed next to Viscount Bearsted – I was on another table. Liz told me that the talk got round to holidays and Viscount Bearsted asked her what we did for holidays.

'*Oh,*' says Liz, '*we often go camping in France with the kids*'. '*Fascinating*' replied the Viscount. '*But tell me, where do you put the nanny*?' Where do you put the nanny became a catch-phrase in the Williams' household.

But in my view Elizabeth Samuel's finest hour arose when she was Chairman of the Public Protection Committee, which inter alia had responsibility at the time for the Fire Brigade. Later the Fire Brigade had its own Authority, which I clerked for a number of years after I had left Shire Hall. The Council were always looking for savings and the Treasurer had a hit list, which he would produce on request. Top of the list was merging the Council's two workshops. The County Surveyor had a very large Workshop with spare capacity, while Tom Ingram, the Chief Fire Officer, had his own much smaller and separate Workshop. So on the face of it, it looked as though money could be saved if the Chief Fire Officer's workshop were closed and the fire engines serviced in future by the County Surveyor's mechanics. The Chief Fire Officer was, however, totally opposed to this suggestion because the County Surveyor's workshop had a reputation for being inefficient.

The proposal to close the Fire Brigade workshop was then placed on the agenda of the County Finance Committee, which Elizabeth had been invited to attend. '*Mr Chairman*' she said '*Before you take such an important decision may I suggest that you visit the Fire Brigade HQ and workshop so that you are in full possession of all the facts*'. It was a reasonable request and Gareth Gimblett, then Council Leader and Chairman of the Finance Committee agreed that there should be a site inspection.

I mentioned that Elizabeth could be cunning. At the time the Brigade had just one extension ladder appliance and this was kept at Slough. It was duly brought to the Fire Brigade HQ at Dee Road, Tilehurst in Reading before the inspection. I was present when the site inspection took place one very foggy morning in November. Gareth Gimblett and most of the Finance Committee were also there as well as Elizabeth. '*Now Gareth*', said Elizabeth, '*you need to get a good view of the site. You and I are going up the extension ladder*'. Gareth went rather pale and declined the invitation. Elizabeth then went around the assembled group, challenging them to accompany her. They all declined apart from David Smith and the two of them then went aloft, disappearing from sight on account of the fog. Eventually they descended; the Group sheepishly dispersed and the suggestion that the Fire Brigade workshop be closed was quietly dropped.

Elizabeth eventually died in harness from cancer. She had been nominated to serve as High Sheriff in 1986-87 but never made it. Had she lived she would have been the first Lady Sheriff of the Royal County since 1185 when the wife of Hugh of St German succeeded her husband.

37
AIR COMMODORE GORDON BLAIR

Gordon Blair was elected to the New County Council in 1974, representing Cold Ash nr Thatcham. He was well-liked by both his fellow Councillors and the staff and was regarded as a safe pair of hands. This was recognized when after the 1977 elections, the Council, which now had a large Conservative majority, elected him as Vice-Chairman of the Council.

A special meeting of the Council had been scheduled for Monday 28th August 1979 and just before I left my house I was telephoned by the Vice-Chairman. I still remember his words: '*Clive, please give my apologies for today's meeting*'. There was a pause and then he added, '*my son has been killed in Northern Ireland*'.

The previous day – Sunday 27th August 1979, the IRA had struck twice with devastating results. First they blew up Earl Mountbatten and several of his family while out in their boat and then they struck again the same day at Warrenpoint. A convoy of Paras was ambushed, killing 6 and then when another force, mainly of Paras but commanded by Lt Col David Blair of the Queen's Own Highlanders rushed to the scene they were also ambushed by another bomb and another 12, including Lt Col Blair, were also killed. Many, including David Blair, were blown to bits.

David Blair was aged 41 and was the most senior officer killed by the IRA. He was married and left a widow and two children - a 10 yr old daughter called Alexander and 8 yr old son called Andrew. He had attended Radley School, nr Abingdon, where there is now a memorial to him. I just took off my hat to Gordon Blair for the way he coped with this tragedy. He just kept going though you could tell how much he was suffering. But understandably he never became Chairman of the County Council.

38
THE HON JEREMY MONSON

On one occasion there was a named vote at a Council meeting, which meant I had to read out the name of every Councillor and they had to say whether they supported the motion, opposed it or had abstained. This information then appeared in the Minutes. It was a weapon that Opposition Groups used to employ occasionally on controversial subjects but as there were 86 County Councillors it was rather a bore to have to read out every name. One of the Councillors was a good friend of mine - Major the Honourable Jeremy Monson. He was 4 years older than me and we had served at the same time in Cyprus during the Eoka insurgency – he with the Grenadier Guards on a short-term commission and I with the Welch Regiment on National Service, though we never met then. One of his duties had been to hang an Eoka fighter but it all went horribly wrong and his platoon took the man's head off. Thereafter Albert Pierrepoint, the official hangman, was smuggled into Cyprus under a pseudonym to carry out executions.

Jeremy's elder brother was Lord Monson of Lincolnshire and the family had both West Indies and East Indies Nabob associations. I later saw the graves of the C18th Col George Monson and his wife Lady Anne Monson, in the South Park Street British cemetery in what is now Kolkota and the family still own an estate near Montego Bay in Jamaica. Even today, the Monsons are in the news. Alexander Monson, who must have been Jeremy's great-nephew, died in a police cell in Kenya in mysterious circumstances in 2014 and the family have been pressing for an inquiry ever since. They have now been told that an inquiry will take place. But I digress. I was reading out the Councillors' names on this named vote and when I arrived at Jeremy it came out as *'Major the Horrible Jeremy Monson'*. It brought the house down and no one laughed more heartily than Jeremy himself. I am pretty sure many of the councillors thought I had done it deliberately, as I had a bit of a reputation as a practical joker, but it was a genuine mistake. Jeremy himself sadly died in 2006.

39
LECKY STANSFELD-TAYLOR

Another amusing story of those days was related to me by Ralph Garbett, a senior solicitor in the County Secretariat. A product of Litchfield Grammar School, Ralph went to Oxford University, where I think he read history and then he qualified as an accountant and ended up in the County Treasurer's Department. He found working with Michael Beasley, the County Treasurer, a real pain – he was not alone in this and the upshot was that he joined the Secretariat and qualified as a solicitor in about 18 months. He was super bright - it took me 3 years to qualify! Digressing again I am still in touch with Ian Pugh, who was hired by the County Council during the 80's from the private sector on a fixed term contract as Director of Commercial Contracts. At the end of his contract he went back into the private sector and became very successful. I later met Ian in the bar of London Welsh RUFC. He told me that in all his time in the private sector, he had never come across such a bright lot of lads and lasses as the solicitors in the County Secretariat and he singled out Ralph Garbett for special mention.

At one Council meeting, which Ralph Garbett was clerking, Lecky Stansfeld-Taylor was in the chair. He had been Chairman of the Education Committee for many years and had been elected Vice-Chairman of the Council but he never made Chairman. However on this occasion the Chairman was not available and in consequence he took the Chair. Lecky was able enough but he had a very ponderous manner, some would say pompous. This was like a red rag to a bull as regards the wilder Councillors on the left and none was wilder than Peter Jones, a Reading University lecturer, who had an impish sense of humour and looks to match. So at some point when Lecky was addressing the Council, Peter Jones could be heard to exclaim '*Silly old fart*' in a voice that resonated round the Chamber. Quick as a flash, David Pilkington, a senior Conservative Councillor, intervened ' *Mr Chairman, if Mr Jones would care to turn his comment into a motion, I am sure it will be passed*'. Which when you come to think of it was extremely witty in a scatological manner of speaking.

AT LINCOLN'S INN – 1980

Left to right: George Matthews: Robert Gray QC; Ted Andrews; the Author.
Robert died in 1996 aged 60; George in 2005 aged 70

George Matthews with Rebecca
(his god-daughter) 1977

MY LETTER TO MR SHERMAN, WRITTEN DURING THE MOVE FROM SHIRE HALL TO SHINFIELD PARK IN DECEMBER 1980

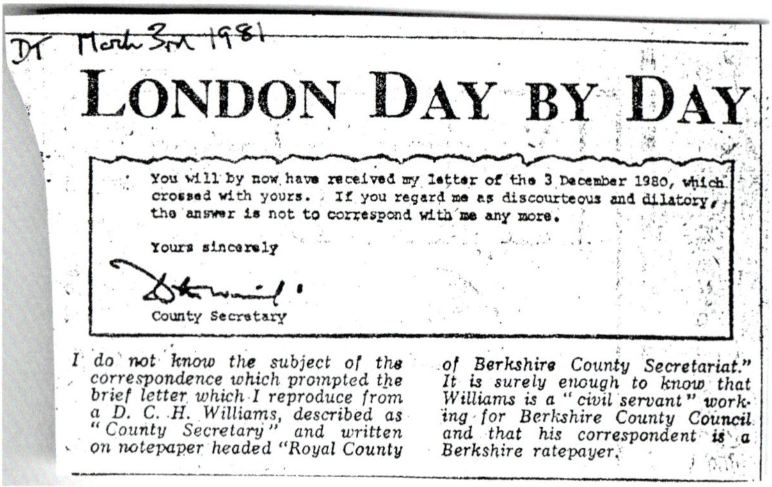

DT March 3rd 1981

LONDON DAY BY DAY

You will by now have received my letter of the 3 December 1980, which crossed with yours. If you regard me as discourteous and dilatory, the answer is not to correspond with me any more.

Yours sincerely

County Secretary

I do not know the subject of the correspondence which prompted the brief letter which I reproduce from a D. C. H. Williams, described as "County Secretary" and written on notepaper headed "Royal County of Berkshire County Secretariat." It is surely enough to know that Williams is a "civil servant" working for Berkshire County Council and that his correspondent is a Berkshire ratepayer.

HM QUEEN ELIZABETH II LEAVES SHINFIELD PARK ON APRIL 2nd 1982 AFTER OFFICIAL OPENING. SHE IS ACCOMPANIED BY LEWIS MOSS CBE DL (CHAIRMAN OF THE COUNCIL). IT WAS THE DAY ARGENTINA INVADED THE FALKLANDS

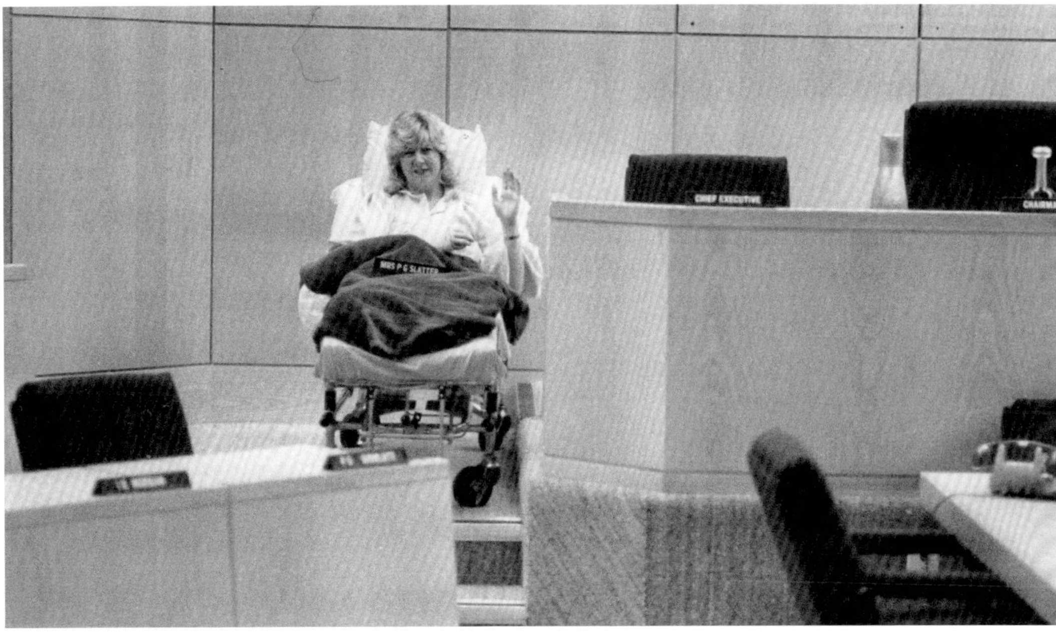

MRS PEARL SLATTER BROUGHT BY AMBULANCE IN 1982 TO VOTE.

Pearl had won Theale in a bye-election shortly before, giving her Conservative Group a majority of just 1. But she had slipped during campaigning and had badly broken her arm – it is incapacitated to this day. But Pearl being Pearl she insisted on coming to Council from her hospital bed to vote.

MY CHILDREN, ROBERT and REBECCA, PRESENT CUDDLY TOYS TO HRH DUKE OF GLOUCESTER FOR HIS YOUNG CHILDREN AT SHINFIELD PARK.

He had previously visited several Berkshire Boys Clubs, as he is President of the Boys Clubs Association – OCTOBER 1982

RETIREMENT OF MRS BELL OF THE REPROGRAPHICS UNIT – 1983

FAREWELL TO DAVID BROWN AND PENNY BROWN (NEE FISHWICK), WHO HAD MET AT THE COUNTY SECRETARIAT, MARRIED, AND WERE MOVING NORTH - 1984

Sam McClew (Gypsy Liaison Officer) next to Author: Ralph Garbett and Michael Bugg next to Penny

MARCH 23rd 1986 – EUROPEAN ENVIRONMENT YEAR 1987

LAUNCH OF GRUNDON'S LITTER BAG SCHEME – printed in every language of the EEC and in the case of the UK – English, Welsh, Gaelic, Urdu & Gujerati

CENTRE – GARETH GIMBLETT (Chairman 1986-89), with BARONESS ELLES MEP and CAPTAIN JOHN MCCUBBIN to his right

MARGARET GIMBLETT standing behind her husband – RON JEWITT (Leader) and AUTHOR behind Margaret

MEMORIAL SERVICE AT ST LAURENCE'S, READING ON MAY 8th 1986 for BOB GASH, who died unexpectedly on 19th April.

AUTHOR ACCOMPANIES IAN MORGAN DL (Chairman – 1983-86)

HARRY TEE (Chief Executive of Reading) behind Gareth Gimblett

LIFE GOES ON – IN THE EDUCATION XMAS GROTTO IN SHINFIELD PARK – XMAS 1986

AUGUST 1987 – THE BOSS – 10 YEARS AS COUNTY SECRETARY & SOLICITOR

Sketch presented to me by my colleagues in the County Secretariat

FAREWELL TO A PENSIVE SIMON DIMMICK – 1988

Simon, then an Assistant County Secretary left to join Blandy & Blandy, the oldest legal firm in Berkshire. He is now their Senior Partner

APRIL 1ST 1989 – THE CENTENARY COUNTY COUNCIL MEETING

LEFT TO RIGHT

Stan Goodchild (Chief Education Officer); David Bowles (County Treasurer); David Ball (Director of Information Services); The Author; Ian Pugh (Director of Commercial Contracts)

APRIL 1st 1989 – THE CENTENARY COUNTY COUNCIL MEETING

LEFT TO RIGHT

Garth Scotford (Chief Fire Officer); Mrs Anne Parker (Director of Social Services); The Author; Bob Clarke (Director of Highways and Planning)

Tony Allen Esq., CBE
(Chief Executive)

40
CORRESPONDENCE WITH BERKSHIRE'S AWKWARD SQUAD

I soon found as County Secretary that a surprising amount of my time was taken up with handling complaints about the County Council. Often the complaint would be sent in the first place to Bob Gash as Chief Executive but invariably he would then pass it on to me and ask my Department to look into the complaint and draft him a reply. In olden days one MP, Bill van Straubenzee of Wokingham used to send us complaints from his constituents about the County Council and asked us for 2 replies – one that he could send to his constituent and the other telling him what we really thought!

41
MAX HEILBUT

I remember one complainant was a Max Heilbut from Bray. He was most unhappy that the Council had granted a consent to dig gravel in the field at the bottom of his garden and he set out to make as much trouble for the County Council as he could. He was a Planning Barrister himself and used his professional training and expertise to full effect. Letter after letter arrived complaining that this and that condition was not being complied with. My staff liaised with the planners and surveyors to reply but nothing we said seemed to satisfy Mr Heilbut. This correspondence went on for 18 months until I got fed up with it. I took all the files and locked myself in a room for 2 days. I then went through the files summarizing the complaints in Mr Heilbut's first letter – then I paraphrased our replies. I then moved on to Mr Heilbut's second letter and did the same, pointing out that he had also complained in his second letter that we had not replied to some of the complaints made in his first, which, of course, we had. I then went through this tedious exercise for the rest of the correspondence – I think there were 8 such missives in total. My secretary, Wendy Freeman, then managed to find one of the typewriters, which had been used for typing old style indictments – it had a carriage 2ft long. This meant that we could get my reply on one sheet of paper and achieve maximum effect. I next wrote to Mr Heilbut and never heard from him again. The game was over.

42
MR SHERMAN

The correspondence with a Mr Sherman of Chavey Down was somewhat similar, though in Mr Sherman's case the cause of the complaint was not gravel extraction but the Council's own waste disposal site at Chavey Down, near Bracknell. Mr Sherman was even more acerbic than Mr Heilbut and always complaining that we did not reply quickly enough to his numerous complaints. Another letter from Mr Sherman arrived in late 1980 shortly before the County Council were due to move from the old Shire Hall in the centre of Reading to the new Shire Hall HQ at Shinfield Park. All our files were packed up for the move but I said to Wendy Freeman *'You must find Mr Sherman's file, so that I can reply to him, otherwise he will only complain again'*. It took her several days but eventually she found the file and I got off my reply. It must have crossed with another letter from Mr Sherman, complaining that I had not replied to his letter and that I was both dilatory and discourteous. So I sent Mr Sherman another reply, which upset him – it was meant to. But Mr Sherman had friends in the Press and I suppose I achieved a fame of sorts with my letter appearing in full in the Peter Simple column of the Daily Telegraph on 3rd March 1981..

Dear Mr Sherman, Thank you for your letter of the 19th. If you find me discourteous and dilatory then I suggest the answer is to stop corresponding with me. Yrs sincerely, D C H Williams

Far from leading to coals being heaped on my head I got messages of congratulation from local government officers all round the country, all of whom had wanted to write similar letters but had never had the guts to do so.

I must have got up Mr Sherman's nose with a vengeance as he then wrote a letter of complaint to Bob Gash, who simply swatted it away, saying that I was well known for my sense of humour. This enraged Mr. Sherman even more and he got Adam McKinlay in the Wokingham Times, to write one of his excoriating, sarcastic pieces complaining more about Bob Gash than me. But as Adam McKinlay always wrote excoriating, sarcastic pieces about everyone, no-one took any notice and that was the end of the Sherman saga.

43
MAJOR BRIAN SHONE

see colour page XIV

The saddest case I had to deal with was Major Brian Shone of Finchampstead. He was well connected – he was a cousin of Selwyn Lloyd, a former Chancellor of the Exchequer and he was a coachman in the Queen's Coronation parade in 1953. After military service during the 2nd World War he became an engineer with the BBC and he then bought a large house and 6 acres of land in Finchampstead. He was a bachelor and much involved in youth activities. The Scouts used to camp on his land at Finchampstead and he had plans drawn up to erect a permanent scouting centre, though he never succeeded in raising the money required to go ahead. He also formed the Berkshire Boys' Choristers group, and twinned it with a similar group from Paris. Nowadays, post Savile, his activities would have come under suspicion but back in the 60's and 70's no concerns were lodged in that regard.

A Roman road used to run from Staines to Silchester and in Berkshire sections of the road still exist and are known as 'the Devil's Highway'. In 1953 all Highway Authorities had to compile a Definitive Map of Public Rights of way. In Finchampstead most of the Devil's Highway runs through National Trust land and the National Trust applied to register that section as a bridlepath. However, the Devil's Highway then ran through an estate owned by a Mr Strauss and he did not want a bridlepath running close to his front door. He argued that the Devil's Highway in his section had only been a forest track and had not been used by the public in general. It so happened that Mr Strauss had served in the war with a lawyer called Scarman, later Lord Scarman, one of the most senior and distinguished lawyers in the country and Strauss persuaded Scarman to appear on his behalf at the resultant local Inquiry. Finchampstead Parish Council were represented by their Chairman, Miss Vaughan-Morgan, who recently died aged 100. Although Miss Vaughan Morgan was quite formidable it was an uneven contest and the Inspector ruled in favour of Mr Strauss. There was an unholy row in the County at this decision and a second Inquiry was held, albeit with the same result. In logic, the County Council should then have taken all the Devil's Highway off the Definitive Map but feelings were running so high that the Council took no action. So we ended up with the absurdity of a cul-de-sac bridlepath. Eventually Strauss' property was bought by a Dr Frederick Gifford, a consulting engineer, and he extended his property to the east and in so doing acquired 200 yards of the adopted Devil's Highway bridlepath. He then built a house at the end of the bridle path! I never understood how he managed to acquire this land – I assume that the land in question must have been owned privately ; and not by the National Trust.

Major Shone had been living in Finchampstead at the time of the Inquiries but as a recent newcomer had been otherwise engaged. Later he became more interested in the history of Finchhampstead and it was not long before he decided to take action about the Devil's Highway. He started standing for public office – for the Parish, where I think he was elected for a time; for the District Council, for the County Council and even for Parliament. I only ever met him face to face twice and that was at the count for two successive County Council elections. By then we were engaging in extensive and somewhat acrimonious correspondence but at the counts we had two very friendly and civilized conversations. His trouble was that he only heard what he wanted to hear.

At a very early stage I told him that I thought the Inspector had made the wrong decision in finding in favour of Mr. Strauss, but that sadly there was nothing that could now be done to reverse it. He just could not accept this. Twice a year he and a group of friends would walk 200 yards into Dr Gifford's property to the end of the bridlepath and out again. That was fair enough and Dr Gifford just had to accept that they were entitled to take such action. But at some point Major Shone got it into his head that the Freemasons had taken over the administration of Berkshire and that he was being thwarted in his efforts to turn the whole of the Devil's Highway into a bridlepath by a vast Masonic conspiracy, of which I was a leading member. I was not best pleased at this, particularly having regard to my experiences with the Masons in Witney, as previously recounted.

Major Shone's next initiative was to write a book on the Devil's Highway and the Heritage of Finchampstead. He sent me an advance copy, which I am afraid I have mislaid. It was a weighty tome, running to hundreds of pages and with numerous coloured maps. It must have cost him a fortune to print as he was self-publishing. Major Shone had a tendency to invent history, of which more anon, but the book started off well enough. It was only after you had read for 40 pages or so, that the Masonic conspiracy started to take over. I featured prominently as the head of the conspiracy but he also had it in for Sir Gerry Vaughan, MP for Reading East and at the time Minister for Health. Sir Gerry was libelled again and again.

Major Shone had also sent a copy of his book to the Department of the Environment and had received a very nice reply from the Private Secretary to Earl Attlee, who was the Under-Secretary of State at the Department. Major Shone had sent me a copy of this letter along with his book and it had been written along the lines of ' what a nice book – many thanks - keep up the good work'. It was obvious that no-one at the Department had taken the trouble to read the book, so I thought I would have a bit of fun. I jotted down the page numbers of the occasions when Sir Gerry Vaughan had been libelled and phoned the Private Secretary and suggested he read those pages. I then waited and about 30 minutes later I heard back from a civil servant in total panic and flying around at about 30,000ft.

Major Shone also told me that he proposed to give a free copy of his book to every bookseller and library in Berkshire. Those were the days when we still had booksellers. This was a step too far, so I upset the Major even more by writing to all Berkshire booksellers and all the County Council's libraries, warning them that Major Shone's book was libellous and they might end up being sued if they stocked it. But interestingly if you google Major Brian Shone, you will find that copies of his books – he wrote several - are still available for sale. But after all this I was surprised by how many funny handshakes I received from Councillors and the like and how often I heard *'Didn't know you were on the square, Clive.'*

My final brush with Major Shone stemmed from his tendency to make up history. Those familiar with the Anglo-Saxon Chronicles will know that they are full of portents of pending doom, culminating in the defeat of the Saxons at the Battle of Hastings in 1066. One of these portents amounted to a stream running red in Finchampstead – one assumes that there is iron ore in the soil, which turns the water red at times of heavy rain. On the basis of this and a few other flimsy historical accounts, Major Shone created the legend of St. Oswald's Well. In spite of the fact there was no well and probably never had been one, he erected a well head and display plaque to commemorate St. Oswald's Well and persuaded the generous hearted Sir Gordon Palmer, then Vice Lord-Lieutenant of the Royal County, to formally open it, accompanied by his Berkshire Boys' Choristers. It made for a good photo, which then appeared in all his later publications to give him an appearance of respectability.

He later discovered a trigonometry point on an early Ordnance Survey map, just where the Devil's Highway came to a stop in Dr Gifford's property. He convinced himself that General Roy had erected this trig point when surveying England in the C18th and he proposed to erect another historical marker at the end of the Devil's Highway to commemorate General Roy's bi-centenary and no doubt to cause maximum grief for Dr Gifford.

It was, of course, all nonsense. The trig point in question was Victorian and General Roy had placed his trig points on the top of hills – not on a flat bridlepath in the middle of a wooded area. I pointed this out to Major Shone and incurred yet more wrath. He then wrote what might be termed his autobiography, entitled 'The Devil in Finchampstead', and I get seven mentions, none of them complimentary!

I then left the County Council in 1989 and that was the end of my dealings with Major Shone. At some point he had sold his original house and land and traded down to free up money to continue his campaign but I suspect that eventually the money ran out and he lost heart when he realized he was getting nowhere. Nevertheless I was very sorry to read in the Reading Evening Post in 1996 that he had been found hanged at his home. He was aged 84.

44
CORRESPONDENCE WITH BERKSHIRE'S WITS

There were occasionally lighter moments as regards my correspondence.

Morley

Mr Morley of Newbury asked to be informed of the Secretary of State's decision on the Berkshire Structure Plan. No doubt fearing the worst he wrote his request on the back of a postcard, showing a gargoyle with its head in its hands.

My reply was short and to the point.

Dear Mr Morley,

Woe unto them that join house to house, that lay field to field, till there be no place (Isaiah 5:8)

Yours sincerely – Clive Williams

Barton

When Desmond Barton, the Chairman of the Newbury Bench and Berkshire Magistrates Courts Committee retired, he wrote a very nice letter of thanks to Roger Penfold, one of the many stalwarts of the Secretariat, who handled the Committee administration for a number of services, including the Magistrates Courts Committee, which I clerked from 1986 – 1996. In his letter Desmond wrote that he was very conscious that his contribution to the work of the Committee had been a very modest one and as for the Computer Sub-Committee, almost nil! As to the latter he recalled at one of the meetings either Norman Rundle or Richard Gibbs (two of the Justices' Clerks in the County) appealing for more VDU's (video display units), which he thought a bit of a shock as hitherto he had thought that a VDU was a Venereal Disease Unit!

On a more sober note he went on to thank Roger also for his support to Ian Playle, the Justices Clerk for Newbury. Ian who was only 34, was travelling with his family through Hungerford on the 19th August 1987 when he encountered Michael Ryan on his rampage. He was shot and rushed off to the John Radcliffe in Oxford. I went to see Ian there but he was on a life support machine and unconscious. He died a few days later, when the machine was switched off. The irony was that Ian Playle had been driving his family down the Bath Road and had he been allowed to continue no harm would have befallen him. But thinking Ryan was in the vicinity of the Bath Road,

Police blocked the Bath Road and diverted traffic round Hungerford Common, and as it happened into the path of Ryan. Ian Playle was one of those who ended up being killed as a result.

Ryan killed sixteen people, including his mother, before turning one of his guns on himself. Coincidentally I knew one of his other victims, a taxi driver called Marcus Barnard. A few months before the massacre I had been on the way from Upper Basildon to Wiltshire, when my car broke down in Hungerford. So I left my car in Hungerford for repair and called a local taxi firm to drive me back to Upper Basildon. They sent Marcus Barnard and we had a pleasant chat along the way.

Milford

I had some crazy correspondence with a Philip Milford, who had moved to Paris, owing the County Council £1,000. He had paid some of the debt, when I sent him a chaser/reminder and received this reply on the 18th May 1987 *Dear Mr County Solicitor, Sir,*

Please sir, sorry sir, but I had forgotten. Very bad of me and I do apologize. Herewith 2 more cheques for 50lbs(Sic) *(one post dated). Once again a very sincere sorry: I will write out the following lines - I must remember the County Council's existence I must remember the County Council's existence I must remember the County Council's existence Especially re a/c P600952 many times and stick it on my shaving mirror, in the loo and above my bed. My arithmetic and sums now come to a majority answer of £600 left Yours very sincerely*

P Milford I must remember the County Council's existence: I must (I used to get this done for 1/- for 50) I must I must I must

On the 25th November 1988 I had another letter from the irrepressible Mr Milford. He must have called at Shinfield Park to see one of my solicitors Penny Fishwick and misheard her name, because 'poisson ecluse' is Fishlock not Fishwick.

But here is his letter:

Dear Monsieur Villiams,

I am desolated to have missed Mme Poisson Ecluse. France has been and is being assailed by things called 'social movements' – i.e strikes – post, nurses, transport etc. Also by those that pay ME. Further my Carte de Sejour (work permit) expired – and I all but ditto. No carte de sejour – no pay - versus no pay slips - no carte de sejour. Many frustrating fiascos later I have got the c-de-s. Now awaiting pay cheques.... So are you from me. Here's one for £12-37p just to get our silly saga into round numbers. £300 left. Also a post-dated item for £50.

As spewed British rail 'We're getting there'. The same does not hold true of Parisian railways... I hope to hear from a suitable surname soon.

I beg you to accept, sir, the intimation of my most distinguished sentiments.

Philip Milford

I felt this reply merited something special by way of a response and with a little help from a fluent French speaker of my acquaintance and Edith Piaf, I concocted the letter below. I did once visit Edith Piaf's grave in the Pere Lachaise cemetery in Paris, where all the French greats are buried, as well as Oscar Wilde.

6th December 1988

Mon Cher Milord, Quand tu ne nous dois rien, Rien de rien, Tu peux retenir, Tous tes biens, Tu sera libere, eleve. Tout ca t-ira bien egal. Pour le moment cependant Nous manquons deux cents cinquante

Je retourne avec plaisir l'expresssion des sentiments bien agreables que tu as exprime et je te prie d'accepter les expressions plus cordiale pour la saison de Noel et l'annee nouvelle, quand j'attend avec impatience le resume de notre correspondence et la remission des sommes encore devants.

Assurement, D C H Williams Notaire de Departement

On 12th June 1989 I received a final letter from Philip Milford. I must have told him that I was on the point of retiring from the County Council.

Dear Mr Williams,

Just received your letter with the sad news. I had long dreamt of bringing my last instalment into you in person just so that we could meet at last. It is not to be, unfortunately and it seems that I will never be able to see you face to face to thank you for a most enjoyable relationship based upon what could have been very unfortunate circumstances.

Believe me when I say I wish you well and hope you are OK. Once again many thanks for all the missives you put your name to. Those letters have done much to improve the image the French have of the stereotyped Englishman.

Once again merci for your good-natured patience, humour and forbearance,

Bonne chance,

Philip Milford

Stronge

A Mr H. B. Stronge of Stubbings, near Maidenhead, once wrote to me in verse, pleading for the County Council to get on with the Stubbings by-pass.

15th December 1982

Dear Sirs,

There's a place in dear old England, in the northern part of Berks,
And of all the county's corners it deserves the highest marks
For the place that's most remembered of any one could see,
It's Maidenhead's own Thicket, on the A four twenty three.

There's a little hamlet, Stubbings, which I hope to glimpse one day
Through a gap between the juggernauts and such like in the way.
It's what they call a 'focal point of heavy road congestion',
And what to do about it? There's been many a suggestion.

A roundabout, a by-pass, or some similar improvement,
But the County Roads Department seems incapable of movement.
And, although the situation's realised the worst of fears
There's been nothing done for years and years and years.

But it's got its compensations, If a chap can wait all night For a vehicle up front to get a chance of turning right, He can thank the County Council for the opportunity
To complete the cross-word puzzle and brew up a pot of tea.

I duly replied in kind

21st December 1982

Dear Mr Stronge,
We are never averse,
To replying in verse,
To someone as witty as you,

We've got just the ticket
For Maidenhead Thicket
And avoiding those wearisome queues

The Surveyor's' drawn a beaut
Of a bypassing route,
For motorists help is at hand.

We just need the cash
From Heseltine's stash
To the tune of 6 million grand

But we've just had a letter
That makes things look better
The prognosis looks good as they say

There is now a good chance
The scheme will advance
And you really will use it one day.

Even though it's in rhyme
These road schemes take time
And land purchase problems are more than a token

But a start is intended
Once '83 is ended
By '86 the route should be open.

And it was!

45

THE RUDEST LETTER I EVER RECEIVED

I have already mentioned that in 1986 I was also appointed Clerk to the Berkshire Magistrates' Courts Committee. There were then 4 Justices' Clerks in Berkshire with the Slough Bench clerked by Mrs Georgina McMasters. Georgina had a strong personality and ran a tight ship. I once went to Slough to meet her on some problem or other and arrived early. So I had to wait until she finished her staff meeting. When her staff emerged, mainly ladies, several were in tears. I asked Georgina about this and she said '*Oh they always have a good cry. They will get over it*'. But even Georgina could not cope with Mr Alan Hardy and I was asked for assistance.

Mr Hardy had made an unsuccessful application to Slough Magistrates Court, when the clerk advising the Magistrate had been Mr Peter Edwards, a senior lawyer at Slough and one of the pleasantest and most inoffensive persons you could imagine. Mr Hardy then launched into a written diatribe aimed at Georgina (which I have lost) and at Peter Edwards, which is reproduced below. As a result Georgina asked me to reply to Mr Hardy, which I did as tactfully as I could, only to receive the rudest letter in response that I ever received during my professional life. It was a masterpiece of its kind and what particularly amused me was that it ended up, Sincerely!

Hardy's original letter to Peter Edwards. A similar letter went to Georgina McMasters.

14th April 1988 Dear Mr Edwards,

They say 'put not your faith in princes'. Well, in respect of this morning's hearing; I might have known better than to put my faith in a right pair of wankers like you and that plonker of a magistrate and you may tell him that from me,

Yours ever,

Alan Hardy

My conciliatory letter to Mr Hardy

25th April 1988 Dear Mr. Hardy,

Thank you for your letter of 13th April. Your description of Mrs McMasters does not accord with the very helpful, courteous and intelligent lady that I know.

May I, however, assure you that although you have obviously taken offence, no offence was intended by Mrs McMasters or any members of her staff on your visits. That said, having looked into your complaints, it does not appear to me that there is any action that I should take.

Yours sincerely,

D C H Williams – Clerk to the Magistrates Courts Committee

Mr Hardy's masterful reply

27th April 1988 Dear Mr Williams, Thank you for your letter of the 25th April.

Imprim is, may I say that my initial letter to you did not ask for any action to be instituted against McMasters as indeed I had taken my own. Had I wished for any to be taken be assured: I would not under any circumstances put my faith in a seat-warming, shit kicking, knighthood-seeking poseur like you!

Incidentally your description of McMasters proves at least one thing – you know f... all about women! No apologies either for the cheap and tatty note-paper. I figured anything superior to it would be akin to feeding caviar to a dog! Now piss off!

Sincerely – Alan Hardy

Postscript

4th May 1988 Dear Georgina,

Mr Hardy is right about one thing. I do not know a thing about women!

Yours sincerely – Clive

46
DEALING WITH THE COUNTY'S GYPSIES

In 1968 the Government passed the Caravan Sites Act, which (inter alia) placed an obligation on County Councils to provide residential sites for gypsies, who wanted to settle down. I recall that the late Sir William Benyon was a member of the County Council at the time and he very generously agreed that Englefield Estates would provide a gypsy site at Burghfield Common – Englefield Estates own about 15,000 acres of land in Berkshire, in addition to 300 houses in Hackney and an estate in Scotland. News of this generosity got abroad and there was then an emergency meeting between the Clerk and the Chief Constable of Thames Valley, as intelligence had revealed dozens of gypsy families were converging on Burghfield Common from all over the South-East in the hope of securing a site.

Slowly and painfully, additional permanent sites were found. Whenever we found a possible site we would try and sell it to the locals. A meeting would be held in the local Village hall but after the first of these I always made sure I was near the exit, as the meetings invariably became incredibly heated. Trying to convince a local community that what they need to make their life complete is a gypsy site, is an uphill, one could say impossible task.

Most gypsies have now settled down in permanent sites or even houses. Horton Parish, south of Slough, which transferred to Berkshire from Bucks in 1974 and where John Milton lived for a time, can claim that 30% of its population has gypsy roots. The local Parish Church even has a separate burial ground for gypsies, where the graves are highly decorated with pictures and objects belonging to the deceased.

But there always was and still is the problem of the Travellers, another name for gypsies. These tended to arrive in Berkshire in the summer and worked their way round the County, offering to tarmac drives, fell trees, buy antiques etc. I found out that many of these families were Irish and had homes in Ireland. They would fly into Heathrow and there was someone in Hounslow, who would hire them caravans and cars for the season. They would then work the Home Counties and at the end of the season fly back to Ireland.

I had on my staff a post for the Gypsy Liaison officer and a small budget to pay the salary and deal with any other problems. The Gypsy Liaison Officer during most of my time as County Secretary was Sam McClew, who was ideal for the role. The gypsies would have had for breakfast the normal local government officer or civil servant but Sam McClew was different. He was a small man but he was a Glaswegian and had served as a merchant seaman. He was as hard as nails and not someone you would want to cross. But he was also a Jehovah's Witness and a very compassionate man and this combination of physical hardness combined with a compassionate nature was just what was required to deal successfully with the gypsies.

We had about 12 lay-bys in the County, where travellers had camped at one time or another. Once a group of travellers arrived in the County, Sam would go and see them and offer them a deal. They could spend 3 weeks working the County, staying in allocated lay-bys, and in return Sam offered to contact the local residents to keep them off the travellers' backs. They were also asked to clear up their litter. If they agreed, which was invariably the case, Sam would then contact the local residents and ask them to hold fire for a week. Then once the travellers had moved on to their next lay-by, Sam would arrange to have the vacated site cleaned. When the next group of travellers arrived they would be allocated a different set of lay-bys. The system worked well and we never had to go to Court to obtain evictions.

47
LICENSING OF SPORTS GROUNDS

Following the Heysel stadium disaster in 1985, the Government brought in a system, whereby Local Authorities had to license Football club grounds and ensure that they were safe for spectators. The power to issue a licence was delegated by the County Council to me as County Secretary but I could call on the Police and Fire Brigade to inspect and advise.

The only football ground in Berkshire subject to the new requirement was Reading Football Club's Elm Park stadium. The Club had been playing there since 1896 and were to continue playing there until 1996, when they moved to the Madejski Stadium. By 1985 Elm Park was feeling its age and was very run down. But Reading were jogging along in the 3rd Division and the average Elm Park crowd was no more than 3,000. Following an inspection the stadium was licensed to hold up to 6,000 spectators and Roger Smee, the then Chairman of Reading Football Club, stated that he was content.

At the start of the 1985-86 season, Reading managed to win their first few games and their home crowds started to grow, until they approached the licence limit of 6,000. At this point Roger Smee desperately started carrying out improvement works and then on a Friday afternoon he would phone me, tell me what he had done and ask for the license limit to be increased. There was no time to send someone down to the ground before the game to assess the position and decide if a licence increase were justified.

Roger and I went back a long way. He had grown up on the Whitley estate and had joined the local Boys Club, which had nurtured his athletic and footballing skills – he was once the Boys' Clubs national 400 yard champion. He also played football professionally for Reading and then Chelsea, where a serious leg injury put paid to his professional career. He then went into property, starting as a site finder for Felix & Pole, the Reading estate agents, and eventually branching out to form his own property empire. But he never forgot his Boys' Club roots and even today he is President of Berkshire Youth, which is an amalgamation of Boys' Clubs and Youth Clubs in Berkshire. I too have had a very long association with Berkshire Boys' Clubs and accompanied Roger, when he sold a surplus Boys' Club site in Southcote to the Clancy brothers. They had offered £10K, which the rest of the Boys Clubs' Trustees thought a very fair price. But by the time Roger had finished with them, they paid £75K. As we trudged off site, Roger said to me '*That's a good example of welly boot negotiation*!' Roger was also at the helm of Reading Football Club, when Robert Maxwell, who owned Oxford United, tried to buy Reading and create a new Thames Valley Club. Although Maxwell had no formal qualifications Roger told me that he had never met a sharper lawyer or accountant than Maxwell.

Returning to the saga, I felt I had no option but to agree the licence capacity increases sought by Roger, though I was sticking out my neck by a mile. Unfortunately the problem grew worse and worse as Reading kept winning. By the time they had won 13 games on the trot – a Football League record – I had increased the licence capacity over the phone to 11,000.

Before the next home game I convened a site meeting with Reading's Divisional Police Commander and the Senior Fire Officer at Reading Fire Station. It was a rather damp evening on the 23rd October 1985 and Reading were at home to Wolverhampton. The three of us stood in Norfolk Road and watched the enormous crowds milling around. You just knew that considerably more than 11,000 wanted to see this game. *'You can't let them in'* said the Fire Officer,' *You will have to close the gates'*. *'If you shut the gates'* said the Chief of Police, ' *we'll have a riot in Norfolk Road'*. *'But it's your decision and the buck stops with you'*, they both said! I did a quick risk assessment and concluded that the chances of Elm Park burning down or the crowd stampeding were far less than there being a riot in Norfolk Road, if we closed the gates. So the gates remained open and to my immense relief Reading drew and the bubble burst. Thereafter gates fell below the approved license figure of 11,000 and the crisis was over.

48
THE GREENHAM PEACE WOMEN

Nowadays the threat of a nuclear war has receded but in the 60's it was taken very seriously and Berkshire with nuclear installations at AWRE Aldermaston (Atomic Weapons Research Authority), ROF Burghfield (Royal Ordnance Factory) and AERE Harwell (Atomic Energy Establishment), would have been wiped off the map if war had broken out. The CND (Campaign for Nuclear Disarmament) were well aware of this and each Easter used to march from Aldermaston to Trafalgar Square, stopping by en route at Warren Row's seat of regional government in Upper Wargrave.

At the time the American Base at Greenham was non-nuclear and did not feature on the CND Easter march. But it was still subject to the occasional anti-USA demonstration. I remember in 1965 being involved in a case in Newbury Magistrates Court at the same time as a number of Greenham Airbase demonstrators were being sentenced for trespass. There was one couple in particular who stood out. Both were tall and very good looking. The man had been a pilot in the RAF but he had become a pacifist and both spoke eloquently and movingly about their beliefs. I never saw or heard of them again but that memory has lingered.

In 1980 the UK Government gave the USA Government permission to site Cruise Missiles at Greenham Common, and these were capable of carrying nuclear warheads. This led to a Group of women marching from Wales to Greenham in September 1981 and establishing the first Greenham Common Women's Peace Camp.

Prior to the 2nd World War Greenham Common had as its name suggests been a Common and one, moreover, where the public had the right to walk and play lawful games. Most of the Common was then requisitioned at the start of the 2nd World War and turned into an air base for American use but there were still areas of the former Common outside the nine mile long perimeter wire, where the public were still entitled to walk and play lawful games. But the Scheme granting these rights did not extend to permitting camping.

Although camping was not permitted the problem was always one of enforcement. Local residents were furious as the camps did no favours for house prices and made it difficult to sell. So the County Council had to be seen to be doing something, no matter how ineffective. Working jointly with the Newbury District Council, two bailiffs were appointed, tasked with removing the unauthorised encampments. However, once the bailiffs had done their work and departed, the Peace Women simply returned and built themselves another encampment. Eventually, of course, in 1991 the Cruise Missiles departed but the Peace Camps had by then become a way of life for some and they stayed. They eventually went in 2000 when the Americans departed and the Common was returned to the District Council. Very wisely and far sightedly, the Council then set up a Charitable Trust to run the former American industrial base and the substantial charitable grants distributed subsequently by the Greenham Common Trust have been gratefully received by many a charity operating in West Berkshire, as I know from personal experience.

I once met two Greenham Peace Women, when they visited the County Council's HQ at Shinfield Park to inspect the Register of Commons. I had to step over one of them, as she was sitting in the corridor outside my office getting in everyone's way, while her friend was inside the adjoining room that held the Register. They then swapped places and rather than have her friend also sitting in the corridor, I invited her into my office, which was big enough to have both a desk and a table. This second peace Woman had a little boy with her, that she called Jay. He must have been at least two, and he had a merry old time running round my office, pulling open any drawers he could reach and scattering the contents all round the room. In the meantime his mother and I sat at opposite sides of the table, trying to have an intelligent discussion.

All of a sudden his mother said '*Jay, come here*', and when he came she sat him on her knee. She then whipped up her jumper and I saw that she was not wearing a bra. Little Jay was then plugged into one well formed breast and then a second. It was like a pit stop as when the refuelling had taken place, he returned with renewed energy to demolish what was left of my office. I thought of the corny old joke, ' *What right have you to do that? 'It is my divine right'. 'Well, your left is not too bad either'*. Then the Peacewoman and Jay left and my secretary, Wendy Freeman, and I spent at least 30 minutes tidying the office, after little Jay's assault. I never even knew the mother's name.

49
THE RENT SERVICE

The Rent Service was set up by the Rent Act 1977 to fix fair rents in the case of rented properties where the landlord did not live on the premises. I think that the service now comes under the Valuation office but in my day it was a hybrid service, funded by the Department of the Environment but administered by the County Council under a Statutory scheme. For the purposes of the scheme I was what was called 'the Proper Officer'. The service really ran itself. There was the Chief Rent Officer, two Rent Officers and 6 supporting staff. They were based in their own office in the centre of Reading and we saw little of them. The Chief Rent Officer was appointed jointly by the Proper Officer and the civil servant in the Department of Environment responsible for the service, and the remaining staff were appointed by the Chief Rent Officer and a senior member of the Secretariat. Disciplinary action followed the same lines. I could suspend the Chief Rent Officer for gross misconduct but dismissal required the consent of the Department.

Once a year I met a Mr Eugene Burr, a very suave civil servant in the Department of the Environment, responsible for the Rent Service, to discuss the service's performance. Berkshire had the only lady Chief Rent Officer in the country, appointed before I became County Secretary - a Mrs Maureen Elliott – and Mr Burr was fulsome in his praise of her. Her output was well above the national average of 25 cases a week – she was managing 40. She sent me her monthly mileage claim for approval – it was normally around 300 miles, which was what one would expect with her work-load. And that really was that. Someone told me that Mrs Elliott had a home in the Isle of Wight. You could not commute from the Isle of Wight to Berkshire each day, so I assumed that she must be living in rented accommodation in the County during the week, returning to the Isle of Wight at week-ends, but that was her business. Also we did seem to make a lot of appointments in the Rent Office, well above the average for the Secretariat as a whole, but it struck me as just one of those things.

One day in 1981 not long after we had moved to Shinfield Park, the Office Manager at the Rent Office made an appointment to see me. She was a very nice elderly Scottish lady, Mrs Isabella Rafferty, known in the Secretariat as Raff. She has since died. In 1980/81 the whole of the County Council had moved from the centre of Reading to new offices at Shinfield Park in south Reading but the Rent Office had remained in the centre of Reading. So something special was afoot, for Raff to want a personal interview. Her opening words were '*Mr Williams I thought you ought to know what is going on*' and she then started her whistleblowing. I was absolutely staggered by what Raff had to tell me. Indeed Mrs Elliot had a home in the Isle of Wight and yes you cannot realistically commute on a daily basis from the Isle of Wight to Berkshire. But she had no accommodation in Berkshire – she did not need it, as she only visited the County on a Friday and then for just half a day. But she was mightily productive in that half day, sitting down with 40 files and fixing the fair rents. Then she filled in her travel claims for all the sites she would have visited if she had been doing the job as it was meant to be done. No-one ever challenged her rent determinations, which suggested to me that the whole service was a waste of money but at the time that was a side issue. It also explained why we were making so many appointments in the Rent Office. Everyone know what was going on, but they were so terrified of Mrs Elliott that they left rather than whistleblow.

I think Raff came to see me on a Wednesday and I immediately went down to the Rent Office to search Mrs Elliott's office, taking my articled clerk Tony Plytas with me. Tony's father was an actor, best known as the chef in Fawlty Towers. We found clear evidence that Mrs Elliot was running an estate agency business in the New Forest and that she also dabbled in the occult, as we came across various spells and incantations. This was a Wednesday and according to Raff, Mrs Elliott never appeared until Friday noon but after we had been searching the office for an hour, suddenly there was Mrs Elliott, in a towering rage. She was a large lady, almost as big as me and she was very quick on the uptake, I will give her that. I told her she was suspended with immediate effect for gross misconduct, whereupon she created an uproar. Then Tony Plytas said ' *Watch out Clive, she has nicked all the exhibits*'. Which indeed she had, and had hidden them under her coat. So then we had a struggle in the middle of the room, until I managed to wrench them back. She then rushed off to telephone Mr Burr. I think he must have confirmed that I had the power to suspend, because she then left the premises and I never saw her again.

The next morning Raff came to see me again and she was in a terrible state. She was so bad that I sent down to the Council restaurant and we managed to find a bottle of brandy to give her a glass. She was in a state because when she had come downstairs that morning in her house she had found her hall mirror cracked from top to bottom. As a result she was convinced that Mrs Elliott had put a curse on her, which I am sure she had and no doubt on me as well. Two years later in 1983 my wife Liz was diagnosed with terminal ovarian cancer and she died in 1986. I also heard later that Mrs Elliott's son had been killed in a road traffic accident but not sure when. Make of that what you will.

But this saga was not yet over. Mrs Elliott had clearly obtained money by false pretences in relation to her bogus travel claims but the Police were not interested in prosecuting.

Even more bizarre and disgraceful was the attitude of the Department of the Environment. I had suspended Mrs Elliott on full pay but I needed the Department's approval to dismiss her. I placed all the facts before Mr Burr and as far as I could see it was an open and shut case. But I just could not get agreement from Mr Burr. He seemed to vanish into thin air. Mrs Elliott appeared to have a hold over him. There was a suggestion that way back he had interested her in joining the service. But as I was getting nowhere with Mr. Burr I decided to go over his head and obtained a personal interview in London with a Mr Robin Sharp, who was an Assistant Secretary in the Department of the Environment. He was very polite but gave no indication that he was going to take any action either. With mounting anger I said '*Look, Mr Sharp, this lady cannot stay as Chief Rent Officer - either she goes or I do*'. To which Sharp replied. '*Mr Williams, I have heard what you say and if you do decide to resign, thank you very much for your services*'.

I have never been so angry in all my life and I left fuming. I decided not to resign but instead to sit tight and see how events panned out. For their part the Department of the Environment decided to take no action either. The potential winner was Mrs Elliott, who remained suspended for several years and would have been on full pay, but for the fact that Ralph Garbett instructed the County Treasurer to stop paying her. My understanding is that eventually Mr Burr retired ; the service was reorganized and her post then disappeared but I don't think she was ever formally dismissed. The case also illustrated the problem with our Civil Service. The top civil servants are bright enough and very good at dreaming up policy but in my experience useless at dealing with difficult problems.

50
ALISON HALFORD

I was once involved in something similar involving the Home Office, when I was Clerk to the Thames Valley Police Authority (1986-1995). Alison Halford was Assistant Chief Constable at Merseyside and applied to become Deputy at Thames Valley in 1989. Colin Smith, the Thames Valley Chief Constable had worked with her and recommended that we place her on the shortlist for interview. But the Home Office stepped in and used their power to blackball her. They couldn't stop us interviewing but said that if we did and wanted to appoint they would refuse their consent. But they would not say why they were taking this line, which was unprecedented. The Police Authority were furious but had to accept defeat and Alison Halford was not interviewed.

We were her 7th rejection for a Deputy post and after her 9th rejection she took a case of discrimination to the Equality Tribunal in 1990. Coincidentally I later discovered that her solicitor at the Equalities Commission, Elizabeth Whitehouse, was a friend of Belinda Goyder, married to Bill Goyder, who succeeded me as Articled Clerk at Shire Hall in 1965, while her barrister initially was Stephen Sedley, now Mr Justice Sedley, who was in the same year as me at Queens' College, Cambridge. For their part the Authority started disciplinary proceedings. Alison Halford subsequently wrote a book entitled 'No Way Up The Greasy Pole' detailing the appalling way she was then treated by Merseyside Police; Merseyside Police Authority and also the Home Office.

I was asked if I would give evidence at her Tribunal Hearing as to what had happened as regards her Thames Valley application. The Police Authority were still smarting at the way they had been given the brush-off by the Home Office and gave their agreement to my going to the Tribunal, which was held in Manchester. There I was grilled by the Home Office's QC, Edwin Glasgow, who started life as a copper. During my cross examination he handed me an internal Home Office memo where I read '*Why on earth does Colin Smith want to interview AH – he must be mad – do you think he is having an affair with her?*' I knew Colin and his wife Pat very well – they were devoted to each other and the inference was outrageous. I said as much to Edwin Glasgow and the cross-examination became quite heated. It was simply that Colin Smith had worked with Alison Halford and thought highly of her. The Home Office, however, had clearly marked her cards and were blind to any other views. In her book Alison Halford recounts that George Bundred, the Chairman of the Merseyside Police Authority was heard to say in a Liverpool pub that the problem with her was that she was a lesbian and this was disrupting the senior command. So on one hand she was a lesbian, on the other having an affair with Colin Smith! It was a case of heads she lost and tails she could not win.

I receive a personal mention in her book: '*My witnesses continued to give supportive and well presented evidence and I could have hugged Mr. David Williams, Clerk to the Thames Valley Police Authority, when on oath he had no hesitation in announcing that my CV for the job had been the best of all the candidates. So keen were they to interview me on the strength of it that his Authority had challenged the Home Office as to why I had not been supported and received the magic tick, thereby refusing me a place on the shortlist. When they could not get the Home Office to change its mind the Thames Valley Authority had no alternative but to dismiss my application*'.

Alison Halford won her Tribunal case – the disciplinary proceedings were dropped and she took early retirement in 1992. She moved over the border into Wales and went on to have a distinguished political career in Wales – she served as a Welsh Assembly member for many years and was and is also involved with a wide range of societies and charities. Although her own career in the Police was ruined, the shabby way she had been treated did lead to major changes. Pauline Clare, who also served at Merseyside, was the first Lady Chief Constable, in her case at Lancashire, while Elizabeth Neville, who was the first Lady Deputy Chief Constable at Thames Valley later became the second Lady Chief Constable – at Wiltshire. There have been several other Lady Chief Constable appointments since, most notably Cressida Dick who is now the Metropolitan Police Commissioner.

51
THE EDUCATION SERVICE

Education used to be far and away the largest Council service, whether measured by budget or employment. About 75% of Council expenditure went on education and some 16,000 of the County Council's 23,000 employees worked in schools and other educational establishments, on full or part-time contracts.

But whereas in the County Secretariat I had 5 solicitors working on social services cases, Andrew Menzies, mostly on his own, very expertly looked after the whole education service. As a result my own involvement with the education service was minimal, though when I did become involved it was nearly always on account of a serious problem.

When I first joined the County Council in 1961, the Director of Education was an imposing individual, called Trevor Whitfield. He had been appointed in 1954 and retired at reorganization in 1974. I only once ever saw him put slightly off his stride and that was one year when the education budget over-ran by £250K. That was a very large sum in those days (several millions in today's money) and there was an almighty furore but he dealt with the crisis very calmly and efficiently and survived. A lesser man might not have.

He had been the sitting Deputy in 1954 and was very well liked. A few years earlier he might well have been appointed without interview but in 1948, Stephen Freeman of Didcot, had persuaded the Council to adopt a policy of advertising all its Chief Officer posts. This Stephen Freeman was an interesting character. He was an engine driver on the GWR and one of those who thought it was 'God's Wonderful Railway.' He used to stand as a socialist, although ERD said he was really a radical. He was illegitimate and his father was said to be from the landed gentry, though I never heard a name mentioned. Somewhat surprisingly he got on well with Sir George Mowbray and in spite of his socialist beliefs, he was the Chairman of the Education Committee at the time of Mr Whitfield's appointment. He was an Alderman by the time I arrived at Shire Hall in 1961 and he eventually died in 1968. There is both a school and a pub in Didcot named after him.

However as regards the appointment of the new Director of Education in 1954, Freeman was at odds with Sir George- Freeman wanting Whitfield and Sir George one of the externals. There were 11 on the Selection Panel, and Sir George thought he could command 6 votes for his preferred candidate. But there were 3 candidates on the final short-list so ERD suggested that each person on the Panel be given two votes and then vote to eliminate the third person. A curious procedure but it was agreed and Whitfield received 10 votes;

Sir George's favoured candidate 6 and the third candidate 5 – one vote was not used. Whereupon Freeman suggested that as Whitfield had received 10 votes he ought to be elected forthwith. Uproar ensued, members of the Panel lost their tempers; personal insults were flung around the room and all the time the three candidates were sitting outside in the corridor, clearly able to hear what was going on. Eventually the Panel calmed down and it was agreed to eliminate the third candidate and vote between Whitfield and Sir George's preference. Sir George was then dumbfounded when Whitfield got the nod by 6-5. Clearly one of Sir George's supporters had changed sides but as it had been a secret ballot, he did not know who was the guilty party. Some time later Col Sir John Aird Bt confessed to ERD it had been him. He just felt that Freeman and the Education Committee members were so keen on having Whitfield it would be churlish to stand in their way. Sir John Aird had been Equerry to the Prince of Wales – later King Edward VIII. I once saw a newsreel of the Prince of Wales and Wallace Simpson larking about in the Mediterranean and there next to them, sitting and bobbing about on a large rubber duck and having a very jolly time was Sir John Aird.

When he retired at reorganisation in 1974, Trevor Whitfield was succeeded by his Deputy Richard Hornsby, a quiet individual, very much the Deputy. In 1978 he phoned me up and asked me to join him when he met Tony Davies, the Head of Reading School, as he had received a complaint from the parent of one of Reading's boarders. I knew Tony a bit as a couple of years previously we had both been on a County Council deputation, that had taken advantage of EU hospitality to be shown round Brussels and to be given an insight into how the EU worked – and more particularly what grants could be applied for. Tony was a very likeable individual. He was very athletic and a natural at ball games – I think he had played cricket for Berkshire. He was not married and Reading School had some boarders. It was his habit to go into the dormitory sometimes of an evening after lights down and chat to the boys. Not the wisest thing to do and the parents of one of the boys felt he had been over-familiar with their son and hence the complaint. It could not be ignored but it was not particularly serious in the greater scheme of things. Tony was shocked when he heard about the complaint and then said '*Clive, what do you advise me to do?*'It was so sad. I could only reply along the lines that we would have to investigate the complaint – we couldn't ignore it, but he needed to get himself a good lawyer. I never saw him again. He owned a shotgun, went home and blew his brains out. Of course, it was all hushed up and nothing was said about the complaint at the Inquest. Overwork was the verdict.

When Richard Hornsby himself retired a few years later, the Education Committee decided that they wanted someone more in the Trevor Whitfield mould to succeed him. They appointed Peter Edwards, a real feisty character, who had been the Deputy Director of Education at Dorset. Dorset County Council was very keen on outdoor education and owned 3 outdoor education centres – Berkshire had nothing. Peter Edwards was also strongly supportive of outdoor education, so he obtained Education Committee approval and then charged his Primary School Adviser, John Wood-Griffiths, with finding a Centre. John had been born in Chester but had North Walian roots and he eventually discovered that Mid-Glamorgan Council, which also had 3 Centres, was prepared to dispose of one of them – at Rhos-y-Gwaliau nr Bala. Peter then approached me and I agreed that the County Secretariat would undertake the legal work to form a charitable trust to acquire and run the Centre, while Peter undertook to arrange for the County Council to supply and pay for the salaries of a Head, Deputy Head and 2 teachers. Geoff Littler in the County Secretariat handled the actual legal work. Peter Edwards and John Wood-Griffiths then drummed up support from the Berkshire business community – Sir William Benyon DL was particularly helpful and became and remained a Trustee right up to his death. So the money was raised to first lease and later purchase the Rhos-y-Gwaliau Centre. Later I too became a Trustee and still am. Eventually in the 90's public sector cutbacks resulted in a gradual reduction of County Council support, so much so that the Trust eventually sold the Centre to two of the teachers; invested the proceeds and the Trust is now solely a grant-making body. The cleaner at the Centre in Rhos is Mary Jones, who has lived in Rhos-y-Gwaliau all her life and had attended school there when it was the village school. Then Mary won £9m on the Lottery. What did she do? – she put in a new kitchen, gave her 4 children some money and carried on cleaning!

It was John Wood-Griffiths, sadly now deceased, who told me about the Basildon school scandal. I have a 1938 photograph of Headmaster Ernest Stanley Nicholas and his wife, on a Basildon school outing. He was still Headmaster in 1974 when he dropped dead in Reading, the year after I moved to Upper Basildon, so I never met him. But he was known as Mr Basildon as he ran the entire Parish. He was Clerk of the Parish Council; Secretary of the Parochial Church Council ; the church organist and the Choir Master and he also helped to found the Parish magazine in 1968 and was its first Editor. There were fulsome tributes paid to him when he died and these have not long been re-printed in the Country Neighbour, as the Basildon Parish Magazine is called, as it has a '44 years ago' column. I also have to confess that he was a fellow Welshman.

One of John Wood-Griffiths' jobs as Primary Schools Adviser was to make sure that schools kept open when crises happened. So after Stanley Nicholas died he went to see the widow, obtained the school keys and opened up. What he found shocked him. It transpired that our Stanley had a second career writing pornography under an assumed name, which he kept locked in a desk in the school. This disclosure was kept very quiet and hence the fulsome eulogies. But after Stanley was buried in Pangbourne cemetery, one evening John received an anguished call from a concerned Basildon resident, asking him to go to Pangbourne cemetery. He went and there he found Mrs Nicholas, drunk, literally dancing on Stanley's grave. He was a wife-beater par excellence and Mrs Nicholas was celebrating her release from his tyranny. My first wife Liz was also buried in Pangbourne cemetery in 1986 and her grave and that of Stanley Nicholas are only 15ft apart. I reflect on this story each time I visit the cemetery because I am pretty certain no-one has ever tended the Stanley Nicholas grave in over 30 years.

On one occasion I was asked to clerk a Disciplinary Appeal Panel. A teacher called Gray had been sacked by Graham Williams, the Deputy Director and had appealed. The man was completely stupid. He had gone around photographing young girls, including his neighbour's 11 yr old daughter, when she was doing handstands in her garden. He had then taken his film to Boots to be processed and Boots were so alarmed at what they had printed that they contacted Graham Williams. Gray's appeal was along the lines that he was interested in art photography. However Frank Butters was chairing the Panel and was a keen photographer. He asked a few technical questions and the answers made it clear the appellant could hardly tell one end of a camera from the other. Appeal dismissed.

The other Disciplinary Appeal I clerked was even more bizarre. It involved the Laboratory Technician at the Holt Girls School in Wokingham. He spent most of his time in the Laboratory and often the curtains were drawn. Then one day loud screams came from the Laboratory. Staff rushed in to find the technician entangled in an industrial vacuum cleaner. It proved impossible to disentangle man and machine, so a stretcher was produced and the technician and the vacuum cleaner were placed on the stretcher covered by a blanket and taken to hospital for disentangling.

The Laboratory Technician was sacked but appealed. His appeal was along the lines that he had forgotten to zip himself up; that he had bent forward to carry out a repair to the vacuum cleaner and somehow he had toppled onto the machine at the same time as accidentally switching it on. As a result his private parts had got caught up in the vacuum blades.

The Panel Chairman on this occasion was Trevor Timperley DFC, a lovely man, who later became the first and only Labour Chairman of the County

Council. I think he earned his DFC flying in Bomber Command during the War. He believed the best of all his fellow men and although the appeal case was totally implausible he wanted to give the appellant every opportunity to make it. He asked if we had the offending vacuum cleaner. We did. I wasn't too sure what he planned to do with it. If he had in mind a reconstruction of the incident I wondered whose private parts were in the firing line. Certainly not the appellant's as I suspected that most of those were still in the vacuum cleaner bag. But the vacuum cleaner was duly switched on and Trevor took out his handkerchief, which he held 6 inches from the blades. Nothing happened. He moved the handkerchief 3 inches away – still nothing. Then an inch away and suddenly there was a great whoosh and what almost sounded like a gulp and the handkerchief was gone. I asked Trevor if he would like me to try and retrieve his handkerchief but he fortunately declined the offer and dismissed the Appeal.

52
THE LONGEST COUNCIL MEETING

For the first part of 1982 – before Pearl Slatter won Theale from a Liberal-Democrat at a bye-election, the Council was being run by the Conservative Group but they did not have an overall majority. It was also a time of rampant inflation. The Council had moved into their new building at Shinfield Park in 1981. It had started life as a £8m project but had cost the County Council £32m by the time it was completed. Pay rises of as much as 10% were not uncommon. When it came to setting the County Council budget in 1982, the Conservative Group proposed a rate rise of 13%; the Liberal-Democrats one of 21% and the Labour Group one of 27%. This was so excessive that I went to see the Group and warned them that they might get the Council surcharged by the District Auditor, if it were passed. I reminded of them of what had happened to Tower Hamlets Council in the 30's. They had fixed so high a rate and had then refused to reduce it, resulting in the entire Council being surcharged and eventually ending up in Wormwood Scrubs, which the Town Clerk had to visit each day to take their instructions. The Group had a good laugh at that and decided to stick with their proposal.

As previously mentioned, Budget meetings were always held on Tuesdays, unlike ordinary County Council meetings which were held on Saturdays. So at 10.30am on Tuesday the budget debate started. The speeches went on all day so it was early evening when the votes were taken. The Conservative Group moved their 13% rate increase and were defeated; the Lib-Dems then moved their 21% increase and they were defeated and finally the Labour group moved their 27% rate rise and they too were defeated. Lewis Moss was Chairman of the Council and he then implemented Standing Orders to suspend the Council meeting, so that the Party Leaders could confer.

The conferring went on all through the night with no Party prepared to concede. But on my advice Lewis Moss held firm and told the Party Leaders that the Council had to fix a rate by law and he would keep the Council sitting until we had a rate.

Eventually just before 7.0am the Council resumed. The Lib-Dem Leader, John Leston, moved a rate rise of 21% and with both the Conservative and Labour Groups abstaining the rate was fixed at 21%. Immediately following this all bar one of the Conservative Chairmen and Vice-Chairmen of Committees resigned. I recall they formed an orderly queue to hand me in their written resignations. The one exception was Neville Auton, the Chairman of the Youth Committee, who couldn't see why politics should intrude into his Committee.

Lewis Moss remained as Chairman of the Council and his Vice-Chairman, Gordon Slater also retained office. But for a time we then had a de facto informal Labour/Lib-Democrat coalition running the Council. At each meeting a Labour or Lib-Dem member of the Committee would be appointed Chairman for the meeting. Then Pearl won Theale and the Conservatives again had a majority.

In total the 1982 budget meeting had lasted 20 hours 30 minutes. I subsequently wrote to the Local Government Chronicle asking if anyone had experienced a longer local government meeting. No-one replied.

COUNTY COUNCIL CENTENARY 1989 – THE COUNTY COUNCIL SONG

Sung by Ernie Wise; Chairman Tony Wiseman and the composer, Colin Preston.
Colin was a member of the County Secretariat and has written many songs and hymns.

JULY 15th 1989 – AUTHOR WITH TONY WISEMAN (Chairman of the County Council).

The author had this plate made by Julian Bellmont of the Aldermaston Pottery and presented it to the County Council, receiving a standing ovation. A second identical plate was made, paid for by the author's friends at Shinfield Park and that is still in the author's possession. (next illustration)

FAREWELL TO SHINFIELD PARK & SECRETARIAT - JUNE 1989

Ron Jewitt (Leader of the Council) doing the honours. Freddy Jones, long since retired, had never set foot in Shire Hall or Shinfield Park since the day he retired but he came back specially for my retirement party.

SEPTEMBER 1987 – Howard Springthorpe (Treasurer) of the Thames Valley Police Authority and I as Clerk were both introduced to Prime Minister, Margaret Thatcher MP at Sulhamstead Police Training Centre, where she was the guest speaker at the Annual Social Gathering of Senior Thames Valley Police Officers. She and husband Denis had to be flown in by helicopter because of IRA assassination threats – the Brighton Grand bombing took place in 1985 and her former personal assistant, Ian Gow, was assassinated in 1985.

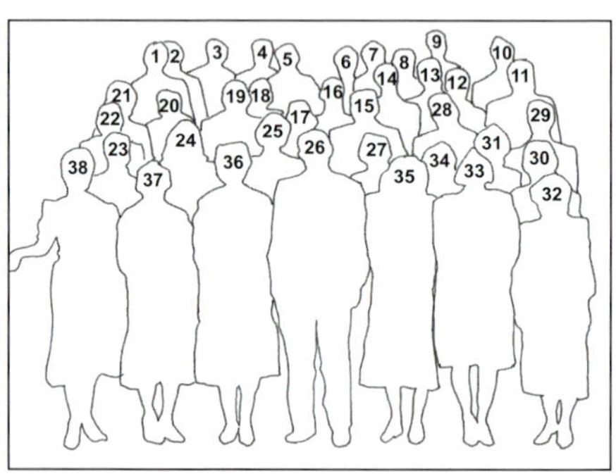

FAREWELL PHOTO ON STEPS OF SHINFIELD PARK – JUNE 1989

1.Colin Lee
2.Geoff Littler
3. Ralph Garbett
4. Ian Robertson
5. Tony Plytas
6. Dean Taylor
7. Colin Wood*
8. Willem Cyrus
9.
10. Graham Lawson
11. Mike Byfield
12. Roger Penfold
13. Chris Green
14. David Over
15. David Weller
16. Andrew Menzies
17. Liz Grugeon
18. Jessica Hill
19. John Killick *
20. Sam McClew
21. Lynda Saunders
22. Colin Preston
23. Julie Fox (Ainsley)
24. Alison Kircher
25.
26. The Author
27.
28. Peter Durrant
29. Stan Walker *
30. Jean Horner *
31.
32.
33. Kate McDonald
34. Katie Hajda
35. Sue Smith
36. Diana Elwes*
37. Joan Klopke
38. Christine Bowyer
*deceased

Foreign Office and to my amazement, was approved without any amendments. So it ended up in a Loyal Address, was duly presented to the Queen of Denmark and is no doubt languishing somewhere in the Elsinore Royal Library.

The Emir of Bahrein came on a Royal visit in 1985, when Ian Morgan was Chairman of the Council. The oil price must have been doing well then because the Emir brought loads of gold and platinum watches with him and everyone who rendered him the slightest service received one. Ian Morgan and Bob Gash went to the Royal Banquet and Ian came away with a gold watch and Bob a platinum one. Bob told me that the Emir's gift to the Queen was a replica of the Royal yacht, Britannia. It was about three feet long and as it was mostly solid gold it literally weighed a ton and had to be carried in by 4 marines.

There was another Royal visit by King Carlos and Queen Sophia of Spain, not long after Bob had died in April 1986, so I accompanied the Council deputation in his place to Windsor. The 12 members of the County delegation were drawn from all three political groups and there was no standard dress code among the men – the Conservatives wore morning dress, while the Opposition wore suits or sport jackets. The Ladies all had hats but no two dresses were of the same colour. The County were required to hand over their Loyal Address immediately following the Royal Borough, whose delegation of 12 men and women were all dressed in identical Council robes and tricorne hats and looked very smart. In contrast the County delegation, when lined up on one side of the room, looked a bit of a rabble and it seemed to me that when the delegation started marching across the room towards King Carlos and Queen Sophia, the Royal couple took several steps backwards. On this occasion there were no invitations to the State Banquet but I did manage to have a look at the Banquet Hall, all laid out with gold plates and cutlery. It was quite a sight.

54

PERSONNEL WARS

I could never understand why with devolved departmental budgeting we had a Central Personnel, later Human Resources Department. But we did and as they had been given the power to veto any regradings, you had to take them with you on any reorganisation.

During my time as County Secretariat we had 3 County Personnel Officers – Richard Painter, who went off to run the local government wing of Lord Ashcroft's empire; Alan Dick, who left to become the Chief Executive of Wyre Forest Council in Worcestershire and Mrs Judy Ratcliffe, who was still there at the time of my departure in 1989.

A year or so after I had been appointed as County Secretary, my Deputy, John Downs, who had been passed over when I was appointed, told me that he had been offered a job with Hays Management Consultants. As we were facing yet another round of budget cuts and I had four very competent Assistant County Secretaries in Alan Ashley, Ralph Garbett, Andrew Menzies and David Over, John Downs posed the question as to whether it was really necessary to replace him as Deputy. He admitted he had an ulterior motive in that if he were not replaced and his post deleted from the establishment, he would be entitled to a redundancy payment of about £3,000. But even taking that into account and giving each of the Assistants something extra for acting up, a major saving could be achieved.

I discussed the proposal with the four Assistants and they were very amenable and supportive. But time was of the essence from John Downs' point of view and in view of this the redundancy proposal was put through Personnel Committee on its own and was agreed. It was a cardinal error on my part, because Richard Painter then blocked the regrading of the four Assistant County Secretaries, for no good reason that I could see. However Richard Painter then left and his replacement, Alan Dick, was a little more flexible but only up to a point. He agreed that just two of my four Assistants could be designated as Deputies and be given an extra increment. It left me with an enormous headache as there was nothing to choose between the four as regards ability and competence. In the conglomerate department that we had become, Ralph Garbett had the widest experience and as the youngest of the four I sensed that Alan Ashley would be the most likely to leave local government. In that I was right – he later went into private practice and now has his own firm in London. But I had long and friendly associations with both Andrew Menzies and David Over. David had been with Berkshire for almost as long as me and I had attended his wedding to Judith in Cleethorpes. Sadly Judith died just two years ago from a brain tumour. So I did not want to hurt two colleagues, whom I regarded as friends. But Personnel had boxed me into a corner - either no-one received any additional money, which seemed grossly unfair, or I bit the bullet and designated two of the four as my Deputies. In the end I opted for designating Alan Ashley and Ralph Garbett. Andrew and David were bitterly disappointed by my decision but were men enough to direct their ire not at me but at the Personnel Department. They lodged a grievance which took on a life of its own and was only settled two years later when their grievance was upheld and they were similarly designated, with their additional increment back-dated to the date of my original proposal. Vindication of a sort but what a waste of time and effort for no good reason.

55
STAN GOODCHILD

Some time after he had left Berkshire to join Lord Ashcroft, I received a call from Richard Painter. Lord Ashcroft had a million or two to invest in academies and in view of Berkshire's reputation, thought he would start by offering Berkshire the money. But Stan Goodchild, the Berkshire Director of Education did not seem interested. Could I help in any way? I had to laugh at this. I had known Stan Goodchild from the days when he had been Head of Garth School in Bracknell in the 70's. From the first moment I met him he pumped me for information on who was who at Shire Hall and how the system worked. It was quite obvious he had ambitions to climb the greasy pole but he was a likeable person nevertheless. Bracknell, from its formation, had attracted numerous computer companies and Stan had persuaded them to give his comprehensive school all their redundant computers. So in the days when computers were a rarety in schools, Garth School was stuffed full of them. His school then went on to win an Award - European Computer School of the Year - and it was at the Award Ceremony I first met Stan. Col Watt and his Conservative colleagues were over the moon at this Award and Stan became their favourite Head. His advice was sought and I believe eventually he was also giving advice to the Conservatives at national level. Whether Stan actually was a Conservative, I was by no means sure - I had him to be more of a Vicar of Bray figure. But the Conservatives obviously thought he was their man and so he eventually ended up as Director of Education. But once Stan landed the top job, we saw a remarkable change in his views. He wanted to hang onto his education empire, not see it whittled away with County schools being replaced by independent academies. I told Richard Painter that in my view he was wasting his time approaching Stan – he or Lord Ashcroft would have to go to the members. Berkshire did eventually get some academies but not financed by Lord Ashcroft.

Stan Goodchild is no longer with us - he too died of a brain tumour. Whether or not there was a connection he was one of the first Chief Officers to acquire a mobile phone and he used to spend all his time walking around with the phone clamped to his ear. When the Rhos-y-Gwaliau Centre nr Bala was facing loss of County Council financial support, I and some of the other Trustees persuaded Stan to travel up to Bala to see the Centre. As we left Berkshire, Stan was as usual on his mobile phone but as we entered Wales, the reception grew weaker and weaker and Stan grew more and more agitated. In the end we managed to convince him that he was going to have to spend 24 hours without a phone call and when that knowledge had sunk in, he relaxed and was very good company.

56
ALAN DICK

When Alan Dick arrived in Berkshire to succeed Richard Painter as County Personnel Officer, the Chief Officers were about to have a farewell dinner for Jimmy Tainsh, the Deputy County Architect. There was a time when the Chief Officers socialized and bonded! The dinner was held at the College of Agriculture, Burchetts Green, and as Alan Dick did not know the County I offered to collect him and take him there. On the way we chatted about this and that and I asked if he had seen Sir Les Patterson on the television the previous evening –Barry Humphries' famous send up of Australian intellectuals. *'Yes,'* said Alan, *'I did see it. How on earth does someone like Sir Les Patterson become Australia's Cultural Attache?'* I didn't know if he were pulling my leg or not but on the whole I think not.

When Alan went to Wyre Forest District Council to be Chief Executive, it was in the news on account of the fact that the previous incumbent (a man) had been forced to resign after having an affair with the Leader of the Council (a lady). As someone uncharitably remarked, they were not going to make the same mistake twice when they appointed Alan. Nor did they and he did them an excellent job.

57
ON NOT BECOMING A CHIEF EXECUTIVE

I applied for number of Chief Executive posts during my time as County Secretary. Initially I failed to get an interview, and after the third time this happened I took advice from Inlogov (The Institute of Local Government Studies) run by Professor Stewart at Birmingham University, where I had attended a 4 month management course in 1971. They were quite blunt – my applications were all about what I had done and not enough about what I was going to do. So for my next application I said that in my view this job requires a, b, c and d and I then spelled out my experience in each of these areas. The new approach worked and thereafter I don' t think I ever failed to achieve an interview, apart from my own County!

I came closest to succeeding at Warwickshire. I hit it off with their Leader, which is normally enough to guarantee success. But Warwickshire were an old-fashioned County and I heard subsequently that after a long discussion I narrowly lost out to the internal candidate. When I came to leave the Interview room I was faced by four identical doors and no exit sign. So taking my courage in both hands I boldly opened what I thought was the exit and was confronted by a broom cupboard. It brought the house down but maybe did not enhance my chances, as it was rather too reminiscent of Peter Sellers' Inspector Clouseau.

On another occasion I went all the way to Fife, having some knowledge of the Kingdom, through my visits with Liz to her grandmother, who lived in Ladybank. It quickly became apparent that I was there to make up the numbers – the token non-Scot - but it was an enjoyable trip all the same. I even used the all night sleeper from King's Cross.

Bucks was my last outing in 1987 and I was accompanied by Christina as there was a reception beforehand, to which partners were invited. Christina has very sensitive people antenna and about 10 minutes after entering the reception she said '*You can forget this one, Clive*'. She was quite right. There was a kind of love-in going on between the Lady Chairman of the Council and the Bucks Chief Education Officer, who was duly appointed.

Bedfordshire, also in 1987, was a fiasco. The Interview Panel consisted of the three party leaders. Some 15 candidates were invited to the first day of interviews and 4 including myself were invited back for a second day. Then after all that no appointment was made! Someone later sent me the local newspaper, which had obviously been well briefed as to what had gone on. The Interview Panel were torn to shreds and made to look complete idiots. They had then tried to counter the criticism by slagging off the applicants. No names were mentioned but I and the other County Secretary, who made the final four, were described as too stolid. I have been called many things in my life but I don't think anyone who knows me has ever regarded me as being 'stolid'. The other County Secretary referred to was David Henshaw, who later became Chief Executive first of Knowsley and then of Liverpool and was knighted for his services. At the time I was impressed by him but I have since read Alison Halford's autobiography 'No Way up the Greasy Pole' and he was the Clerk of the Merseyside Police Authority, which dealt with her case so disgracefully. Merseyside was obviously a difficult Authority but Henshaw was not a lawyer and there are times when a legal training is an advantage.

But the most bizarre Interview I attended was at Hereford and Worcester. This had been a shot gun marriage – two Counties which were chalk and cheese had been merged. Worcestershire was basically Conservative but Herefordshire was essentially Independent/Liberal. However, instead of just 3 party leaders for this Interview you had an Interview Panel of 15, divided into 5 groups of 3, each with a different topic and limited to 45 minutes each. In other words each candidate was subjected to 5 interviews, each of 45 minutes.

My first Interview was with a Panel charged with finding out my views on Law and Order and the Lieutenancy. The Panel comprised a Mr Moffat, the Conservative Leader of the combined County, another Worcestershire Conservative and someone called George, who was an Independent from Herefordshire. It has to be said that Mr Moffat was an imposing figure. He was a huge man, around 20 stone, who had been a colonial officer.

As by this time I was both Clerk of the Thames Valley Police Authority and Clerk of the Berkshire Magistrates Committee, as well as Secretary to the Berkshire Advisory Committee, I thought there was nothing that this Panel could ask me which would floor me. How wrong I was.

George opened the questioning. '*Mr Williams, why do you want to work in Hereford & Worcester with a bunch of raving idiots like these* ?' – pointing at his Conservative colleagues. I was wondering if I dared reply along the lines of '*Well, I am a raving idiot myself, so I should feel at home*', but before I could get out a word Mr Moffat intervened '*That's a bit much, George, why do you say that?*' George then started outlining his grievances and in a thrice an almighty argument developed. I was then totally ignored for about 20 minutes as they slugged it out in front of me, proving second by second that they really were raving idiots.

Eventually they remembered why they were there and I was asked a second question, only slightly less odd than the first and again having no relevance whatsoever to the supposed subject matter of the interview. It was asked by Mr Moffat. *'Mr Williams, if you saw a garage with three parking spaces marked out for the Lord Lieutenant, Chairman of the Council and Chief Executive, what* would *you think?'*. This was a trick question – apparently the Lord Lieutenant had a coveted covered parking space and the Leader of the Council did not – a source of great resentment on the part of Mr Moffat. I twigged what was behind the question and gave an appropriate toadying answer, expressing surprise that someone as powerful and important as the Leader of the Council should be left out when it came to the vital task of allocating car park spaces.

There was only time for one more question, which in some ways was the oddest of the lot. I still don't really know why it was asked.

'Mr. Williams, if you travel 18 miles south of Birmingham' – I am pretty good on my geography, so I took a chance and said *'You arrive at Meriden, the geographical centre of England'*. This impressed them but they had only just started. *'Now if you go east you go through 5 counties. How many counties do you go through if you travel west?'* I thought quickly – Shropshire, Powys and Ceredigion, so I replied *'Three'*. *'No, just one'* replied Mr Moffat.' *'I don't understand that'*, said I, *'You have got Shropshire, Powys and Cere*digion'. *'We never said anything about W*ales,' riposted Mr Moffat and that was that. End of interview!

Robin Hodgson was the front runner for this position. Robin and I had both been Assistant Solicitors at Oxfordshire County Council and were good friends. His subsequent career had taken him to Essex, where he was County Secretary. But at the end of the first day's interviewing, Robin had had enough and in spite of being pressed to stay, he withdrew. He later achieved his ambition and became Chief Executive at Hants County Council. I soldiered on and made the shortlist for the second day but was not surprised and was indeed rather relieved when no appointment was made. As in the case of Bedfordshire County Council, Worcester and Hereford Council then persuaded their Treasurer to take over the position.

58
1986 – MY ANNUS HORRIBILIS

ERD died in February 1986. He was 80 so he had had a good innings, for one who was short, corpulent and who claimed never to have taken a day's exercise in his life.

But much worse was to come. On 1st April 1986 my wife Liz died of ovarian cancer at the age of only 40. My daughter Rebecca was just 11 and my son Robert only 9. Liz had been terminally ill since 1983 when the cancer was first detected at such a late stage that she was given just twelve months to live. But Liz was always a fighter and she extended that to 3 years. I knew what was coming but it was still a very difficult time, and even more so for my children.

see colour page XXI

Then three weeks later Bob Gash died at the age of just sixty. He had been attending a conference in Oxford and he and his wife Rosamond were staying in a hotel in Oxford, when Bob just passed away peacefully in his sleep. Bob had always had a drink problem, which must have contributed to his early demise. He once said to me *'I am not an alcoholic, Clive – I am a dipsomaniac.' 'I didn't know there was a difference, Bob'* I replied. *'Oh Yes'* he said and explained that dipsomaniacs are subject to binges but can then go for periods – sometimes for years - without imbibing. Alcoholics drink all the time.

He put his problem down to Christ Church College, Oxford. It was and probably still is dominated by public school entrants. Bob was a Grammar school boy and was just ignored. As Xmas approached he was very lonely and so he bought a bottle of whisky and invited all his stair to join him. They were happy to drink his whisky but this he claimed kicked off his problem. Up to then he had hardly ever drunk alcohol.

There used to be a pub behind Shire Hall, called the White Lion. Sometimes after work Bob would invite me to join him there for a drink. Whisky was his tipple but he drank doubles and could drink several without any apparent effect. But if he continued he would suddenly crash out. I enjoy a drink but I quickly learnt not to try and keep up with him.

His drinking got him into all kinds of scrapes. The worst occasion was in 1976 when the legendary Geoff Hallett, Manager of Barclays Bank in Reading – they were the County Council bankers - invited Bob and the County Treasurer around to the Bank for a Xmas drink. Mike Beasley, the County Treasurer wisely declined and sent his Deputy, Geoff Ellis, in his place. At the time I was Bob's Assistant and I feared the worst. I was not disappointed as at 4.0pm I received a call from the Bank to the effect that Bob was feeling unwell, so could I come and collect him. I had a two door Austin Allegro at the time, so I took Howard Davies with me and we drove round to the Bank in Market Place. After hammering on the door we were let in and then taken past the tellers to Hallett's office. The Deputy Bank Manager, a Mr Wilson, opened the door and he was the only one of the four still compos mentis. Geoff Ellis was a giggling wreck; Geoff Hallett could not stand up and Bob was unconscious. Everywhere you looked there were whisky bottles – some full; some empty; some half full; some a third full. So Howard and I carried Bob out of the Bank and somehow managed to squeeze him into my Allegro.

We couldn't take him back to Shire Hall, so we went to his home in Shiplake. Unfortunately Rosamond was not at home, but his mother was, so we made our excuses as best we could and left. Bob's mother then died a fortnight later. Whether the incident contributed to her demise no-one could say but the shock led to Bob going on to the wagon for several years.

It was a wonder successive County Council Chairmen did not take him to task over his drinking but Bob could charm the birds from the trees when he had to and as his drinking bouts were intermittent he managed to get away with it. He could also tell a story against himself. Lewis Moss, who was Chairman from 1980-1982 always used to go ski-ing at Xmas time and one year he was ski-ing in the Dolomites when a ski-ing party there at the same time got themselves killed in an avalanche. On his return the Chairman discussed this incident with Bob and said *'The trouble was – they went off piste'*. But he pronounced piste as pissed – not peest and to Bob pissed had only one meaning. '*Oh, serve them right, then*', said Bob and received one very odd look from Lewis Moss.

59
TONY ALLEN

The Council decided to appoint headhunters to find Bob's replacement in 1986. I applied but the timing was all wrong for me and in the event no internal candidates were interviewed.

see colour page XXIV

The successful applicant was Tony Allen, slightly younger than myself, who had started life as a solicitor but had moved into local government management at an early age. He had already held the post of Chief Executive for the London Borough of Hammersmith & Fulham for ten years by the time he was appointed at Berkshire.

Compared to Bob Gash it was a case of chalk and cheese. Bob Gash had been like the Chairman of a Board, happy for Chief Officers to get on with running the place and only becoming involved when there were problems. Ralph Garbett once said to me that he liked working for Bob as he was only interested in sixes – he couldn't be bothered with singles. It was an apt metaphor. In contrast the new Chief Executive had a clear idea of what he wanted to achieve and was hands on in making sure his aims were implemented.

Shortly after taking up his appointment he assembled all the senior Council officers in the Council Chamber for a pep talk. Referring to his background he announced that he was a Unitary man and not in favour of two tier local government. I thought that was an extraordinary statement from someone who had just been appointed Chief Executive of a County Council. But in a sense he was ahead of his time, since as I later found out, his concept of Unitary government in Counties was to abolish the District Councils and hand all the powers to the County Council. That is the position nowadays in Counties such as Wiltshire, Somerset and Cornwall. But it was never going to happen in Berkshire in the 80's, when the six Districts were too strong and too closely aligned with the Members of Parliament. So when Unitary government arrived in 1998, long after I had left Berkshire, it was the County Council that got the chop. Though from all the joint working relationships that are now being formed between the Unitaries, one could be forgiven for thinking that the County Council is in the process of being re-constituted.

In 1986 the Council was again under Conservative control and had set its new Chief Executive a brief to raise efficiency. Some services were privatised and to make sure the Council was not ripped off, a new Chief Officer Post of Director of Commercial Contracts was created and as previously mentioned was filled by Ian Pugh, recruited from the private sector on a fixed term contract.

60
DAVID BALL

It was also decided to extend computerization, until then mainly confined to a main frame computer located in the County Treasurer's Department. I arrived one day in Shire Hall at Shinfield Park to find the building overflowing with large cardboard boxes marked ' Apricot Computers'. I then learned that the Council had appointed a new Director of Computing (Information Systems), who had previously worked for Apricot Computers. The Council had strict rules on competitive tendering, which had been by-passed in this instance and I raised my concerns with the Chief Executive. I received a somewhat hostile reception as he had been personally involved in what had gone on and had secured what he thought was a very good deal for the Council. But I persisted and the upshot was that David Ball, the new incumbent, signed a declaration that neither he nor any other member of his family had obtained any financial benefit from the transaction that had just taken place, that amounted to £500K. I found that difficult to believe but in the absence of any evidence to the contrary I had to let the matter rest.

David Ball was quite a character. He was a person who said what was on his mind and did not mince his words. On one occasion he bought a curry in the Shire Hall restaurant and told the chef that it was inedible. The chef got on his high horse and said *'Well cook it yourself if you think you can do any better.'* Which was precisely what David Ball did. One day at Shire Hall we were treated to the sight of David Ball cooking and serving 150 curries. I was one of his customers and there was no doubt that he knew how to cook a curry. It was excellent.

However, his inability to suffer what he regarded as fools gladly, led to some spectacular fallouts with other Departments. The Council had a Supplies Department, which all Departments were required to use, rather than make their own purchasing arrangements. David Ball used them as little as possible and when Norman Coulbeck, the County Supplies Officer politely reminded him of Council Standing Orders, his reply was along the lines that the Supplies Department were not worth using as they were a useless bunch of incompetents. In fact Norman Coulbeck was a perfectly competent officer – it was really a clash of two cultures, i.e traditional local government and the world of commerce.

But I don't buy in to the black and white view that some take of the private and public sectors. Without the private sector we wouldn't have a public sector but to work efficiently the private sector needs to have an efficient public sector.

And having myself worked for 28 years in local government and 20 years in the private sector, I have come across outstanding and useless employees in both sectors. I would also mention the experience of my personal secretary, Marion West (sadly now deceased), who went off to work in the private sector for 50% more pay. She was interviewed three times before her future employers were convinced that someone from local government could undertake the job. Within a year she was back in local government – she couldn't take the boredom any more. She just sat around all day twiddling her thumbs – at Shire Hall she had to work flat out from the moment she entered the building, and faced with a choice of boredom and high pay and hard work and lower pay, she wisely opted for the latter.

My final David Ball story relates to 1988, when he somehow found out that my Department were engaged in a child care case where one of the defendants was a Norman Cuckoo Hughes. He observed in a memo headed '100 things about the County Council ' that *the Director of Information Systems keeps a cuckoo clock in his office; this is the only cuckoo that is nailed to the wall; the other 2,498 cuckoos freely roam Shire Hall*'.

61
COST CENTRE MANAGEMENT

The Departments that remained in-house at Shire Hall embarked upon cost centre management. The Chief Executive identified 400 cost centres and each distinct cost centre was given a budget and told to manage within it. The County Secretariat had always run itself this way, so it was no shock to the system. In fact not long after my appointment as County Secretary in 1977 we had undertaken a voluntary internal exercise and had reduced our budget by 5%. Then the Council in its wisdom decided at the next budget meeting to cut all departments by 5%, and to make that happen a freeze was put on replacing any vacancies. My protest that we had already done the exercise and should be exempt fell on deaf ears and we ended up with a 10% cut.

In any organisation, the turnover of staff is higher at the bottom of the scale than at the top and the result of this freeze on filling vacancies was that we were reduced to just one part-time clerical post, whereas we had had two previously. When our part-time officer fell ill on one occasion I and a Committee clerk ended up spending two hours sorting the post and then going round the Department delivering it. I subsequently mentioned this to the then Conservative Leader, Christopher Ward, a solicitor in private practice in Reading. I got no sympathy. '*The partners always open the post in our office*' said Christopher. *'But you have a 100 or so items of mail'* I replied *'We have over a thousand. If you want me to spend my time distributing the post, fine, but it is no way to run an army'*. It always makes me smile when I hear politicians of any political hue stating that they will balance the books by making huge efficiency savings. Such savings can be made but as we live in a democracy and politicians like to get re-elected, the really tough decisions tend to get deferred or kicked into the long grass.

62

SOURING OF RELATIONSHIPS

Returning to 1986, in addition to the introduction of cost-centre management, a number of departmental reorganisations were started but one consequence of this exercise in management change and drive towards cost efficiency was to sour relations at Shire Hall at both officer and member level. Some of the change was attributable to a change in management style. Bob Gash had been a genial, albeit distant, boss. If a complaint arrived – one normally had at least two to three a week, Bob Gash would simply pass them on and ask me to investigate and report back. Tony Allen kept himself much more to himself; was far more forceful and did not suffer fools gladly. Under Tony Allen, complaints were still passed on to me to investigate but accompanied by a lengthy critique, with an assumption that someone in the organisation was at fault. It was almost as if my Department were guilty until they could prove themselves innocent. There was no sense of partnership or working to a common goal. As you might imagine, that approach did not go down well. On one occasion I received a memorandum from the Chief Executive complaining that someone in my department had withdrawn an item he had personally written from the Information Technology Panel Agenda. He had not agreed to this, so would I kindly get a grip on my Department? I showed the memo to Joey Rowe, Head of Committee Administration in the County Secretariat, who promptly blew a gasket. It transpired that Joey had been phoned by the Chief Executive's Secretary and had been asked to withdraw the item in question. Presumably the Secretary had made a mistake but was too afraid of her boss to own up!

63
JOEY ROWE

John Rowe, known universally as Joey, was a very old friend of mine from the time when we formed two-thirds of the Shire Hall Rugby Club front row. He had and still has an irrepressible sense of humour and was always the life and soul of the County Secretariat. A Cornishman, he was built for mining, being broad shouldered but short of stature. During my time as County Secretary he applied for and was shortlisted for the post of Clerk to the Scilly Isles Council. The whole Council was involved in the interviews, including the two representatives from the tiny island of Bryher, one of whom was a giant of a man, 6'6" tall with long black hair and beard and a gold ring in his ear. On being introduced Joey, all 5' 5", looks up at the giant and says ' Where's your parrot then?' The giant roared with laughter and they more or less offered Joey the job on the spot. But Joey's wife Kathy, sadly now deceased, had second thoughts when she realized that there was then no secondary school on the Islands so that their then teenage girls would have had to be boarded in Cornwall. So after much agonizing Joey returned to Shire Hall.

Joey was Deputy Clerk at Newbury Rural District Council before joining the Secretariat. On one occasion I went with an Assistant County Planning Officer, called David Patterson to discuss a planning problem in Newbury District. Joey was there representing the District Council and David Patterson started to introduce me very formally to Joey – '*Mr Rowe, this is Mr Williams....*'. Joey cut him short. '*No introductions needed*' he said, ' *Mr Williams and I are old lovers*'. You should have seen the look on David Patterson's face.

On one occasion they were digging up the car park. I was standing besides this large hole when Joey walked by and asked '*What's up? Has the Chairman lost 50p?*'.

Prior to the Royal Opening of Shinfield Park in April 1982, Joey posted an 'official' notice on the Secretariat Notice-Board. It informed the Department that a special loo had been installed for her Majesty's use and a volunteer lady was needed to sit on it for an hour or so before the visit to 'warm it up' before possible royal usage! To Joey's amazement and slight consternation this spoof resulted in 5 ladies of the Secretariat volunteering to perform this vital civic function. Whether they then believed Joey's explanation that their services would not in the event be required as the Queen had deputed the task to one of her Ladies-in-Waiting, I have my doubts, but suffice to say that Joey managed to get away with it without being torn limb from limb.

64
MANAGEMENT TEAM RE-ORGANIZATION

Another indication of the growing estrangement between me and the Chief Executive arose when he reorganized his Management Team and left me off. However, he stated that the Chief Officers could as a Group elect an additional two members of the Management Team. I put my hat in the ring but was not elected – I think the Chief Fire Officer and County Librarian were the successful candidates. This was a real shock to the system and severely bruised my amour-propre. In the aftermath for the first time I started thinking about pursuing a career outside local government. In the event my omission did not do any real harm. If anything were decided I found out about it quickly enough. I also reflected that my failure to get elected was probably more a case of old scores being settled on the part of some Chief Officers, who resented the former dominance of the Clerk, than a reflection on my personal abilities.

However, by 1988 Shire Hall was a very unhappy place. There was widespread unhappiness among the staff and an underground satirical magazine entitled 'Managers Health &(In) Efficiency' was doing the rounds. Here are two extracts :

PERSONAL COLUMN

OBITUARY

Chief Officers Management Team – of boredom, after a long illness. No flowers. Donations to Distressed Gentlefolk Association; Help the Aged and Exit

FOR SALE

APRICOTS

Large stock, stoned and rather bruised but still OK for trifles, curries etc Ext 3900

(As previously mentioned the County Council had bought £500K of personal computers from a firm called Apricot, where the Director of Information Technology, who loved his curries, had previously worked.)

65
SOURING OF RELATIONS AT MEMBER LEVEL

Relations also soured at member level. On 5th May 1988 at the Annual Meeting of the Council I was asked to take the Chair while the Council approved the Conservative Group's nominations for Chairmen and Vice-Chairmen of the Council's Committees. I was not very happy at this suggestion –it was actually contrary to the Council's Standing Orders - but I was assured that it would be a formality. However when it came to the Personnel Committee Vice-Chairmanship, Ron Jewitt, the Conservative Leader stated that he was not in a position to put forward a nomination. Quick as a flash, John Leston, the Alliance Leader, saw an opportunity to make mischief and nominated Mr Trevor Brown, a Liberal-Democrat member of the Committee as Vice-Chairman. Trevor Brown was a lovely man but he had never chaired a Committee in his life and he would have been totally out of his depth if he had been elected. He was as much taken aback as everyone else by John Leston's action. Immediately there was uproar in the Chamber and my attempts to restore order and get the Conservatives off the hook severely back-fired; instead of shouting at each other, all parties rounded on me. The Chairman of the Council, Gareth Gimblett, and the Chief Executive were on the platform with me but I was left to get on with it. The meeting quickly descended into pandemonium and in the end I had had enough. I apologized for my part in the shambles that had just taken place and then announced my resignation as County Secretary and walked out of the Chamber. There was a stunned silence as I left.

Not long after I arrived home the phone started ringing and Peter Leigh, the County Property Officer, who was a longstanding colleague, kindly drove all the way from his home in Wokingham to Upper Basildon to persuade me to change my mind and withdraw my resignation. It took a long time but eventually I cooled down, and withdrew my resignation, which was gratefully accepted. But deep down I knew that this was the final nail in the coffin and after this incident I resolved to quit local government when the first suitable opportunity occurred.

The local paper, the Reading Evening Post, now defunct, really went to town on the Council, publishing the following editorial on May 9th 1988

'They put one of their most respected officers in an impossible position, pilloried him when he could not reply and did not lift a finger to help him.

Instead they asked him for a public apology. As a professional and honourable man, the county secretary both apologized and resigned. Fortunately, after colleagues and councillors pleaded with him over the week-end he announced today that he would stay on. It would have been a sorry day for the County if it had lost one of its most senior and experienced officers as result of political horseplay that got out of hand.

Not a single councillor would seriously claim Mr Williams was the tool of any political party. Yet in the heat of the moment that was the allegation they flung in his face. As Council leader Ron Jewitt says it was an appalling abuse of power by politicians. Councillors now readily admit it is they who bear the real responsibility.

THEY asked Mr Williams to supervise the election of the Personnel sub-committee Vice-Chairman in breach of their own standing orders.

THEY were responsible for the bungle which let the opposition nominate their own candidate, Trevor Brown, after the Tories declared none of the ruling group was standing. It was then as the pandemonium had already erupted, Mr Williams made his procedural error of calling a vote for Councillor Brown, who by rights should have been automatically elected.

Mr Williams's real mistake was not thinking fast enough on his feet at the end of a long day while surrounded by shouting and screaming politicians. The incident was all the more shocking because it was out of character with the normally civilised proceedings. But Berkshire's councillors now have a long way to go to regain the respect of both their officers and the electorate. '

Three days after the AGM, Chairman Gareth Gimblett wrote to me and my colleague Chief Officers apologizing on behalf of the Council for the way I had been treated, writing as follows:-

'I write concerning the deplorable events that marred the Council meeting last Saturday which, as some of you know, I condemned at that time and when I resumed the Chair. The behaviour of some County Councillors and the attacks made on the integrity of the County Secretary were inexcusable, and may certainly have undermined the confidence of some Chief Officers in the Council's proceedings.

No Chief Officer should be placed in the exposed position that the County Secretary found himself in last Saturday. Indeed, the Standing Orders of the Council are framed so as to avoid such a situation. In future the election of Chairmen and Vice-Chairman of Committees must be conducted as part of the normal agenda of the Council, so that the handling of any problems which arise becomes the direct responsibility of the Council Chairman – an elected member rather than an Officer.

The chaos of last Saturday was an aberration which could have been avoided and will not occur again during my period of office as Chairman. I am most conscious that the good working of this Council depends very much on continuing mutual trust and confidence between members and officers. If such trust and confidence has been lost as a result of Saturday's events, I am anxious that they should be restored as quickly as possible.' Gareth Gimblett – Chairman of the County Council

Frederick Gareth Robert Gimblett CBE DL was a biologist, who had been a lecturer at Reading University. He was a fellow Welshman and coincidentally his family roots also lay in Clydach, Swansea Valley.

Relations between the political groups on the Council remained sour during my remaining time at the Council. On 5th October 1988 John Leston, Leader of the Alliance Group issued a lengthy Press Release accusing the Tories, and by implication the Chief Executive, of mismanagement on a wide range of issues. The 'macho management style' prevailing at Shire Hall was criticized as was plummeting staff morale. The Tories were also criticized for the procedure followed in appointing the former County Quantity Surveyor as County Property Officer.

According to John Leston in his Press Release '*The Tories' record in recent months is a new and powerful script for 101 ways in how not to run a Council. They have forced out or alienated Chief Officers, presided over a totally unacceptable level of staff turnover, got themselves into a crisis over how to handle competitive tendering, have conducted totally bogus and insulting so-called 'consultations', and run up a bill to date in excess of a quarter of a million pounds employing outside consultants to help them do all this*'.

Following this broadside Mrs Liz Grugeon, The Branch Secretary of Berkshire County Officers NALGO, wrote to Gareth Gimblett on behalf of her members on 18th October 1988, stating that John Leston was only saying what she had been saying for months without anyone taking her seriously, so would the Council now discuss the issues raised? I have to add that Liz Grugeon was a well-respected member of the staff of the Secretariat, very much a moderate, level-headed lady and not at all a firebrand or militant.

However a copy of her letter was passed to the Chief Executive and the following day she received the following reply:

'I am sure you will have heard by now the references made to your interest in this item. It was also commented upon that you did not even have the courtesy to send a copy to the Leader of the Council or myself. Apparently you rate the press as more important.

On the substance of what you say in your letter, I made the point to the Committee that in the past twelve months I cannot remember any occasion when you have approached me about matters of staff morale. Your Union have commented on some of the departmental reorganisations during consultation programmes, but not one time, as far as I am aware, have you or your union taken any steps to bring your general concerns on behalf of the staff about morale or any other important matter to the attention of top management.

I am sure your Union would have more support and more credibility if it sought to discuss management matters with management in a responsible and constructive way. Expressing your views via elected Members and the press is not what I would regard as either appropriate or constructive in the first instance.'

A J Allen – Chief Executive

As David Over said to me recently, by 1992, three years after I had left, no-one at Shire Hall agreed with anyone on anything, apart from just one thing – everyone disliked the Chief Executive! He had many good points to make – but his cold, clinical approach did not endear him to anyone. Not that that would have bothered Tony. He had one very thick skin and always gave the impression that he was indifferent to personal criticism and really did not care what people thought about him. After he had left Shire Hall he became a Governor at Newbury College and he then chaired the Governing Body for several years. But he became unpopular there as well and eventually he could not get anyone to second him when he stood for re-election as Chairman. I can not think of anyone else who in that position would not then have walked away from the College, but Tony simply reverted to becoming a back-bench Governor.

66
THE CENTENARY COUNCIL MEETING

see colour pages XXIII-XXV

One of my happier memories from this period was the celebration of the County Council's centenary on 1st April 1989. I suggested that we held a light-hearted County Council meeting, with everyone dressing up in Victorian clothes. To my surprise this was agreed and as the photographs included in the book show, everyone entered into the spirit.

I also felt it would be appropriate to have a centenarian as guest of honour, so I advertised in the local press and had three replies – all ladies. I arranged to meet them but the first died before the meeting took place. The second lady was in a County Council home in Maidenhead. I went there and met the centenarian and her niece. The niece said '*Auntie – here's the nice Mr Williams from Shire Hall. Would you like to go to the Centenary meeting in Reading?*'. '*No, I wouldn't*' replied her aunt very firmly. The poor niece was very embarrassed.

That left just Mrs Rose Diggens of 50, Watlington Street in Reading. She lived in a basement flat and when I entered she was sitting there with her hat and coat on and clutching her hand-bag – ready to go! She looked 80; her son was with her – he was 70 but looked 50 and the granddaughter must have been 40 but looked 20.The whole family was in a time warp. '*But Mrs Diggens, the meeting is not for two months*' I said!

She made the meeting all right and what a story she had to tell. There were 6 Diggens boys in Thatcham – all butchers and all enlisted in the 1st World War and 5 survived. She was a Thatcham girl as well and went into service in Ealing during the War. When her fiancé returned they were married and they set up a butcher's shop in Watlington Street, running it for 50 years. Her father was a well-digger in Reading. She could remember him getting up at 4.am on a Monday morning to walk to Reading, returning Saturday tea-time, with his money hidden under his socks on account of the fear of being robbed by foot-pads.

67
EARLY RETIREMENT

In Spring 1989 I applied for and was granted early retirement in the next round of voluntary redundancies. I was not replaced as County Secretary – the Committee side of the Secretariat was placed under the Chief Executive but my post as County Solicitor devolved on two of my close colleagues – Ralph Garbett and David Over while Andrew Menzies, the third Assistant County Solicitor at that time became the County Council's Monitoring Officer, charged with ensuring that everyone acted legally and obeyed the rules.

I decided to leave the County Council with good grace. The previous three years had been difficult but had been outweighed by the many previous good times. At my final Council meeting in July 1989, when William Anthony (Tony) Wiseman was Chairman, I presented the Council with a very nice ceramic plate, bearing the County Council coat-of-arms, made by Julian Bellmont at the Aldermaston pottery. I received a standing ovation in return which rather took me aback but it was a very pleasant gesture on the Council's part. The plate disappeared in 1998 but has recently come to light in the County Record Office. I also have another in my possession, presented to me by my colleagues at Shire Hall.

see colour pages XXVI-XXIX

By the time I came to leave there was talk of unitary government in the air. It was known that John Redwood, the Member of Parliament for Wokingham was in favour and at the time he was an influential member of the Government. Christina asked Tony Wiseman, the new Chairman, what action the Conservatives were taking as regards the proposal to bring in unitary government. She remembers his reply very clearly '*Christina, I can assure you of one thing. Berkshire will not fight for its own survival.*' I knew that the Labour Group supported the break-up of the County Council, as they were strong in Reading and Slough, and stood to gain control there, as indeed has proved to be the case. But I never understood why the Conservative Group were initially of the same persuasion.

So at first it was only the Liberal Democrat Group that argued the case for retaining a County Council. Later when it transpired that Berkshire would the only historic County to be abolished, the Conservative group changed its mind but by then it was too late.

The County Council took a long time to die – it was not finally dissolved until 1998. The final Liberal Democrat Chairman of the Council was also the first and only Lady Chairman – Mrs Ann Risman OBE, married to Bev Risman, a former English Rugby Union International. Ann is an old friend and so Christina and I were invited to several of the closing ceremonies.

68
SALE OF SHIRE HALL- 1988

The County Council was created in 1888 and decided to establish itself in Reading – the County town had previously been Abingdon and the first Clerk, Mr Morland came from Abingdon. He did not retire until he was 81 and in later years he often used to find himself ending up in Bristol as he would fall fast asleep by the time his train reached Didcot, where he was meant to change for Abingdon.

see colour pages I-III *and* V

Initially the County Council leased and then bought a row of three houses in the Forbury, owned by Suttons Seeds and sited next to the firm's seed repository. By 1912 the County Council had built its new Shire Hall for £16,000, with all the windows facing the Seed repository having to be frosted over, to stop County Council staff spying on what the Sutton Seed employees were about in their seed repository.

As already mentioned the seed repository and Forbury House next door were demolished in 1961 to make way for the Prudential's rather hideous office block, which was built on stilts, as the original Reading County Borough plan was to run the Reading IDR (Inner Distribution Road) through the Forbury.

The new Shire Hall was never large enough from day one to house all the Council's staff. By 1961 it housed only the Clerk's and Treasurer's departments and by the time the move to Shinfield Park took place in 1980/81, only the Chief Executive and his staff, plus the County Treasurer and his Department were accommodated in Shire Hall. The Secretariat occupied a two story terrapin on land owned by the County Council next to the Abbey Gateway – the other 11 Departments were scattered around Reading in rented accommodation.

Shire Hall was redundant on the move to Shinfield Park in 1981 but it took 7 years to find a buyer. This was the Grosvenor Estates (the Duke of Westminster's property Company), who eventually turned the building into an hotel – the Forbury Hotel. They paid £1.5m. But having bought the building the Company ran into a planning problem as regards usage. Although I had left the County Council and was working at Field Seymour Parkes, they approached me and I gave them an affidavit which set out the uses of the building dating back to 1961. This did the trick and they obtained their consent.

By way of thank-you they later invited me to their monthly luncheon in Grosvenor Square. I went along to join a crowd of architects, surveyors, valuers,

thought, trapped in her car, they obligingly and very speedily cut off the top of her car and lifted her out of what was now an open top car! You couldn't make it up and, of course, not a word was said to the Fire Authority.

The Thames Valley Police Authority in those days had a Chairman, Vice-Chairman and Deputy Chairman and by convention, each County held one of these positions. Dr Peter Phillips OBE actually lived in Cookham but was Chairman of Bucks Policy Committee and Deputy Chairman of TVPA. As if that were not enough he also Chaired the Authority that ran the Royal Berkshire and Battle Hospitals in Reading. He also had an art gallery, specializing in the Staithes artists – I bought several works from his gallery over the years. I hit it off with Peter (sadly now deceased). He came from a very poor part of Cardiff but had worked his way up and become a successful engineer, before immersing himself in public service. He persuaded me to join his Health Authority. It was voluntary work but interesting, though one never felt really in control. Then the Government decided to set up the New Health Authority framework. By this time I was his Vice-Chairman and I worked with him in submitting nominations to fill the new Trusts. All our nominations were accepted except mine. I was rejected by the Minister, Brian Mawhinney (now Lord Mawhinney), as having no health experience! Apparently the administrator who had handled the paperwork had used my old CV. Peter was so embarrassed by this that he persuaded me to become Secretary to his Trust at a salary of £5K a year, which is what all the Non-Executive Directors then received under the new system. So I added Secretaryship of the Royal Berks & Battle Hospitals (NHS) Trust to my clerking portfolio. If it moved in Berkshire I clerked it! I remained as Secretary until Peter stood down in 2001 and was replaced by Colin Maclean OBE.

In 1996 I saw an advertisement for Clerk to the Lincolnshire Police Authority. I knew that the Deputy Clerk at Lincolnshire County Council also handled police matters and was very competent, so I assumed he would be appointed. But Lincoln is a beautiful city, which I had once visited when Roger Forshaw moved there from Berkshire to work for Lindsey County Council, as it then was, and I thought a day out in Lincoln would be enjoyable, so I submitted an application. At the interview I discovered that the Deputy Clerk had withdrawn and there was no real competition. But I made it clear that I would not move to Lincoln – I would spend 2 days a week on the job, if appointed, and would commute, staying overnight if necessary. And I asked for a fee of £35K a year. Much to my amazement they offered me the job. I still did not understand why until the end of my first week. I then discovered it was all to do with the Chief Constable, Peter Bensley. He had been the Deputy and had been passed over twice before they gave him the top job. It was a big mistake, because he did not realize that times had changed. As he saw it was his job to police Lincolnshire. If he needed additional resources then he needed to call a meeting of the Police Authority to vote him what he needed. But he did not see the role of the Police Authority as any more than that – certainly not setting policy. In his view all policing was operational and that was down to him.

The Police Authority knew that this was not how the new system was meant to work but they needed an experienced Clerk to stand up to the Chief Constable and fight their corner. I was that experienced Clerk and hence the offer of the post. To be fair to Peter Bensley once he knew how the system was going to operate, he was fine and I never had any problems with him.

I really enjoyed Lincolnshire. It is a large county in area with 1000 Parishes (Berkshire has 100) and as it has no motorways, it is operating 30 years behind the rest of the country. They really know how to feud in Lincolnshire; there were some rare old battles when I was there, mainly centred on the Cathedral, though the County Council was also often involved. Coincidentally David Bowles, the former Treasurer at Berkshire was appointed as Chief Executive of Lincolnshire, though we never met there. The Lincolnshire County Council Treasurer and then Treasurer of the Police Authority was Roger Buttery. We got on like a house on fire and are still in touch.

I have many happy memories of Lincolnshire. The Police Authority had its HQ at Nettleham, just outside Lincoln. You can find the ruins of the Bishop's Palace there, where Edward 1 was presiding when he created his son Prince of Wales. But travel south and you reach Sempringham, where there is a ruined nunnery. After Prince Llewelyn of Wales was killed near Builth in 1284, all his male relatives were put to death. But he had a 6 month old daughter called Gwenllian and killing females was not permitted. So Gwenllian was sent to the nunnery at Sempringham and stayed there for the rest of her life. She died in 1337 and was buried at Sempringham. Her grave is unknown but when I visited in 1999 there were fresh daffodils at the entrance to the site, commemorating the last true Princess of Wales.

Occasionally Christina used to join me and we used to explore Lincolnshire. It took us a whole weekend just to go round the Cathedral and Castle. The Castle has on display the Lincolnshire copy of Magna Carta – all Counties were given a copy but many have disappeared. The Castle also has the original Chapel, which was designed so that prisoners could not see each other; just the preacher. The only prisoners who could see each other were those in the front row. They would have been the ones who had been condemned to death and they had to sit there with their coffins in front of them. This regime of forced solitude was eventually abandoned, as it was driving too many prisoners mad.

On another occasion we visited Hull. There is a lane there called ' the Land of Green Ginger'. I had heard about it and had always wanted to see it. It is in the medieval part of the City. We liked Hull but we were there on a Friday night. It seemed as though all the men were in the bars and pubs, while the women linked arms and marched arm in arm down the main street. The sight of 15 women aged from 50 to 18, with linked arms, marching towards you is quite terrifying but fortunately I had Christina there to protect me.

There are 7 District Councils in Lincolnshire and the Police Authority used to hold quarterly Consultative meetings in each District. I used to attend most of these with either the Chairman or Deputy Chairman of the Police Authority and the local Area Commander. They could be held in the most out of the way places. You would be driving round this fen in the mist, hoping to hell you would not drive into a drain, as the Fen waterways are called, searching for the village hall. When you found it, it would be totally isolated, with scarcely a house in sight. Yet once you walked through the doors, the place would be packed and you wondered where on earth they had all come from.

The meeting that stands out most in my mind was at Castle Bytham, near Stamford, in south Lincolnshire. Beforehand the Area Commander almost apologized that there was so little crime, so I assumed a short and easy meeting. Quite the reverse – I think the local Councillor was standing for re-election and had made law and order her theme. In the process she had wound up her constituents. We were subject to a barrage of criticism and one would have thought that Castle Bytham was the subject of an out-of-control crime wave. By the end of the meeting we were quite shell-shocked. When the audience had departed there was just one local resident left. He came down and introduced himself. He had not long moved to Castle Bytham from Manchester. He wanted to be accepted into his new community, so he had not said anything during the meeting but he wanted us to know that he had just had to listen to the biggest load of twaddle he had ever heard. There had been more crime in a week in the street where he used to live in Manchester than in the whole of Castle Bytham in a year. He thought the Police in Lincolnshire were doing a magnificent job, so keep it up. We left feeling much better.

My time in Lincolnshire came to an end when Peter Bensley reverted to type. He had a protégé female officer, Dena Fleming, whom he promoted to Inspector. Then there was a falling out – the fault for this would need to be apportioned as in some ways Dena Fleming was a mirror image of Peter Bensley. She then took a case to an Employment Tribunal and the Chief Constable defended it, even briefing a Queen's Counsel. But not a word was said to me as Clerk or to the Police Authority. We only found out about the case when it made the national papers. The Authority were naturally furious.

10th DECEMBER 1998 – Invested with the OBE at Buckingham Palace by the Prince of Wales.
Honour received for services to the community of Berkshire.
I was accompanied by Christina and my daughter, Rebecca, and son, Robert.

CHRISTINA SWORN IN AS HIGH SHERIFF OF THE ROYAL COUNTY OF BERKSHIRE AT THE CROWN COURT, READING, ON APRIL 2nd 2009.

She is the second member of her family to have held the office of High Sheriff but there was a gap of 426 years!

CHRISTINA WITH HER CHAPLAINS – FATHER BRUCE BARNES (left) and FATHER DOMINIC GOLDING (right)

Christina's theme for her Shrieval Year was 'Bringing the Generations together'. Together we devised a 'Beating-the-bounds of Berkshire' charity walk to raise funds for Age Concern (Berkshire). 18 walks were researched with historical commentary, covering 139 miles and taking place in May 2009. Berkshire Youth's 'V' Volunteers helped with marshalling and transport and the author's Pangbourne Rotary Club were also involved. Prince Philip agreed to act as Patron and started us off. Colin Preston (to left of Author) was there in his capacity as Chairman of Age Concern (Woodley)

Kay Everett – a Trustee of the Charity was also a Freeman of Reading, so we exercised her right to drive a flock of sheep across Caversham Bridge, followed by a flock of human sheep from Thameside School. The sheep came from John Bishop of Rushall Farm and the shepherd's smock – an authentic copy – was supplied by the Museum of English Rural Life.

Finish of walk at Windsor Park. We raised £6,000. Christina and the author walked 100 miles but Jeff Gardner (holding the B-t-B stick) and his wife Carole, walked the entire way. Theresa May MP and her husband walked the Maidenhead leg. The stick was afterwards presented to the Museum of English Rural life.

LAUNCH OF BERKSHIRE GARDENS TRUST – JULY 2009 at ENGLEFIELD HOUSE

Christina with the Hon Mary Bayliss (Lord Lieutenant) and all the Berkshire Mayors (of both Town and Borough Councils) and the Chairman of West Berkshire District.

Formation of the Berkshire Gardens Trust was Christina's initiative. Berkshire was the last County to form a County Gardens Trust.

PRESENTATION OF A HIGH SHERIFF CERTIFICATE TO STEPHANIE STEEVENSON (Mayor of Thatcham), in recognition of Thatcham's Litter Pick.

PRESENTATION OF A HIGH SHERIFF CERTIFICATE TO ANNE DEWING,
who had organized an Upper Basildon Clean-Up.

PRESENTATION OF A HIGH SHERIFF CERTIFICATE TO MRS NAOMI ROBINSON JP DL on the occasion of her 90th birthday. Naomi was Chairman of Keep Berkshire Tidy, through whom Christina and the Author first met. She died in March 2018, aged 98.To the author's best knowledge until her death she was the oldest surviving County Councillor.

VISIT TO BERKSHIRE FIRE SERVICE AT WHITLEY ROAD FIRE STATION -
Fire Authority Chairman and Iain Cox (Chief Fire Officer) in attendance

Unlike the County's Finance & General Purposes Committee, who flinched at the challenge laid down by the Hon Elizabeth Samuel, Christina had no qualms about ascending to the heights in the Brigade's Hydraulic platform.

With JOHN ALVIS (High Sheriff of Somerset) and four other High Sheriffs at the Somerset Crown Court Service, held in Wells Cathedral.

Processing down Guildford High Street, flanked by the High Sheriffs of East and West Sussex, on the way to Surrey Crown Court Service.

PRESENTATION OF SHRIEVAL CERTIFICATE TO
SIR WILLIAM BENYON DL AT ENGLEFIELD HOUSE

TOPPING OUT CEREMONY FOR NEW DOLPHIN CENTRE AT PANGBOURNE 2009

Note the Shrieval flag on the Jag. Fixed on by a magnet, it comes off if you drive over 20mph. So you have to find somewhere quiet a few hundred yards from your destination; fix it on and then drive very slowly!

OPENING PANGBOURNE ROTARY CLUB'S ART EXHIBITION
AT PANGBOURNE VILLAGE HALL – APRIL 2010

With Peter Harris (President); John Rowell (now deceased) and Author

HIGH SHERIFF'S RECEPTION – JUNE 2009 at BRADFIELD COLLEGE

During her Shrieval Year Christina undertook around 350 engagements.
The author accompanied her to about half of these.

THE AUTHOR WITH HIS GRAND-SONS GEORGE & HENRY WILLIAMS -

Clewer Infants School, Windsor - 2016

THE AUTHOR WITH CHRISTINA AND PROFESSOR DWARKA NATH (TUTU) BOSE -

Visit to House of Lords - 2016

AUTHOR WITH HIS DAUGHER REBECCA (BECKY)
AT DULWICH COLLEGE - 2017

Sir Ernest Shackleton sailed the James Caird 700 miles from Elephant Island to South Georgia to rescue the crew of the Endeavour after it was crushed in the ice. The author and Christina will be visiting South Georgia in January 2020

WITH DAVID OVER ON TOUR IN 2017.

Facing a bleak future two former County Solicitors entertain the punters as best they can.

house backed onto a private street, which was a cul-de-sac and he took it upon himself to create his own private car park by fencing off most of it. Later he built a wall. My friend, Anthony Cosslett, lives on the other side of the private street and objected to Mr Morris's actions, as did many others. A protest meeting was held but when Morris saw this on returning from work, he drove his car into the protesters putting three of them, including Anthony Cosslett, in hospital. The Police took no action but when some time later, the protesters decided to knock down the wall that had by now been built, Morris called the police and it was the protesters who were all arrested. When they were released without charge at midnight and returned home, there was Morris to jeer at them, so he had obviously been tipped off by one of his police friends. Later Morris attacked Anthony Cosslett and beat him unconscious. There was a witness but yet again no action was taken. I did my best to get some justice for my friend but sadly I failed. All that was achieved was to get rid of the unlawful enclosure. Thames Valley Police and Lincs Police were not perfect but I like to think this degree of corruption would never have been allowed to take place in the policing areas with which I was associated. It saddens me that the worst police corruption I have ever personally encountered took place in my home town.

71
VOLUNTEERING

Sidney and Beatrice Webb were well-known Socialists at the start of the last Century and they founded the Fabian Society. Beatrice Webb once said that she and Sidney had a perfect marriage: '*Sidney takes all the big decisions and I decide which are the big decisions*'. That sums up my parents' marriage to a T. My mother was the power behind the throne and what she said went. As mentioned in the Preface, I come from a teaching family, yet when I was 7 I remember my mother saying '*You will be a teacher over my dead body*'. She meant what she said and both I and my younger brother, Paul, ended up as solicitors. She was probably right. I remember telling her about my promotion in 1969 to Assistant Clerk at Berkshire on a salary of £2,800. She replied, '*I am very pleased for you Clive but you do realize that you are now earning more than your father and I think that is an absolute disgrace.*' Which it was – my father was then Deputy Head of Cardiff High School, the most successful state school academically in the whole of Wales and yet his pay was below that of a third-tier County Council officer.

My mother also had strict rules on honesty – there were no shades of grey. I remember my father was once laying down a cement path. He had almost finished the job when he ran out of sand. We lived at the top of a hill and very conveniently the Council had placed a bunker of sand near the front of our house. I never saw it used and I think it must have been intended to assist horse-drawn transport struggling to climb the hill in winter. But as when I was growing up there were no longer any horse-drawn transport, the sand just lay there unused. So my father nipped out and got a shovelful of this sand to finish his path. But he was spotted by my mother and she made him put it back. In consequence he had to trek up to the village with his barrow and buy a whole barrowful of sand, most of which he did not need. But as far as my mother was concerned the sand in the bunker was Corporation property and taking it would be stealing. As I wrote at the start of this paragraph – there were no shades of grey.

It was also my mother's strong belief that it was your duty to try and put back more into society than you drew out. So this was ingrained in my psyche from an early age and inevitably this led me into volunteering. At Cambridge I was active during the annual Poppy Appeal / Rag Day - one year I was my College joint organizer along with my friend John Labrum. Our College raised £350 - a considerable amount in 1960 and there were over 20 Colleges participating. We spent a happy day shaving a Belisha Beacon and polishing the brass studs.

This built up a queue of vehicles stretching back a very long way, all of whom were taxed to be allowed to drive over our handiwork.

SAMARITANS

When an Articled Clerk at Shire Hall I volunteered to become a Samaritan. Once a fortnight I would go to St Giles' Church Hall in Southampton Street and then man a phone for the whole night. I received very little training but mostly you just needed to be there to listen and be sympathetic. But there was one rather horrible individual, who lived off begging and was known to treat his mother abysmally. Then he would phone the Samaritans, say he was going to kill himself, and look for sympathy. I was subjected once to this but then I had a second encounter. He phoned me and said he was going to throw himself under a train. I replied. '*It is now 9.00pm; if you can get down to the station by 9.25pm, you will be in time to catch the 9.30pm train*'. This was a bit brutal and probably not in the training manual but it had the desired effect. All talk of suicide was forgotten and instead he entered into a tirade against me for not caring. In his case I didn't. Ironically a few weeks later he was killed by a train but it was an accident, not suicide. He was begging down at the station; someone on a train offered him some money just as the train started to pull out of the station and running to take the money from the out-stretched arm, he slipped and fell between the platform and the train. A gruesome end for an unpleasant individual.

YOUTH WORK

Working with young people has been at the heart of much of my volunteering. When I first moved to Upper Basildon in 1973 it was clear that the Village needed a Youth Club as there was nothing else for young people to do. So I and a friend Kelvin Bryon started one in the Village Hall. It was very hard work but quite rewarding in a masochistic kind of way. One problem was Frank Dixon, Chairman of the Village Hall Committee. The Village Hall had been erected in the 30's and showed its age. But Frank and his wife were keen ball-room dancers, so the floor had been brought up to ball-room standard. This meant that every Friday evening was spent running the Youth Club and every Saturday morning saw Kelvin and myself crawling round the floor, polishing out the scratches made by the Youth Club. When after 4 years Kelvin moved to Pangbourne it was no surprise that I could not find anyone to step into his shoes and the Youth Club closed.

But in 1977 I then started taking some of the former Basildon Youth Club members down to the Pangbourne Youth Club, which was held in what is now known as the Dolphin Centre. In what seemed no time at all I became

Chairman of the Management Committee running the Centre. The Centre was leased by the County Council from the Parish Council and when in 1998 the County Council was replaced by West Berkshire District Council, the District Council took over the Lease. The District Council then decided to re-build the Centre at a cost of £1.3m, if the Management Committee would contribute £300K. So I formed a fund-raising Charity in 2005 and eventually raised £350K. I knew Stuart Tagg, who was the Chief Executive of the Greenham Common Trust and duly submitted an application for a grant. I have previously mentioned how far-sighted West Berkshire Council were to set up this Trust to run the former American industrial estate at Greenham Common – it has kept many a Charity in West Berks afloat. Anyway one day Stuart Tagg phoned me at home. He said '*Clive, we are going to give you one hundred and fifty*'. My immediate thought was '*how stingy – I was hoping for a few thousands at the very least*'. Fortunately I kept silent. Just as well, as the Greenham Trust gave us £150K. Three years ago the West Berkshire Council said it could no long take responsibility for the volunteers operating out of the Centre, so the fund-raising Charity was turned into an Operating Charity for volunteers. The latest twist in the saga is that budget constraints are such that the District Council now wants to get shot of all responsibility for running the Centre. So the Operating Charity are submitting a bid to take over the running of the whole Centre.

I have had two other attempts to run a Youth Club in Upper Basildon. When Ann Schlee and I were Church Wardens, we obtained the agreement of the then Vicar, the Rev Alan Hogarth, and the PCC (Parochial Church Council) to use the Church Centre. Then James Tyrrell (now sadly deceased) and I, plus a band of volunteers from the Church started another Youth Club. It ran for 5 years but some of the boys were wild and at times uncontrollable. One Jamie Smith, on one occasion, walked in football boots right over James' beloved veteran Jaguar car. It scratched it from one end to the other and how James managed to keep his cool is beyond me. But I heard a year back that the said Jamie Smith now has a steady job and is a model citizen, so maybe we did some good.

But after the Youth Club folded some of the boys, including Jamie Smith and his brother Ricky, were very keen to play football. James Tyrrell had attended Bradfield School and had played soccer for England schools. He discovered that there was an indoor 5-a-side League being run at the Northcroft Centre in Newbury and although they were all men's teams, we could enter a team with our 14 and 15 year olds. So we entered and although our boys did their best and never gave up, each week they received a pasting. On one occasion we were due to play Cold Ash and the Smith brothers had with them their cousin, down from London, who asked if he could come along to watch. He was a little lad, who looked about 12, so we squeezed him in. At half-time it was Cold Ash 8 – Basildon Boys 0. Each half was 15 minutes, so Cold Ash had been scoring a goal every two minutes. The cousin then said that he had played a bit, so could he go on as a replacement. We had nothing to lose so Jamie Smith came off and his cousin went on. The next 15 minutes were extraordinary. Our pint-sized Pele pulverized the opposition. They just could not cope with him. He scored 7 goals and would have won the match had he had a few more minutes. He admitted afterwards that he had been on the books of Brentford FC since he was 9!

Three years ago I had another go at starting the Youth Club, but this time paying for a Leader. The money comes from the School House fund. The Church owns the School House, which I manage ; it is rented and the surplus can be used for Youth Projects. After a sticky start the Club has taken off and we have a membership of 27. This is so large that we have had to hire an Assistant Youth Leader.

The Club meets in the New Village Hall in the Dixon room. But it also uses the Bruton room. Frank Dixon has already been mentioned. He and his wife had no children and when the Dixons died they left their sizeable estate 'to the village' to build a new Hall. The Brutons did likewise. The result was that Basildon has one of the finest Village Halls in the County. I became Chairman of the the Village Hall Trust in 2017. They were short of Trustees and I volunteered.

My other youth volunteering involves the Berkshire Youth Charity, where I was Company Secretary for many years and am now a Trustee. This is an amalgamation of the Berkshire Boys Clubs Association and Berkshire Youth Clubs. It runs some Youth Clubs and provides a range of services to its 150 affiliated Clubs, As mentioned previously the President of Berkshire Youth is Roger Smee MBE.

NAOMI HOUSE

In the 90's I chaired the Reading, Wokingham and Bracknell Committee that raised £500K for Naomi House in Sutton Scotney,Hampshire. The building cost £4m to erect and the Naomi Trust need several millions a year to run it. It provides respite care for children with terminal illnesses and their families. Mrs Sue Balchin MBE, formerly Clerk of the Berkshire General Commissioners of Income Tax was on my Committee and was a great help – she knew everyone in Wokingham and Bracknell but sadly she too has passed away. It is surprising how easily the money rolls in if you have a good cause.

Penny West, who owned Horncastle Garage, put on a Fashion Show and Auction and raised £25K. She is no longer with us either. Dylan Williams at the Basildon (Tomb Farm) Shooting School laid on a Charity Day. There were 70 present and the auction raised £12K. In Bucklebury we tracked down the very English grand-son of Dr Scholl of Chicago, who was a Trustee of the Scholl Foundation that grant aids children's causes all round the world. That resulted in another £50K.

UNIVERSITY OF READING

I also had an 8 year stint from 1995-2003, as a Council Member of Reading University. This appointment arose from a chance meeting with the then Vice-Chancellor, Professor Roger Williams, originally from Tredegar, Monmouthshire. The University received their money's worth from me. I chaired several disciplinary Committees, as well as the Working Party, which considered what action the University needed to take in response to the Dearing Report. I was also Chairman of the St Patrick's Hall Committee. Where I failed was in not persuading the University Secretariat to emulate the County Council system of Agenda presentation, where all major reports had a one page succinct summary sheet, setting out what Councillors were being asked to approve and what it would cost if they did. Not rocket science but it worked and if they wanted more, Councillors could read the appendices. University Council agenda ran to 400 pages. They invariably came out late and were so obtuse that I, and I suspect most other Council members, never had the time or indeed energy to work their way through such a great morass of paper. What infuriated me was that every so often the University Secretariat would seek ideas on how the University could become more efficient in its administration. I would respond and refer to the County Council system and I would then see my suggestion kicked into the long grass. The reality was that the senior dons, who ran the University, liked to take the necessary decisions without Council interference, so the complex, unreformed system suited them perfectly. After my two terms of 4 years I did not seek re-election.

WATLINGTON HOUSE

In 2005 when I was still working at FSP, Philip Seymour, then Senior Partner, asked me if I would become a Trustee at Watlington House. The building stands in Watlington Street and was built by a Samuel Watlington in 1688 and extended around 1760. It provides accommodation for charities and was saved from destruction in 1930. It had previously housed Kendrick Girls School. The Trust was effectively run by Architects – John Beach (Chairman), Matt Andrews, and Ken Major, who lived close by and was the effective Manager.

The Treasurer was a retired Bank Manager. A caretaker, who didn't seem to do much, and his wife, had a flat on the top floor. The whole building had a tired look and the so-called garden was no more than a muddy parking lot. The Tin Hall at the rear, that had been put up many years previously by the School, was in such a state that it could not be used. It needed something done but at the time I had my hands full elsewhere. Then Ken Major died and the Treasurer resigned. The Chairman, John Beach, was obviously a very sick man – in fact he died not long after – so that left just Matt Andrews and me. So Matt became Chairman and I became both Secretary and Treasurer. What I then discovered horrified me – the Trust had only a few thousand pounds in the bank. It was so bad that I had to lend the Trust £10K to keep it going.

9 years of hard work followed but today the Trust has an income of £80K a year - £12K of which comes from the refurbished Tin Hall. The House is fully occupied; the roof has been fixed; the garden has been re-designed, thanks to the Berkshire Gardens Trust and looks outstanding and the Trust has £50k in the bank. As my mother would have said: '*I am glad about that.*'

THE OLD BLUECOAT SCHOOL, THATCHAM (OBS)

In 2004 I was contacted by Bobbie Wootton, who as Bobbie Collins had been the County Councillor for Thatcham. She wanted help with saving the Grade 1 listed Old Bluecoat School, which is one of Thatcham's best-known buildings. It started life in 1307 as a Chapel and was renovated by Lady Winchcombe in the C18th as a school for poor boys from Thatcham and surrounding areas. They were given blue coats to wear and the name has stuck. There were similar Blue coat schools in Newbury and Reading. The latter still exists but is located nowadays in Sonning.

The Charity school closed during the Great War, when the Headmaster went off to help the war effort in France. The building, however, continued to be used as a classroom until the 60's. Then it was leased to an antique dealer and became an antiques shop for a number of years but by 2000 it was empty. The Newbury Rural District Council had acquired the freehold of the building when it ceased to be a charity school, and when the Newbury RDC was abolished in 1974, the freehold passed to West Berkshire District Council. Around 2003 the District Council announced it was going to sell the building on the open market. Bobbie Wootton objected and won the backing of Thatcham to persuade the District Council to change its mind and retain the building for community use. So the upshot was that the freehold of the property was transferred to the Thatcham Town Council and they in turn granted a 99 year lease to the newly formed Thatcham (Old Bluecoat School) Charity, which I had set up. I became a Trustee and in 2005 after the

Chairman, Peter Allen, died unexpectedly, I replaced him as Chairman.

The building was as good as derelict when I became Chairman but now it is a thriving centre, used by a wide variety of groups and societies most days of the year. It cost £175K to put the building to rights. The Greenham Common Trust generously donated £60K; the Veolia Foundation £40K. Other Trusts gave over £50K between them and the balance came from individuals. Simon Witcomb, a musical accountant with a practice in Thatcham was the inspiration behind the monthly tea & cake concerts, which are held on Sundays from 4 -5pm. These are well written up in the Newbury Weekly News and the publicity attracts many hirers, who hitherto had been unaware that the building could be hired.

OBE

see colour page XXX

In 1998 right out of the blue I received a letter from Prime Minister Tony Bair, advising me that I was being recommended for an honour – an OBE (Officer of the Order of the British Empire). As I discovered later, 1998 was the year when the voluntary sector had been singled out for special recognition. I still don't know for certain who put me up, though I have my suspicions. I have to say that my first instinct was to refuse it as I am somewhat sceptical of the honours system. I know many individuals who deserve honours but have never been recognized, while I also know a number of individuals who have received honours, but don't in my view deserve them. However, in my case the award was to be in recognition of community service and Christina and my children thought I should accept and so on 10th December 1998, we duly turned up at Buckingham Palace, parked in the courtyard, saw some of the Royal Collection of pictures and I received my OBE from Prince Charles. On the same occasion June Whitfield, the actress, became a Dame and Wayne Sleep, the dancer, an OBE.

72
ROTARY

Rotary has become a big part of my life, so it needs a mention. John Wood-Griffiths was a member of the Caversham Rotary Club and was always trying to persuade me to join the his Club. I demurred because the Club met each week at lunch time and by the time I would have travelled from Shinfield Park to Caversham and back and attended the meeting, 2½ hours would have elapsed and that would have been too much out of my working week.

Then the Caversham Club came up with a new suggestion – to form a 'daughter' Club, based on Pangbourne and meeting Monday evenings. John Kirk, the senior partner at Field Seymour Parkes, lived in Pangbourne and was President of the Caversham Club at the time. He recruited me. Ron Jones, then Head of Theale Primary school was also recruited, while John Wood-Griffiths, who lived in Whitchurch Hill recruited a neighbour, Dick Hoskins. Coincidentally Dick, Ron and myself are all welsh and are still Club members.

From such humble beginnings the Club has prospered. Lady members first joined in the late 90's and Club membership has hovered around the 30 mark. The Club is involved in activities for both young people and the elderly. Fund raising has always played a prominent part in the life of the Club and we now have 5 fund-raising events each year, raising around £20K for charity. I run two of these events – both art shows where we sell local artists' work on commission and I help out in the other three cases. I have also served two terms as President and one as Secretary.

It is a constant battle nowadays for service clubs, such as Rotary and the Lions, to attract new members and if Club membership falls below 20 then the Club will be at risk. This happened a few years ago to Caversham. It had 45 members when the Pangbourne Club was formed, but Caversham membership had dropped so low by 2012 that the Club folded. Robin Borthwick then joined Pangbourne, the Club he had helped set up in 1989, along with the Rev Derek Spears, formerly Vicar of Earley St Peter's, who after retirement moved to live in Mortimer, which is part of Pangbourne Club's patch.

73
LONDON WELSH RUGBY FOOTBALL CLUB

I have already mentioned an encounter with Ian Pugh, former Director of Commercial Contracts at Shinfield Park, in the bar of London Welsh RFC at Old Deer Park in Kew. Ian's grandsons play for London Welsh Juniors and he sponsors their team.

The rise and fall of London Welsh in the era of professional rugby merits a book to itself – maybe one day it will be written, but it would be a Herculean task, such are the passions that are aroused. The Club was founded in 1885 and for the last 60 years has played its rugby at Old Deer Park in the shadow of the Kew Gardens Pagoda. Kew Gardens, the Rugby grounds of London Welsh and London Scottish and the Mid-Surrey Golf Club are all royal estate, with low rents but with expansion very strictly controlled.

The heyday of London Welsh RFC was in the late 60's and early 70's. They were English-Welsh Champions in 67-68 and 70-71 and supplied 7 players for the British Lions 1971 tour to New Zealand, 5 of whom played all the Tests. This is a record for any Club. The 5 'Immortals' were John Dawes, who captained the Lions and is still Club President; JPR Williams; Gerald Davies; Mervyn Davies (now deceased) and John Taylor. Mike Roberts and Geoff Evans were also on the tour party.

Hindsight is a wonderful thing and the Club should have capitalized on its success, which even in those amateur days saw crowds of 4,000 turn up at Old Deer Park to watch the team, by buying its own ground and allowing for future expansion. But it was comfortable at Old Deer Park and comfortable with its amateur status. Other Clubs were far more ambitious and by the 90's London Welsh had lost its pre-eminence and had sunk to playing in the lower leagues of London rugby.

Enter on the scene my friend Kelvin Bryon. Kelvin is the same age as myself and grew up in Newport, Monmouthshire. His wife Pat is a Welsh-speaker from Llanelli. Kelvin and Pat moved to Upper Basildon in 1971 and I met Kelvin and Pat not long after Liz and I moved there in 1973. He had not long formed his Company, Basildon Chemicals Ltd, but it was very early stages and the Company then comprised just Kelvin, his then business partner Roger Packe and Pat.

20 years on and Basildon Chemicals Ltd was prospering. At the same time Professional Rugby was finally recognized by the authorities in 1995, and the London Welsh Committee then decided to try and raise some sponsorship, so

that they could strengthen the team and begin the climb up the leagues. Kelvin was one of those who responded to the sponsorship request and thus began his association with the Club. From being one of a number of sponsors, Kelvin ended up as the main and at times the sole sponsor, and while he has deep pockets, professional rugby at the elite level requires ultra deep pockets. Eventually in part for financial reasons and in larger part on account of his wife's deteriorating health, Kelvin handed over control of the Club to a property developer - Trevor Owen Stanley- a Welshman from Anglesey, who promised major investment. However this never materialized and in 2016 the professional arm of London Welsh was dissolved. London Welsh RFC is now again a purely amateur club, still playing at Old Deer Park but in Division 6 of the Hertfordshire /Middlesex League.

I started going to London Welsh games as Kelvin's guest in the 1990's. By this time the Committee that used to run London Welsh had been succeeded by a Company, with Kelvin as Chairman. He then asked me to become a Director and I then remained a Director on and off until the arrival of Trevor Owen Stanley in 2014. I had always had my doubts about Trevor Owen Stanley and his associate Chris Samuelson, who also became a Director, as they had previously been unsuccessful in an attempt to take over Reading FC. Ian Wood-Smith of FSP, who was at the time a Director of Reading had told me that Reading doubted they could deliver on what was being promised, and ended the negotiation.

Another off period was in 2009, when the Club experienced financial difficulties and went into administration. It was bought by a Company called Saudi Global owned by a Neil Hollinshead. Bank drafts were handed over showing that the Company was good for several millions. Although by this time London Welsh had run out of funds, Kelvin put in £400K of his own money to pay off the creditors. But Neil Hollinshead was a crook. The bank references were forged and the money meant for the creditors went into his own pockets. He then fled to Saudi-Arabia but eventually returned to the UK. He was arrested and went down for 7 years for fraud. So Kelvin bought back the Club and put even more of his money into it.

Quite remarkably and in large part due to Kelvin's dogged determination, London Welsh twice made it to the Premiership in 2012/13 and 2014/15. But the Club came up against the cabal, that runs professional rugby in England and the cabal won. Back in 1995, 13 Clubs with major financial backers formed a Company to run professional Rugby. And because they were taking all the financial risks, they made most of the rules – rather than the English RFU. Originally they wanted a sealed league with no relegation – the norm is two for promotion and two for relegation. In the end there was a compromise with just one promotion and one relegation. Then they divided up the money to make sure that the original 13 Clubs were at a financial advantage to see off any potential newcomers. When London Welsh was in the Premiership in 2012 and 2014 it received just £1.5m a year from the Premiership; the other Clubs in the Premiership received over £4m a year. Even Bristol, who had been defeated by London Welsh and stayed in the Championship, received more money from the Premiership than London Welsh did, owing to Bristol's founder member status.

The final protection barrier was ground ownership. Having done a deal to rent the Kassam Stadium in Oxford for Premiership games, London Welsh were told that they could not be promoted because they did not own the ground. On pointing out that 3 other Premiership Clubs also rented their grounds they were told that the Premiership had granted 3 special exemptions, and to grant a fourth would undermine the integrity of the Premiership. It took legal action to get the Premiership to accept that London Welsh could be promoted and play their games at Kassam.

In fact only one Club – Exeter – has broken the Cabal's grip. They sold their original ground for major development and bought another. They also have a wealthy backer and enjoy substantial home support. Last year they even won the Premiership. But lacking all three of these basic essentials, London Welsh paid the price and were relegated each time they were promoted.

Probably my happiest memory was the second game against Bristol in the 2014 play-offs. Bristol had won the league by a mile but there is no automatic promotion. The top team plays the 3rd and the 2nd team plays the 4th, both home and away. Then the winners of those two encounters play each other again, home and away. London Welsh had come 4th in the division and so had to play Leeds, who had come 2nd. It was very close with each side winning at home but London Welsh ended up scoring more points overall. Bristol beat the 3rd placed team, so it was Bristol-v-London Welsh to see who would be promoted. The first game at Kassam resulted in a London Welsh victory 27-8. But we knew the return in Bristol would be a humdinger. It would be the last in their old stadium before moving and when Kelvin and I turned up it was packed with a crowd of 12,000. There were a handful of London Welsh supporters but 10,000+ Bristolians can make an awful lot of noise. They had also all been given little Bristol flags to wave. Bristol went 10 points into the lead and suddenly 27-18 looked a lot less comfortable than 27-8. But London Welsh defence held on; Bristol became more and more frantic and then started making errors. With about 10 minutes to go the crowd realised it was not going to happen; they grew silent and in the end London Welsh not only won on points but ended up pinching the game 21-20. It was a wet evening and we left the stadium walking on air but also walking across thousands of abandoned Bristol flags. I picked one up as a trophy – still have it somewhere. The Premiership season that followed was a total disaster – London Welsh lost every game, setting a new record it would rather not have had and winning just one bonus point. So I forget about that and just remember that wet June evening in Bristol in 2014.

74
BALC (BERKSHIRE ASSOCIATION OF LOCAL COUNCILS)

Although I have never served on a Parish or Town Council I have been President of BALC for over 20 years. I owe this appointment to a Berkshire eccentric called Geoff Hill (1924-2010), whom Christina first met when she was a member of the Executive Committee of the Berkshire Environment Trust from 1989-1992 and Vice-Chairman from 1990-1992. Geoff was the Chairman. He was a passionate environmentalist and was very much involved in the Berkshire CPRE. He was just as passionate about local democracy and was a member of Hurley Parish Council for 40 years. He also became Chairman of BALC, which represents the interests of Berkshire's Parish and Town Councils.

But he was a genuine Berkshire eccentric. His domestic life was tragic – he had an Australian wife, who had eventually given up on him and had returned to Oz with one of his daughters. The other daughter was severely handicapped and in a home. She has since died. So he lived on his own with his cat called 'Oi' in a cottage in Ashley Hill woods, quite near the old Dewdrop Inn at Burchetts' Green, reputedly the haunt of highwaymen in past times. Rather like Miss Abery he allowed his property to revert to nature and on the last occasion I visited him at Burchett's Green, I could not find the place. Eventually he emerged through what appeared to be a solid hedge.

Geoff was always falling out with people and one day he sacked my predecessor as President, a barrister called Clifford Joseph, and persuaded me to take his place. I found that it was the job of the President to chair BALC's AGM, and as at the time the Association was as good as broke – it has since put its financial house in order - we had some lively AGMs in the early years. I attend most of BALC's Executive Committee meetings and very occasionally get wheeled out as an elder statesman to help resolve problems.

I was one of Geoff's two executors – he left a residue of £400K for youth causes but as he had been a Gurkha officer, and the Gurkhas are based at Watlington House, I persuaded my co-executor to use £20K of the residue of the estate to fund the 'Geoff Hill Memorial Garden' at Watlington House. The Watlington House Trust put in another £20K and then enlisted the help of the Berkshire Gardens Trust (BGT) to design the garden. One of the BGT members, Gaila Adair, who has since become a Trustee at Watlington House, is a professional garden designer and undertook the task of garden design, assiduously researching the history of contemporary C17th and C18th gardens, to create a garden in keeping with the date of the House. As already mentioned the

House was built in 1688 and extended around 1760. The result has been the creation of a very beautiful garden that considerably enhances the House.

I also acted as Geoff's literary editor and published his Memoirs. He was always writing and I have included the following piece entitled 'Boots', from which you will understand why I regarded him as a loveable eccentric. I have no doubt it all happened exactly as he has written.

Boots by Geoff Hill

My old black boots clearly show that the wearer is a tramp, who picked them up from a ditch, but the truth is that my poor old feet could not bear the pinching of some newer boots that I possess.

A Local Government colleague kindly pointed out that my old boots were excessively worn at the external corners of the heels. He refrained from describing them, or me, as down-at-heel. I replied that I was not in the habit of walking behind myself and I had not noticed this phenomenon.

However I took the point, kindly meant no doubt, and recently visited a shoe shop. I was attended by a well-proportioned shop girl and I told her that I had heard of BOGOFF and wondered if I bought one shoe, I could get the other free.

She said that they didn't do free boots and that I would have to buy a pair.

I said that in that case, could I have a discount for quantity?

She said that if I wanted a discount for quantity I would have to buy all the boots in the shop. I replied that I thought that was a bit excessive. Perhaps she had not noticed that I was not a centipede and only had two feet. She said that she had observed that fact.

I said in that case can I have discount for cash. She replied that the shop only sold goods for cash at the marked price.

I said that I didn't appear to be getting far with her and added 'Giss us a kiss.

She gave me a peck on the forehead and I said ' That's not much of a kiss' to which she replied ' If you want any more than that, you will have to marry me'.

I said I already had two wives and if I married her she would get me convicted for trigonometry.

She replied 'You should have thought of that before you came into the shop'.

I said that before I came into the shop I didn't realize that she had such a fine pair of er, eyes.

She said 'Thanks for the compliment, but you appear to have come to the wrong shop'.

I gave her a bow and made as though to beat a retreat but eventually she sold me a good pair of brown boots and we parted all smiles.

75
LITERARY PURSUITS

In the 80's I was asked if I would write a few articles on the local history of Basildon for the junior page of the Basildon Parish Magazine, ' the Country Neighbour', which comes out monthly. It was known I was interested in history and indeed that has always been the case. I remember at the age of 5 being shown round the Roman remains at Caerleon, near Newport, Monmouthshire, by 'Uncle' Jacob Gabriel, a relative by marriage, who was the honorary curator, and I can still recall the stories he told me. Was it not the Jesuits who said that if they had the care of a boy until 7 they had him for life? In my case if was Uncle Jacob Gabriel and history.

I had sufficient material in my possession to provide a couple of brief articles, which is all that I had been asked for, and if I had stuck to my brief what follows would never have happened. But what material I had I knew was very incomplete. Miss Swadling's brief History of Basildon was a major part of my source material and her history stopped abruptly at 1910, which I knew was when Major Morrison inherited the Basildon estate. I later discovered that she had based her History in large part on the Victoria County History of Berkshire, which goes no further than 1910.

So something compelled me to write a fuller history, necessitating a little researching of my own. I knew a Leslie Cram, who worked at Reading Museum and I asked him what material the Museum held on the Parish of Basildon. He took me to their repository and they had three drawers stuffed full of stone axes and the like just from Basildon alone. The earliest was dated to 500,000BC. So I started writing articles for Junior County Neighbour,with the first going back to 500,000BC and then as I researched further, I worked my way through the centuries to modern times. In total there were 12 monthly Articles. I actually found that the Articles generated more interest among adults than youngsters, but this encouraged me to keep researching.

My research took me all round the world, combining research with holidays. In South Africa, Christina and I stayed in Durban and visited the reconstruction of Dingaan's Kraal; Captain Allen Gardiner, the Basildon born missionary, is credited with being the founder of Durban and was the first missionary to try and bring Christianity to the Zulus. We also came across his picture in Swaziland and Lesotho, where he also worked. We also went to Spion Kop, where Major Morrison (referred to in the next paragraph) was a scout with the British Army and where we found the grave of the brother of the lady, who later became his first wife.

In Margaret River, West Australia we stayed at Basildene Manor – a B&B, built by a Percy Willmott. The Willmotts are descendants of Sir Francis Sykes Bt, who built Basildon Park. Percy and his younger brother Frank emigrated to Western Australia at an early age; their sister Theresa became a companion to Miss Ellen Morrison, who ran the Basildon estate for her brother Charles and then inherited it in 1910 on his death. But she died only months later and left her companion around £5m in today's money, part of which Theresa passed on to her brothers, who invested in property. As a result of this visit to Western Australia we became great friends of Del Willmott and his wife Jen – Del being Frank's grand-son. We last stayed with them in July 2017 at their apartment in Jolimont, near Perth.

It is the research that takes the time and I have spent many a happy hour ploughing through documents looking for what I call the golden nugget. But you always have this feeling that another golden nugget is in the next folder and if you stop now you will miss it and will later look foolish if you publish now. So you keep researching and the paper pile grows and grows. It was like that with my father. He became interested in tracing the history of the families, who had lived in the Wentloog levels – a flat and very wet area of land about 10 miles long by 5 miles wide, lying between Cardiff and Newport and besides the River Severn, that had been drained by the Dutch in the C17th. Gradually our house filled up with paper as my father researched and researched. Finally I recall my mother saying in exasperation '*Elwyn, for God's sake do something with it!*' So he wrote up his material, sent it to his alma mater - University College, London, and he became Dr Elwyn Williams.

The original Articles for the Country Neighbour were written in 1992 and after two years' research in 1994 I self-published my History of Basildon, printing 1,000 hard back copies. They filled up Honeycroft House but they sold gradually and by 2003 they had all gone. In the meantime further research had revealed some errors, so in 2004 I self published an amended, improved 2nd Edition, this time of 500 copies. I have about 50 left.

Over the years Tutu Bose has visited the Williams' household from time to time, when in the UK or passing through to attend an academic conference. He always pressed on us an invitation to reciprocate and stay with him in Kolkota, as it now is, and in 1998, Christina and I took him up on his invitation. Tutu lives near and took us to see the famous South Park Street cemetery, where the great and good of the East India Company were buried from 1770-1830. It is well preserved and has an excellent guide book. No expense was spared by the families of the deceased in commemorating their departed and the result is an extravaganza of mausoleums and tombs of all shapes and sizes, elaborately carved and decorated. There was also what appears

see colour page XXXIX

to have been a competition to have the tallest mausoleum and that honour goes to Sir William Jones, the former Chief Justice of Bengal. He was obviously a brilliant man, as he learnt all the main Indian languages – Sankskrit, Urdu & Hindi and also founded the Asiatic Society, which remains today India's premier scientific society. According to the guide book, as plain Mr Jones, he was once presented to the King of France – Louis XVI - as follows: '*Sire, allow me to introduce Mr Jones – a most remarkable man, who speaks every language under the sun except his own*'. Although of Welsh stock, Jones had been raised in England, had attended Harrow School and was a non-Welsh speaker.

But of even more interest to me was the obelisk mausoleum right next to Sir William Jones – that of Catherine Sykes. She was the first wife of Francis, later Sir Francis Sykes of Basildon and had died one assumes of puerperal fever as she died only 10 days after giving birth to her second son. She was just 23. This was in 1770. Sir Francis was 40 and had made his fortune, so after his wife's death he quit India and the Company and returned to England. As we toured the cemetery I came across other Berkshire connections. Col Monson and his wife Lady Ann Monson are buried side by side – the Hon Jeremy Monson, formerly Vice-Chairman of Berkshire County Council, was later most helpful as he was a descendant. There were several Vansittart graves – the Smiths of Shottesbrooke Park are Vansittarts. The Hon Rose Aylmer is buried there. She was only 20 and a victim of cholera. The famous lines by Walter Savage Landor from his 'Ode to Rose Aylmer' are inscribed on her tomb. She was the niece of Sir Henry Russell, Chief Justice of Bengal, who later bought Swallowfield Park.

The upshot of this was that I started to research East Indian connections with Berkshire and the more I researched the more I found. There were so many that in the C18th Berkshire was known as the English Hindoostan. With the Crown at Windsor and Parliament at Westminster, Berkshire was a good location, particularly as many of the returning 'Nabobs', as they were known, bought themselves seats in Parliament. Sykes, for example,bought up Wallingford, which returned two Members of Parliament. He was MP for Wallingford for many years and the other seat went to his nominee. Nabob is the Anglicization of Nawab, which is an Urdu word, meaning deputy. When the Great Moghul Emperors of India created their empire they divided it into provinces and placed a Deputy or Nawab in charge. But in time as the power of the Emperor waned these Nawabs were seen to be rulers in their own right. From Nabob we get the words 'nob' and 'snob'.

After 10 years' intermittent research I discovered 31 stately homes in Berkshire with Nabob associations. In 5 cases, there were two Nabob ownerships at different times. Only Sir Francis Sykes built a new house - Basildon Park; in every other case existing property was purchased. Some of the houses have been demolished but most still stand and most are still in private hands, though in East Berkshire, these are mainly Middle –Eastern hands. Eventually in 2010 I self-published 'the Nabobs of Berkshire'. I again printed 1000 copies and have 180 left.

As a consequence of visiting the South Park Street cemetery in Kolkota and writing my Nabobs book, I was persuaded to join BACSA (the British Association of Cemeteries in South-East Asia), which gives grants to maintain East Indian Company cemeteries. I have now become their Publicity and Communications Officer.

In 2006 I wrote and self-published a booklet 'Lest we Forget' - the History of Basildon's War Memorial. About 30% of the able-bodied men of Basildon Parish died in the 1st World War – the average across the UK was 12%. So as part of the research, Christina and I spent 3 days driving through France and Belgium visiting all the cemeteries or memorials where Basildon Men are either buried or commemorated. To put their deaths in context I prefaced the booklet with potted histories of the 1st and 2nd World Wars. One of these Basildonians, Pte Frederick Cresswell is buried in Mendinghem cemetery near Poperinge, Belgium. The place name sounds Flemish but we discovered that it was all a joke. There was a field hospital in that location, that they were originally going to call 'Endinghem' but it was felt that even for the Tommy's warped sense of humour, that was a bit too much, so it was changed to 'Mendinghem'. Another hospital close by was called 'Dosinghem' and a third 'Bandageinghem'. Eventually the hospitals departed but the cemeteries remained.

'Basildon in Postcards' was another publication in 2013, brought out jointly with David Thomas of the Forge, Upper Basildon, who owns one of the three collections of postcards that featured. In 1902 the Post Office allowed cards to be divided, so that you could write the address on one side and a message on the other. That left the front free for a picture. This change, coupled with the efficiency of the Post Office meant that postcards became the favourite form of communication. Within a few years of 1902 millions were being sent and entrepreneurs started bringing out cards showing views from villages, such as Upper and Lower Basildon. So we had 100 different views of Upper and Lower Basildon from around 1910 to work on.

My most recent work, published in 2018, has been a booklet featuring a Potted History of Padworth, written for my friend and fellow Rotarian, Brian Jenkins. Brian is an entrepreneur and his latest business venture has been to acquire the Old Rectory in Padworth and turn it into a hotel, specializing in the marriage market. The booklet is intended for the hotel's guests.

Interestingly, Shinfield Park is now owned by the Wood Group, which is a Scottish family business. The Woods were Scottish fishermen, who owned land near Aberdeen, which was developed as a port to serve the off-shore oil industry. Brian Jenkins had founded Patol to make fire-fighting equipment and the Woods tried to buy his business but he refused. Brian was in for some major government contracts at the time and he had a factory in Wales working for him. But he then ran into cash flow problems and arranged an overdraft with the Royal Bank of Scotland (RBS) to tide him over. But suddenly he was told by RBS that they were calling in their loan and he had three days to find the money elsewhere. He failed and lost his business, which was then bought by the Woods. Not long after Patol were awarded the major contracts he had been working for, so the Woods benefited, not Brian. He was not best pleased either to later find out that Sir Ian Wood was a Director of RBS. Fortunately for Brian he and his wife owned his Business HQ personally – it was not a Company asset. So Brian being Brian he then started another business, the Jubilee Nursery, which has been very successful. He also found after a time that all his old Patol clients were returning to him as they were not happy with the way Patol was being run. Eventually he even bought back the name Patol at a knock-down price. But his experiences would have broken a lesser man.

I have one further project in the pipeline and that is an account of three West Berkshire personalities. Surprisingly one of these is the author D H Lawrence. He and his German wife, Frieda von Richthofen, a cousin of 'the Red Baron', were thrown out of Cornwall in 1918 as in the hysteria of the time Frieda was suspected of spying. A friend lent them her Cottage in Hermitage and then in August 1918, when the friend needed the cottage herself, another friend let them have 'The Myrtles' in Pangbourne. John Webb, a painter and decorator now lives in Minehead but 20 years ago he lived next door to Myrtle Cottage, Upper Basildon, which at one time was in the Parish of Pangbourne. He told me that groups of Japanese tourists had started to visit to look at the cottage where the great D H Lawrence had lived. I knew that was a nonsense but no-one knew where 'the Myrtles' was. So I did some detective work and found the right house – nowadays 38, Reading Road, Pangbourne. I then discovered that Reading University holds summaries of Lawrence's letters and I have used this material to paint a picture of Lawrence and the life he and Frieda led in West Berkshire.

The second personality is Captain Allen Gardiner (1797-1853), the Basildon missionary to whom reference has already been made in connection with his attempt to convert the Zulus to Christianity. He then went to South America where in 1853 he tried to convert the Yamana Indians in Tierra del Fuego. They turned hostile and Gardiner and his 5 companions starved to death in

1853. In 2014 Christina and I went on a South American cruise from Santiago in Chile to Buenos Aires in Argentina. In Ushaia we visited the Museum of the Yamanas, who are now no more, in that the last pure-blooded Yamana Indian died in the 50's and later in the Beagle Channel, we sailed past Picton Island, which was Gardiner's last base. So I now have sufficient material to complete the story of this unsuccessful missionary.

The third personality is Lady Craven of Benham (1730-1828). She married young and had 7 children with Lord Craven but the marriage then fell apart. She then met the Margrave of Ansbach, who was also unhappily married and she became his mistress. The Duke's summer Court was held at Triesdorf near Ansbach, where she built a theatre to perform her plays – she built another at Benham. The ducal buildings at Triesdorf still stand and are now owned by the local College of Agriculture, the former Principal of which is my good friend Horst von Zerboni di Sposetti, whom I first met as a result of a Rotary twinning. At one point Lady Craven went on a remarkable coach trip around Europe, meeting all the Heads of State, including the Empress Catherine the Great. As she journeyed she wrote letter after letter to the Margrave,which were later published and give a vivid portayal of society life in Europe not long before the outbreak of the French Revolution. When Lord Craven and the Margrave's wife both died within a short space of time, the two married very quickly, greatly upsetting society. The Margrave then agreed to give up his Dukedom to the King of Prussia, in return for an annuity, and he and his wife then moved to England, where they divided their time between Benham and London. The Margrave died in 1806 and was buried in Speen. Lady Craven, as was, later moved to Florence, where she died in 1828. Interestingly the Hon Osbert William Craven was elected to the first Berkshire County Council in 1888 to represent the Uffington division. His address was given as Ashdown House, now owned by the National Trust.

76
THE LIEUTENANCY, THE MAGISTRACY AND THE SHRIEVALTY

The Lieutenancy dates back to Tudor times and the Lord Lieutenant is Her Majesty's representative in the Royal County. The Clerk to the Lieutenancy used to be the Clerk and later Chief Executive of the County Council. Now the senior officer at Reading Borough Council fulfils the role. The Lord Lieutenant is empowered with royal consent to appoint a number of Deputy Lieutenants to assist him and in 2005, the then Lord Lieutenant, Sir Philip Wroughton appointed Christina as one of his Deputy Lieutenants. She was then the youngest DL and is now the longest serving lady DL. All the Unitary Councils hold citizenship ceremonies at least once a month, with anywhere from 20-30 new citizens being sworn in on each occasion. The ceremony is taken by the local Superintendent Registrar but normally a DL and the Mayor (or Chairman in the case of West Berkshire) are present. I have accompanied Christina to many of these ceremonies in the past 13 years, mainly to Slough and Bracknell. She gives the assembled company a talk on the history of the County and the local Borough; the Mayor adds a few words; Christina then hands over the registration certificates individually and at the end we all sing the National Anthem. Then there are photographs. I never cease to be staggered by the range of nationalities applying to become British Citizens – from every continent in fact. Invariably those applying have lived in the UK for least 7 years and all have good jobs and are well settled. You also sense their pride in becoming British Citizens. There were two Algerians on one occasion and I asked them why they were applying to become British rather than French citizens. Their reply was straightforward. They had gone to France, where after 5 years they still felt unwelcome. So they moved to Bracknell, where they felt so at home that they now wanted to make their home here permanently.

Assessing applicants for the Queen's Awards for Voluntary Service is the other main activity for Deputy Lieutenants. All applications are assessed in depth by two Deputy Lieutenants and are then judged on a County Basis before being assessed nationally. Christina normally carries out at least two of these assessments each year.

ERD was very proud of the fact that he was appointed a DL and Bob Gash was always mortified that he was not. Sir Gordon Palmer was Lord Lieutenant for most of the time that Bob was Chief Executive and I always suspected that Lady Palmer may have had a hand in that decision. She was formidable and you crossed her at your peril, though I always got on well with her. Her son, Lord Palmer, owns and runs Manderston, the stately home in the Scottish Borders, famous for its silver staircase. Christina and I have undertaken several motoring holidays in Scotland, but have never managed to visit Manderston on the one day in the week that it is open to the public. However on one occasion we knew that Naomi Robinson was staying with her great friend Lorna Palmer at Manderston Lodge, so although the House would not be open, we decided to visit anyway on our way back home. It was bucketing down with rain and as we drove into the village we saw a youngish man and an old girl in a ditch cleaning it out. I stopped to ask the way to the Lodge and was amazed when the old girl who answered turned out to be Lady Palmer!

The County Council involvement with the Magistracy dated back to the creation of Magistrates Courts Committees, by virtue of the Justices of the Peace Act 1949. The service was paid for by a Home Office grant of 80%, with 20% coming from the County Council rate precept. The Committee was Clerked in my time by ERD and later Bob Gash, with the Committee work being undertaken by Freddy Jones and then Roger Penfold. The Committee was made up of magistrates drawn from the County's Benches, each of whom had its own Justices Clerk, mostly part-time, though as time went by the part-timers gave way to full-time legally qualified appointments.

My involvement with this service, prior to Bob Gash's death in 1986, was limited to work in relation to the appointment of new magistrates. But only a few days after Bob had died I was approached by Len Reynolds, Chairman of the Magistrates Courts Committee, who asked me to take over as Clerk. Len is dead now – I attended his funeral. He was a lovely man, who had been Head of Desborough Grammar School in Maidenhead. He had also had a distinguished war, serving in small boats in the Mediterranean, for which he was awarded the DSO. He also became the Navy's official war historian for that branch of the service, writing two scholarly and comprehensive tomes. He was also one of those approached by John Wood-Griffiths, who had agreed to become a Trustee of the Rhos-y-Gwaliau Outdoor Education Trust, which is how I already knew him.

I accepted the offer and held the post of Clerk to the Berkshire Magistrates' Courts Committee until 1994. The service then went over to full-time Chief Executive appointments, at which point I bowed out. I had some modest successes during my time as Clerk. I was involved in senior appointments below those of Justices Clerk and the system I inherited was one of dead man's shoes. It was assumed in the service that if anyone retired the person next below them would automatically be promoted. In Maidenhead I broke that system and with two persons applying for a vacancy I promoted the junior over the senior.

Shock horror and it did not make me a popular person but it was the right thing to do and the junior in question – a lady – is now a Judge.

Len also asked me to draw up a scheme for reorganizing the County's Benches. For example Slough had a very full and varied work load but found it difficult recruiting Magistrates. Maidenhead next door had no problem recruiting Magistrates but its work load consisted mainly of road traffic offences. Merging the two made good sense to me and Len, who was Chairman of the Maidenhead Bench agreed. So Len and I went to a meeting of the Maidenhead Magistrates to seek their support. It was not forthcoming. The opposition was led by a very senior Magistrate, Rosemary Thomson. I got on well enough with her but she was dead set against any closer association with Slough, for no good reason that I could see. But she was influential and persuaded the entire Bench, apart from their Chairman, to her point of view. As a result she killed the reorganization, which went down the Swannee, apart from the merger of Reading with Bradfield & Sonning. I had to laugh when Rosemary later became Chair of the Magistrates Association and used to go round the country urging her fellow magistrates not to be parochial and to embrace reform! She had as much success as I did and in 2005 Magistrates Courts Committees were abolished. It is difficult to find a Magistrate who is happy with the way the service is currently run and I like to think that had the Berkshire Magistrates accepted my re-organization proposals in 1986, they would have had a better chance of surviving but that is probably wishful thinking on my part.

When I became County Secretary in 1977, I also became Secretary to two Advisory Committees – one for the appointment of General Commissioners of Income Tax and the other for the Appointment of Magistrates. Both were chaired by the Lord Lieutenant with the actual committee work being undertaken by Roger Penfold MBE. As the positions went hand in hand with the Clerkship of the Magistrates Courts Committee, with the agreement of the then Lord Lieutenant, Johnny Henderson, I remained as Secretary of both until 1994. In 1995 Sir Philip Wroughton succeeded Johnny Henderson as Lord Lieutenant and asked me to become a member of the Advisory Committee on the appointment of General Commissioners. He also asked me to suggest the names of ladies, who might be interested in becoming General Commissioners, given that all the existing Commissioners were male, though they did have a lady Clerk in Sue Balchin MBE, as mentioned before, now sadly deceased.

An old College pal of mine, Nigel Candler, (who sadly died in 2006), lived near Hungerford with his wife Margaret, and I coaxed Margaret into applying to become a General Commissioner and having applied she was appointed. Then she in turn persuaded my Christina to apply and so Christina joined her as a General Commissioner in 1998. Christina then rapidly rose through the ranks. She chaired the Reading Division from 2001-2003; the County from 2004-2009 and South Central England from 2007-2009. In 2009 General Commissioners were abolished but Christina was one of a handful of former General Commissioners, who applied and were successful in being appointed in 2009 to the National First Tier Tribunal: Tax Chamber. Under the new system cases are heard by a QC or Judge and Christina sits with him or her.

As Christina relates the story, she was told by Sir Philip in 1998 that she was joining the Advisory Committee on the Appointment of Justices! These are normally 7 year appointments but she served until 2010. She was Chairman of the Appointments Panel from 2001-2010 and Chairman of the West Berkshire Advisory Sub-Committee from 2007-2010. Her appointment as a Deputy Lieutenant took place in 2005 and no doubt resulted from the favourable impression she had made on Sir Philip.

The Shrievalty is much older than the Lieutenancy and dates back to King Alfred, who divided his kingdom into shires and initially appointed a reeve or steward to manage the royal possessions in each Shire. The Shire reeve or sheriff grew in power and by the time of King Edward the Confessor was responsible for tax collection, law enforcement and raising the County fyrd. Nowadays the High Sheriff's residual responsibility is to have regard to the welfare of the judges, which is undertaken in several ways including holding a Crown Court service at the start of the judicial year.

The High Sheriff is a royal appointment and there is a local consultancy panel that submits two names each year. Applicants have to show some community involvement and a scandal free past. The post is unremunerated but there are costs involved, which the High Sheriff has to foot. Some High Sheriffs push the boat out and one spent £250,000 in a year but the norm is nearer £10,000. If you are in line to be appointed High Sheriff, you know 4 years in advance, which gives you time to prepare.

see colour pages XXXI-XXXVIII

Christina received the nod in 2005 and became High Sheriff in 2009-2010. She was the first lady High Sheriff of the Royal County of Berkshire, already to be a Deputy Lieutenant (DL) and the first of either sex to be such since Sir William Benyon in 1995-96. I acted as her Secretary. During the year she attended 350 functions and meetings and I accompanied her to about half. She has always been interested and involved in mental health issues, and served as a non-executive director of Berkshire Healthcare (NHS) Trust, being elected Governor for West Berkshire, when it became a Foundation Trust, then Lead Governor for the whole Foundation Trust. She has also sat as a Mental Health Act Manager for the Trust for 17 years, and also sits in that capacity at the

Elysium (formerly Priory) Hospital at Thornford Park, Thatcham. Not surprisingly, therefore, Christina made mental health one of the themes for her year. This resulted in a visit to Broadmoor, which was fascinating. What one finds as High Sheriff is that people open up to you. High Sheriffs only hold office for a year and are seen as neutral and no threat. This meant that senior public service managers, such as say the Chief of Police at Reading, the Head of Reading Prison or the Senior Director at Broadmoor Hospital were quite happy to talk openly about the problems they faced. There was nothing that Christina as High Sheriff could do to resolve them but the mere fact of being there and providing a friendly listening ear must have been of some therapeutic benefit.

Walking around Broadmoor it was impossible to work out who were the staff and who were the patients, and I have to say that on the whole the patients looked more normal than the staff. I recalled the time when I was Vice-Chairman of West Berkshire Health Authority and we had an incident at Boroughcourt Hospital. Two young offenders from Nuffield Remand Centre were sent each day on day release to work in the grounds at Boroughcourt. One of the lady patients was a nymphomaniac and approached them for sex but they declined. Unfortunately one day when having their lunch they came across some homebrew, that had been made by the patients as part of some mis-guided therapy programme. The homebrew was lethal and having drunk a couple of glasses the two young men became blind-drunk. This time when the lady patient approached them they obliged her. They were so drunk that when they arrived back at Nuffield they started fighting with the Remand Centre staff. Initially this turned them into heroes among the other inmates but when it got out that they had been having sex with a mentally handicapped patient, their fellow inmates turned against them. It got so bad that they had to be placed in protective custody and they were eventually moved to another prison.

Nuffield complained to Boroughcourt as to what had gone on and I ended up chairing an Inquiry to try and get to the bottom of the matter. I use the phrase advisedly because nearly all the staff at Boroughcourt were male and as far as I could tell they were all gay and had recruited each other. One was the Mayor of Reading. The general line was that the lady patient liked sex, so what was the problem? They clearly knew what had been going on but had decided to take no action. But as for pinpointing liability they all clammed up and I got nowhere. I thought it is a funny old world where the remand prisoners at Nuffield better reflect public opinion than the people we appoint to look after the vulnerable in society.

Returning to the Shrievalty, at the time I was Vice-Chairman of Age Concern (Berkshire) and Christina agreed that we would organize a 'Beating the Bounds of Berkshire' charity walk to raise funds for the charity. I devised a series of 18 linked walks around Berkshire and wrote a historical commentary. Berkshire Youth kindly arranged for their Volunteer organization to help with administration. Prince Philip agreed to become Patron, (with Christina as High Sheriff as Vice-Patron) and to start the walk at Windsor in return for 10% of the monies raised. The start was quite amusing. Prince Philip duly arrived and went around the assembled company chatting away. He addressed one young man, who ignored him. So he said '*How the hell are you going to hear what I am saying with those bloody things clamped over your ears?*' This had the desired effect and the young man in question removed his headphones. Theresa May MP and her husband Philip walked the Maidenhead leg and it has to be said that Christina received more support from Theresa May during her shrieval year than from any other Berkshire MP.

One of the Trustees of Age Concern (Berkshire) was Kay Everett, who had been Mayor and had been granted the Freedom of the Borough. Freemen of Reading are entitled to drive a flock of sheep across Caversham bridge, so as a publicity stunt I prevailed upon John Bishop of Rushall Farm to bring a flock of sheep to Reading. The Museum of English Rural Life kindly lent me a copy of an authentic shepherd's smock and hat and the local Thameside Primary school also turned out dressed as sheep. It was all great fun and attracted the publicity we were after.

The walk took place in May 2009 and the total route was 139 miles. One couple Jeff and Carole Gardner walked the entire route. Christina and I managed about 100 miles over the 9 days. In total the walk raised £6,000.

Another couple, Brian and Jools Anderson, gave us an authentic Beating-the-Bounds wand or stick, which was carried round the whole route. You can see it in one of the photographs. Afterwards Christina presented it to the Museum of English Rural Life.

FOOTNOTE

Ellis Roger Davies (ERD), my father's oldest friend, best man and my godfather, came to Berkshire in 1935 as Deputy Clerk of the County Council. I arrived in the County as his Articled Clerk in 1961 and my career with the former County Council, other public bodies, institutions and charities, continues to this day. Likewise Christina's professional, charitable and ceremonial role in the Royal County continues today and into the future. That represents 83 years of family commitment to this remarkable Royal County. I hope that this account of that long period will be of interest, and on occasions amusement, to all those who read it.

This is not the end. It is not even the beginning of the end.
But it is, perhaps, the end of the beginning.

Winston Churchill – 10th November 1942, celebrating the Allied victory at El Alamein

Veni, Vidi, Laboravi, Scripsi!

ACKNOWLEDGEMENTS

Copyright in the photos of the County Council in 1971, 1974 and 1977 is vested in the County Record office and the photos are included with the County Archivist's consent. Other illustrations are either taken from the newspaper which the former County Council published in 1988 to commemorate its centenary or are from the author's own archives.

The author is grateful to those colleagues who have either contributed their own stories and/or helped the author to correct his fading memory. Where this has been the case their contributions have been acknowledged in the text.

Special thanks are due to David Over, who has given the author a great deal of assistance and also undertook proof reading .

But this book would never have seen the light of day without the support and encouragement of my beloved wife Christina. Most of it was written some years ago but the author then experienced what can only be described as writer's block and the project was shelved . Christina has encouraged me to resurrect the project and has made many helpful suggestions, enabling me to bring it to fruition. As always I owe her my deepest thanks.

Clive Williams OBE

May 2018

INDEX